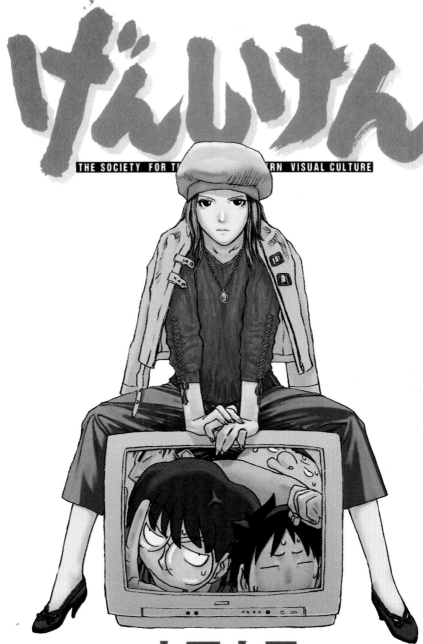

げんしけん

THE SOCIETY FOR T… RN VISUAL CULTURE

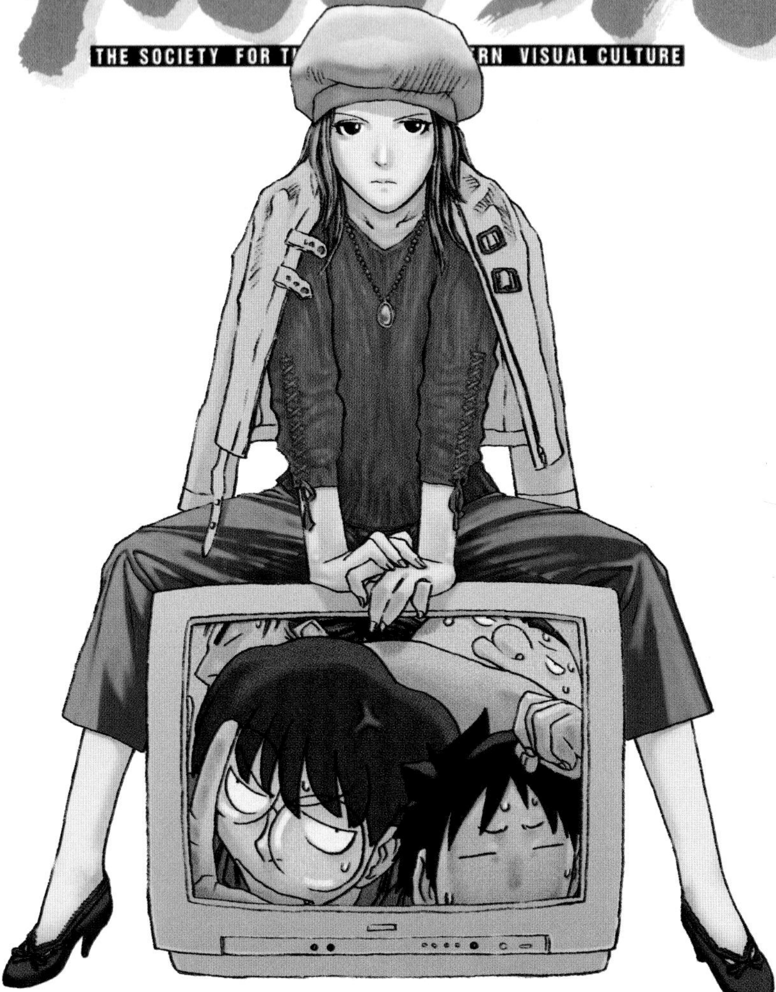

木尾士目

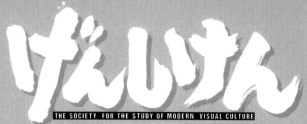

THE SOCIETY FOR THE STUDY OF MODERN VISUAL CULTURE

Vol.1
CONTENTS

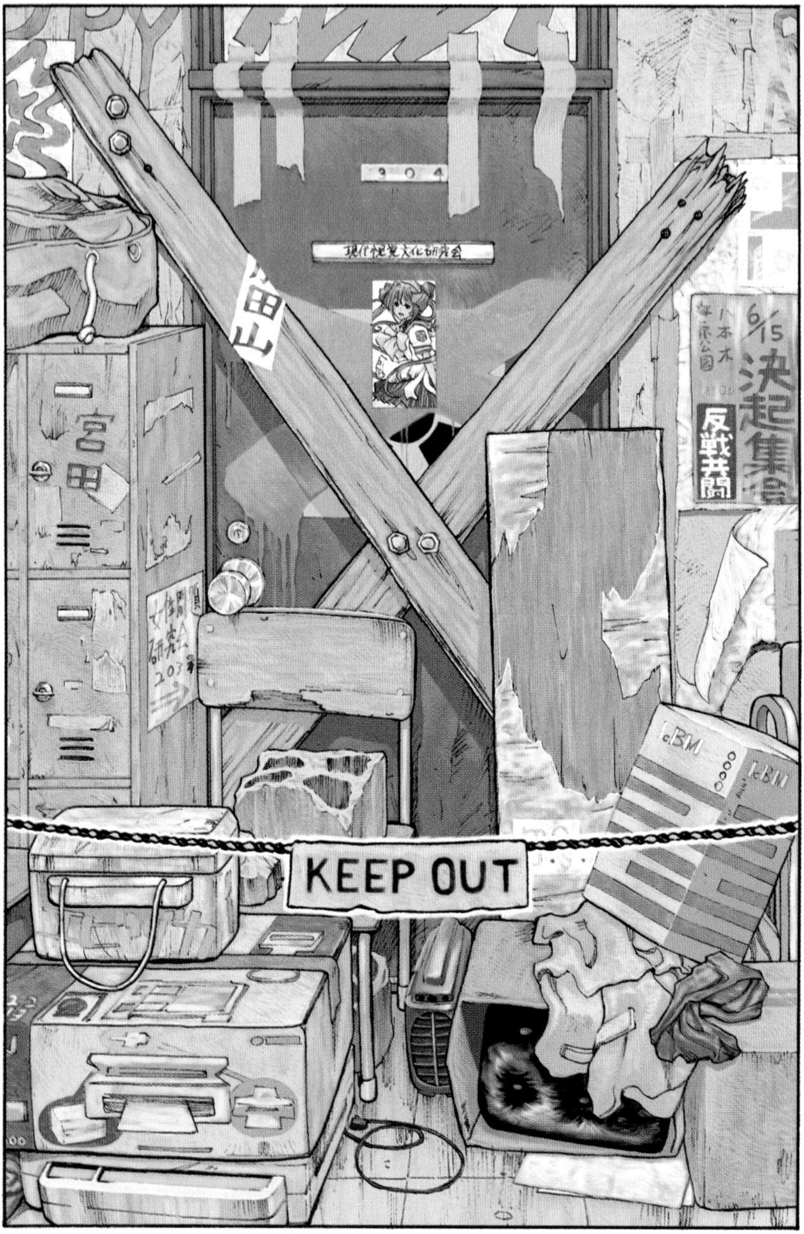
304
現代視覚文化研究会
宮田
6/15
決起集会
反戦共闘
IBM
KEEP OUT

第1話　現視研

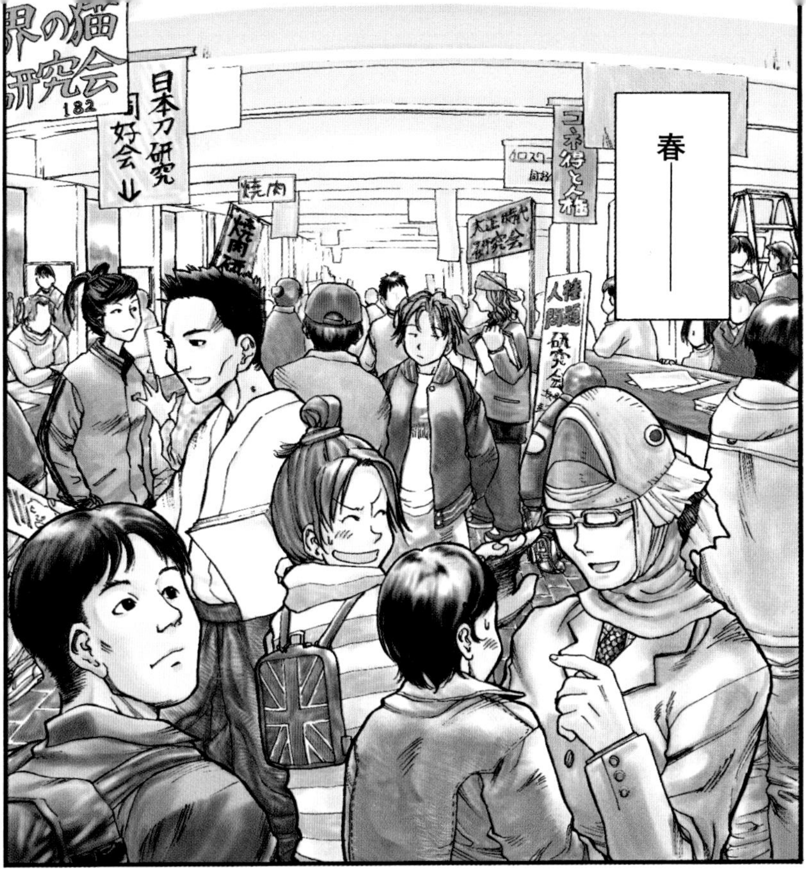
春——
大正時代研究会
焼肉
日本刀研究
好会

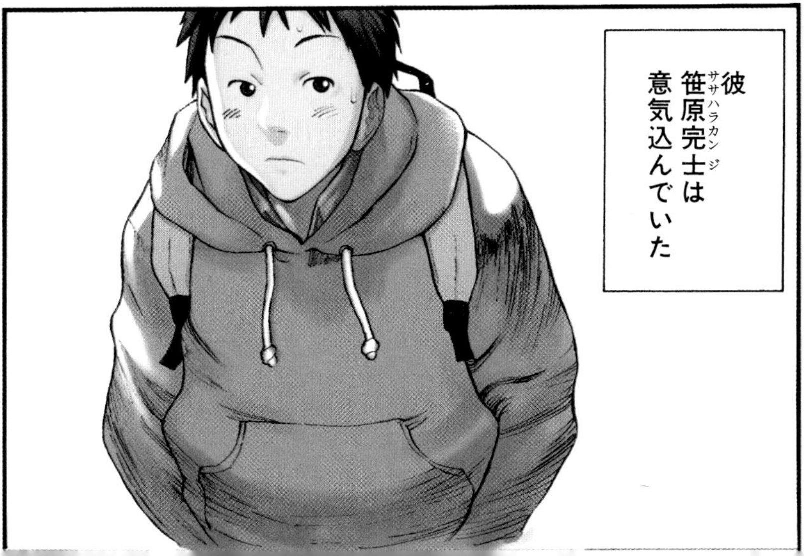
彼
笹原完士（ササハラカンジ）は
意気込んでいた

GENSHIKEN

1

KIO SHIMOKU

TRANSLATED AND ADAPTED BY
David Ury

LETTERED BY
Michaelis/Carpelis Design

BALLANTINE BOOKS · NEW YORK

Genshiken, Volume 1 is a work of fiction. Names, characters, places, and incidents are the products of the author's imagination or are used fictitiously. Any resemblance to actual events, locales, or persons, living or dead, is entirely coincidental.

A Del Rey Books Trade Paperback Original

Published in the United States by
Del Rey Books, an imprint of
The Random House Publishing Group, a
division of Random House, Inc., New York.

First published in Japan in 2002 by
Kodansha Ltd., Tokyo
This publication rights arranged through
Kodansha Ltd.

Printed in the United States of America

Del Rey Manga website: www.delreymanga.com

Library of Congress Control Number:
2005922043

ISBN 0-345-48169-0

Lettering—Michaelis/Carpelis Design
Associates Inc.

9 8 7 6 5 4 3 2 1

GENSHIKEN

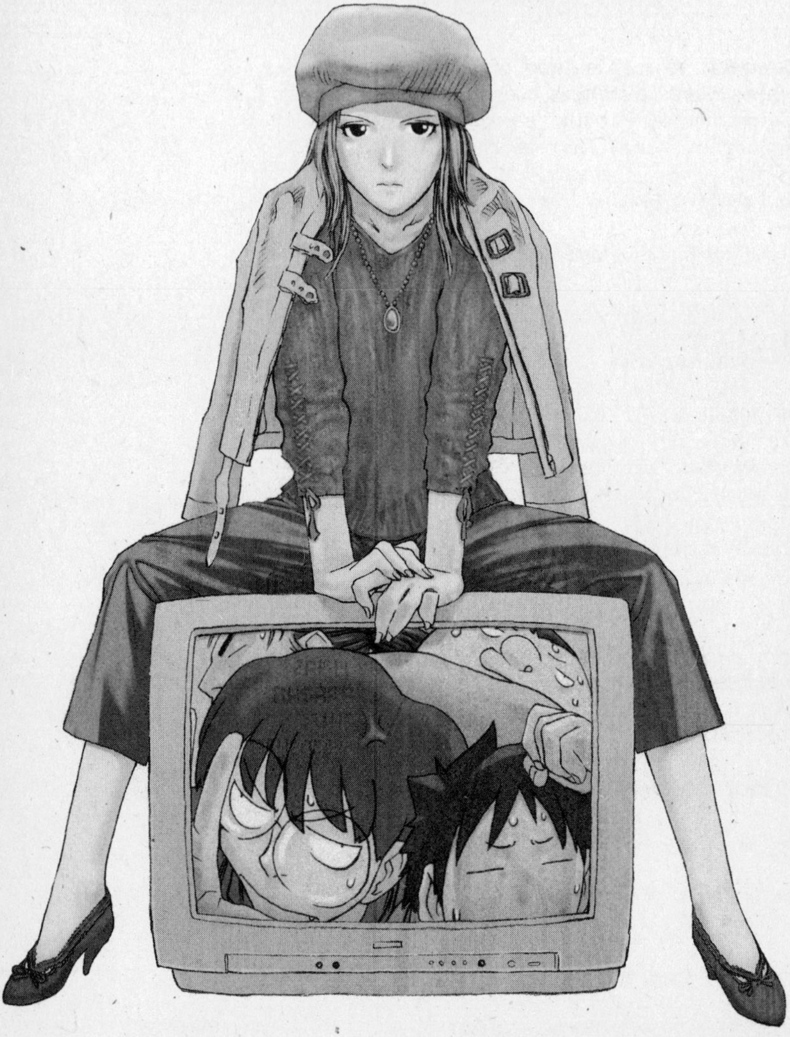

Contents

PROFILE

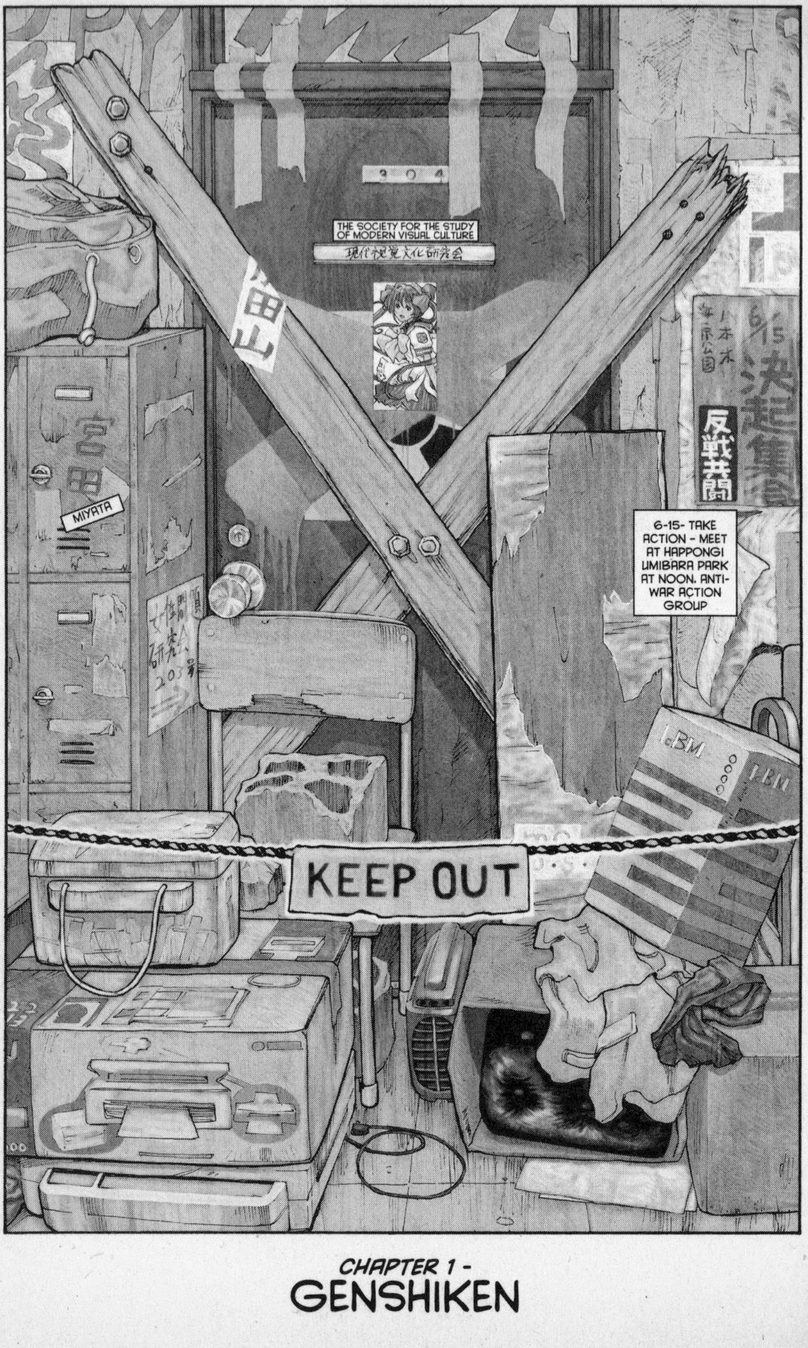
304
THE SOCIETY FOR THE STUDY OF MODERN VISUAL CULTURE
現代視覚文化研究会
反戦共闘
6-15- TAKE ACTION - MEET AT HAPPONGI UMIBARA PARK AT NOON. ANTI-WAR ACTION GROUP
宮田
MIYATA
IBM
KEEP OUT

CHAPTER 1 -

GENSHIKEN

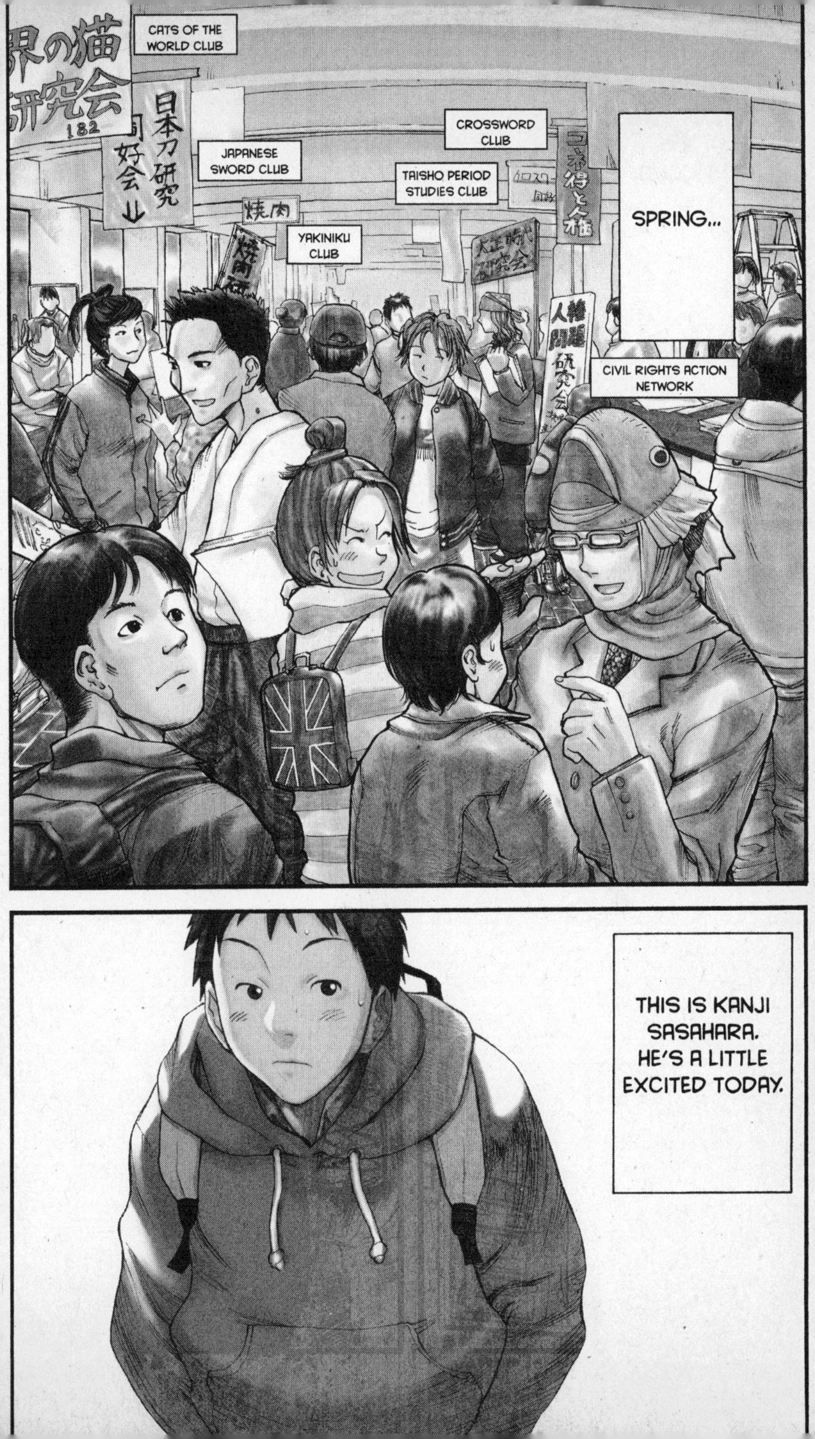
SPRING...
CROSSWORD CLUB
CIVIL RIGHTS ACTION NETWORK
TAISHO PERIOD STUDIES CLUB
CATS OF THE WORLD CLUB
JAPANESE SWORD CLUB
YAKINIKU CLUB
THIS IS KANJI SASAHARA. HE'S A LITTLE EXCITED TODAY.

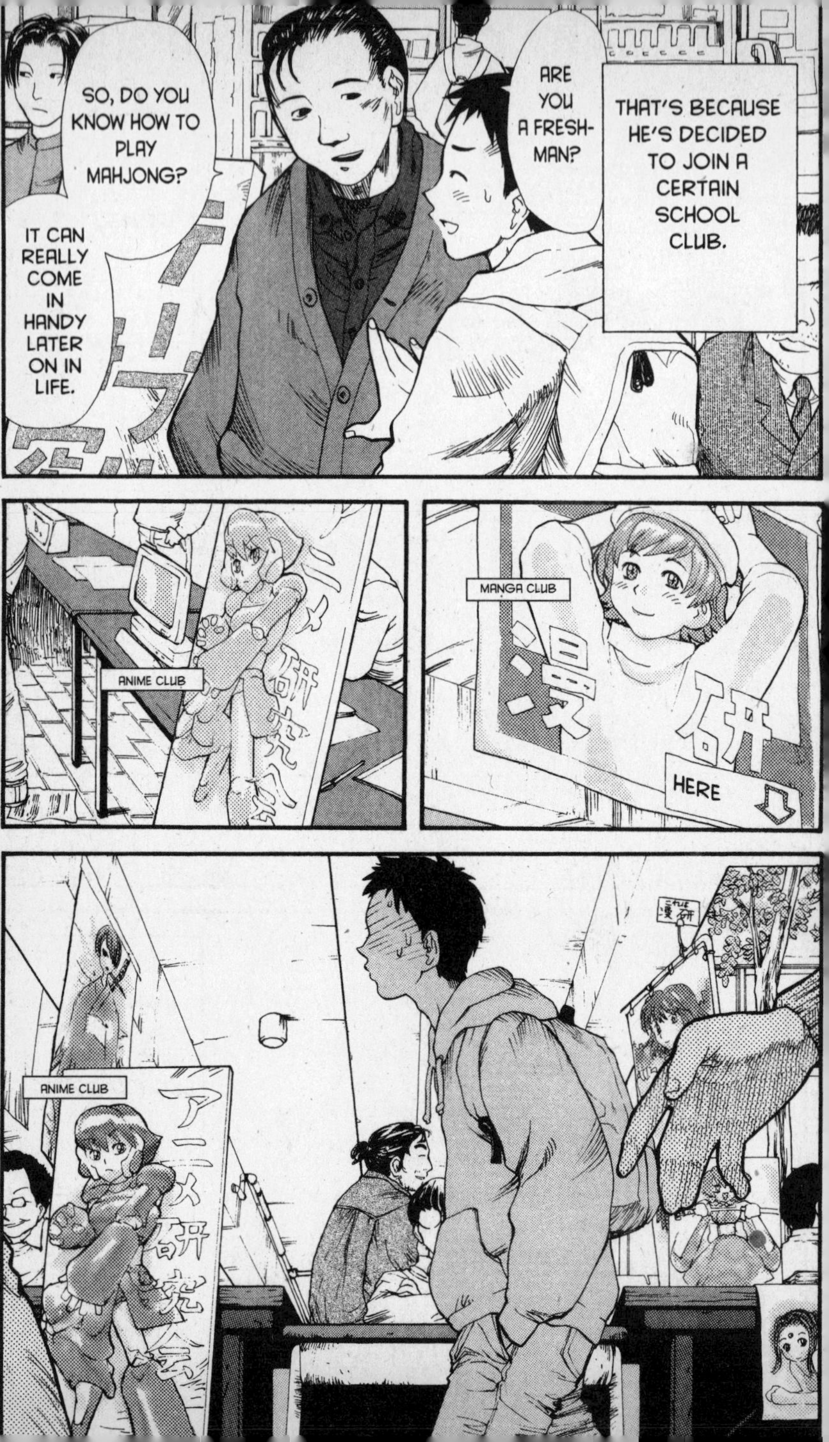
THAT'S BECAUSE HE'S DECIDED TO JOIN A CERTAIN SCHOOL CLUB.
ARE YOU A FRESHMAN?
SO, DO YOU KNOW HOW TO PLAY MAHJONG?
IT CAN REALLY COME IN HANDY LATER ON IN LIFE.
MANGA CLUB
漫研
HERE
ANIME CLUB
漫研
ANIME CLUB
アニメ研究会

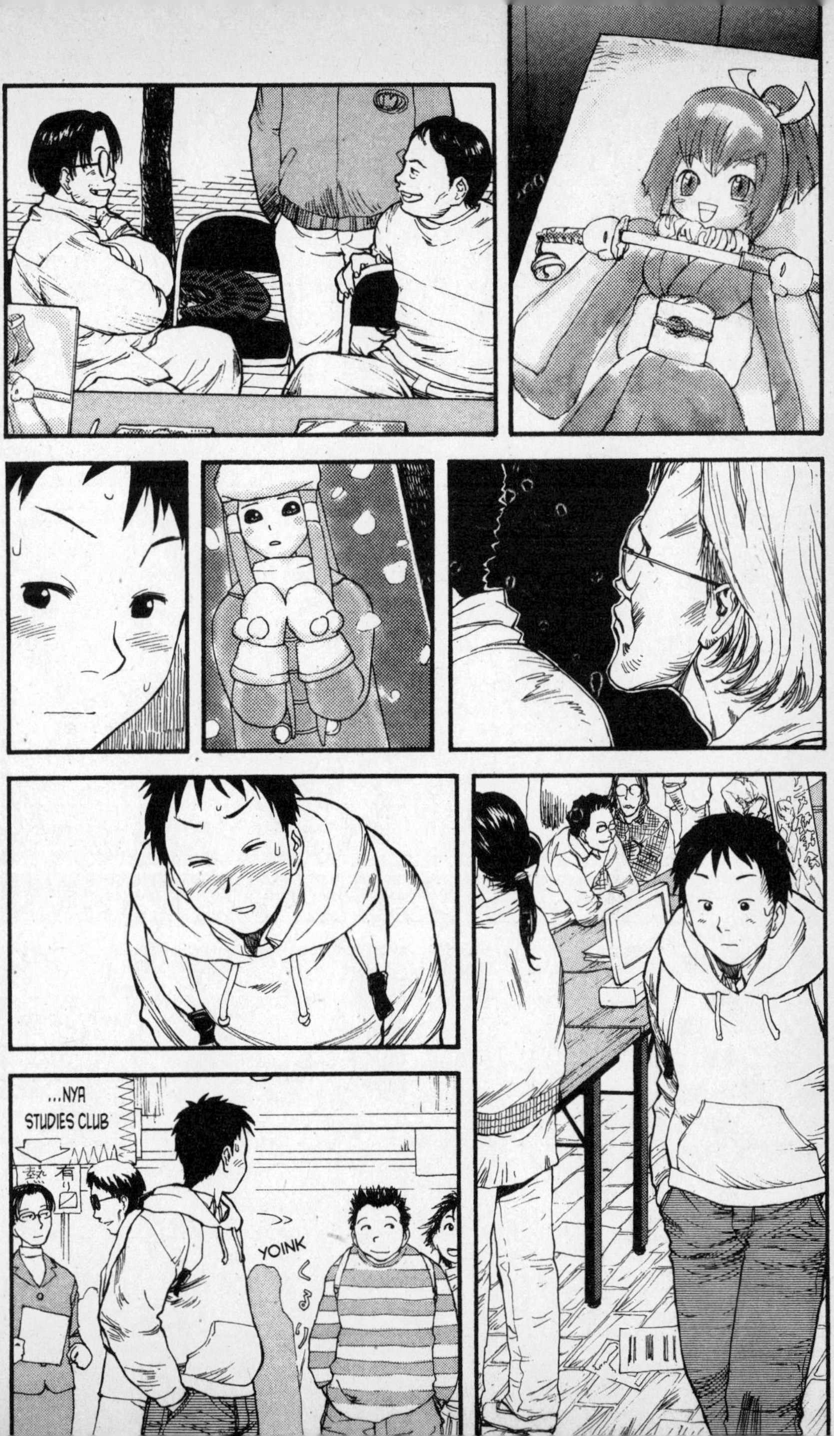
...NYA
STUDIES CLUB
YOINK
くるり

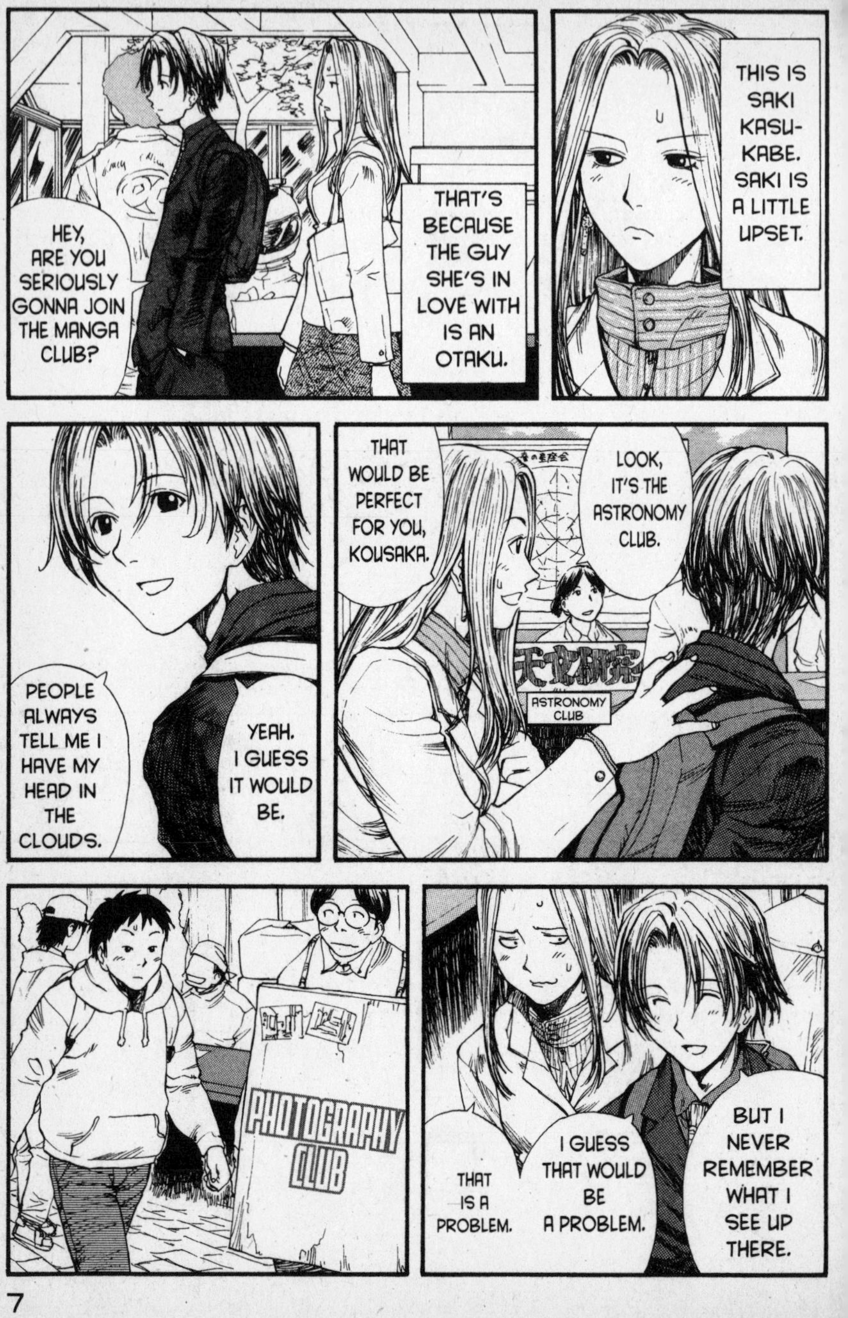
THIS IS SAKI KASUKABE. SAKI IS A LITTLE UPSET.
THAT'S BECAUSE THE GUY SHE'S IN LOVE WITH IS AN OTAKU.
HEY, ARE YOU SERIOUSLY GONNA JOIN THE MANGA CLUB?
LOOK, IT'S THE ASTRONOMY CLUB.
THAT WOULD BE PERFECT FOR YOU, KOUSAKA.
ASTRONOMY CLUB
YEAH. I GUESS IT WOULD BE.
PEOPLE ALWAYS TELL ME I HAVE MY HEAD IN THE CLOUDS.
BUT I NEVER REMEMBER WHAT I SEE UP THERE.
I GUESS THAT WOULD BE A PROBLEM.
THAT IS A PROBLEM.
PHOTOGRAPHY CLUB

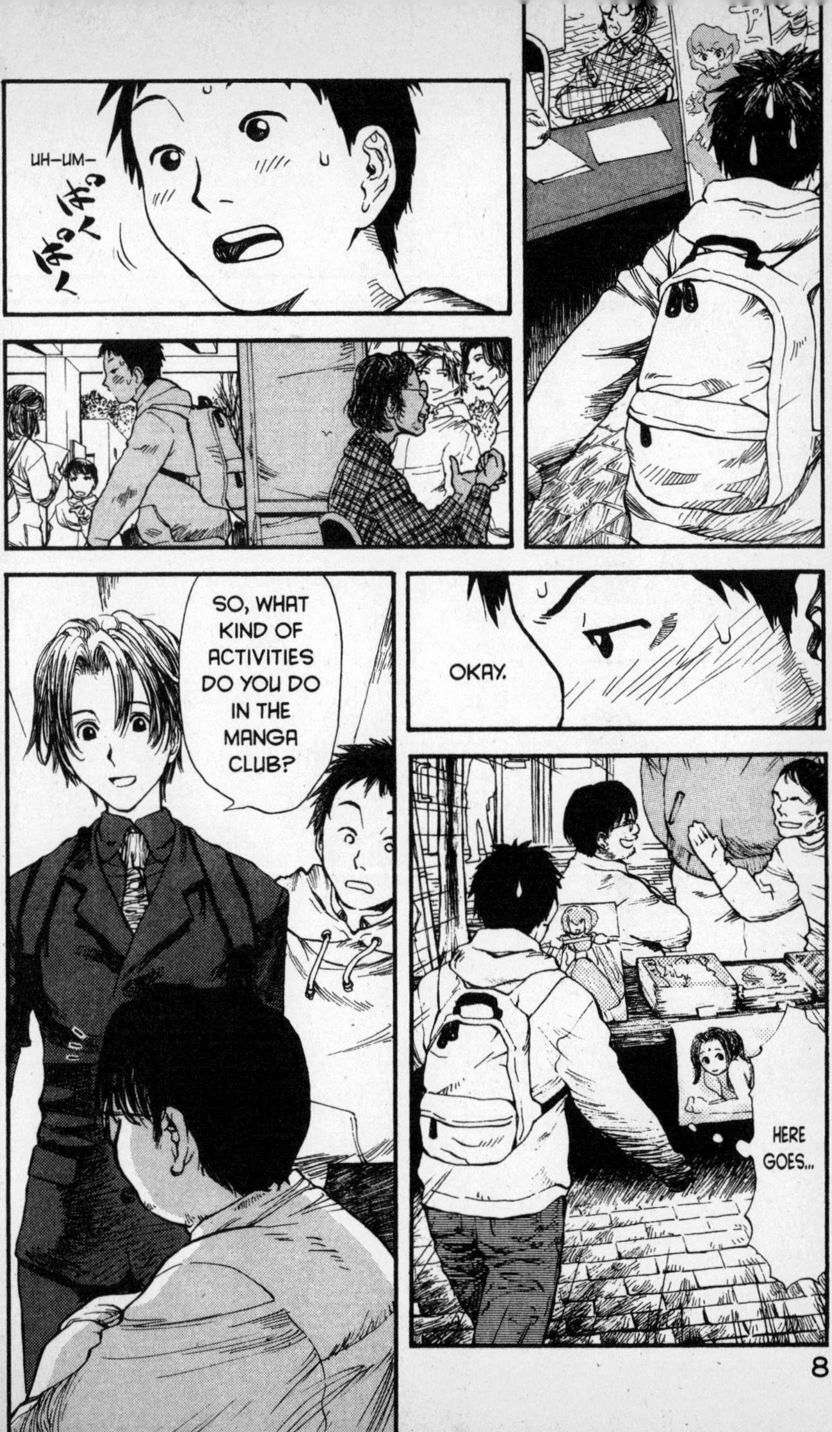
UH-UM-
OKAY.
HERE GOES...
SO, WHAT KIND OF ACTIVITIES DO YOU DO IN THE MANGA CLUB?

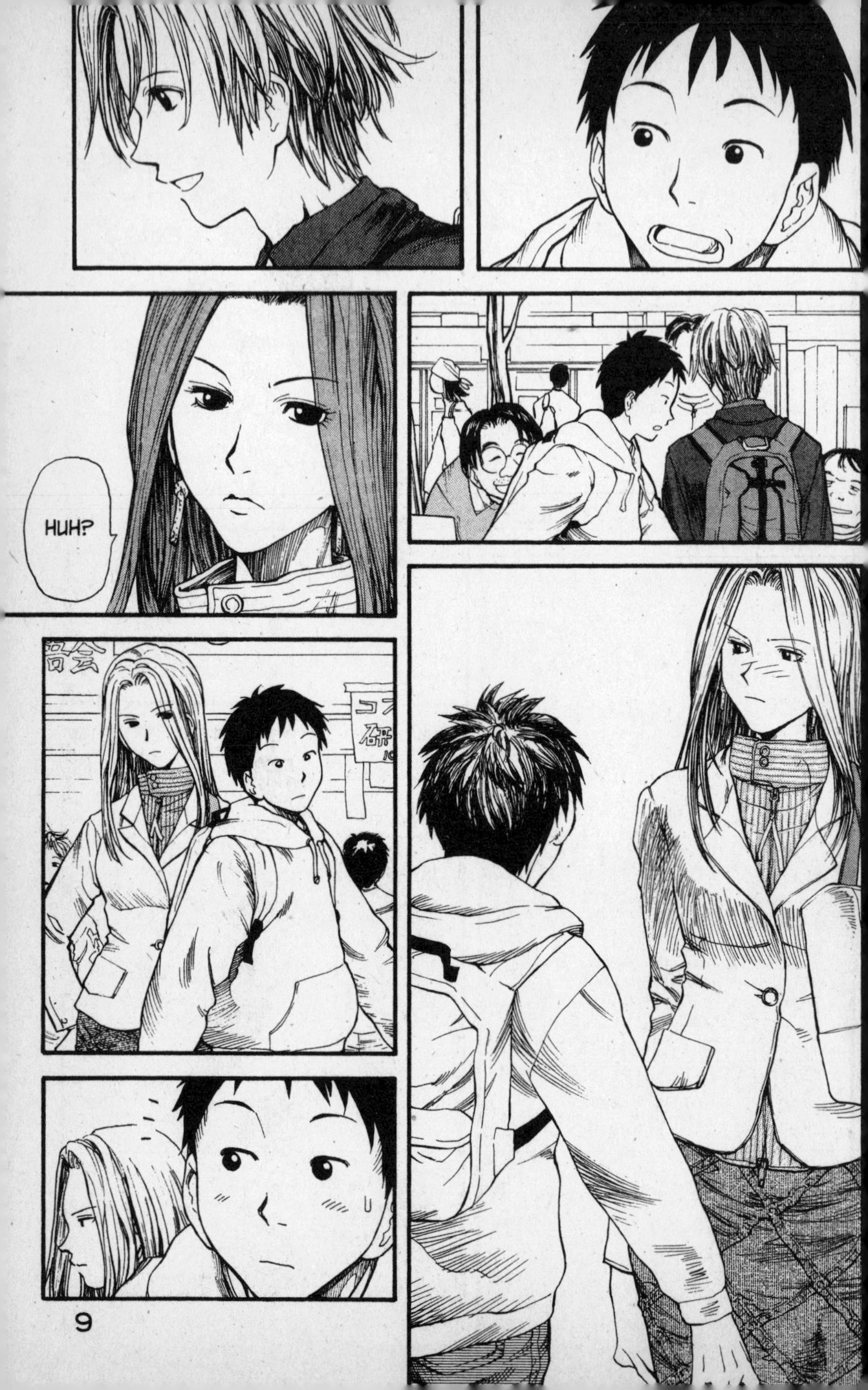
HUH?

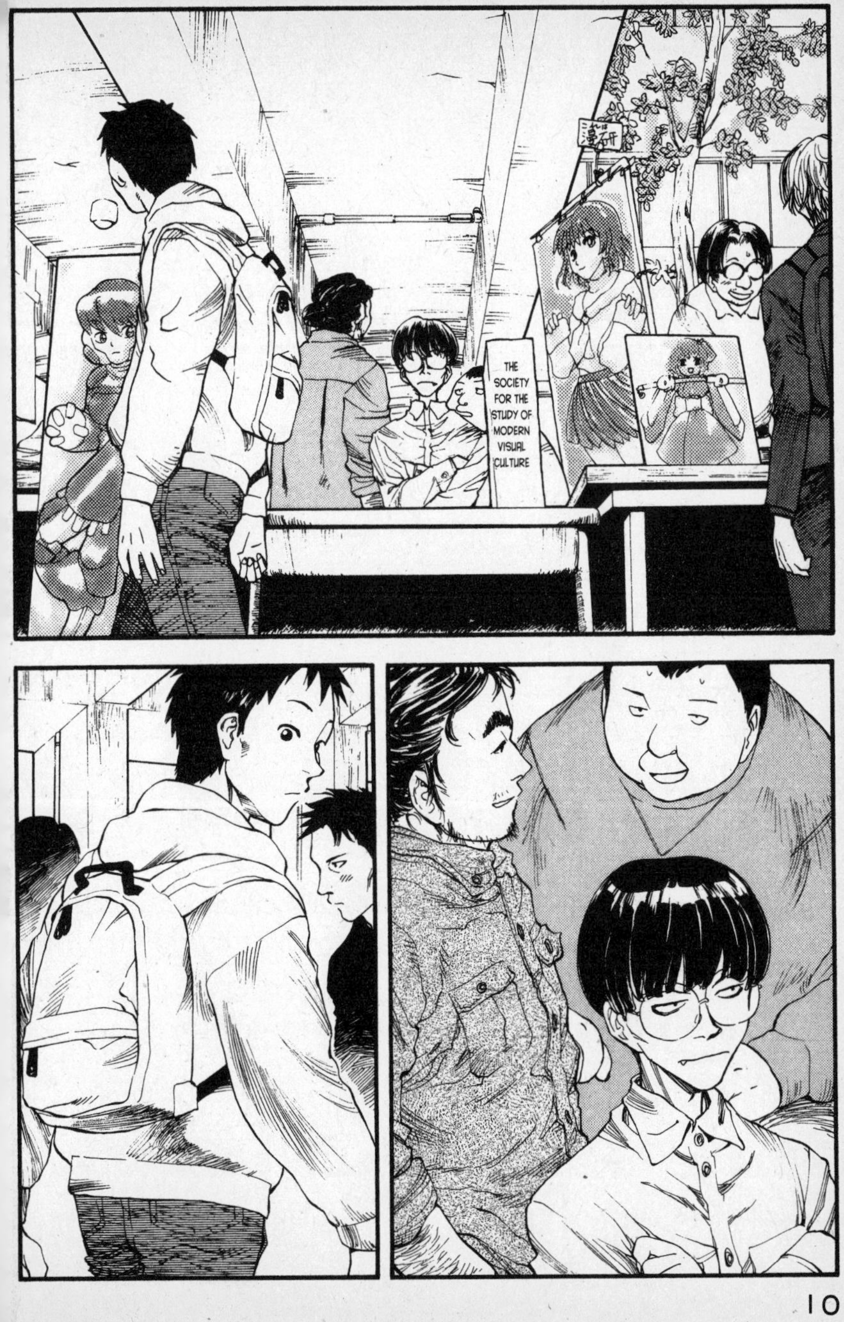
THE SOCIETY FOR THE STUDY OF MODERN VISUAL CULTURE

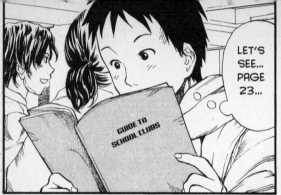

LET'S SEE... PAGE 23...

GUIDE TO SCHOOL CLUBS

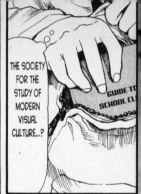

THE SOCIETY FOR THE STUDY OF MODERN VISUAL CULTURE...?

GUIDE TO SCHOOL CL...

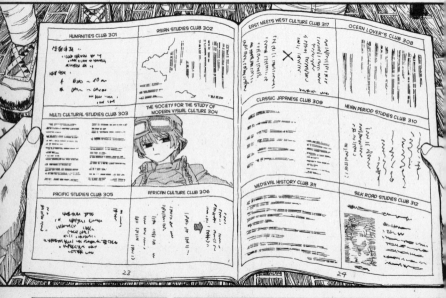

HUMANITIES CLUB 301	ASIAN STUDIES CLUB 302	EAST MEETS WEST CULTURE CLUB 317	OCEAN LOVER'S CLUB 308
MULTI CULTURAL STUDIES CLUB 303	THE SOCIETY FOR THE STUDY OF MODERN VISUAL CULTURE 304	CLASSIC JAPANESE CLUB 309	HEIAN PERIOD STUDIES CLUB 310
PACIFIC STUDIES CLUB 305	AFRICAN CULTURE CLUB 306	MEDIEVAL HISTORY CLUB 311	SILK ROAD STUDIES CLUB 312

23   24

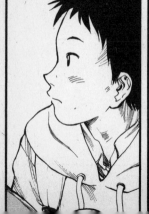

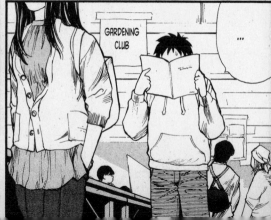

GARDENING CLUB

...

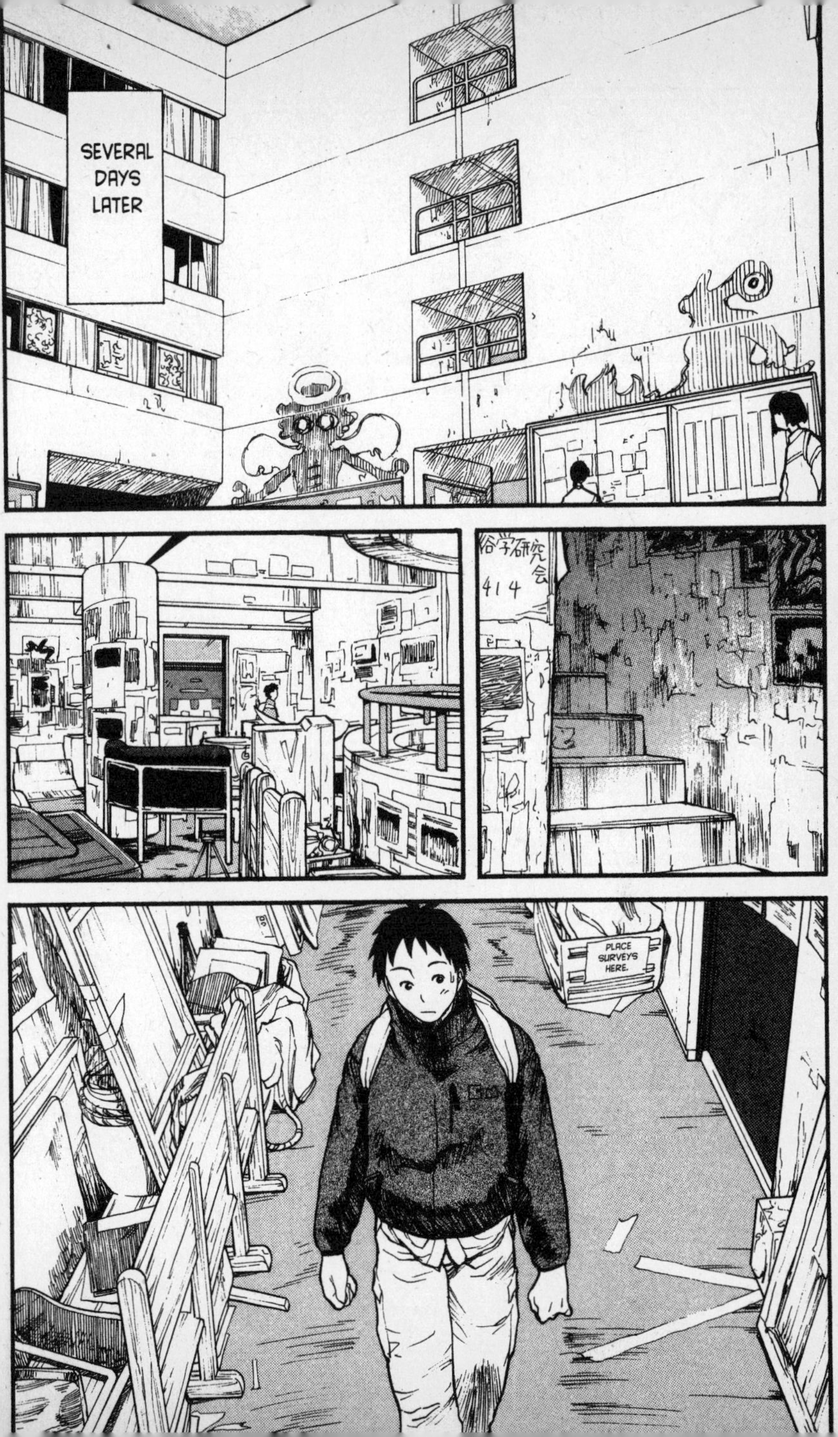
SEVERAL DAYS LATER
俗学研究会
414
PLACE SURVEYS HERE.

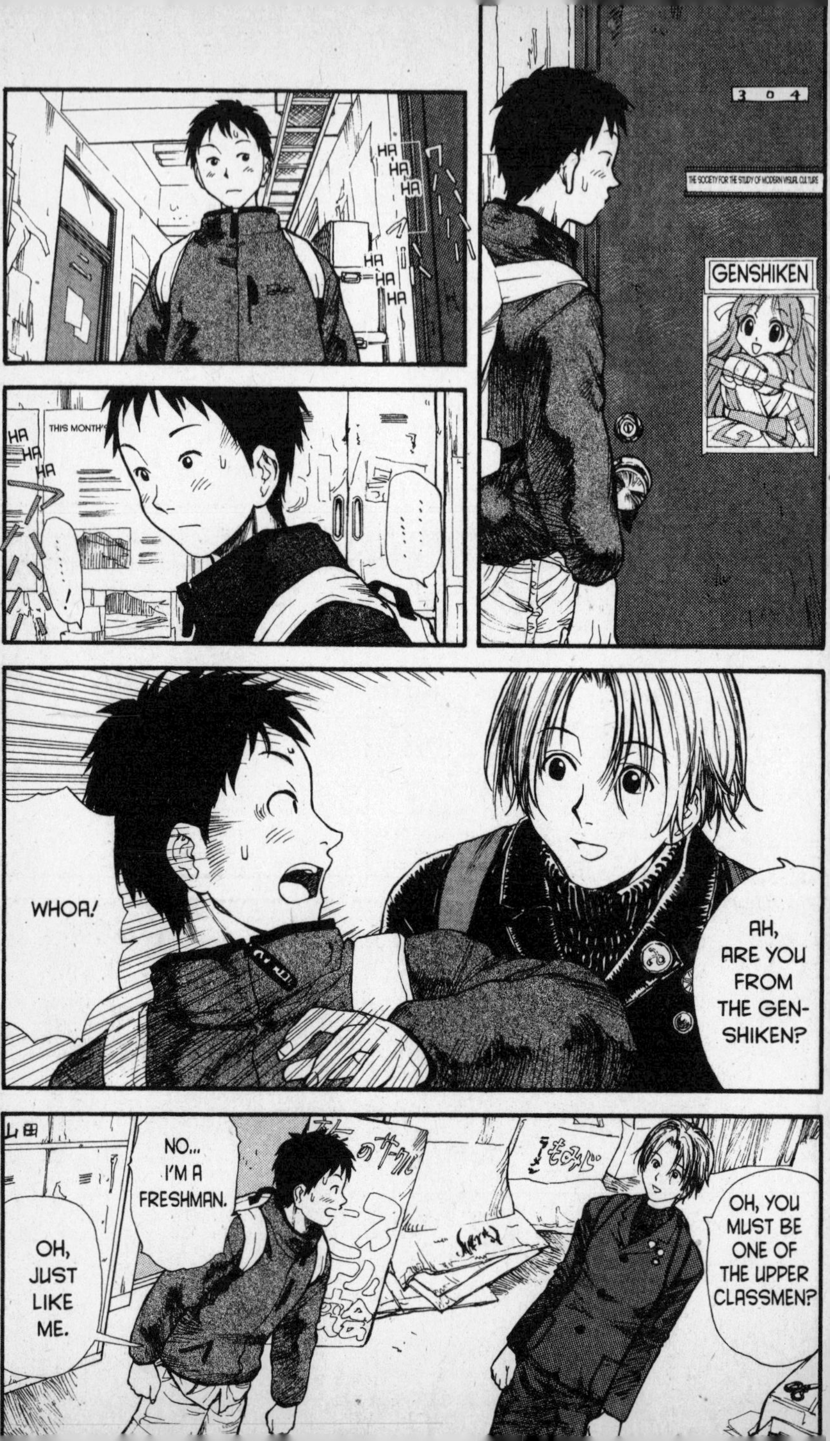

304
THE SOCIETY FOR THE STUDY OF MODERN VISUAL CULTURE
GENSHIKEN
HA HA HA
HA HA HA
HA HA HA
THIS MONTH'S
......
......!
AH, ARE YOU FROM THE GEN-SHIKEN?
WHOA!
OH, YOU MUST BE ONE OF THE UPPER CLASSMEN?
NO... I'M A FRESHMAN.
OH, JUST LIKE ME.

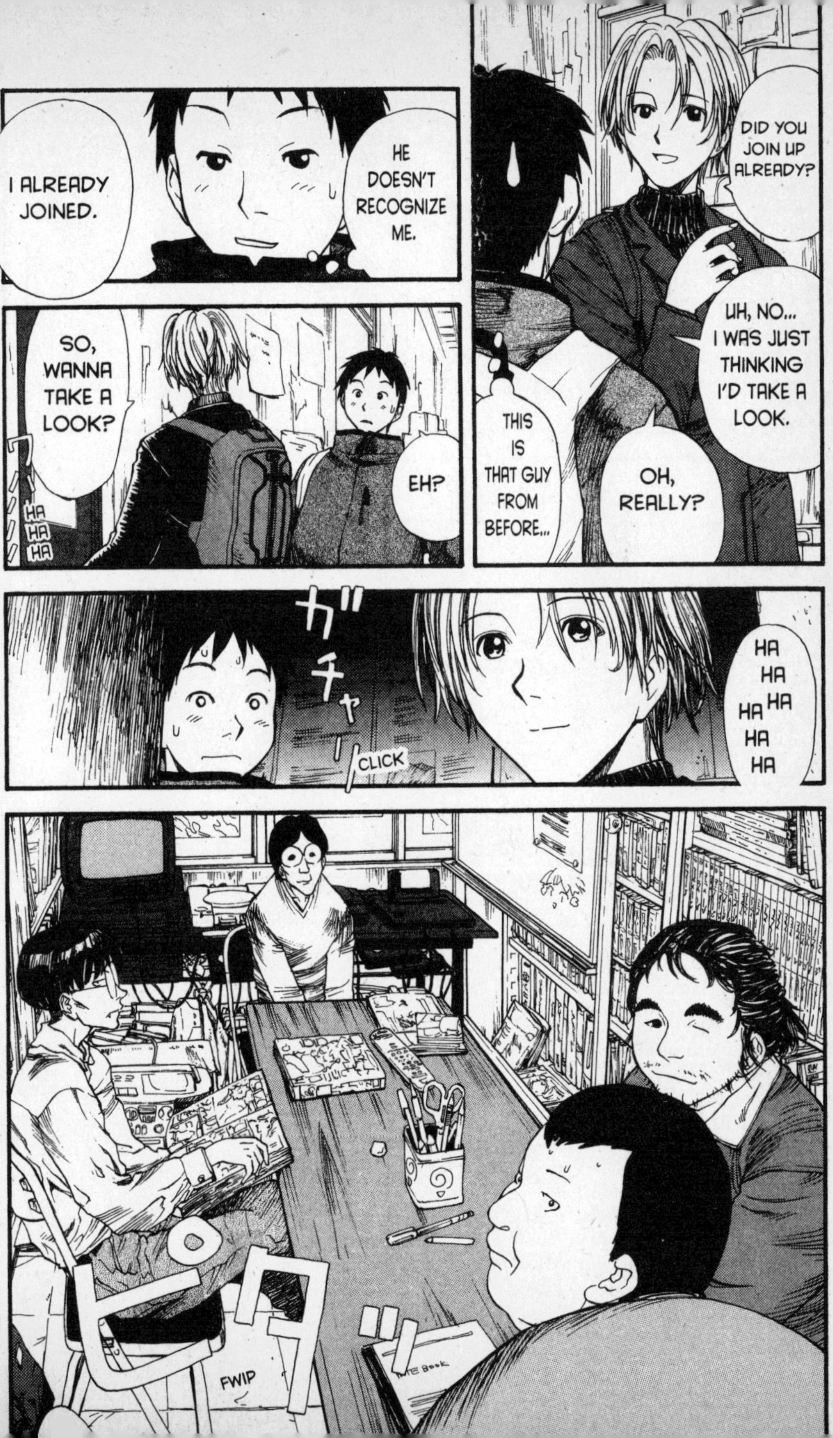
DID YOU JOIN UP ALREADY?
UH, NO... I WAS JUST THINKING I'D TAKE A LOOK.
OH, REALLY?
THIS IS THAT GUY FROM BEFORE...
HE DOESN'T RECOGNIZE ME.
I ALREADY JOINED.
EH?
SO, WANNA TAKE A LOOK?
HA HA HA
HA HA HA HA HA HA
CLICK
FWIP

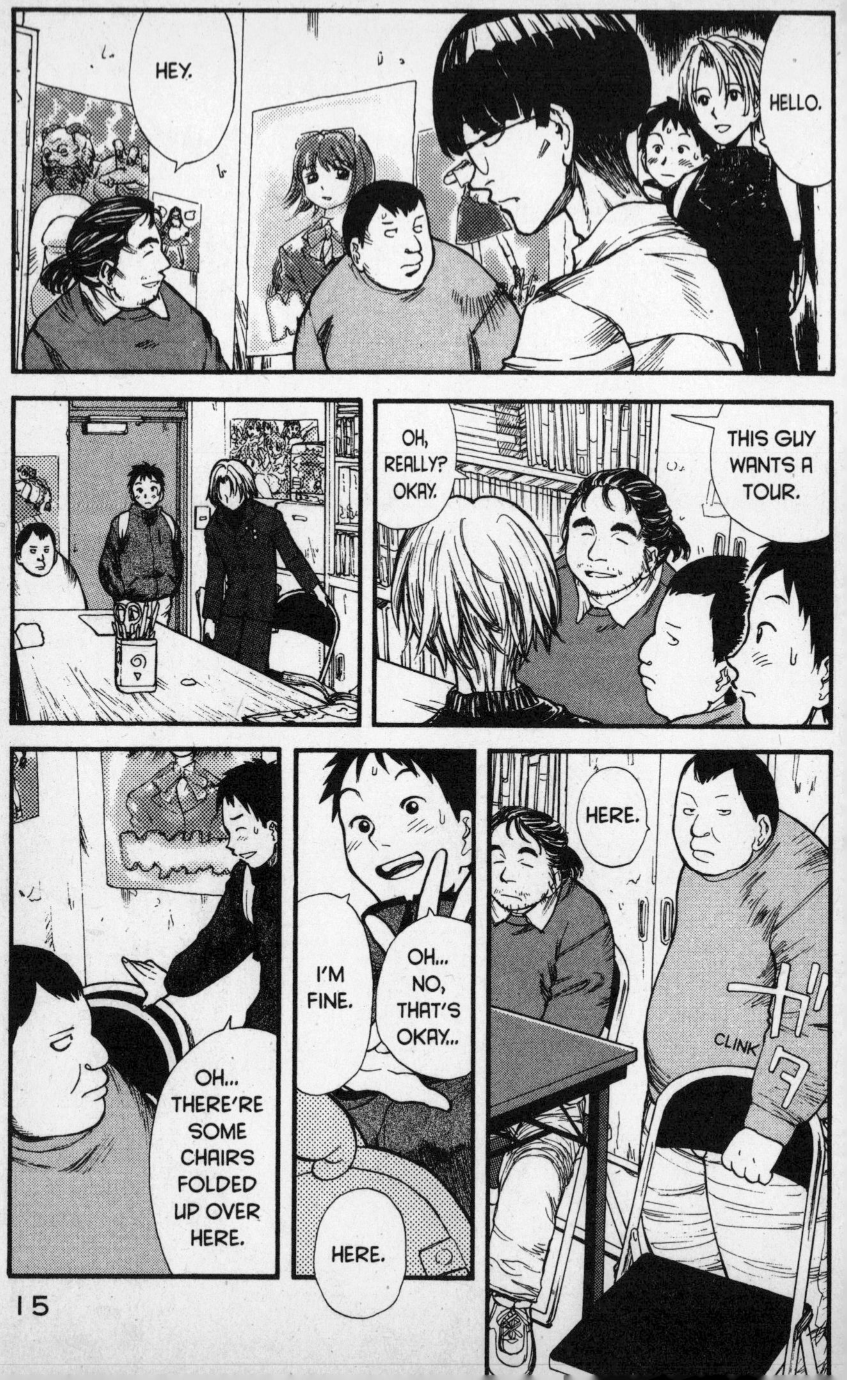
HELLO.
HEY.
THIS GUY WANTS A TOUR.
OH, REALLY? OKAY.
HERE.
ガタ
CLINK
OH... NO, THAT'S OKAY...
I'M FINE.
HERE.
OH... THERE'RE SOME CHAIRS FOLDED UP OVER HERE.

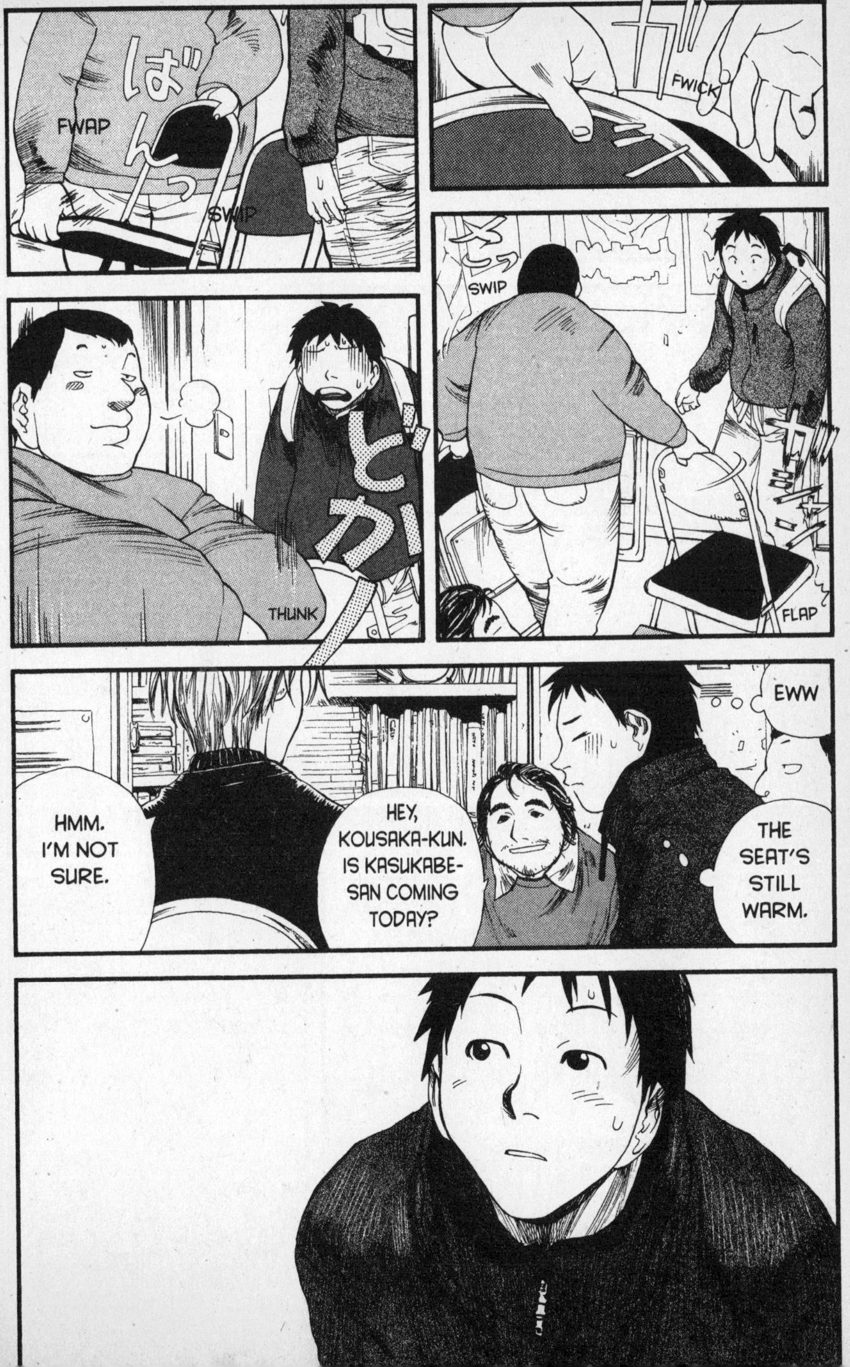
FWICK
ばんっ
FWAP
SWIP
SWIP
FLAP
THUNK
EWW
THE SEAT'S STILL WARM.
HEY, KOUSAKA-KUN. IS KASUKABE-SAN COMING TODAY?
HMM. I'M NOT SURE.

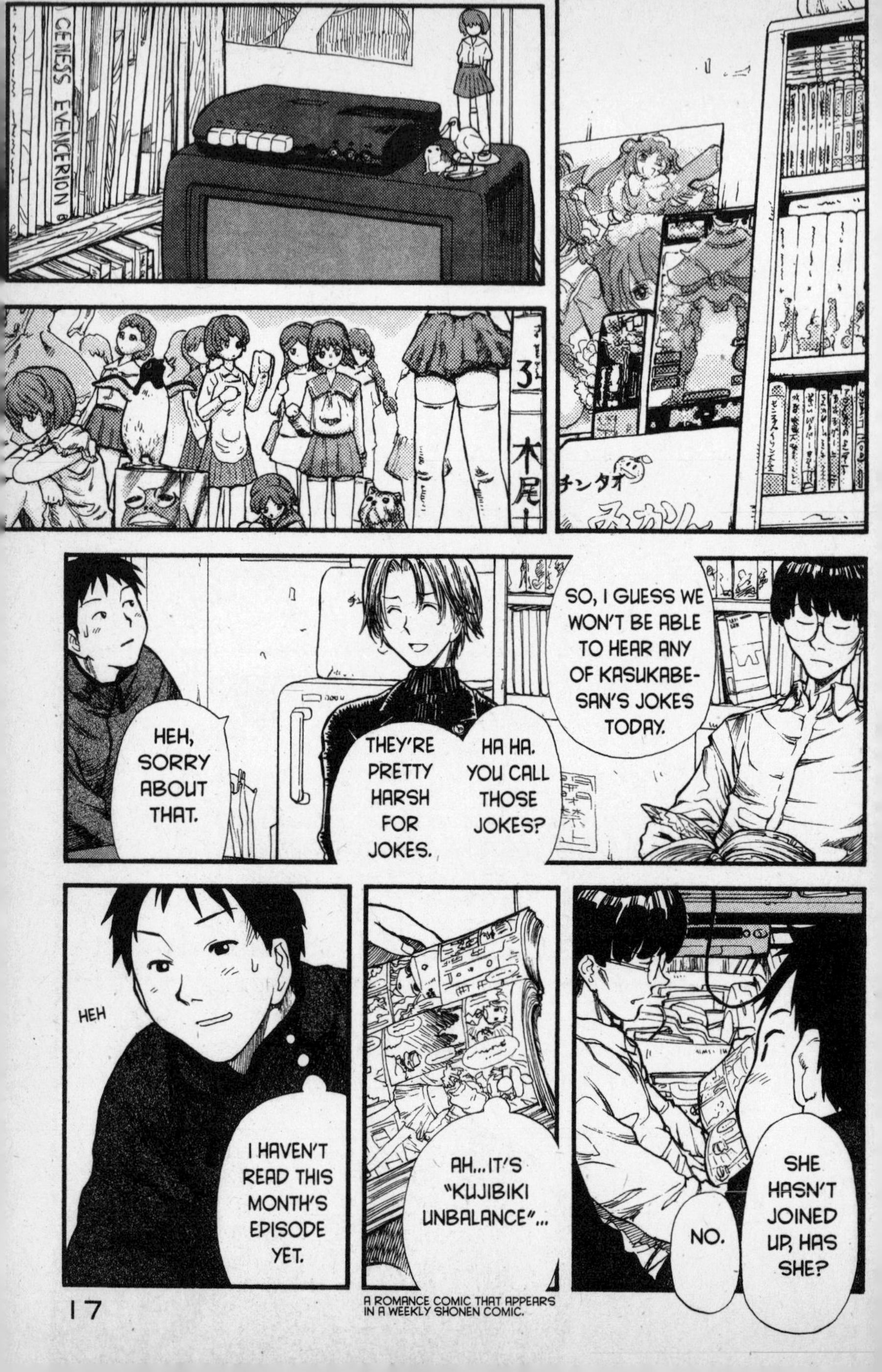
SO, I GUESS WE WON'T BE ABLE TO HEAR ANY OF KASUKABE-SAN'S JOKES TODAY.
HA HA. YOU CALL THOSE JOKES?
THEY'RE PRETTY HARSH FOR JOKES.
HEH, SORRY ABOUT THAT.
SHE HASN'T JOINED UP, HAS SHE?
NO.
AH...IT'S "KUJIBIKI UNBALANCE"...
HEH
I HAVEN'T READ THIS MONTH'S EPISODE YET.

A ROMANCE COMIC THAT APPEARS IN A WEEKLY SHONEN COMIC.

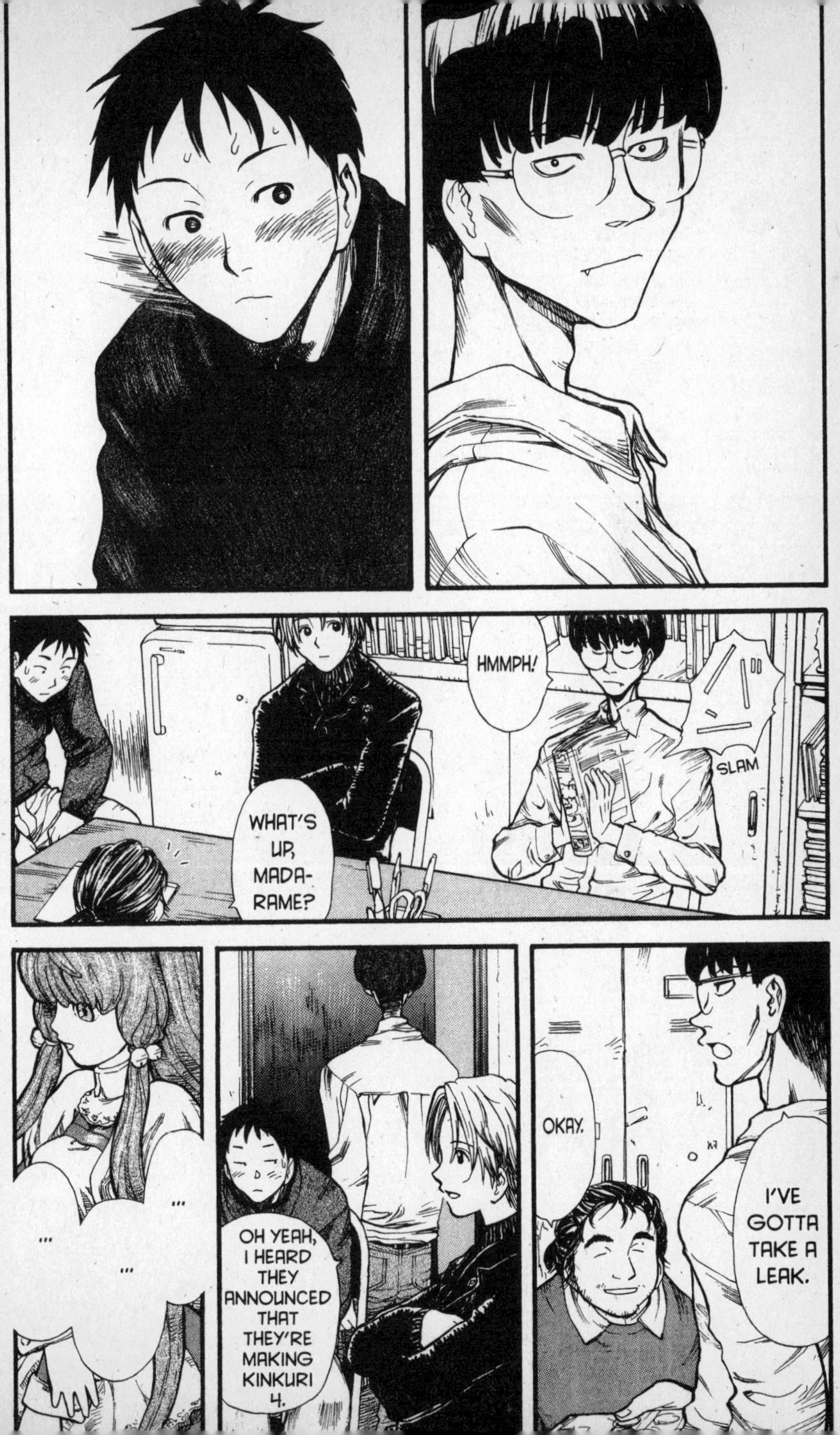
HMMPH!
SLAM
WHAT'S UP, MADARAME?
I'VE GOTTA TAKE A LEAK.
OKAY.
OH YEAH, I HEARD THEY ANNOUNCED THAT THEY'RE MAKING KINKURI 4.
...
...
...

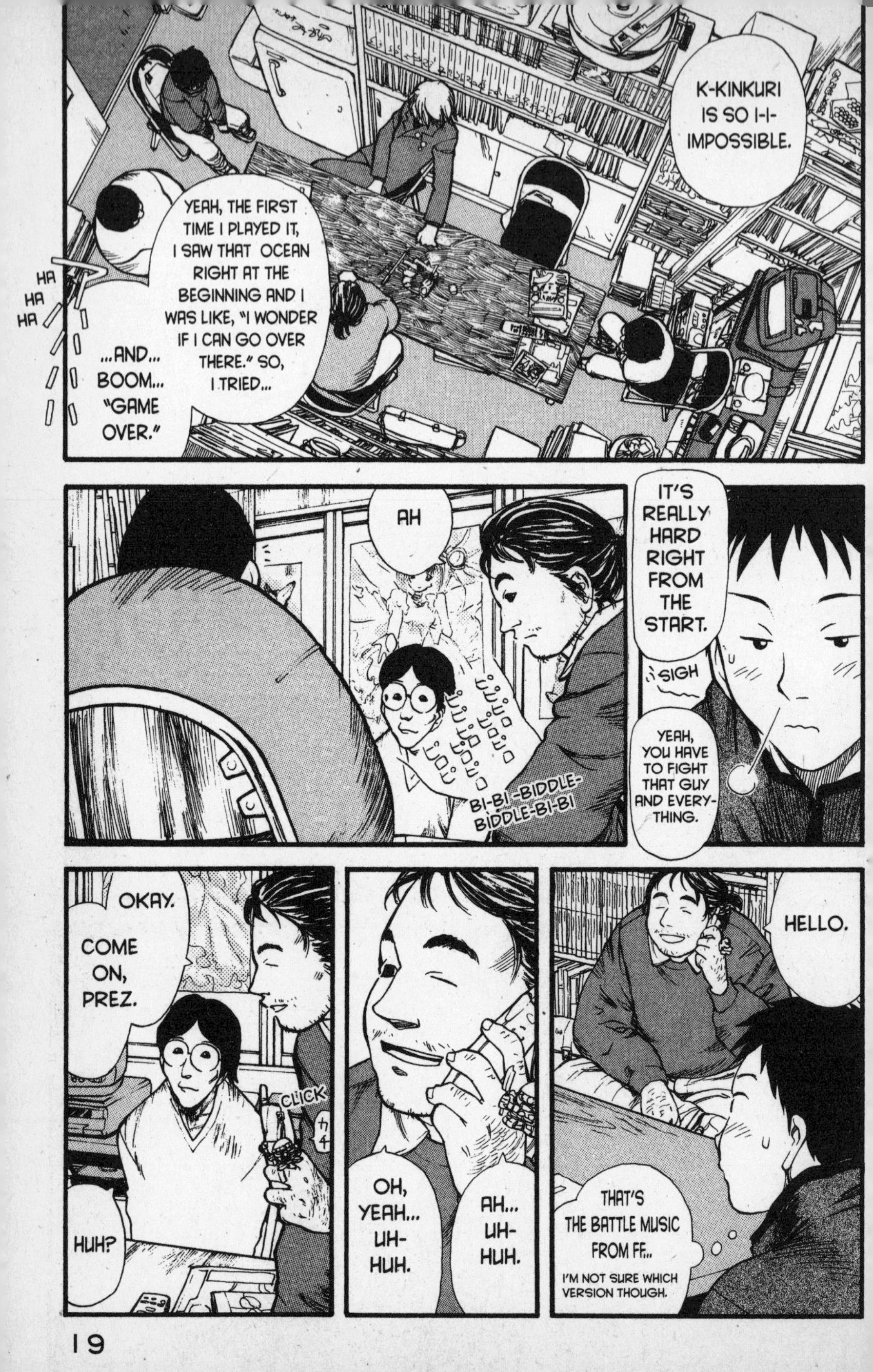
K-KINKURI IS SO I-I-IMPOSSIBLE.
YEAH, THE FIRST TIME I PLAYED IT, I SAW THAT OCEAN RIGHT AT THE BEGINNING AND I WAS LIKE, "I WONDER IF I CAN GO OVER THERE." SO, I TRIED...
...AND... BOOM... "GAME OVER."
HA HA HA
IT'S REALLY HARD RIGHT FROM THE START.
SIGH
YEAH, YOU HAVE TO FIGHT THAT GUY AND EVERY-THING.
AH
BI-BI-BIDDLE-BIDDLE-BI-BI
HELLO.
THAT'S THE BATTLE MUSIC FROM FF...
I'M NOT SURE WHICH VERSION THOUGH.
AH... UH-HUH.
OH, YEAH... UH-HUH.
OKAY.
COME ON, PREZ.
CLICK
HUH?

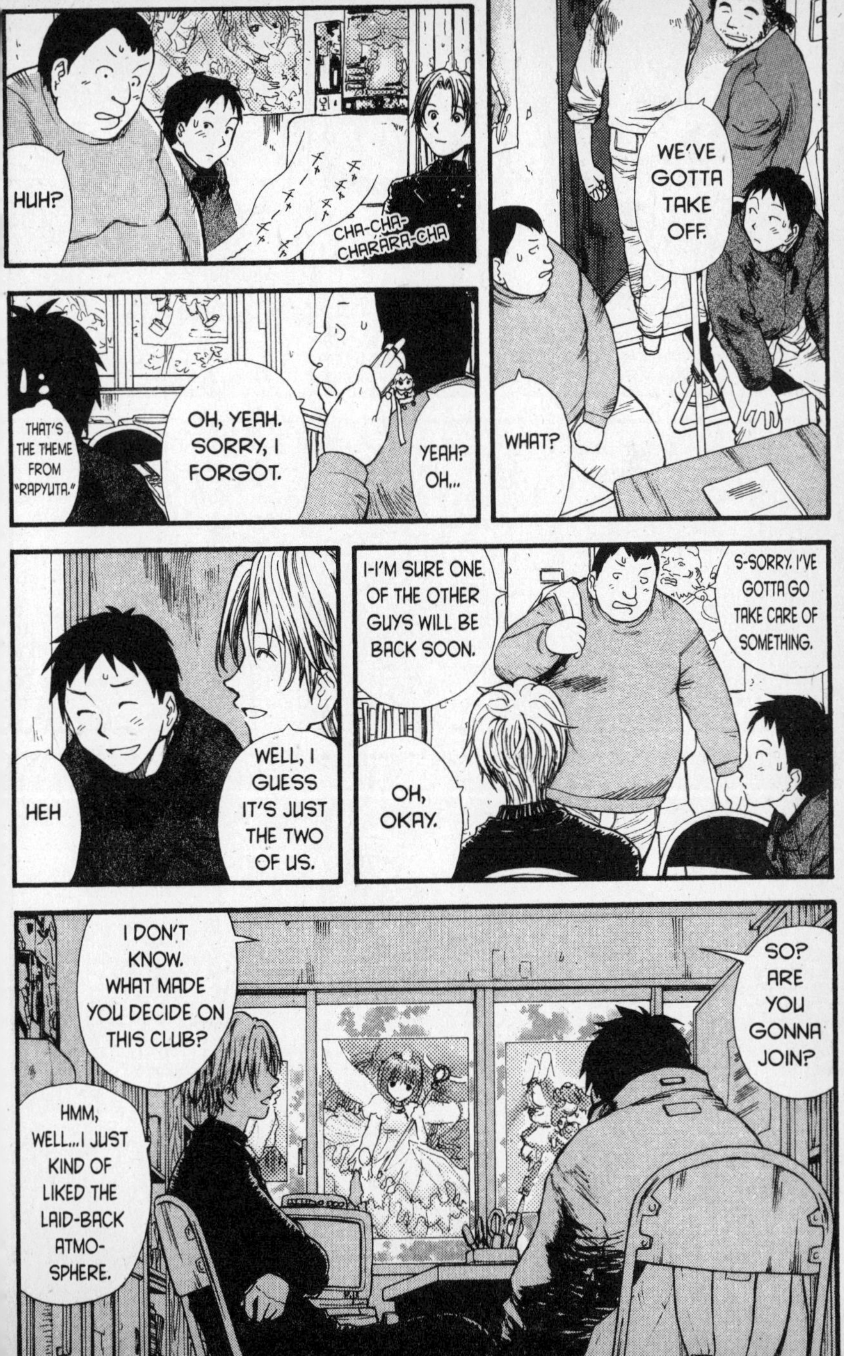
WE'VE GOTTA TAKE OFF.
WHAT?
HUH?
CHA-CHA-CHARARA-CHA
YEAH? OH...
OH, YEAH. SORRY, I FORGOT.
THAT'S THE THEME FROM "RAPYUTA."
S-SORRY. I'VE GOTTA GO TAKE CARE OF SOMETHING.
I-I'M SURE ONE OF THE OTHER GUYS WILL BE BACK SOON.
OH, OKAY.
WELL, I GUESS IT'S JUST THE TWO OF US.
HEH
SO? ARE YOU GONNA JOIN?
I DON'T KNOW. WHAT MADE YOU DECIDE ON THIS CLUB?
HMM, WELL...I JUST KIND OF LIKED THE LAID-BACK ATMO-SPHERE.

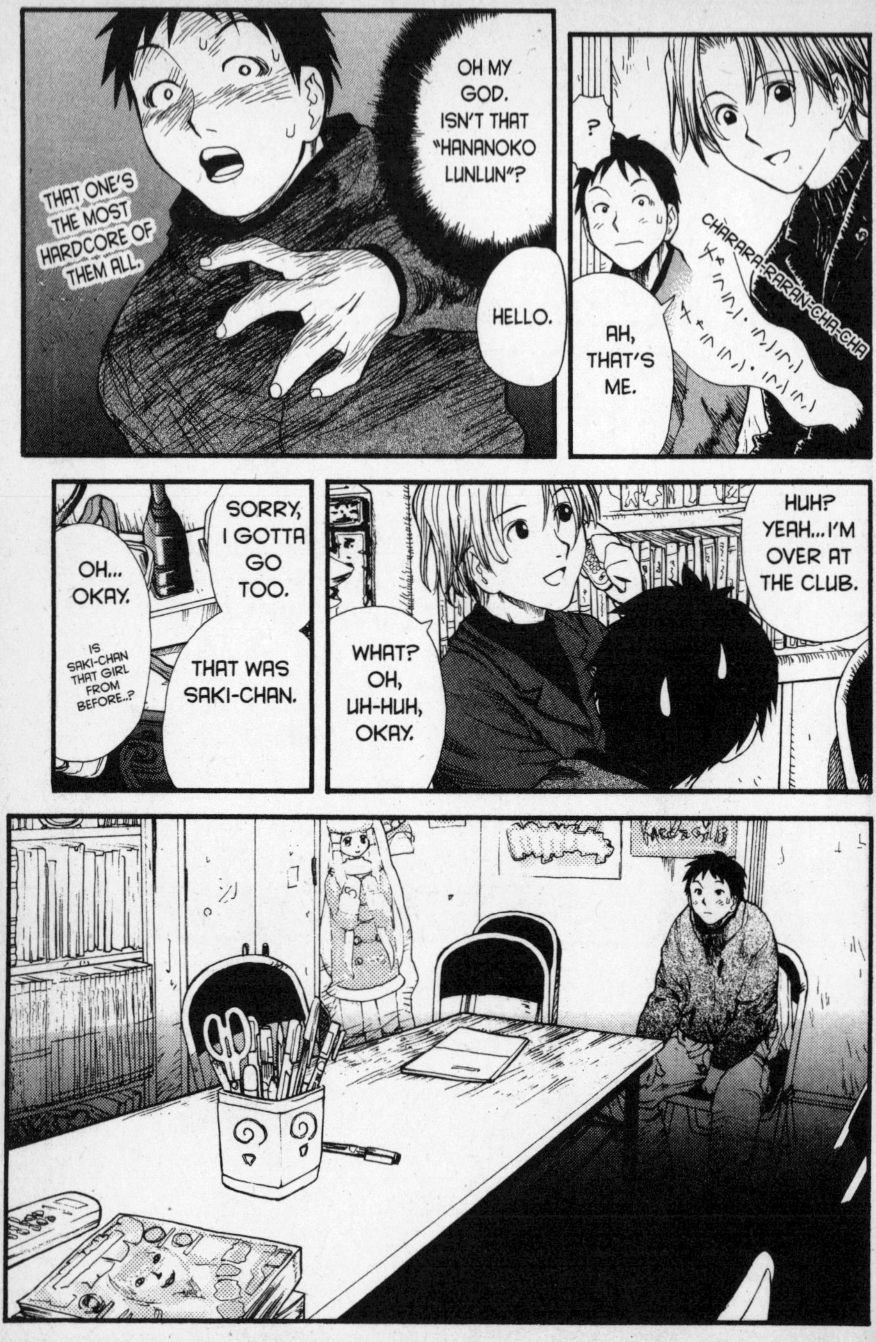
?
CHARARA-RARAN-CHA-CHA
AH, THAT'S ME.
OH MY GOD. ISN'T THAT "HANANOKO LUNLUN"?
HELLO.
THAT ONE'S THE MOST HARDCORE OF THEM ALL.
HUH? YEAH...I'M OVER AT THE CLUB.
WHAT? OH, UH-HUH, OKAY.
SORRY, I GOTTA GO TOO.
THAT WAS SAKI-CHAN.
OH... OKAY.
IS SAKI-CHAN THAT GIRL FROM BEFORE..?

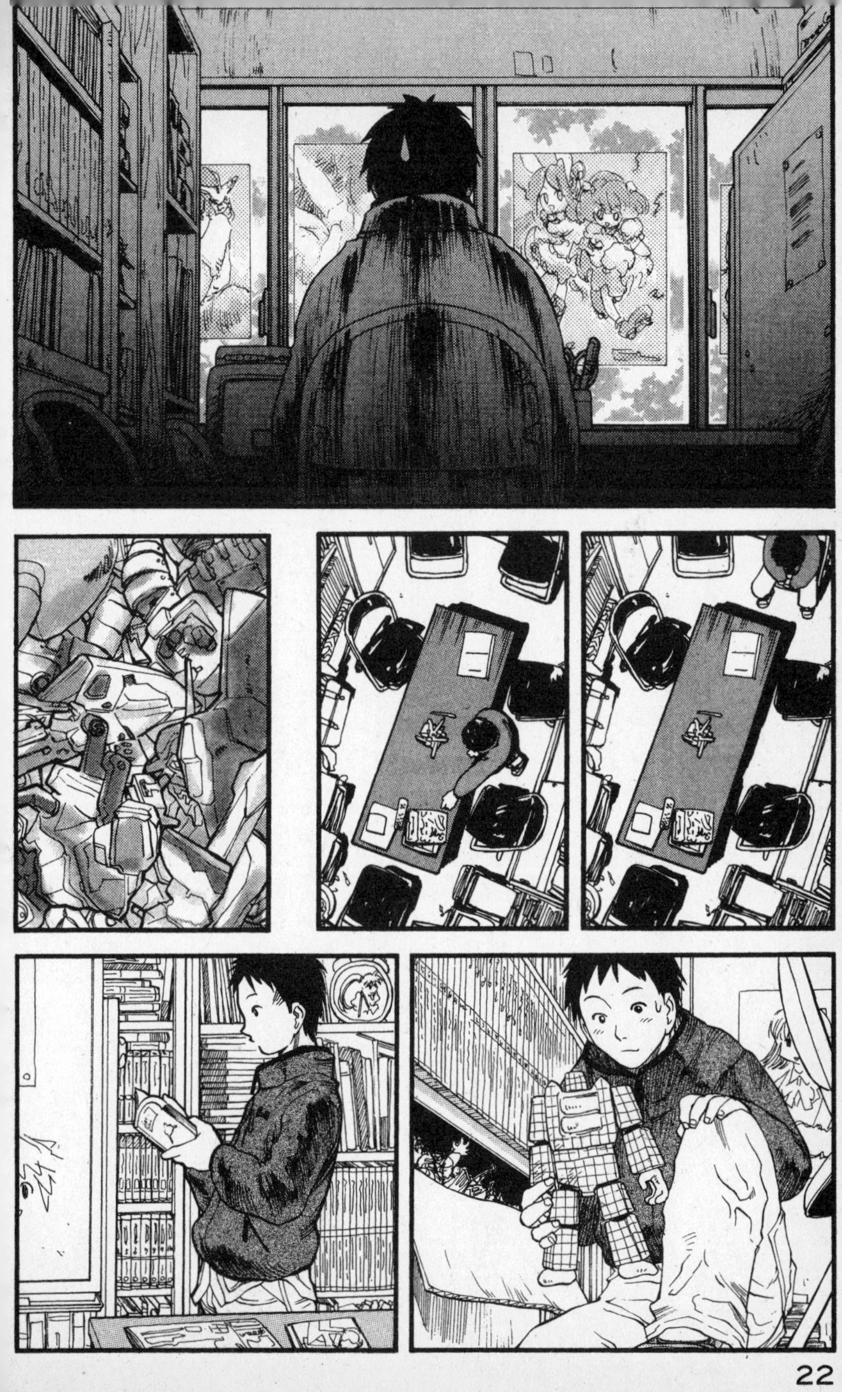

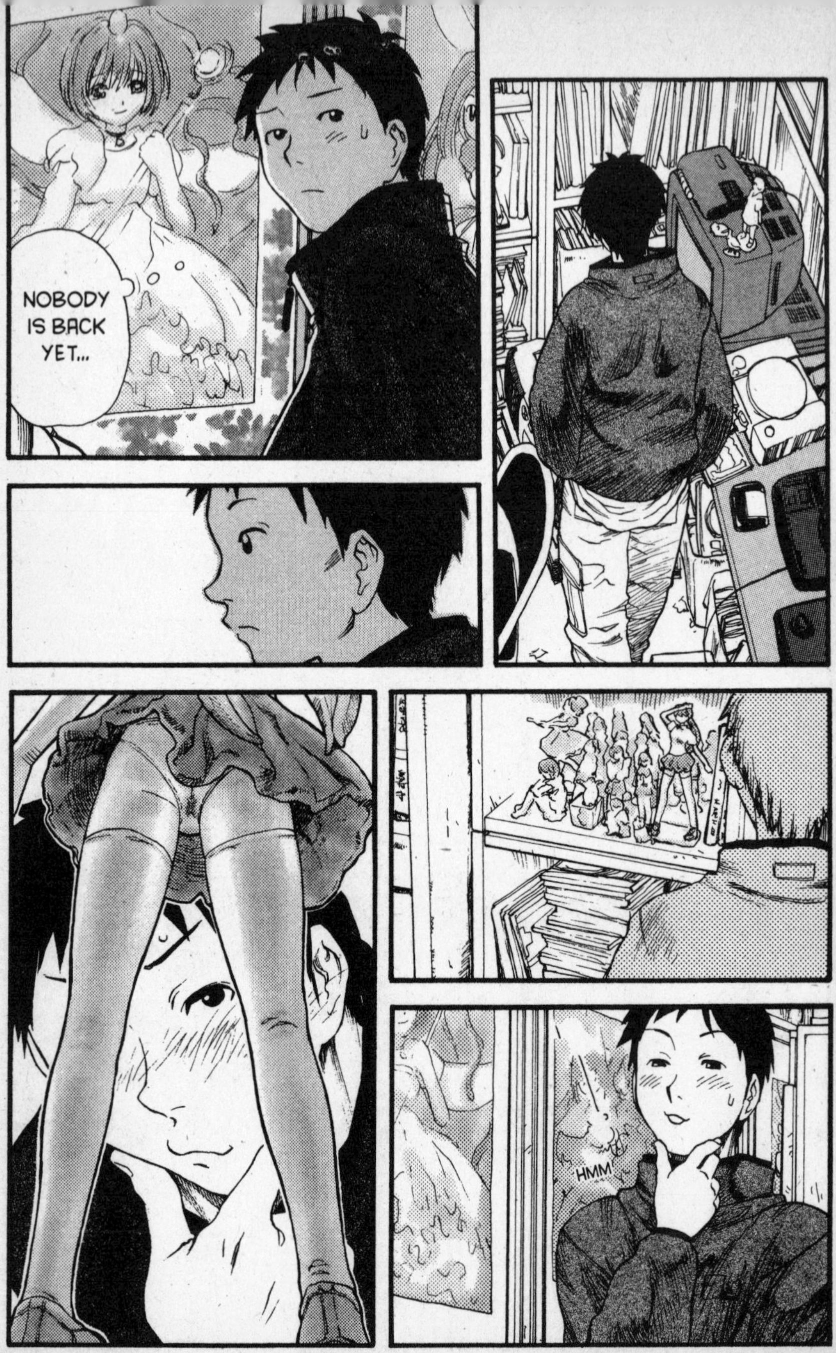
NOBODY IS BACK YET...
HMM

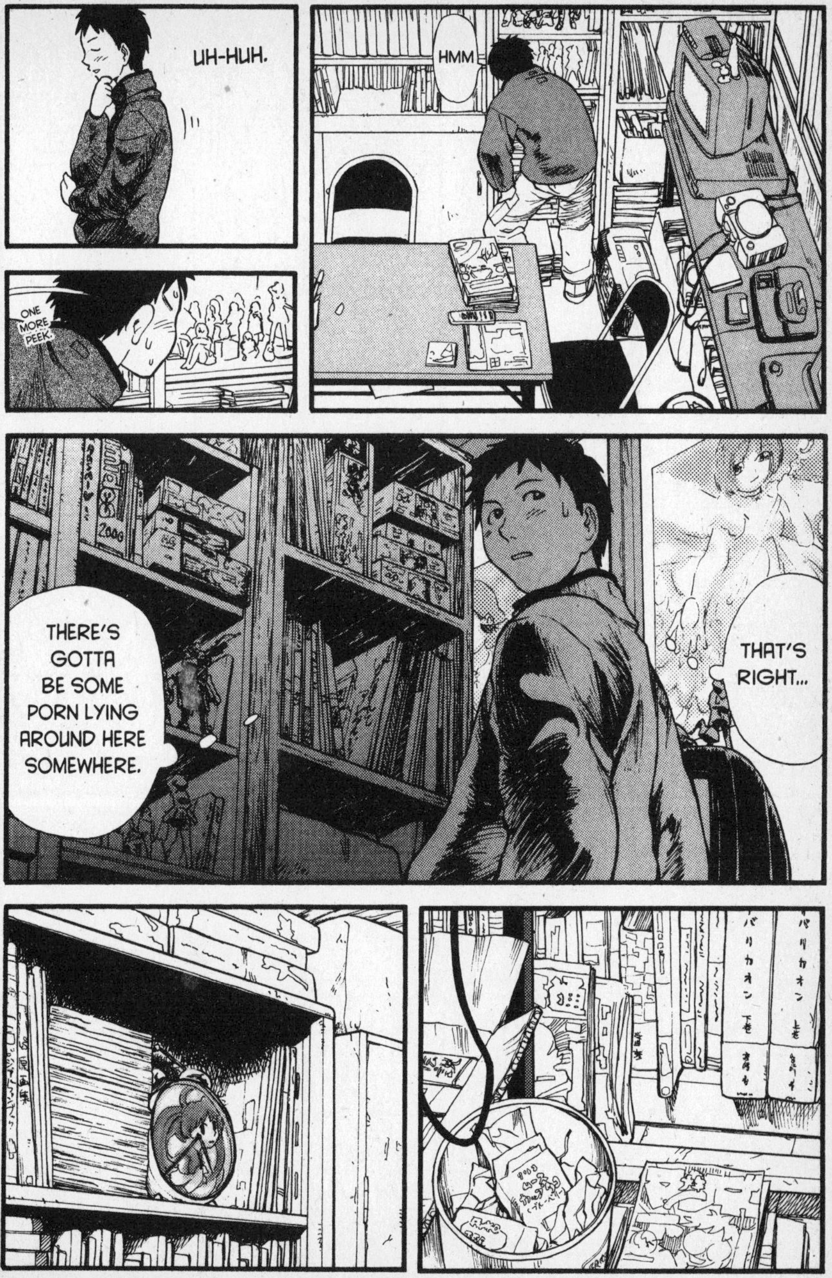
HMM
UH-HUH.
ONE MORE PEEK.
THAT'S RIGHT...
THERE'S GOTTA BE SOME PORN LYING AROUND HERE SOMEWHERE.

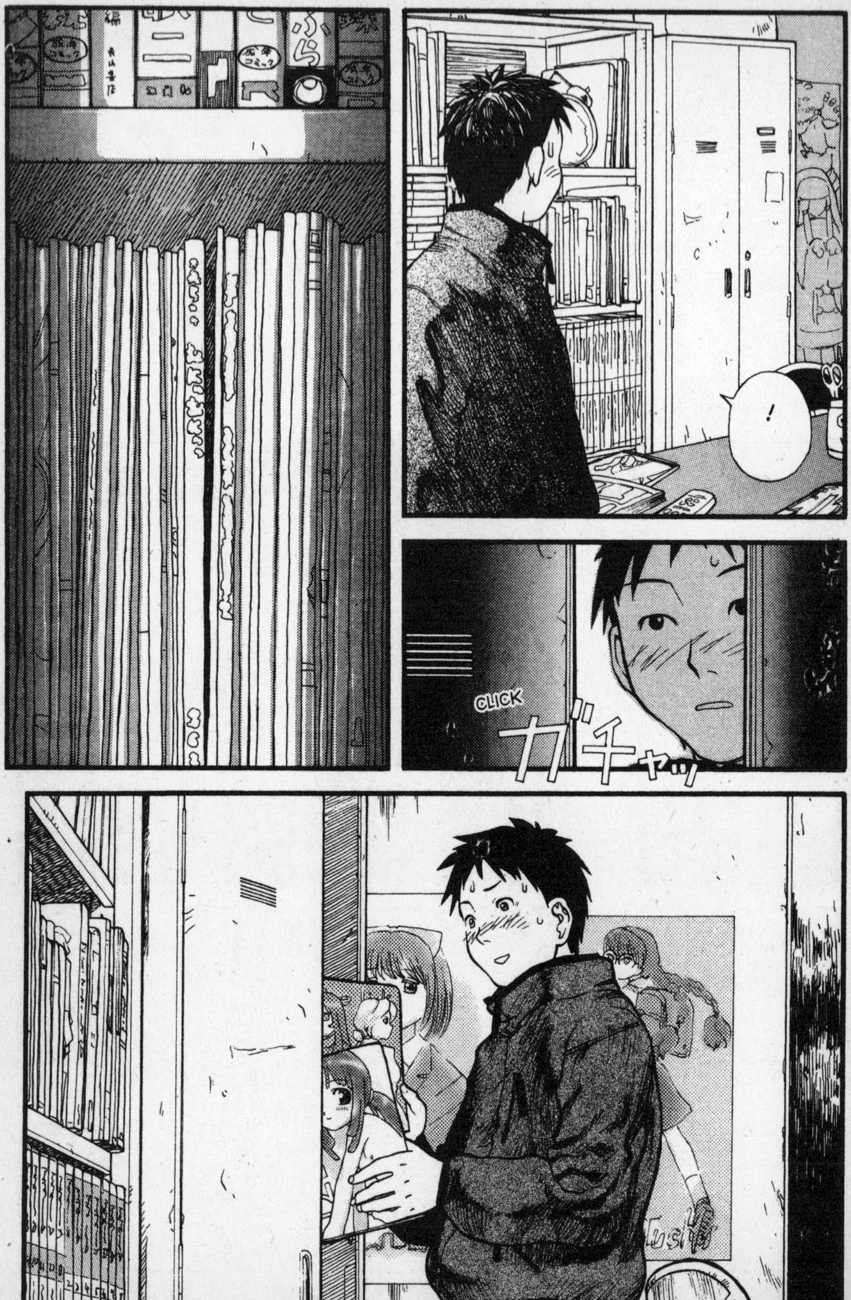
!
CLICK
ガチャッ

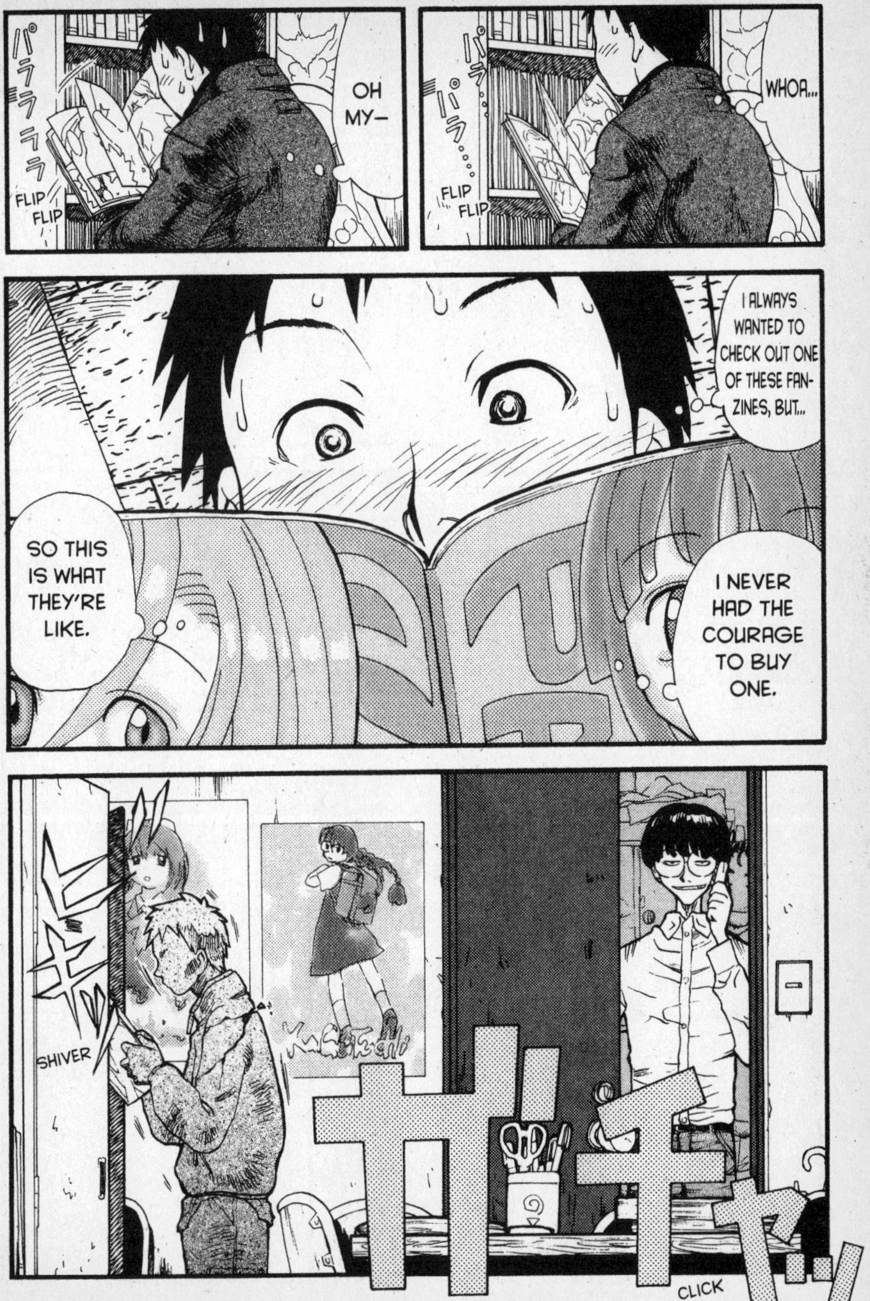

WHOA...
FLIP FLIP
OH MY—
FLIP FLIP
I ALWAYS WANTED TO CHECK OUT ONE OF THESE FAN-ZINES, BUT...
I NEVER HAD THE COURAGE TO BUY ONE.
SO THIS IS WHAT THEY'RE LIKE.
CLICK
SHIVER

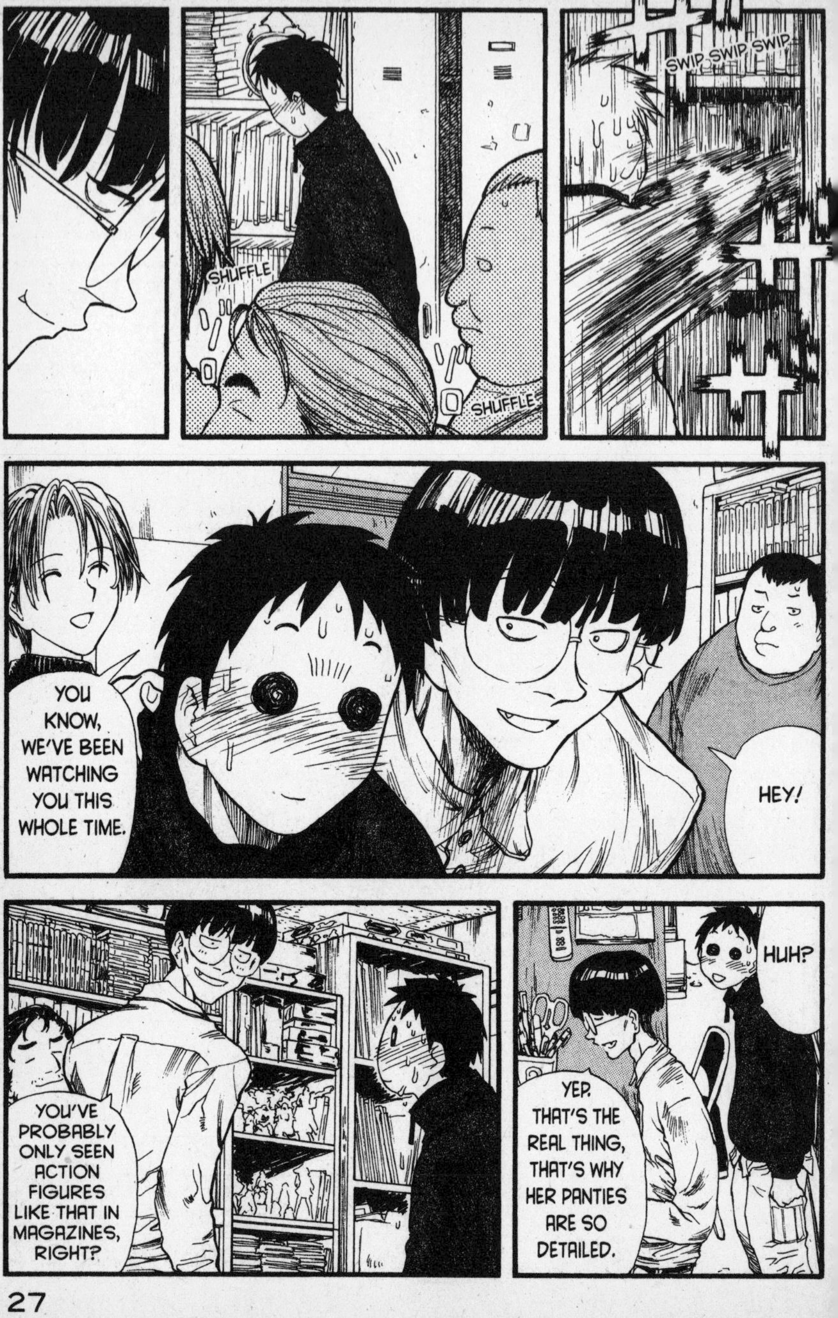
SWIP SWIP SWIP
SHUFFLE
SHUFFLE
HEY!
YOU KNOW, WE'VE BEEN WATCHING YOU THIS WHOLE TIME.
HUH?
YEP. THAT'S THE REAL THING, THAT'S WHY HER PANTIES ARE SO DETAILED.
YOU'VE PROBABLY ONLY SEEN ACTION FIGURES LIKE THAT IN MAGAZINES, RIGHT?

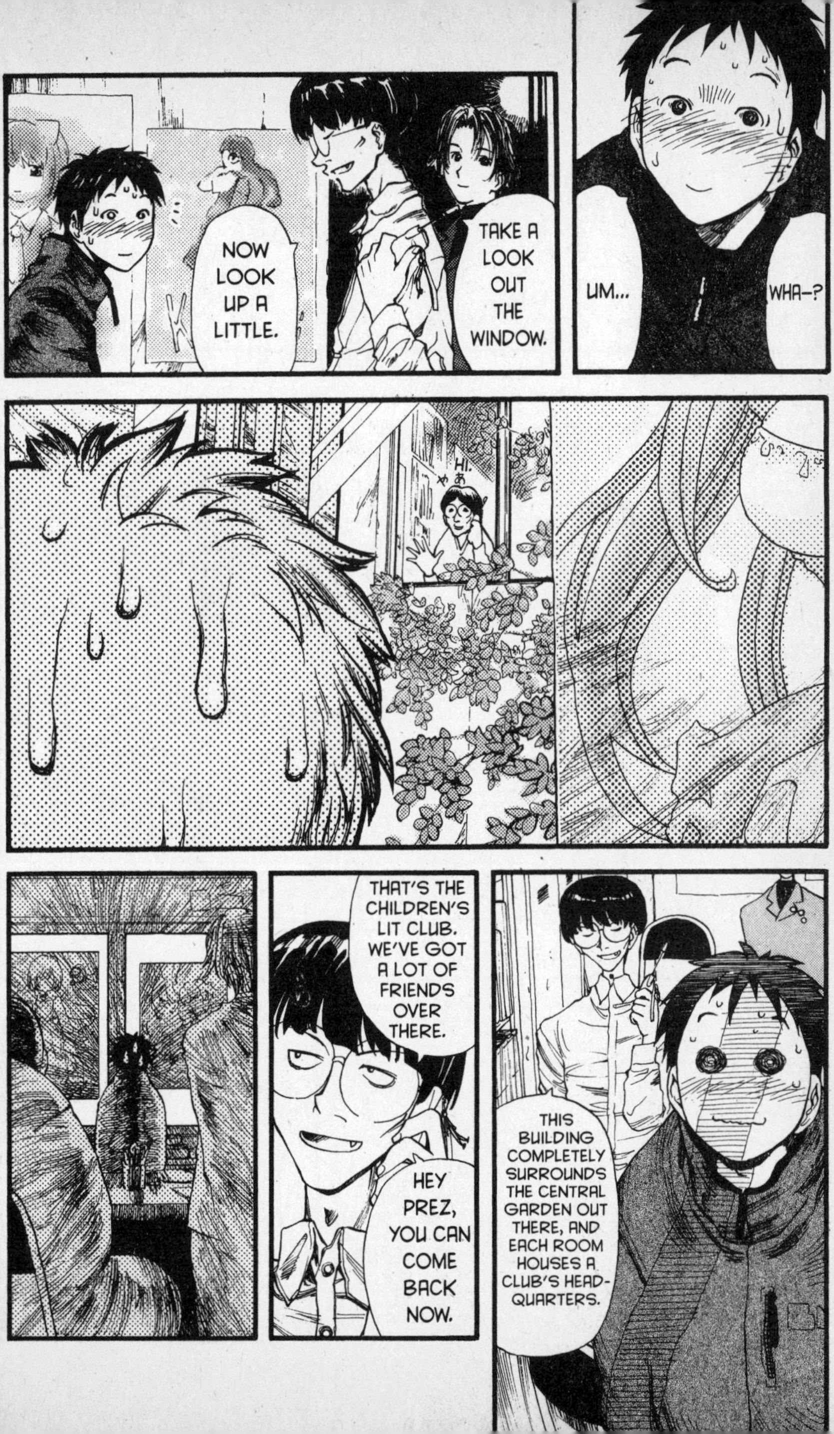
WHA-?
UM...
TAKE A LOOK OUT THE WINDOW.
NOW LOOK UP A LITTLE.
HI.
やあ
THIS BUILDING COMPLETELY SURROUNDS THE CENTRAL GARDEN OUT THERE, AND EACH ROOM HOUSES A CLUB'S HEAD-QUARTERS.
THAT'S THE CHILDREN'S LIT CLUB. WE'VE GOT A LOT OF FRIENDS OVER THERE.
HEY PREZ, YOU CAN COME BACK NOW.

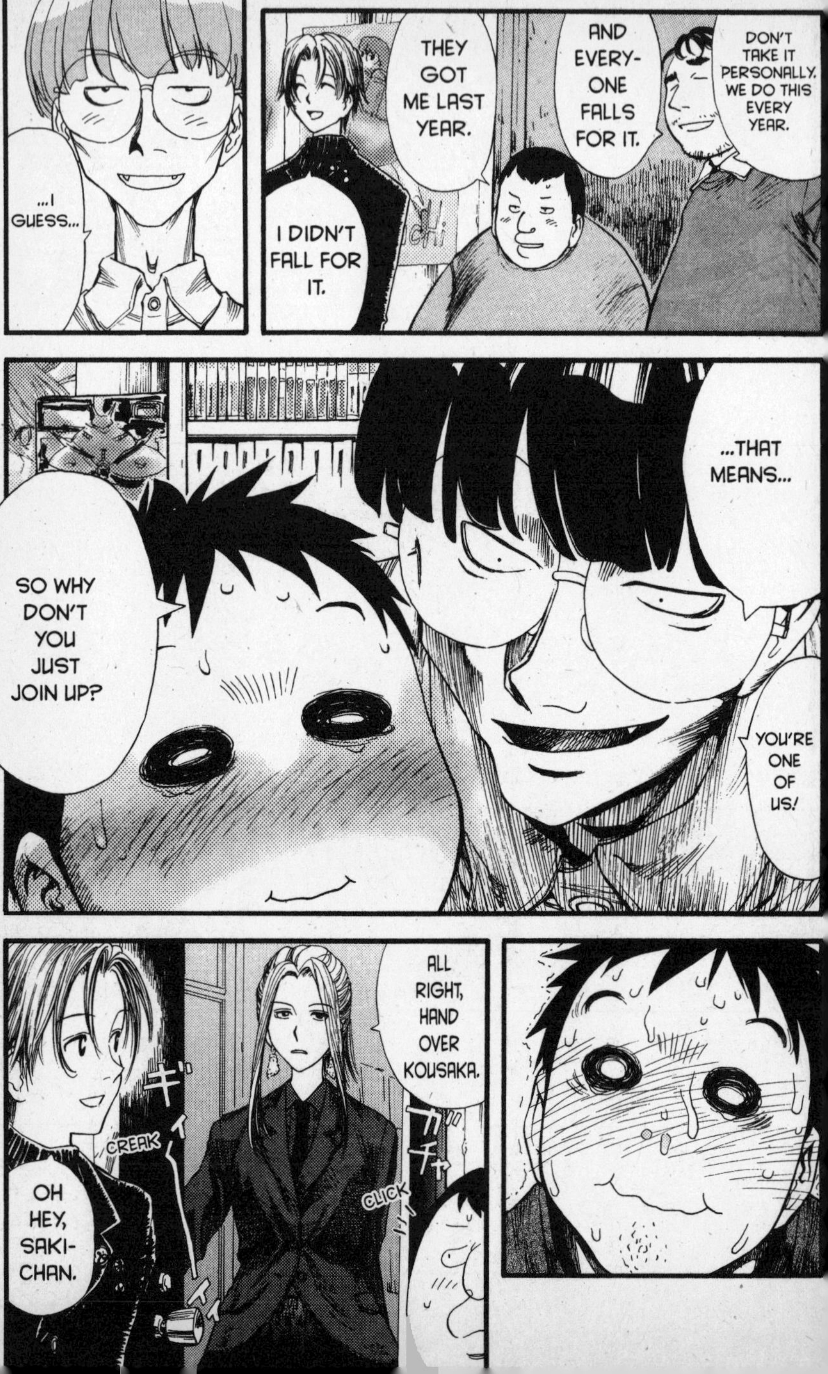
DON'T TAKE IT PERSONALLY. WE DO THIS EVERY YEAR.
AND EVERY-ONE FALLS FOR IT.
THEY GOT ME LAST YEAR.
I DIDN'T FALL FOR IT.
...I GUESS...
...THAT MEANS...
YOU'RE ONE OF US!
SO WHY DON'T YOU JUST JOIN UP?
ALL RIGHT, HAND OVER KOUSAKA.
ガチャ
CLICK
ギィ
CREAK
OH HEY, SAKI-CHAN.

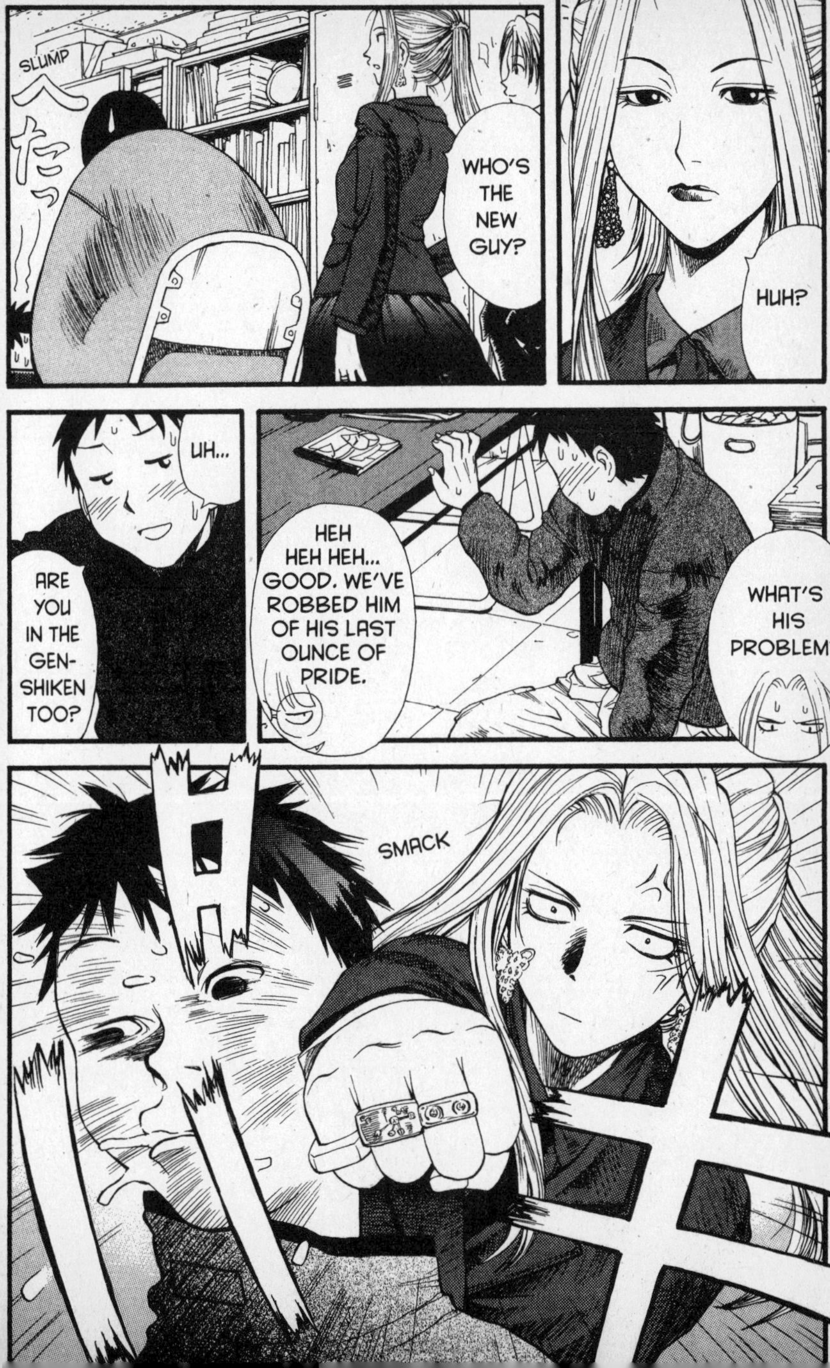
HUH?
WHO'S THE NEW GUY?
SLUMP
へたっ
WHAT'S HIS PROBLEM?
HEH HEH HEH... GOOD. WE'VE ROBBED HIM OF HIS LAST OUNCE OF PRIDE.
UH...
ARE YOU IN THE GEN-SHIKEN TOO?
SMACK

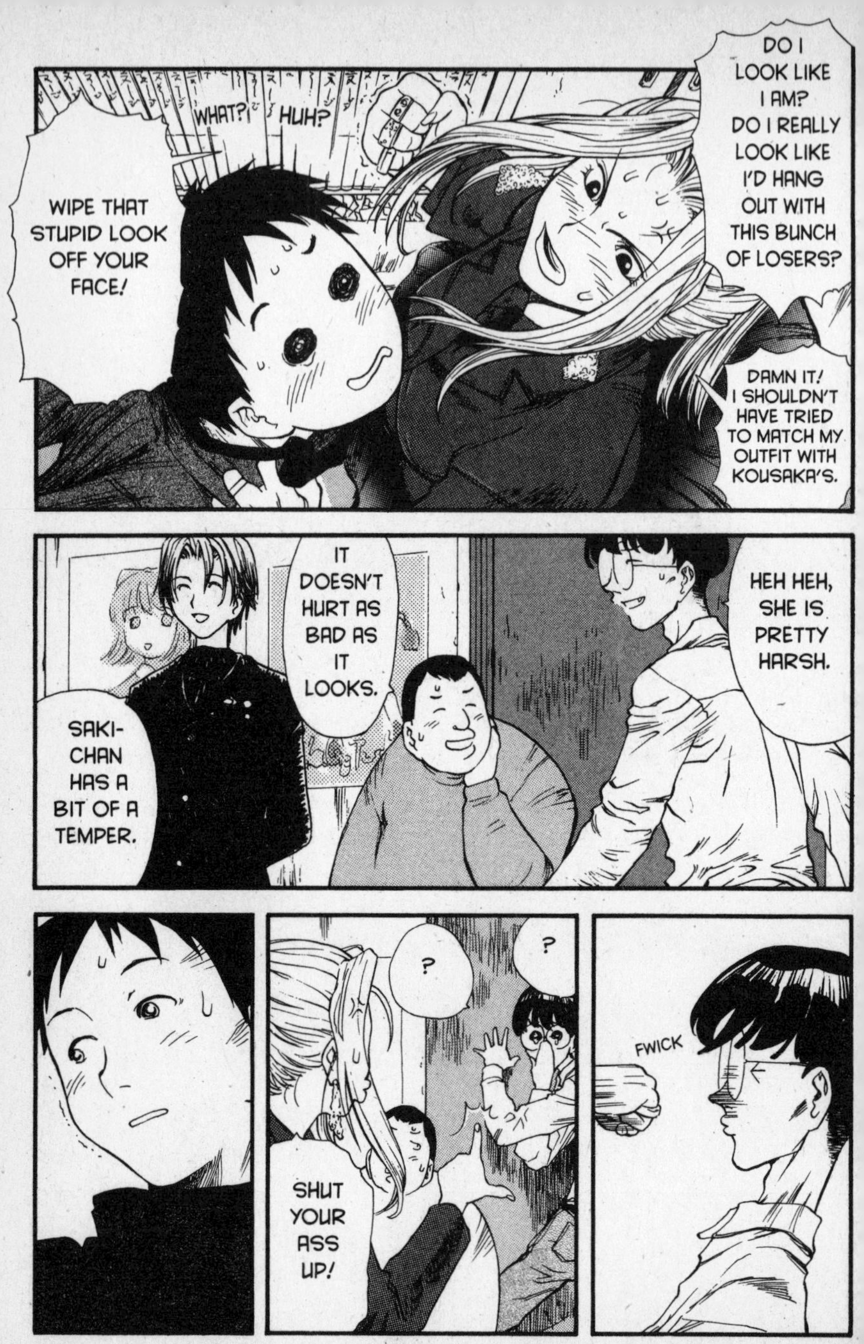
DO I LOOK LIKE I AM? DO I REALLY LOOK LIKE I'D HANG OUT WITH THIS BUNCH OF LOSERS?
HUH?
WHAT?
WIPE THAT STUPID LOOK OFF YOUR FACE!
DAMN IT! I SHOULDN'T HAVE TRIED TO MATCH MY OUTFIT WITH KOUSAKA'S.
HEH HEH, SHE IS PRETTY HARSH.
IT DOESN'T HURT AS BAD AS IT LOOKS.
SAKI-CHAN HAS A BIT OF A TEMPER.
FWICK
?
?
SHUT YOUR ASS UP!

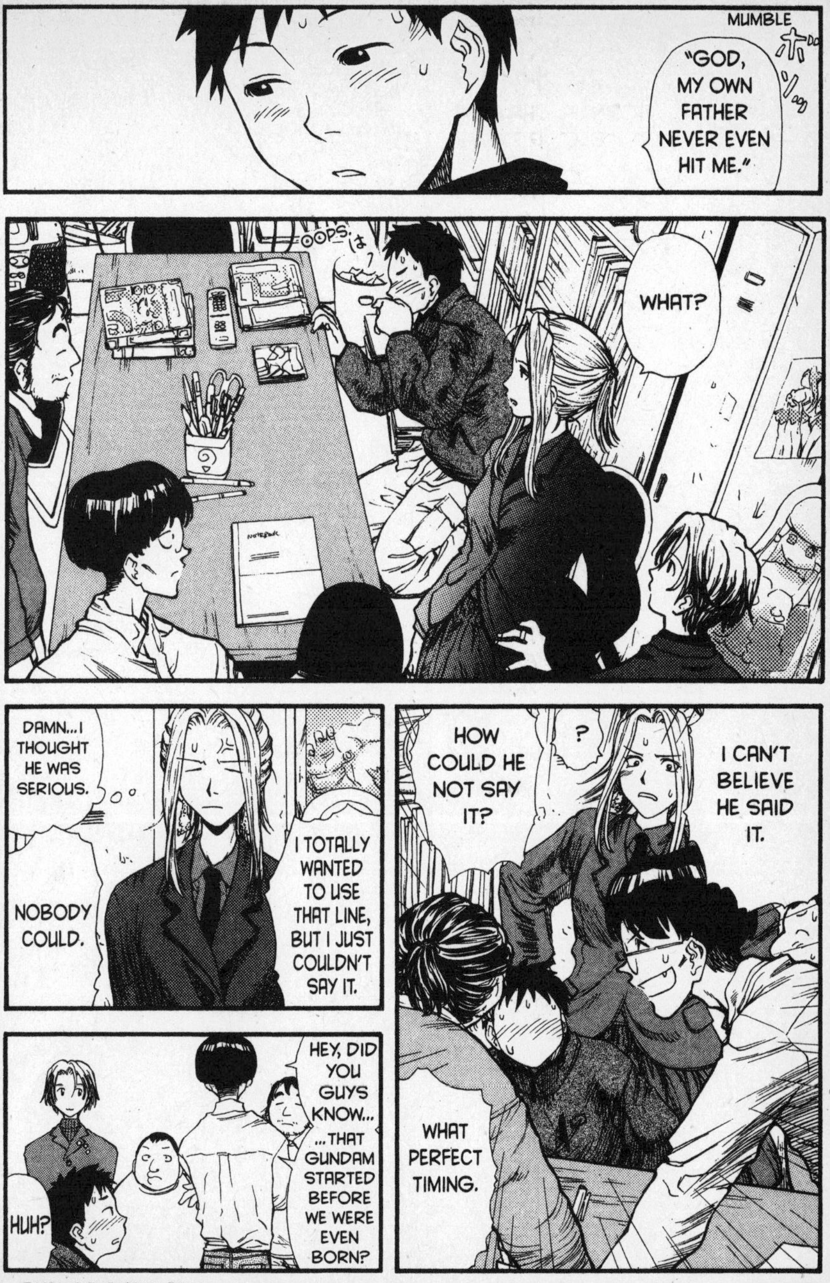
MUMBLE
"GOD, MY OWN FATHER NEVER EVEN HIT ME."
WHAT?
OOPS.
I CAN'T BELIEVE HE SAID IT.
?
HOW COULD HE NOT SAY IT?
WHAT PERFECT TIMING.
I TOTALLY WANTED TO USE THAT LINE, BUT I JUST COULDN'T SAY IT.
DAMN...I THOUGHT HE WAS SERIOUS.
NOBODY COULD.
HEY, DID YOU GUYS KNOW...
...THAT GUNDAM STARTED BEFORE WE WERE EVEN BORN?
HUH?

SASAHARA KANJI

PROFILE

KANJI SASAHARA

BORN JANUARY 13TH

BLOOD TYPE B

FAVORITE MANGA

PANTHER VS PANTHER

BERSERKER

FAVORITE ANIME

PATWABER

FAVORITE VIDEO GAME

DRAGON FEST 3

THE CHAMP OF FIGHTERS 95

FAVORITE FIGHT GAME CHARACTERS

YAGAMI-KUN

FUCHIKAEI

ERIC

ZABEL

BASARA THE BEHEADER

*THESE ARE THE CHARACTER'S CHOICES AND DO NOT NECESSARILY REFLECT THE AUTHOR'S TASTES.

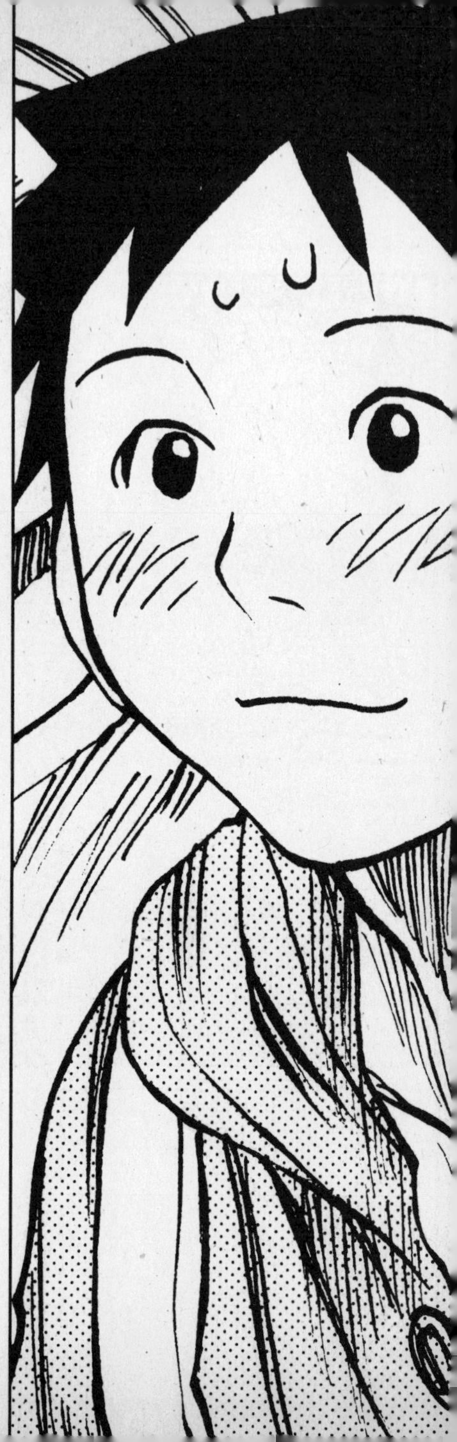

CHAPTER 1 - MOMENTS LATER

CRYING OVER SPILT MILK

BY THE WAY...
YOU CAN BORROW ANY BOOK YOU WANT.
GO AHEAD
NO... THAT'S OKAY.
REALLY, THAT'S—
...
IT'S TOO LATE NOW.

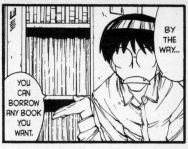

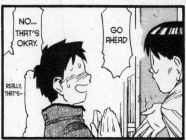

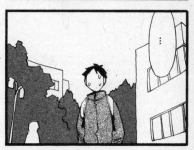

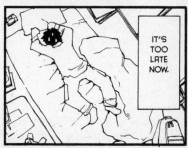

CHAPTER 2 -
PREPARE TO BE PERSECUTED...

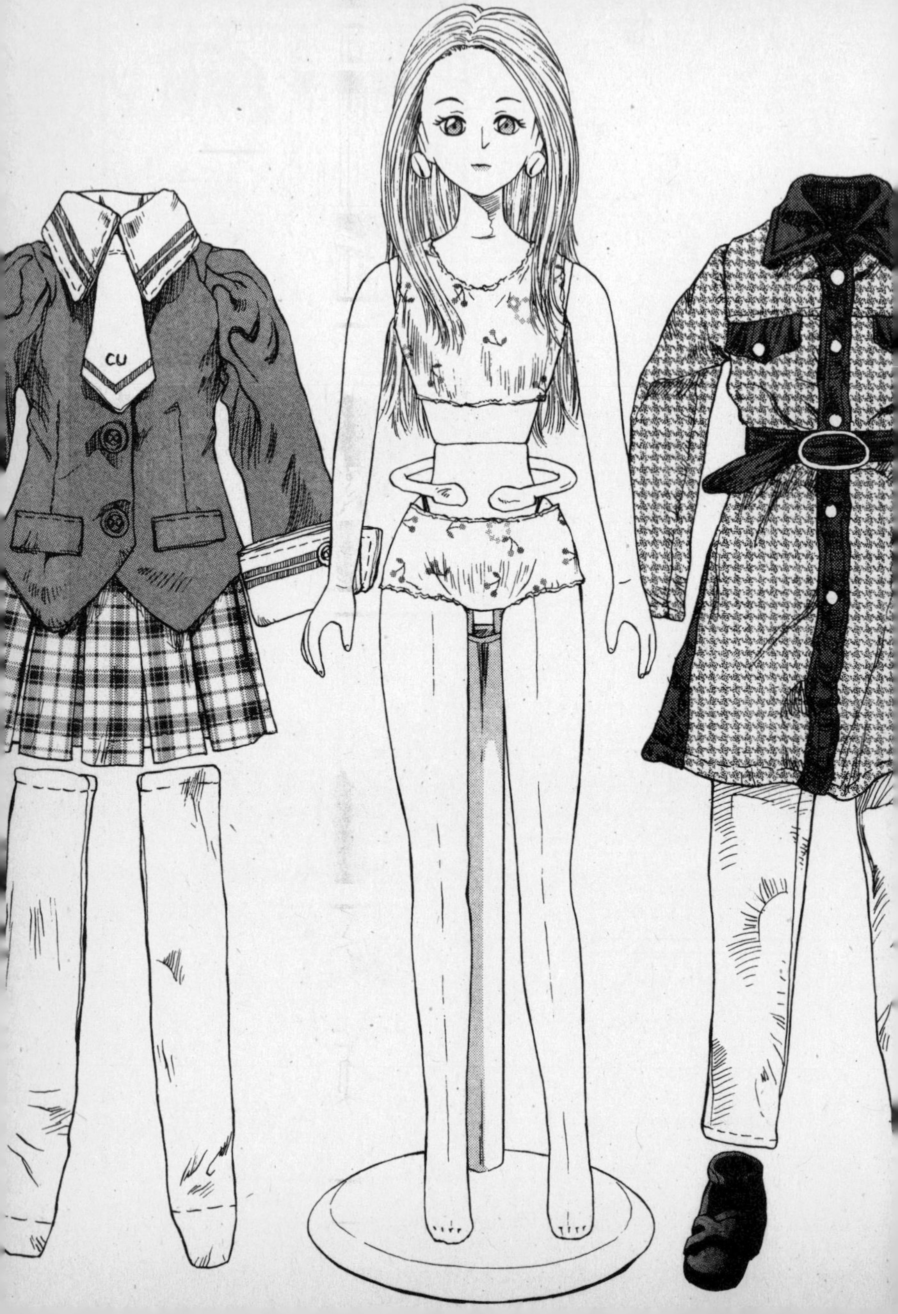

CU

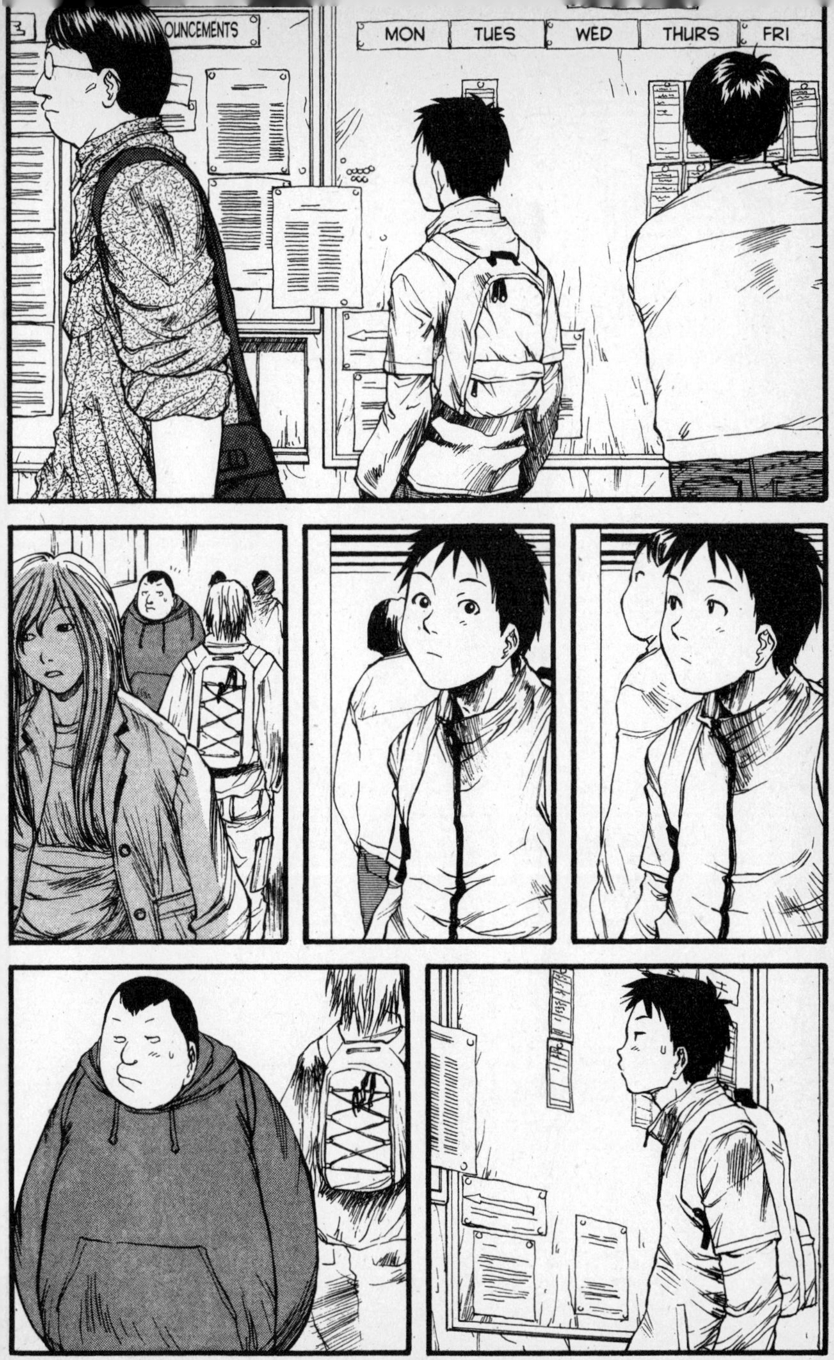
OUNCEMENTS
MON
TUES
WED
THURS
FRI

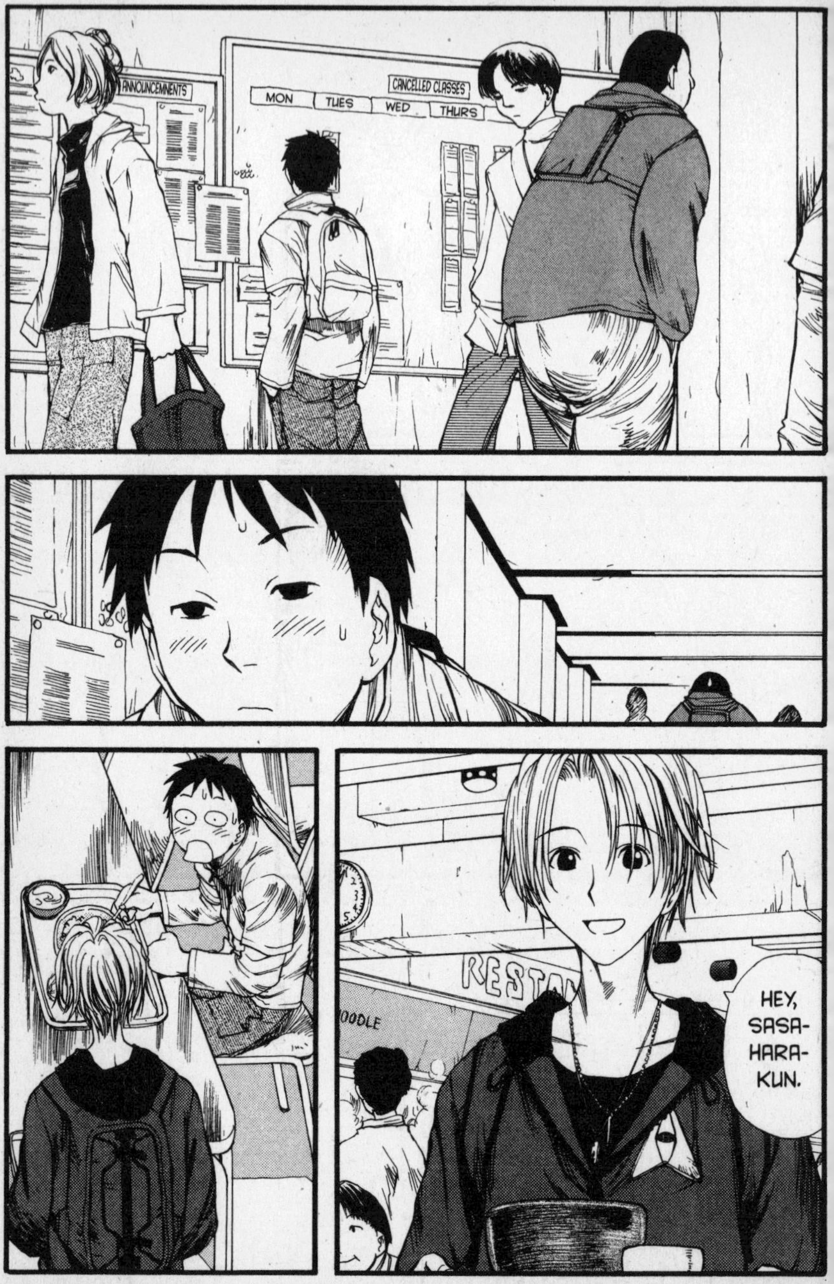
ANNOUNCEMENTS
CANCELLED CLASSES
MON
TUES
WED
THURS
HEY, SASA-HARA-KUN.

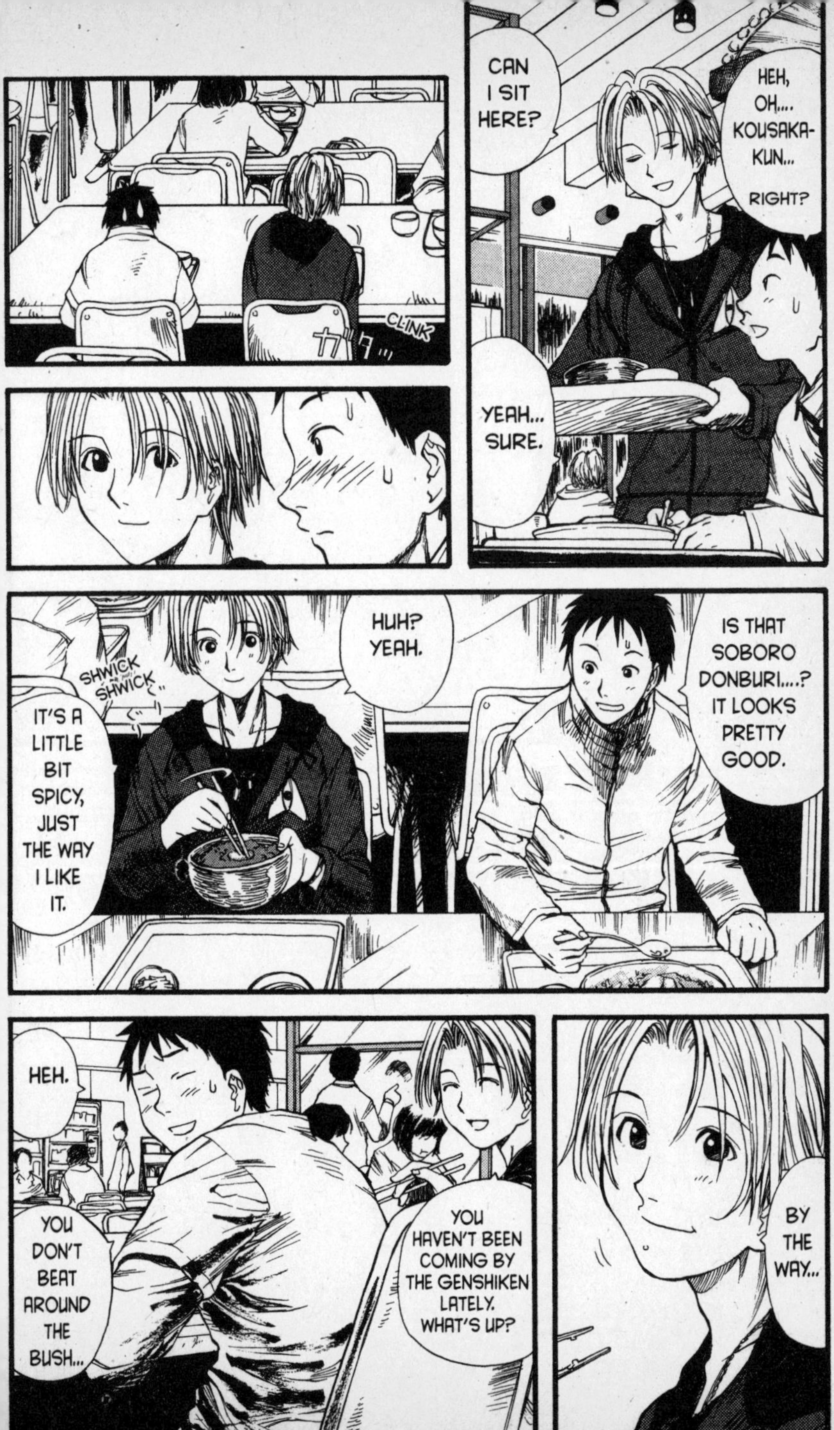
CAN I SIT HERE?
HEH, OH.... KOUSAKA-KUN... RIGHT?
YEAH... SURE.
CLINK
IS THAT SOBORO DONBURI....? IT LOOKS PRETTY GOOD.
HUH? YEAH.
SHWICK SHWICK
IT'S A LITTLE BIT SPICY, JUST THE WAY I LIKE IT.
BY THE WAY...
YOU HAVEN'T BEEN COMING BY THE GENSHIKEN LATELY. WHAT'S UP?
HEH.
YOU DON'T BEAT AROUND THE BUSH...

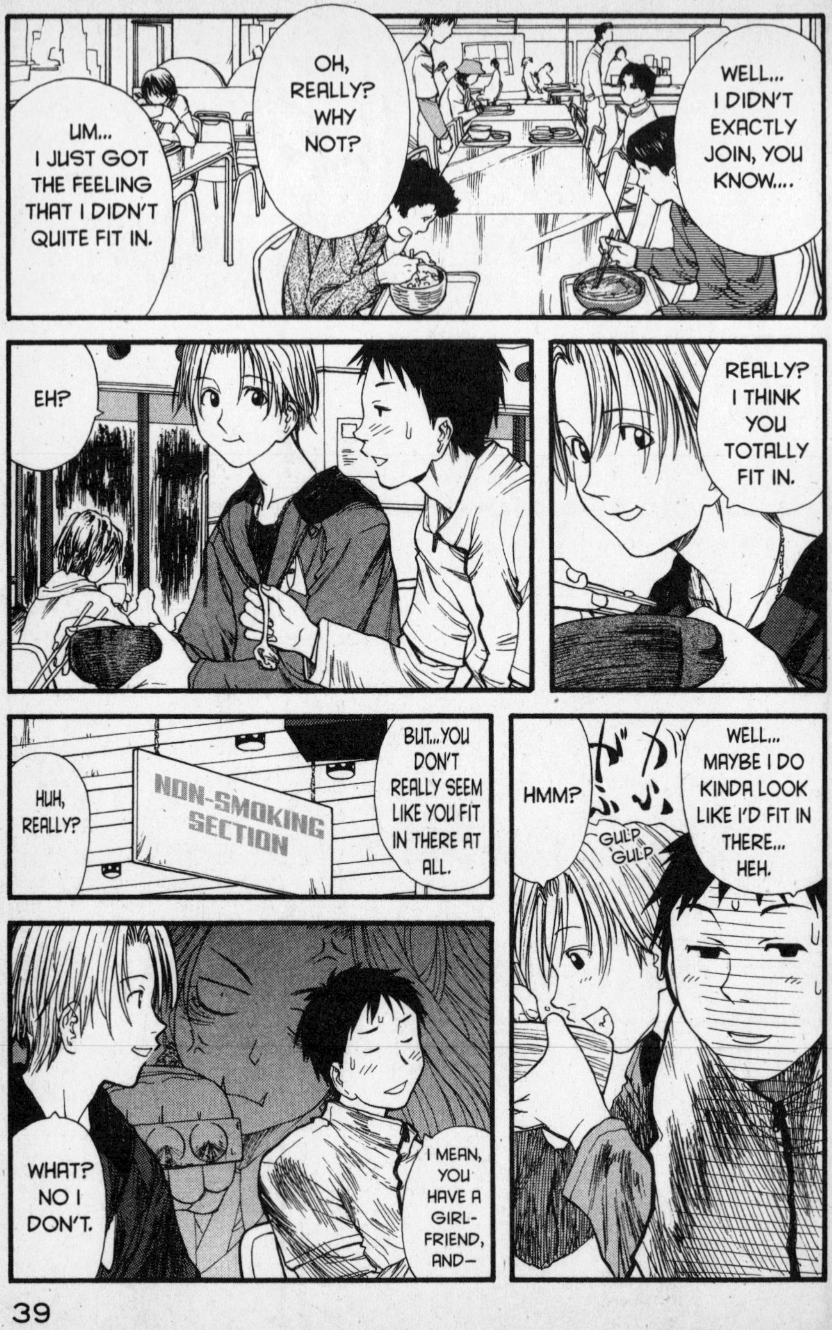
WELL... I DIDN'T EXACTLY JOIN, YOU KNOW....
OH, REALLY? WHY NOT?
UM... I JUST GOT THE FEELING THAT I DIDN'T QUITE FIT IN.
REALLY? I THINK YOU TOTALLY FIT IN.
EH?
WELL... MAYBE I DO KINDA LOOK LIKE I'D FIT IN THERE... HEH.
HMM?
GULP GULP
BUT...YOU DON'T REALLY SEEM LIKE YOU FIT IN THERE AT ALL.
NON-SMOKING SECTION
HUH, REALLY?
I MEAN, YOU HAVE A GIRL-FRIEND, AND—
WHAT? NO I DON'T.

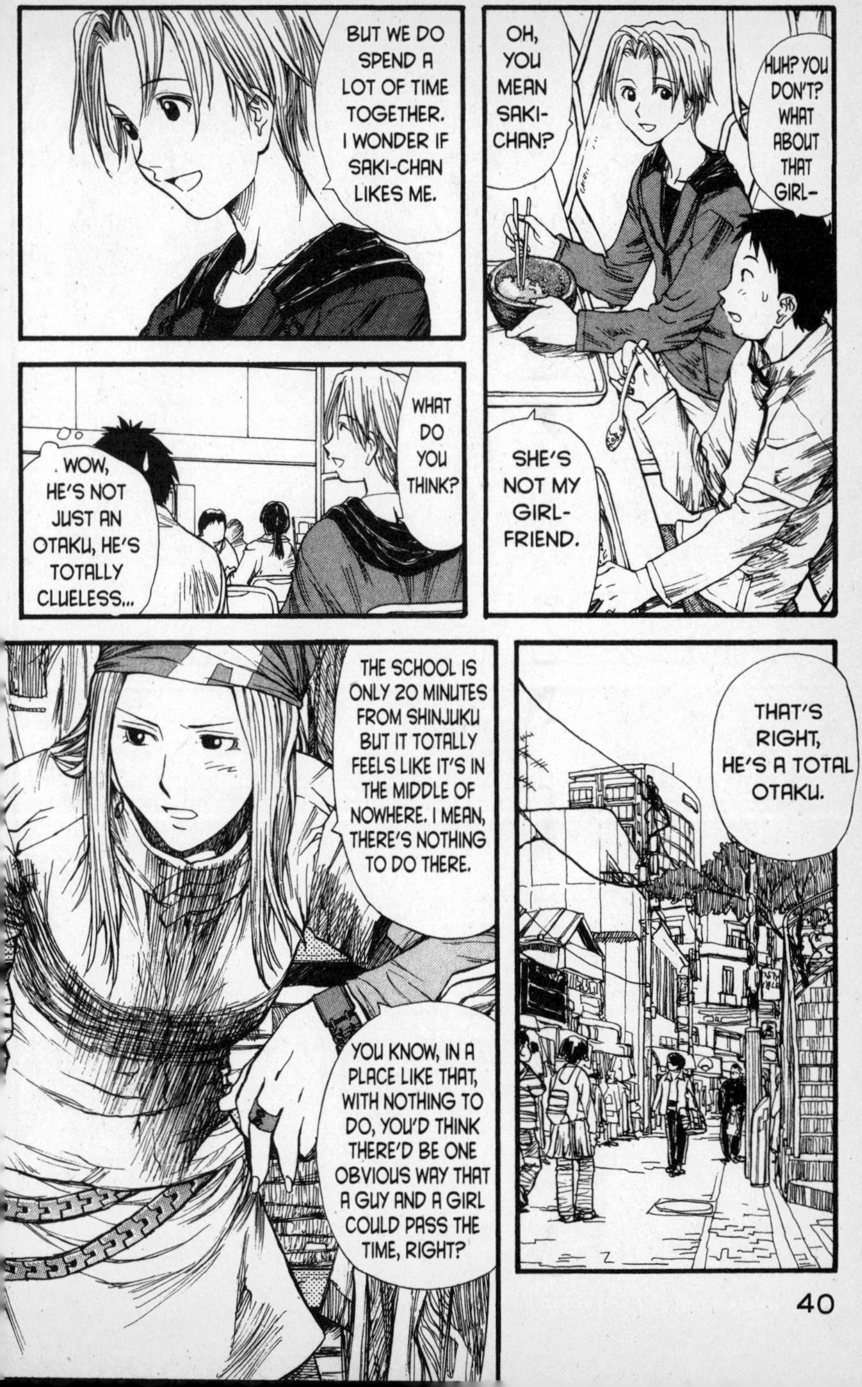
HUH? YOU DON'T? WHAT ABOUT THAT GIRL-
SHE'S NOT MY GIRLFRIEND.
OH, YOU MEAN SAKI-CHAN?
BUT WE DO SPEND A LOT OF TIME TOGETHER. I WONDER IF SAKI-CHAN LIKES ME.
WHAT DO YOU THINK?
. WOW, HE'S NOT JUST AN OTAKU, HE'S TOTALLY CLUELESS...
THAT'S RIGHT, HE'S A TOTAL OTAKU.
THE SCHOOL IS ONLY 20 MINUTES FROM SHINJUKU BUT IT TOTALLY FEELS LIKE IT'S IN THE MIDDLE OF NOWHERE. I MEAN, THERE'S NOTHING TO DO THERE.
YOU KNOW, IN A PLACE LIKE THAT, WITH NOTHING TO DO, YOU'D THINK THERE'D BE ONE OBVIOUS WAY THAT A GUY AND A GIRL COULD PASS THE TIME, RIGHT?

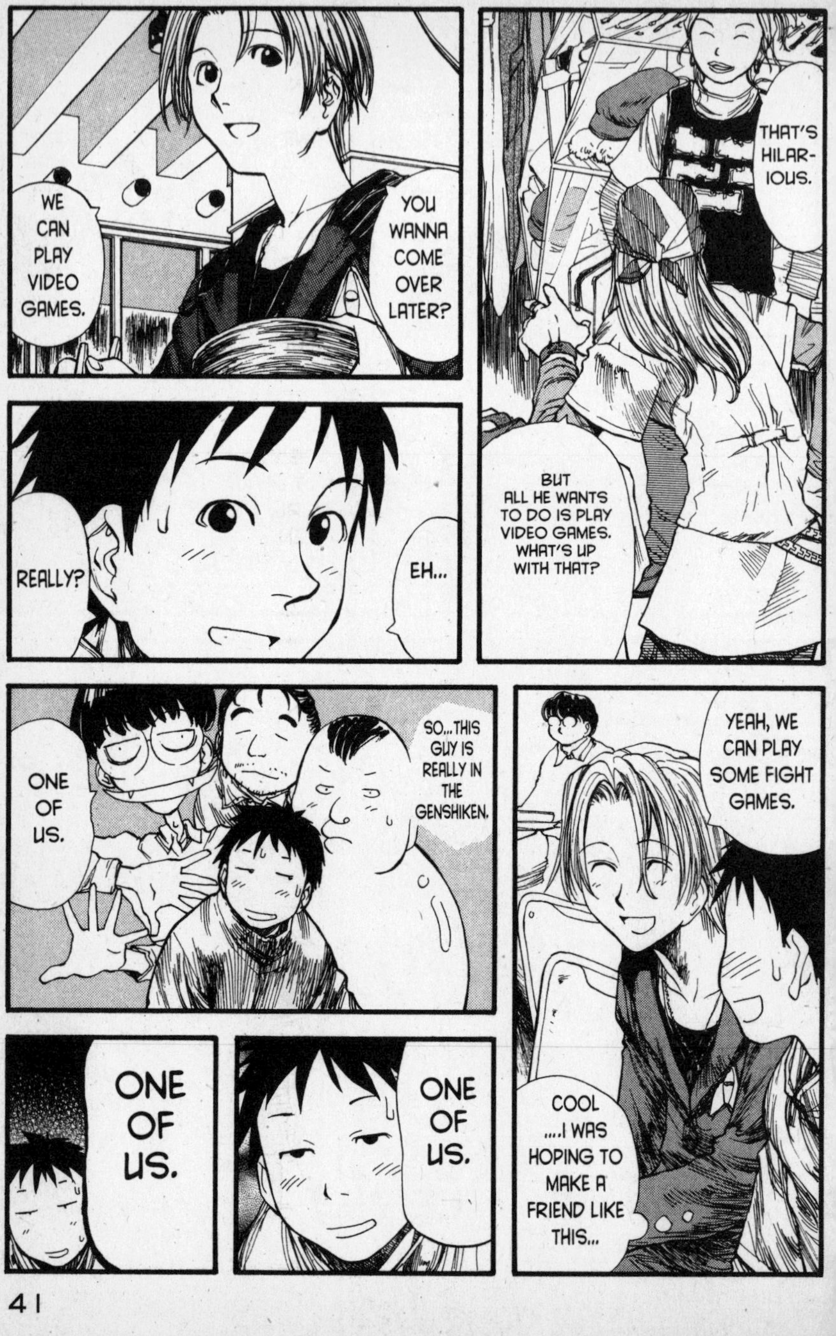
THAT'S HILAR-IOUS.
BUT ALL HE WANTS TO DO IS PLAY VIDEO GAMES. WHAT'S UP WITH THAT?
YOU WANNA COME OVER LATER?
WE CAN PLAY VIDEO GAMES.
EH...
REALLY?
YEAH, WE CAN PLAY SOME FIGHT GAMES.
COOL ....I WAS HOPING TO MAKE A FRIEND LIKE THIS...
SO...THIS GUY IS REALLY IN THE GENSHIKEN.
ONE OF US.
ONE OF US.
ONE OF US.

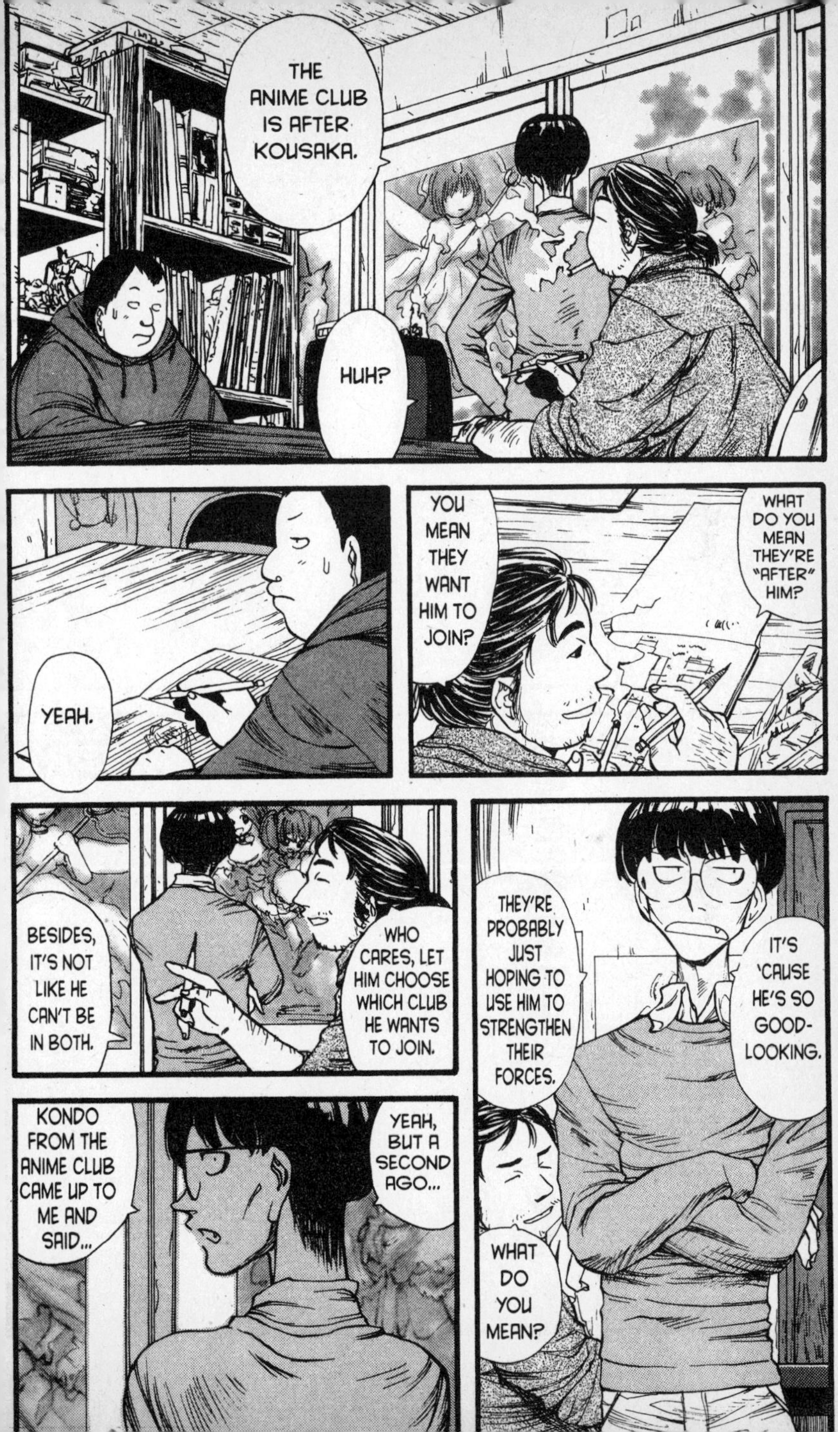
THE ANIME CLUB IS AFTER KOUSAKA.
HUH?
WHAT DO YOU MEAN THEY'RE "AFTER" HIM?
YOU MEAN THEY WANT HIM TO JOIN?
YEAH.
IT'S 'CAUSE HE'S SO GOOD-LOOKING.
THEY'RE PROBABLY JUST HOPING TO USE HIM TO STRENGTHEN THEIR FORCES.
WHAT DO YOU MEAN?
WHO CARES, LET HIM CHOOSE WHICH CLUB HE WANTS TO JOIN.
BESIDES, IT'S NOT LIKE HE CAN'T BE IN BOTH.
YEAH, BUT A SECOND AGO...
KONDO FROM THE ANIME CLUB CAME UP TO ME AND SAID...

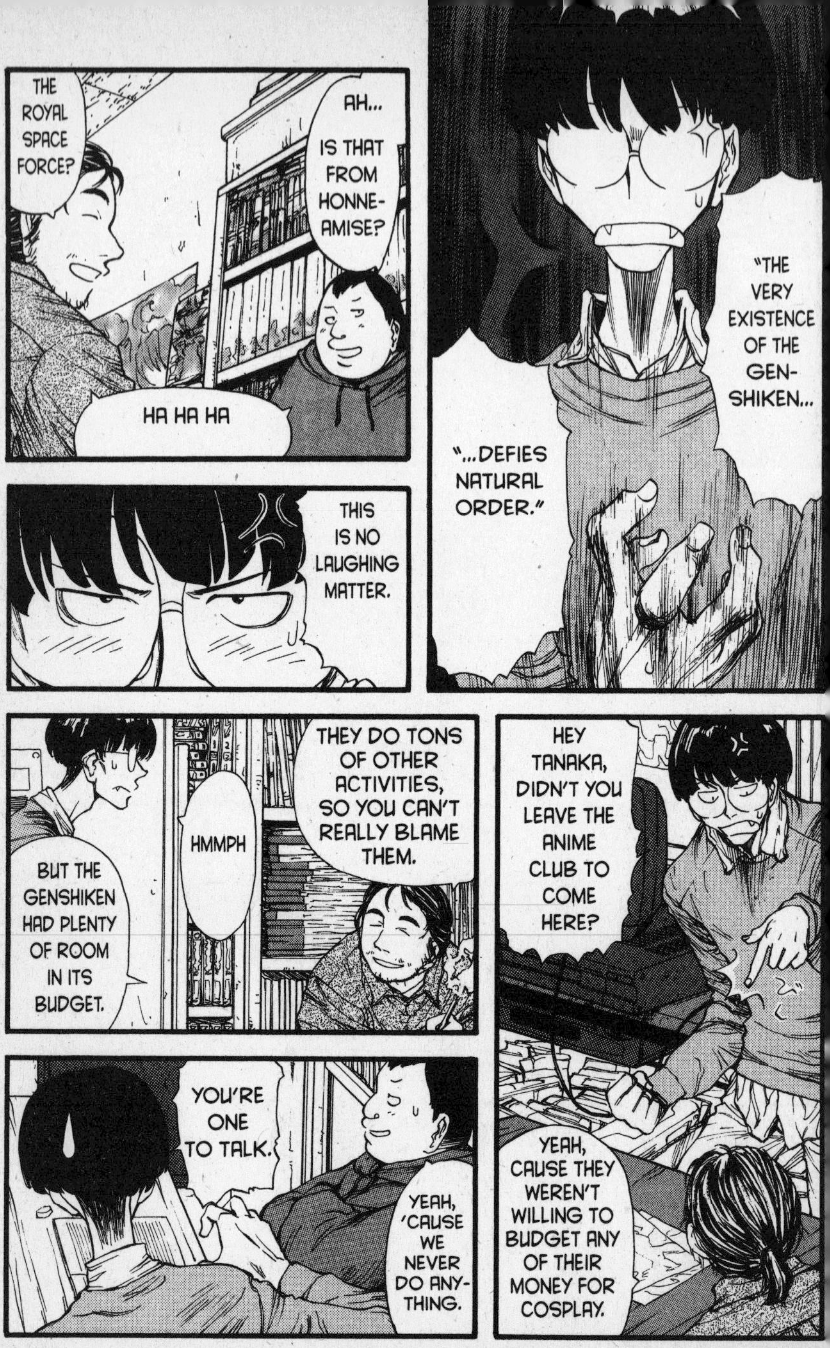
"THE VERY EXISTENCE OF THE GEN-SHIKEN...
"...DEFIES NATURAL ORDER."
AH... IS THAT FROM HONNE-AMISE?
THE ROYAL SPACE FORCE?
HA HA HA
THIS IS NO LAUGHING MATTER.
HEY TANAKA, DIDN'T YOU LEAVE THE ANIME CLUB TO COME HERE?
YEAH, CAUSE THEY WEREN'T WILLING TO BUDGET ANY OF THEIR MONEY FOR COSPLAY.
THEY DO TONS OF OTHER ACTIVITIES, SO YOU CAN'T REALLY BLAME THEM.
HMMPH
BUT THE GENSHIKEN HAD PLENTY OF ROOM IN ITS BUDGET.
YEAH, 'CAUSE WE NEVER DO ANY-THING.
YOU'RE ONE TO TALK.

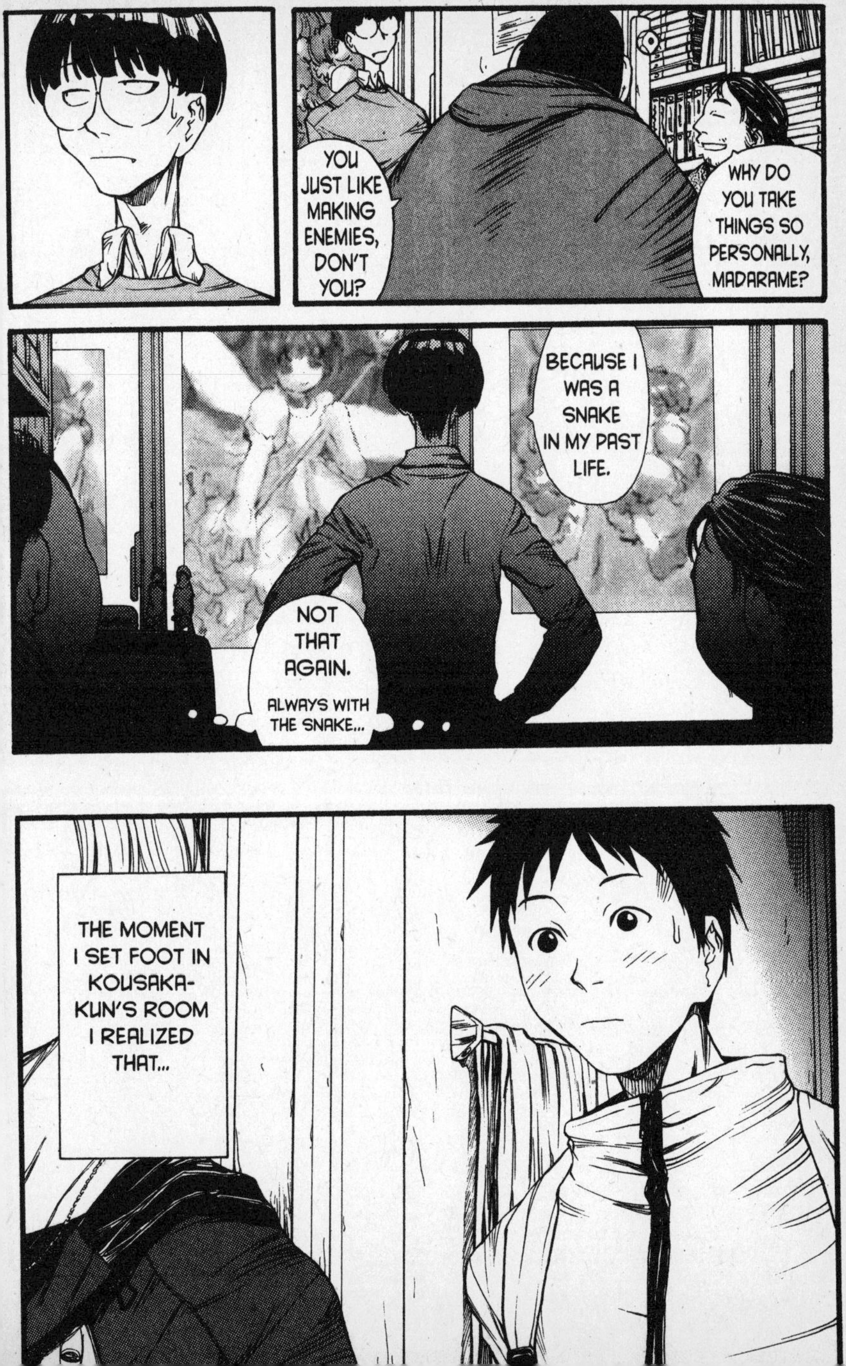
WHY DO YOU TAKE THINGS SO PERSONALLY, MADARAME?
YOU JUST LIKE MAKING ENEMIES, DON'T YOU?
BECAUSE I WAS A SNAKE IN MY PAST LIFE.
NOT THAT AGAIN.
ALWAYS WITH THE SNAKE...
THE MOMENT I SET FOOT IN KOUSAKA-KUN'S ROOM I REALIZED THAT...

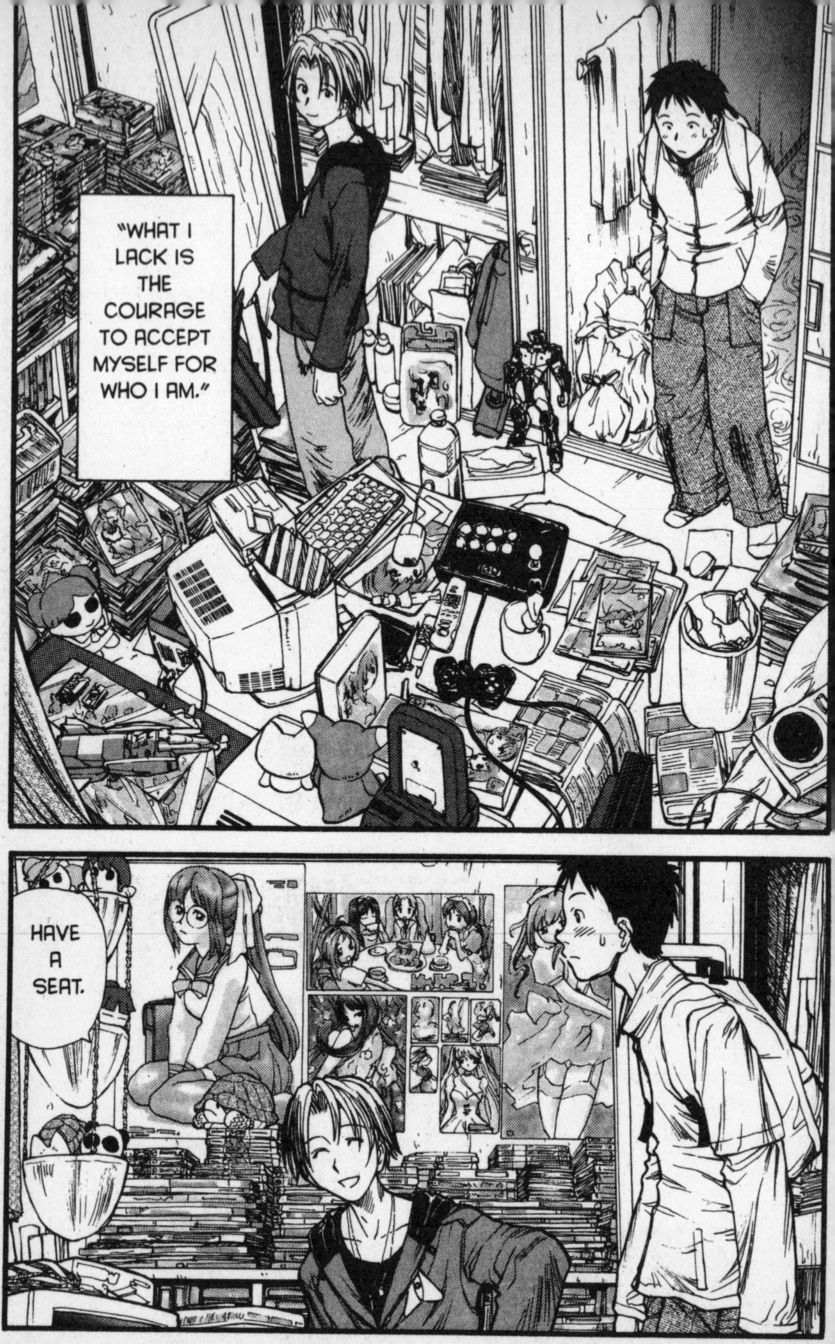
"WHAT I LACK IS THE COURAGE TO ACCEPT MYSELF FOR WHO I AM."
HAVE A SEAT.

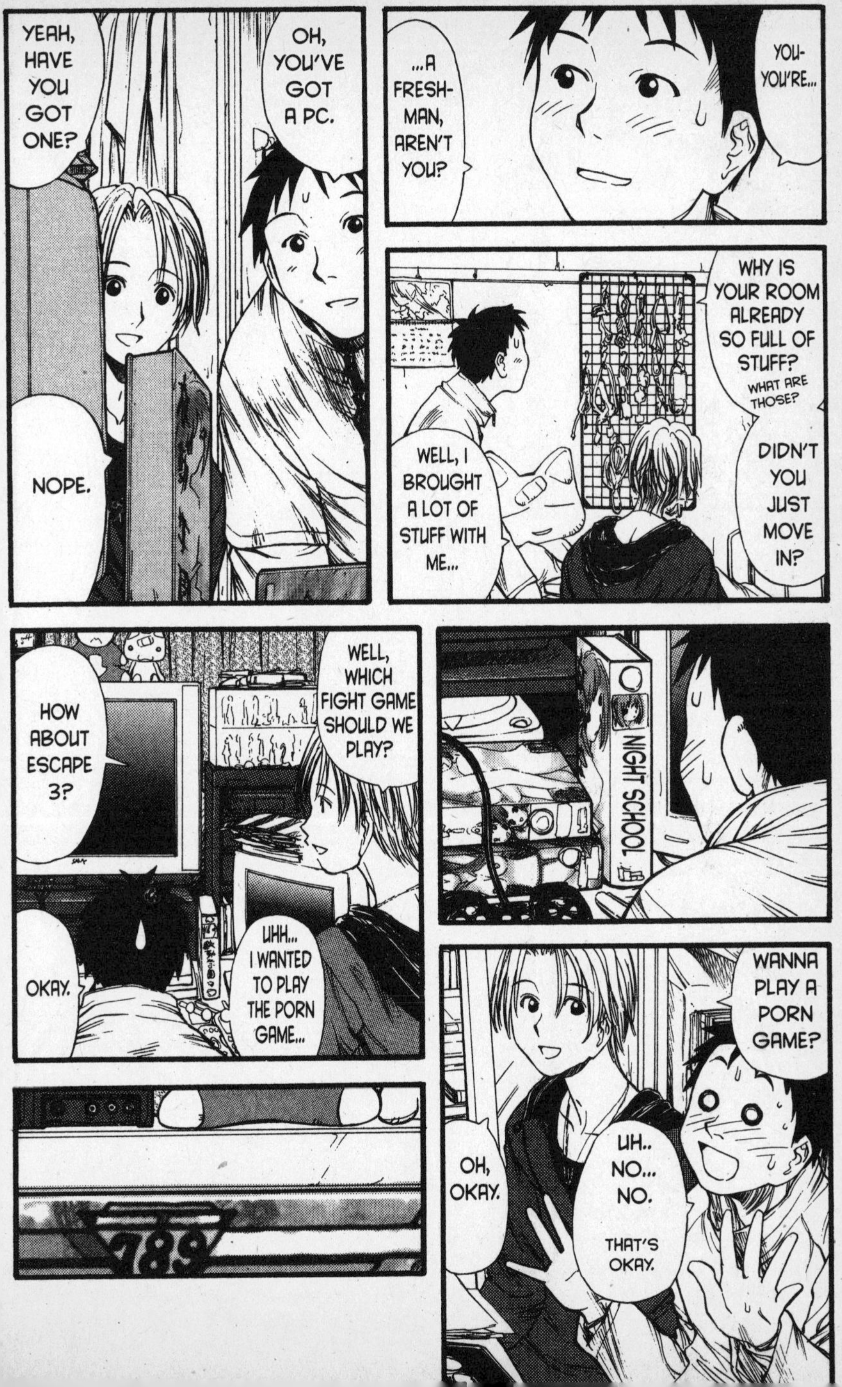
YOU- YOU'RE...
...A FRESH-MAN, AREN'T YOU?
WHY IS YOUR ROOM ALREADY SO FULL OF STUFF?
WHAT ARE THOSE?
DIDN'T YOU JUST MOVE IN?
WELL, I BROUGHT A LOT OF STUFF WITH ME...
OH, YOU'VE GOT A PC.
YEAH, HAVE YOU GOT ONE?
NOPE.
NIGHT SCHOOL
WANNA PLAY A PORN GAME?
UH.. NO... NO.
THAT'S OKAY.
OH, OKAY.
WELL, WHICH FIGHT GAME SHOULD WE PLAY?
HOW ABOUT ESCAPE 3?
UHH... I WANTED TO PLAY THE PORN GAME...
OKAY.
789

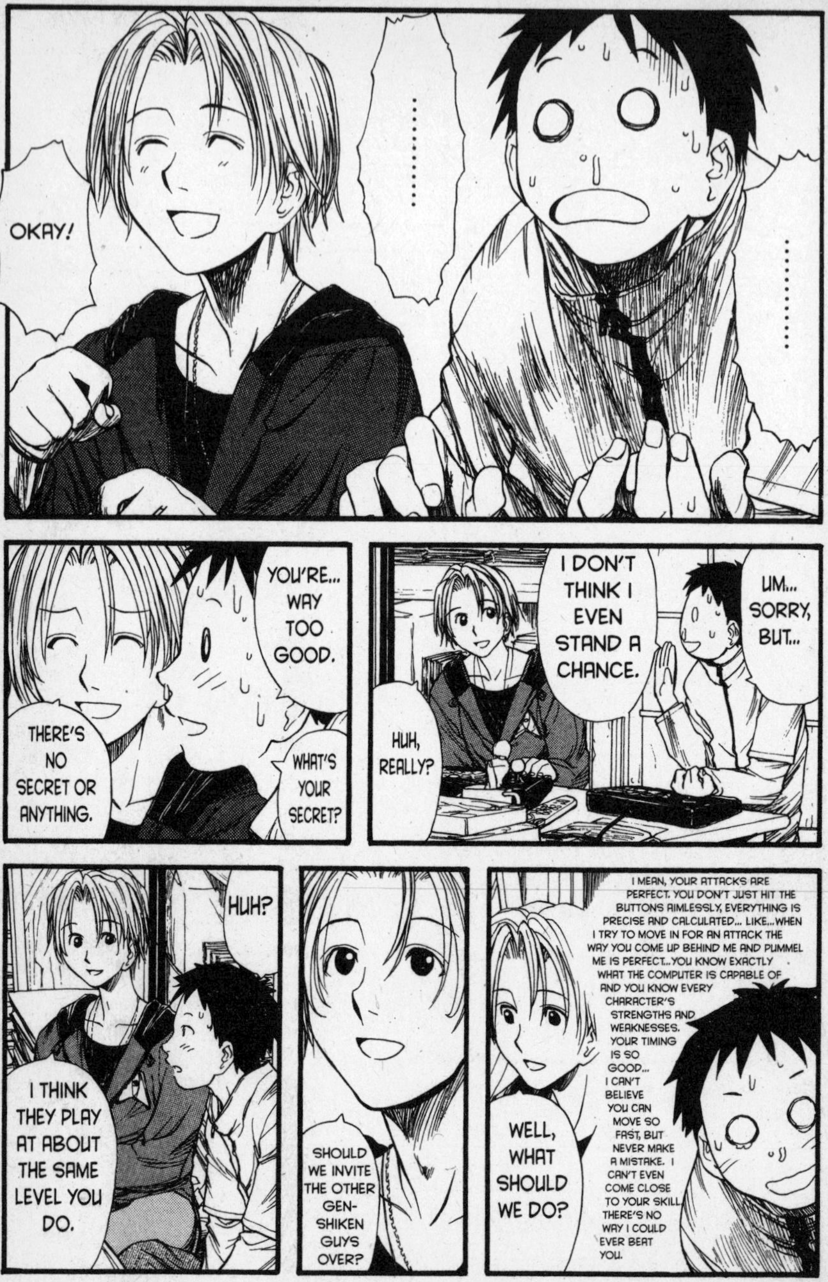
......
......
OKAY!
UM... SORRY, BUT...
I DON'T THINK I EVEN STAND A CHANCE.
HUH, REALLY?
YOU'RE... WAY TOO GOOD.
WHAT'S YOUR SECRET?
THERE'S NO SECRET OR ANYTHING.
I MEAN, YOUR ATTACKS ARE PERFECT. YOU DON'T JUST HIT THE BUTTONS AIMLESSLY, EVERYTHING IS PRECISE AND CALCULATED... LIKE...WHEN I TRY TO MOVE IN FOR AN ATTACK THE WAY YOU COME UP BEHIND ME AND PUMMEL ME IS PERFECT...YOU KNOW EXACTLY WHAT THE COMPUTER IS CAPABLE OF AND YOU KNOW EVERY CHARACTER'S STRENGTHS AND WEAKNESSES. YOUR TIMING IS SO GOOD... I CAN'T BELIEVE YOU CAN MOVE SO FAST, BUT NEVER MAKE A MISTAKE. I CAN'T EVEN COME CLOSE TO YOUR SKILL. THERE'S NO WAY I COULD EVER BEAT YOU.
WELL, WHAT SHOULD WE DO?
SHOULD WE INVITE THE OTHER GEN-SHIKEN GUYS OVER?
HUH?
I THINK THEY PLAY AT ABOUT THE SAME LEVEL YOU DO.

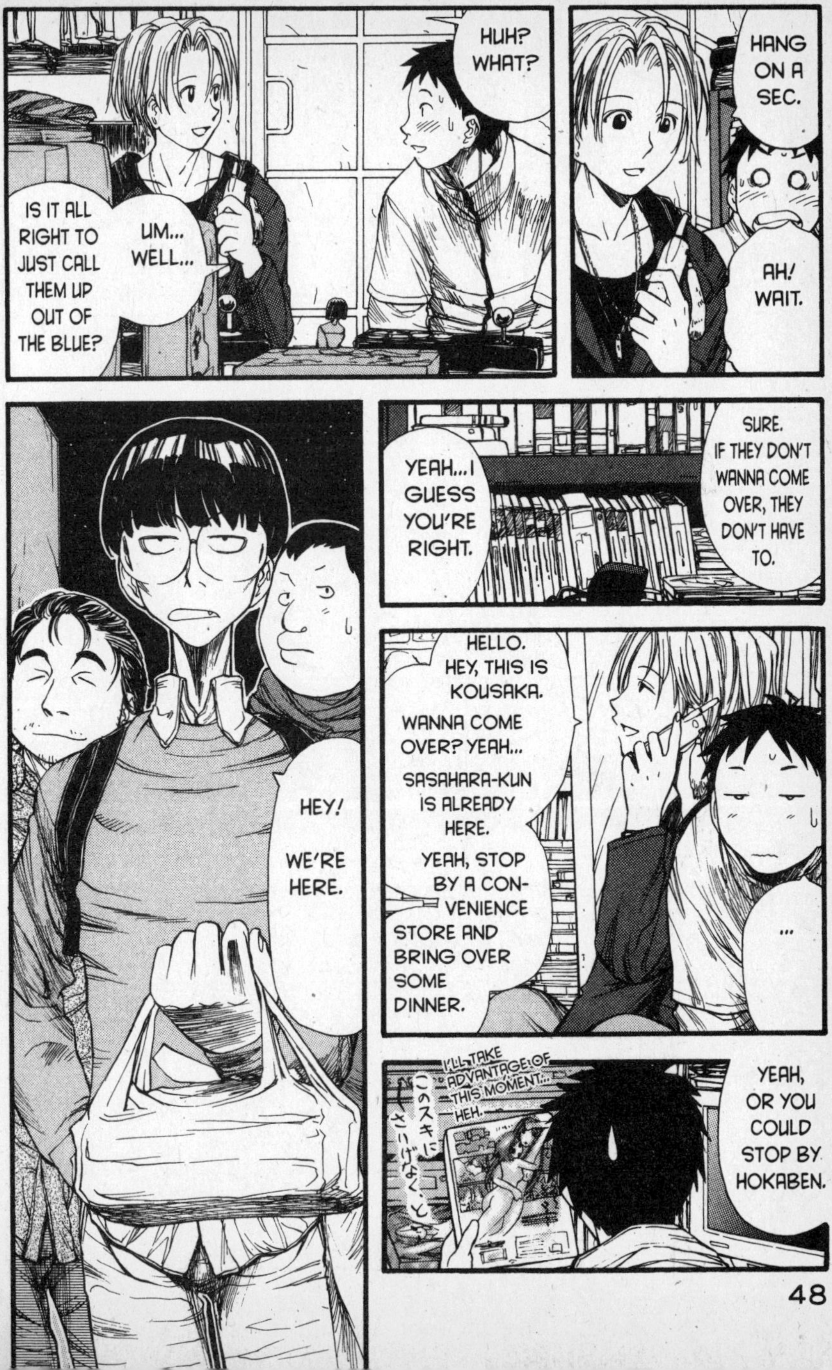
HANG ON A SEC.
AH! WAIT.
HUH? WHAT?
UM... WELL...
IS IT ALL RIGHT TO JUST CALL THEM UP OUT OF THE BLUE?
SURE. IF THEY DON'T WANNA COME OVER, THEY DON'T HAVE TO.
YEAH...I GUESS YOU'RE RIGHT.
HELLO. HEY, THIS IS KOUSAKA. WANNA COME OVER? YEAH... SASAHARA-KUN IS ALREADY HERE. YEAH, STOP BY A CON-VENIENCE STORE AND BRING OVER SOME DINNER.
...
YEAH, OR YOU COULD STOP BY HOKABEN.
このスキに さりげなく、と
I'LL TAKE ADVANTAGE OF THIS MOMENT... HEH.
HEY! WE'RE HERE.

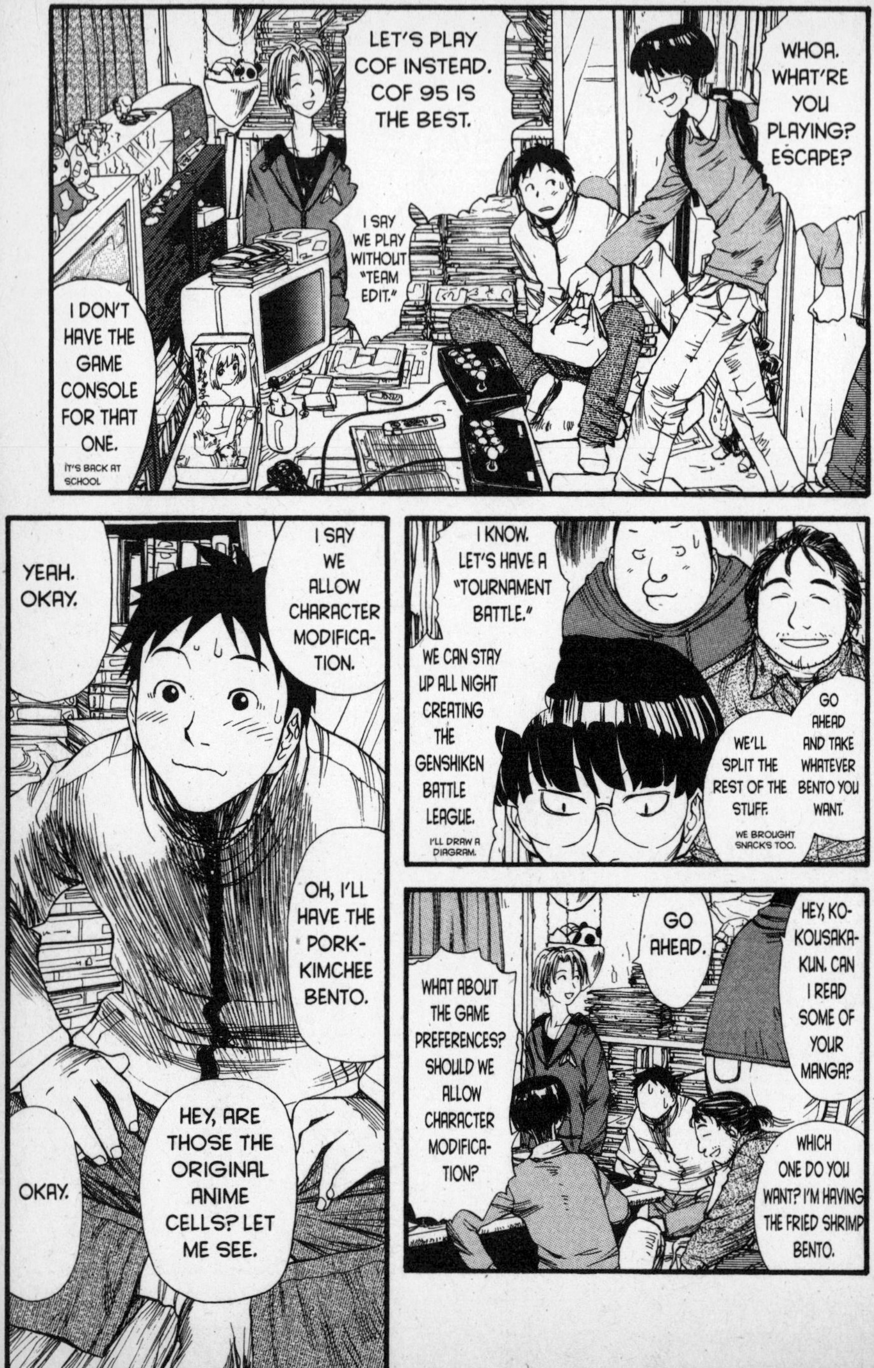
WHOA. WHAT'RE YOU PLAYING? ESCAPE?
LET'S PLAY COF INSTEAD. COF 95 IS THE BEST.
I SAY WE PLAY WITHOUT "TEAM EDIT."
I DON'T HAVE THE GAME CONSOLE FOR THAT ONE.
IT'S BACK AT SCHOOL
I KNOW. LET'S HAVE A "TOURNAMENT BATTLE."
GO AHEAD AND TAKE WHATEVER BENTO YOU WANT.
WE'LL SPLIT THE REST OF THE STUFF.
WE BROUGHT SNACKS TOO.
WE CAN STAY UP ALL NIGHT CREATING THE GENSHIKEN BATTLE LEAGUE.
I'LL DRAW A DIAGRAM.
HEY, KO-KOUSAKA-KUN. CAN I READ SOME OF YOUR MANGA?
GO AHEAD.
WHICH ONE DO YOU WANT? I'M HAVING THE FRIED SHRIMP BENTO.
WHAT ABOUT THE GAME PREFERENCES? SHOULD WE ALLOW CHARACTER MODIFICATION?
I SAY WE ALLOW CHARACTER MODIFICATION.
YEAH. OKAY.
OH, I'LL HAVE THE PORK-KIMCHEE BENTO.
HEY, ARE THOSE THE ORIGINAL ANIME CELLS? LET ME SEE.
OKAY.

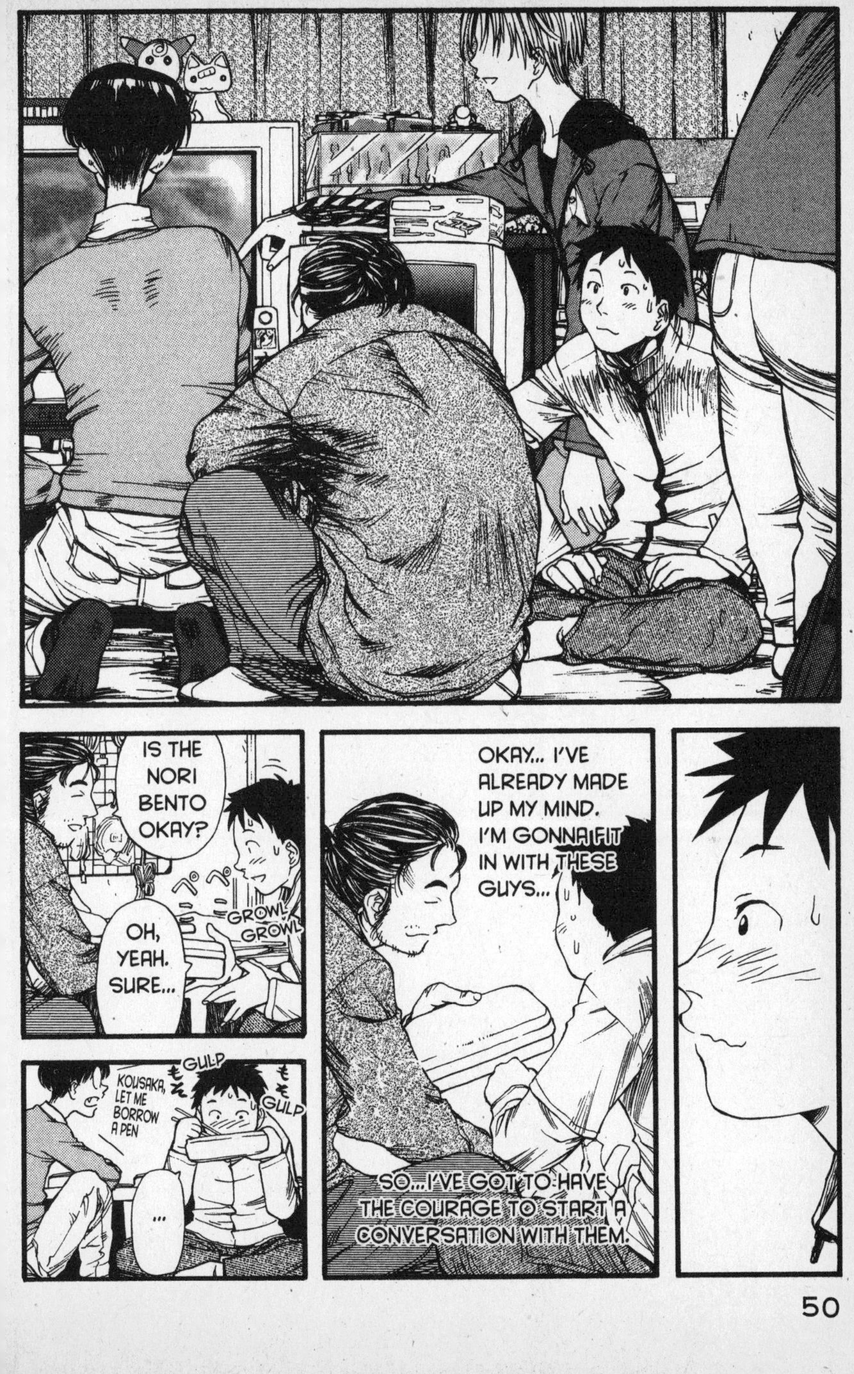
OKAY... I'VE ALREADY MADE UP MY MIND. I'M GONNA FIT IN WITH THESE GUYS...
SO...I'VE GOT TO HAVE THE COURAGE TO START A CONVERSATION WITH THEM.
IS THE NORI BENTO OKAY?
GROWL GROWL
OH, YEAH. SURE...
GULP GULP
KOUSAKA, LET ME BORROW A PEN
...

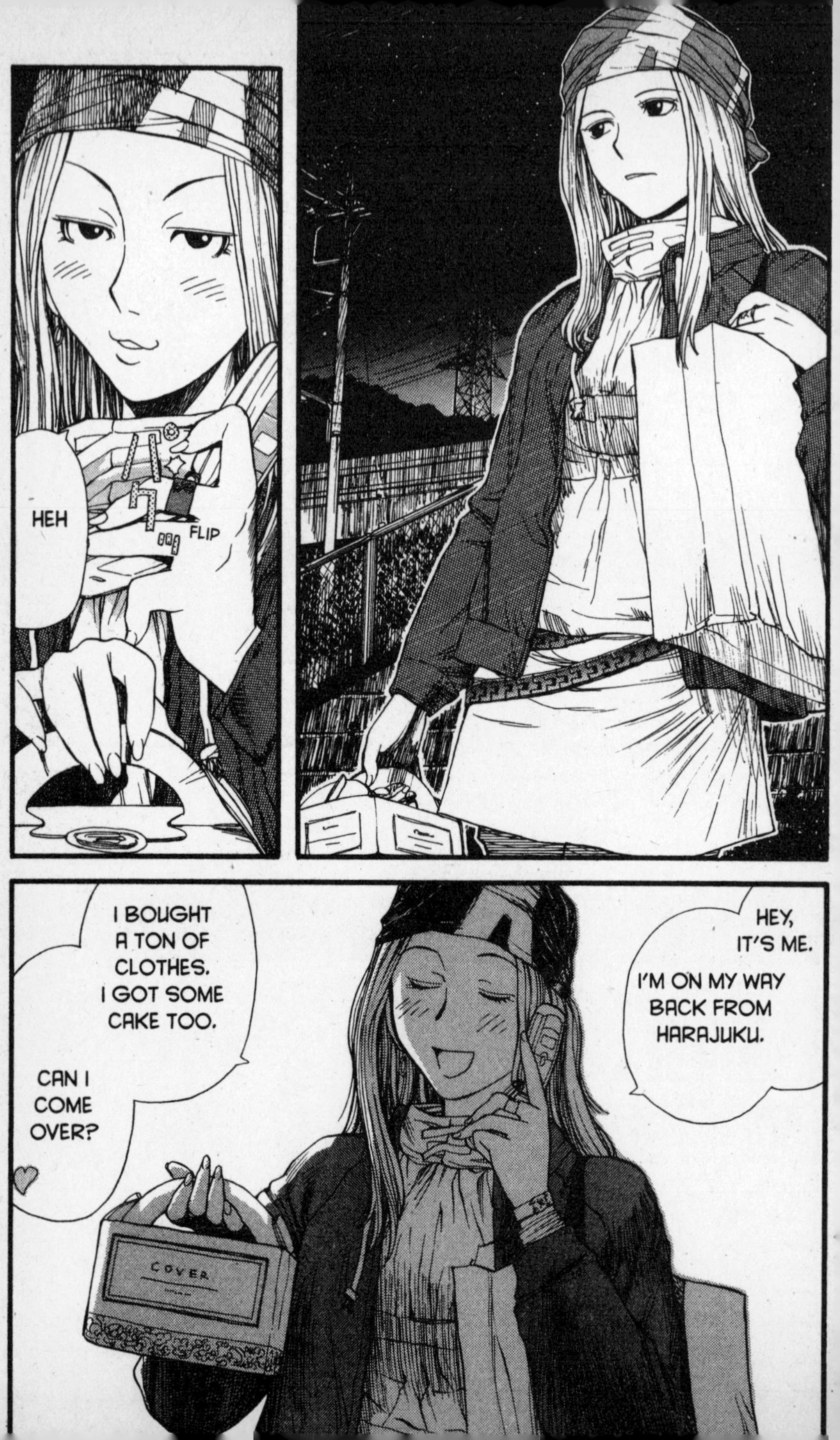
HEH
FLIP
HEY, IT'S ME.
I'M ON MY WAY BACK FROM HARAJUKU.
I BOUGHT A TON OF CLOTHES. I GOT SOME CAKE TOO.
CAN I COME OVER?
COVER

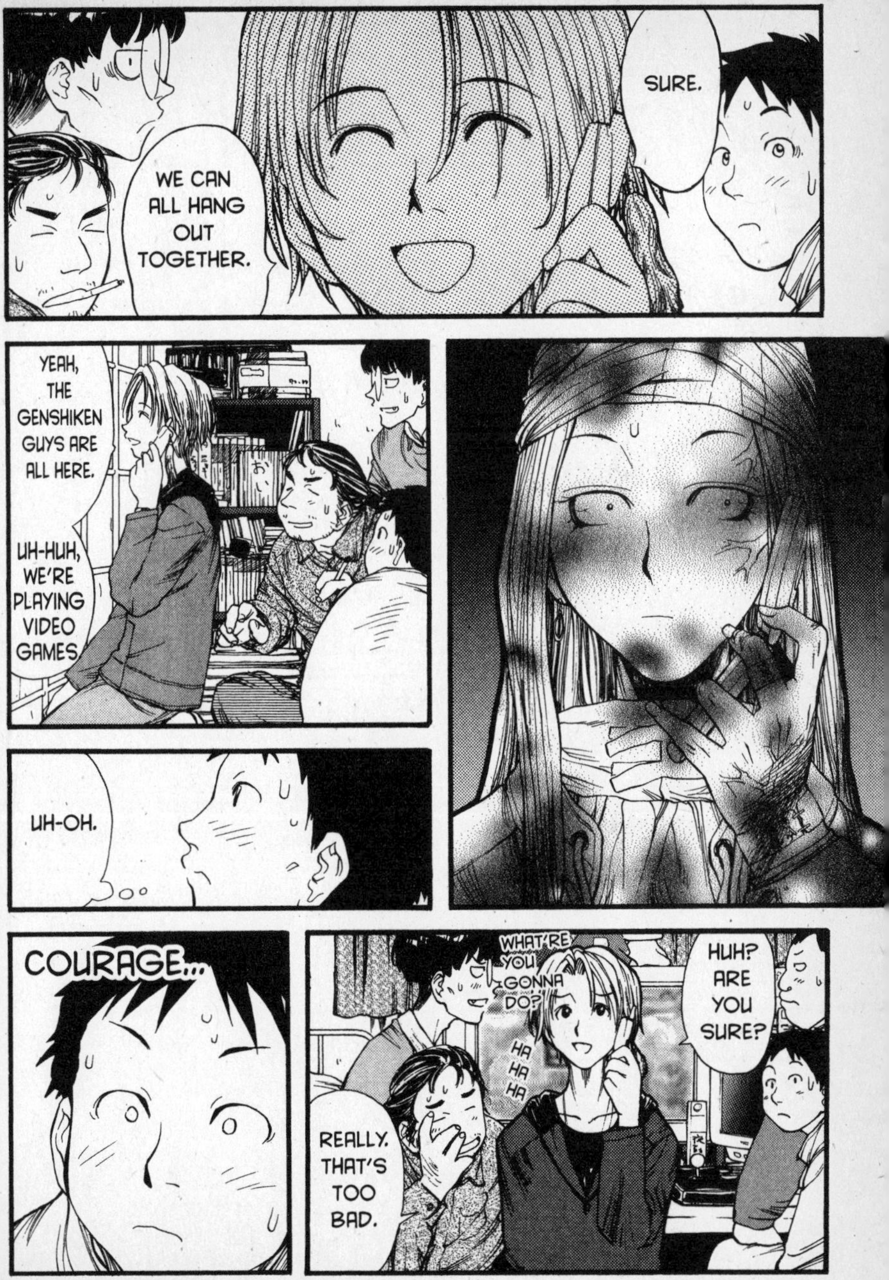
SURE.
WE CAN ALL HANG OUT TOGETHER.
YEAH, THE GENSHIKEN GUYS ARE ALL HERE.
UH-HUH, WE'RE PLAYING VIDEO GAMES.
UH-OH.
HUH? ARE YOU SURE?
WHAT'RE YOU GONNA DO?
HA HA HA HA
REALLY. THAT'S TOO BAD.
COURAGE...

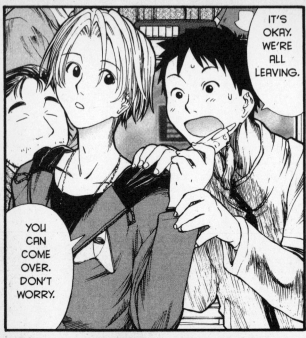

IT'S OKAY. WE'RE ALL LEAVING.

YOU CAN COME OVER. DON'T WORRY.

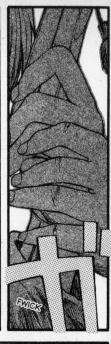

FWICK

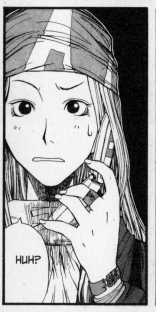

HUH?

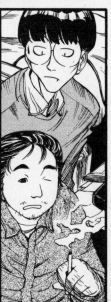

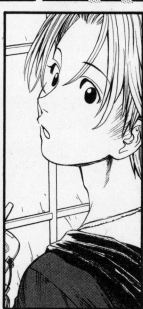

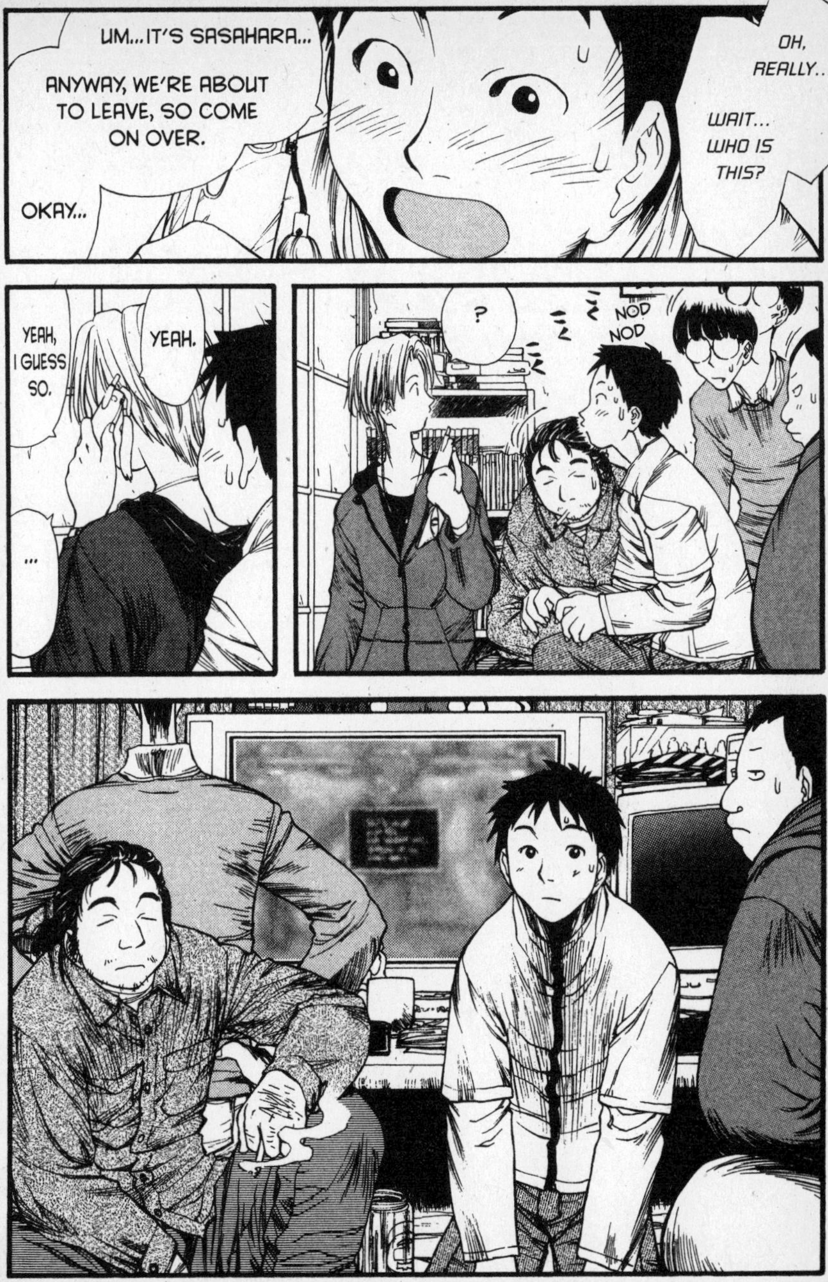
OH, REALLY...
WAIT... WHO IS THIS?
UM...IT'S SASAHARA...
ANYWAY, WE'RE ABOUT TO LEAVE, SO COME ON OVER.
OKAY...
?
NOD NOD
YEAH.
YEAH, I GUESS SO.
...

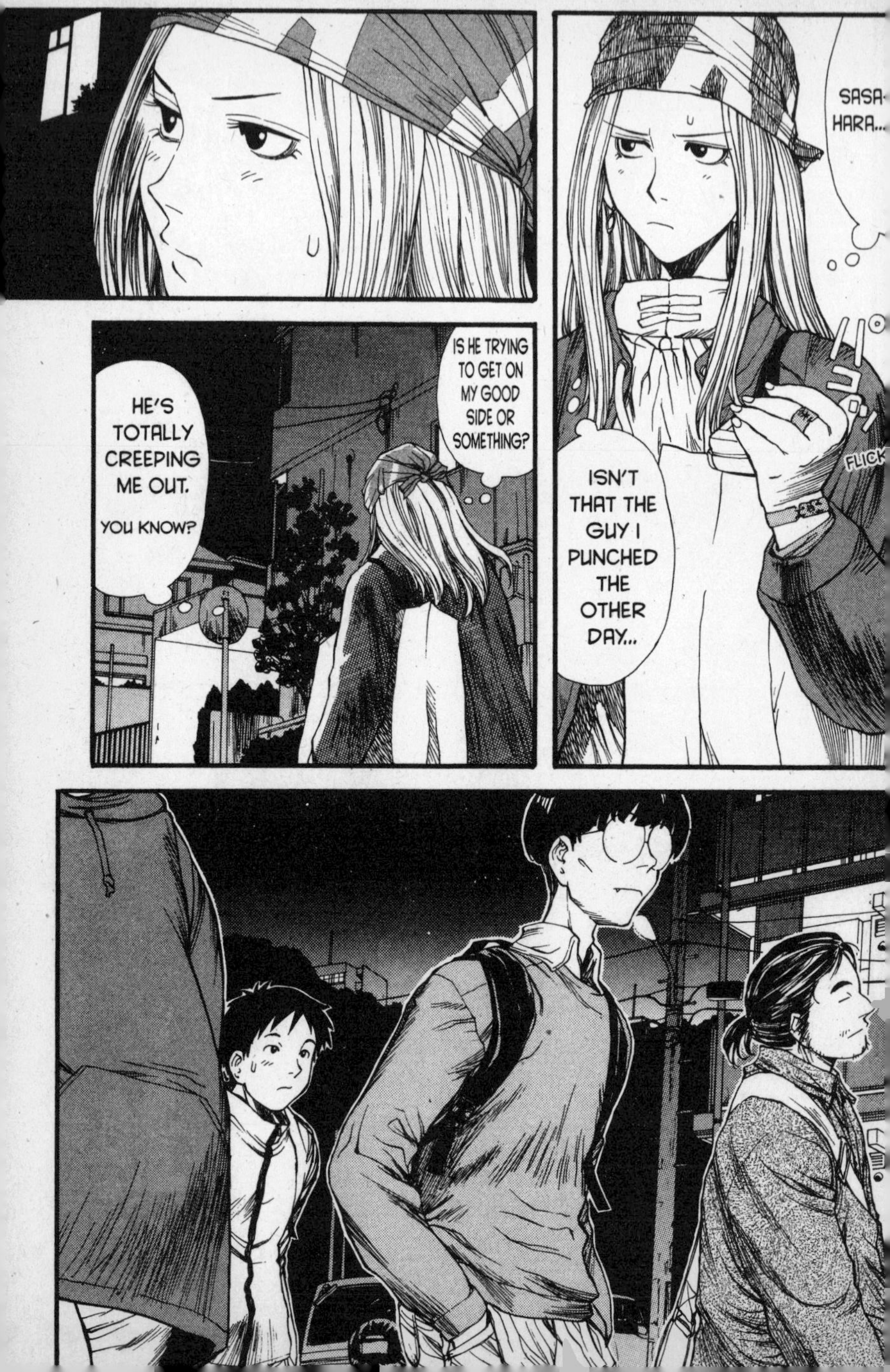
SASA-HARA...
FLICK
ISN'T THAT THE GUY I PUNCHED THE OTHER DAY...
IS HE TRYING TO GET ON MY GOOD SIDE OR SOMETHING?
HE'S TOTALLY CREEPING ME OUT.
YOU KNOW?

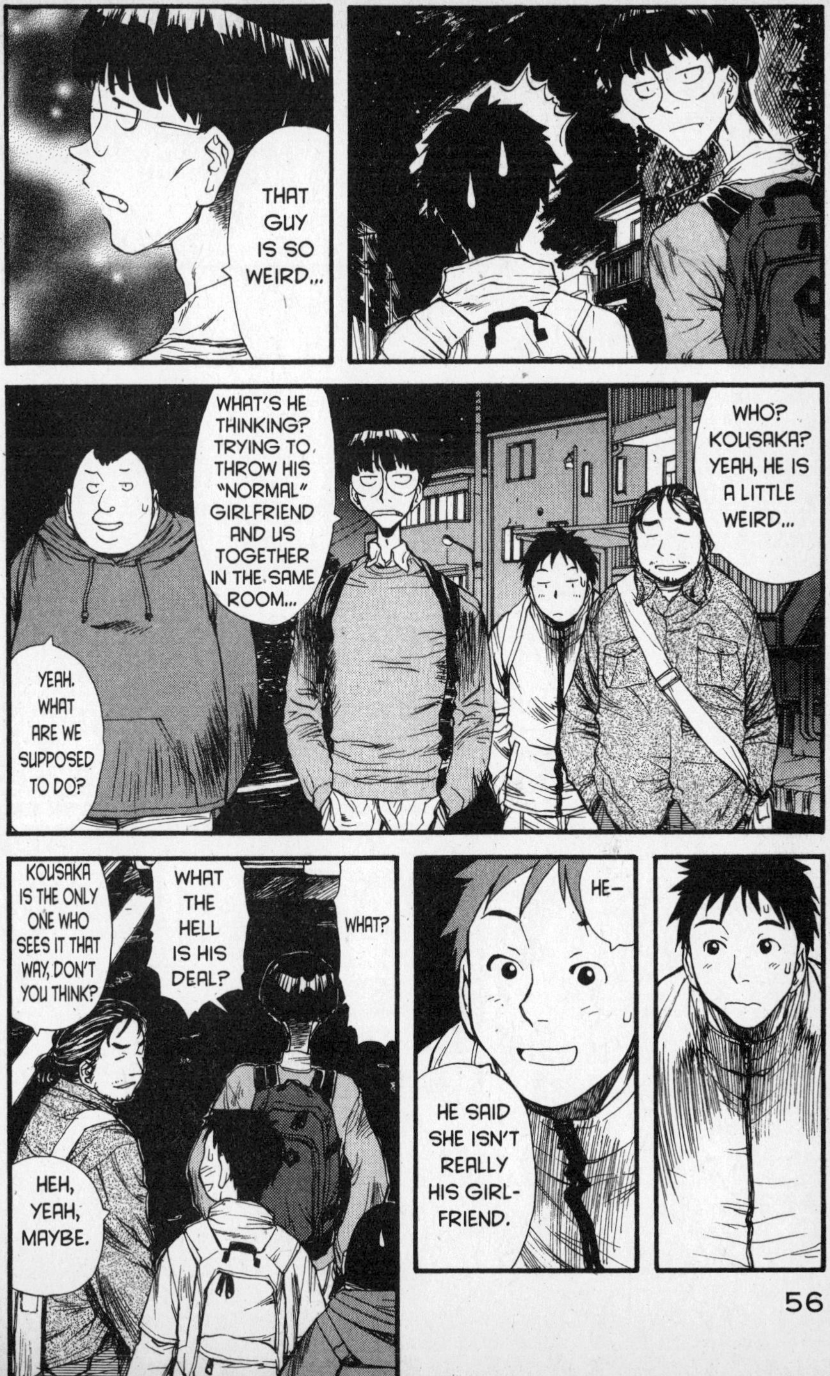
THAT GUY IS SO WEIRD...
WHO? KOUSAKA? YEAH, HE IS A LITTLE WEIRD...
WHAT'S HE THINKING? TRYING TO THROW HIS "NORMAL" GIRLFRIEND AND US TOGETHER IN THE SAME ROOM...
YEAH. WHAT ARE WE SUPPOSED TO DO?
HE-
HE SAID SHE ISN'T REALLY HIS GIRL-FRIEND.
WHAT?
WHAT THE HELL IS HIS DEAL?
KOUSAKA IS THE ONLY ONE WHO SEES IT THAT WAY, DON'T YOU THINK?
HEH, YEAH, MAYBE.

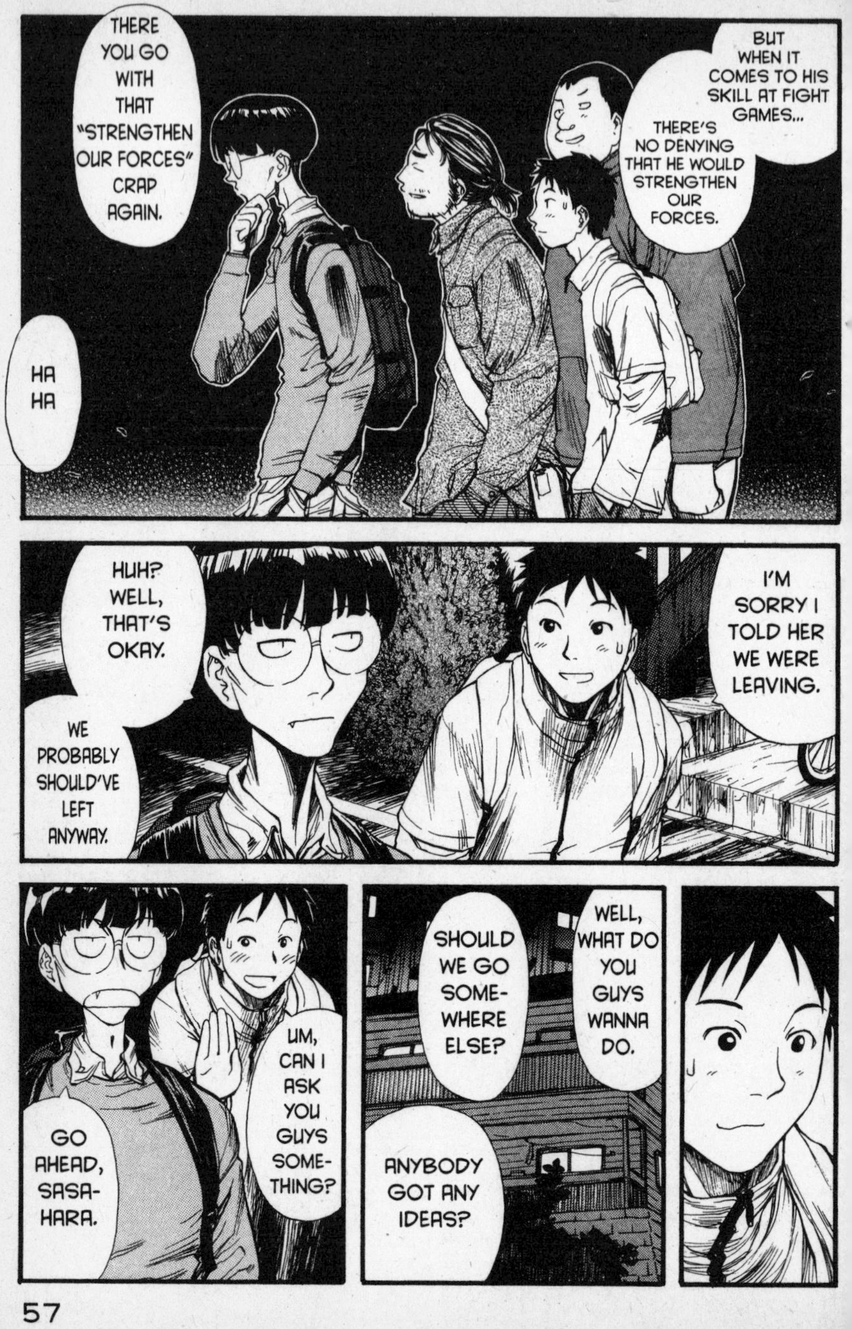
BUT WHEN IT COMES TO HIS SKILL AT FIGHT GAMES...
THERE'S NO DENYING THAT HE WOULD STRENGTHEN OUR FORCES.
THERE YOU GO WITH THAT "STRENGTHEN OUR FORCES" CRAP AGAIN.
HA HA
I'M SORRY I TOLD HER WE WERE LEAVING.
HUH? WELL, THAT'S OKAY.
WE PROBABLY SHOULD'VE LEFT ANYWAY.
WELL, WHAT DO YOU GUYS WANNA DO.
SHOULD WE GO SOME-WHERE ELSE?
ANYBODY GOT ANY IDEAS?
UM, CAN I ASK YOU GUYS SOME-THING?
GO AHEAD, SASA-HARA.

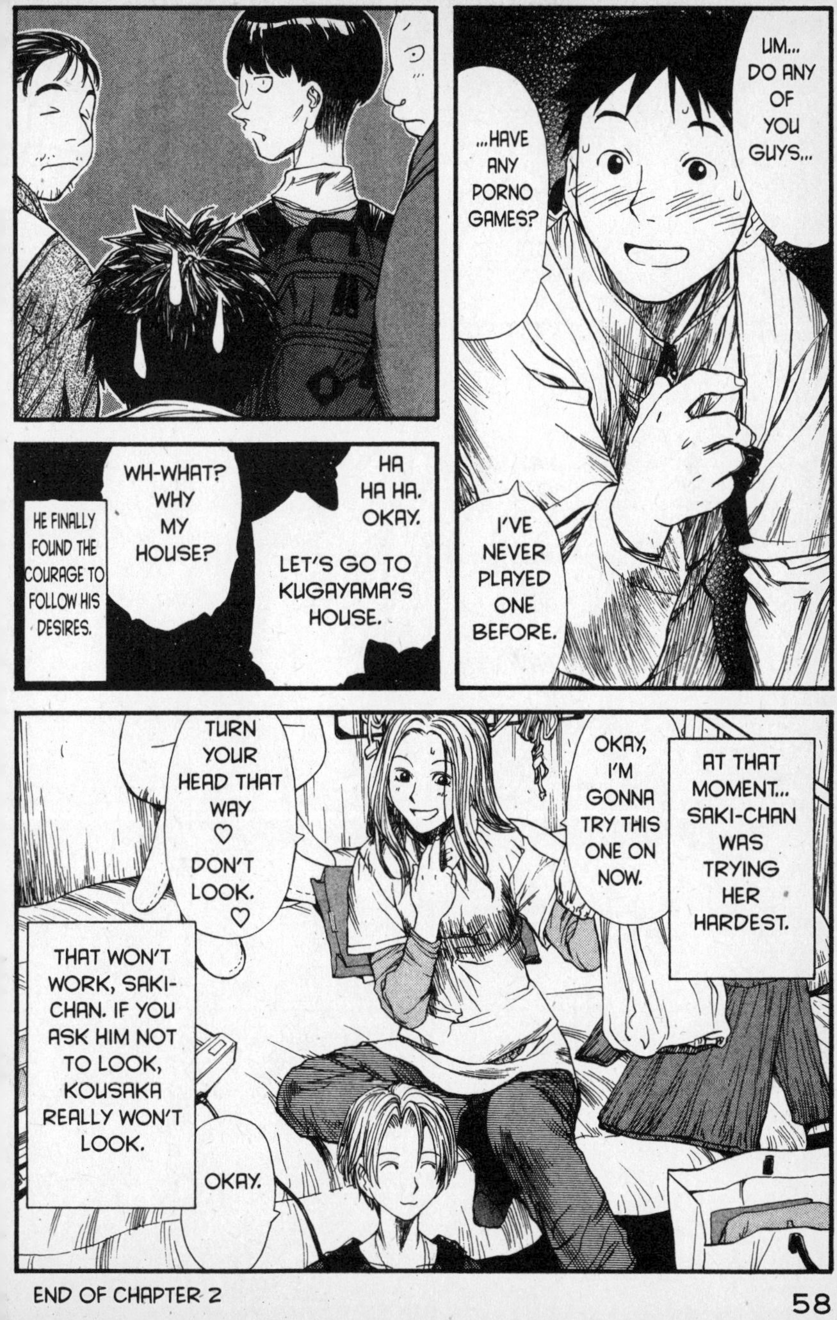
UM... DO ANY OF YOU GUYS...
...HAVE ANY PORNO GAMES?
I'VE NEVER PLAYED ONE BEFORE.
HA HA HA. OKAY.
LET'S GO TO KUGAYAMA'S HOUSE.
WH-WHAT? WHY MY HOUSE?
HE FINALLY FOUND THE COURAGE TO FOLLOW HIS DESIRES.
AT THAT MOMENT... SAKI-CHAN WAS TRYING HER HARDEST.
OKAY, I'M GONNA TRY THIS ONE ON NOW.
TURN YOUR HEAD THAT WAY ♡ DON'T LOOK. ♡
THAT WON'T WORK, SAKI-CHAN. IF YOU ASK HIM NOT TO LOOK, KOUSAKA REALLY WON'T LOOK.
OKAY.

END OF CHAPTER 2

KOSAKA MAKOTO

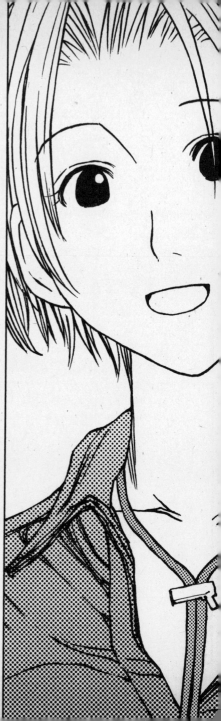

PROFILE

MAKOTO KOUSAKA

BORN FEBRUARY 2ND

BLOOD TYPE B

FAVORITE MANGA

THE MYSTERIOUS ADVENTURES OF DADA

FAVORITE ANIME

PRETTY MUCH ANYTHING

FAVORITE VIDEO GAMES

FULL ARMOR

STREET MASTER 2

DRACULINA HUNTER

FAVORITE FIGHT GAME CHARACTERS

JULIETTE

SAKAMOTO

TAKIKEN

GOKI

*THESE ARE THE CHARACTER'S CHOICES AND DO NOT NECESSARILY REFLECT THE AUTHOR'S TASTES.

THE PERFECT CHOICE

KUGA-YAMA'S HOUSE
OKAY, WHICH PORNO GAME DO YOU WANNA PLAY?
UH... UMM...
OKAY, I WANNA PLAY "MY HEART." IT STARTED OUT AS A PC GAME AND THEN THEY MADE IT INTO A HOME VIDEO GAME.
GEEZ, YOU'RE REALLY GETTING SUCKED INTO THE OTAKU WORLD.
SO, WHICH CHARAC-TER?

CALM DOWN

カチ CLICK
THEIR "DOWN THERE HAIR" IS THE SAME COLOR AS THEIR REGULAR HAIR, ISN'T IT?
HUH? OH, YEAH. IT IS.
カチ CLICK
I MEAN, I'VE SEEN PHOTOS IN MAGAZINES, SO I KNEW IT WAS, BUT...
JUST SHUT UP AND WATCH.

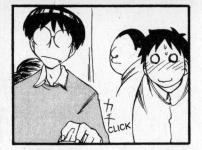

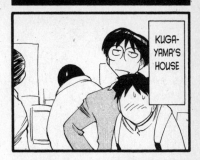

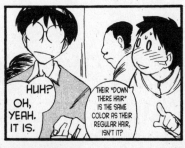

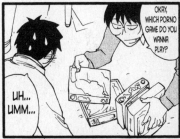

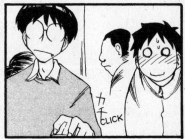

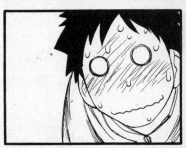

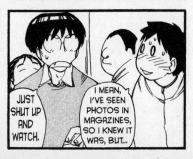

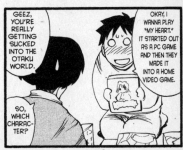

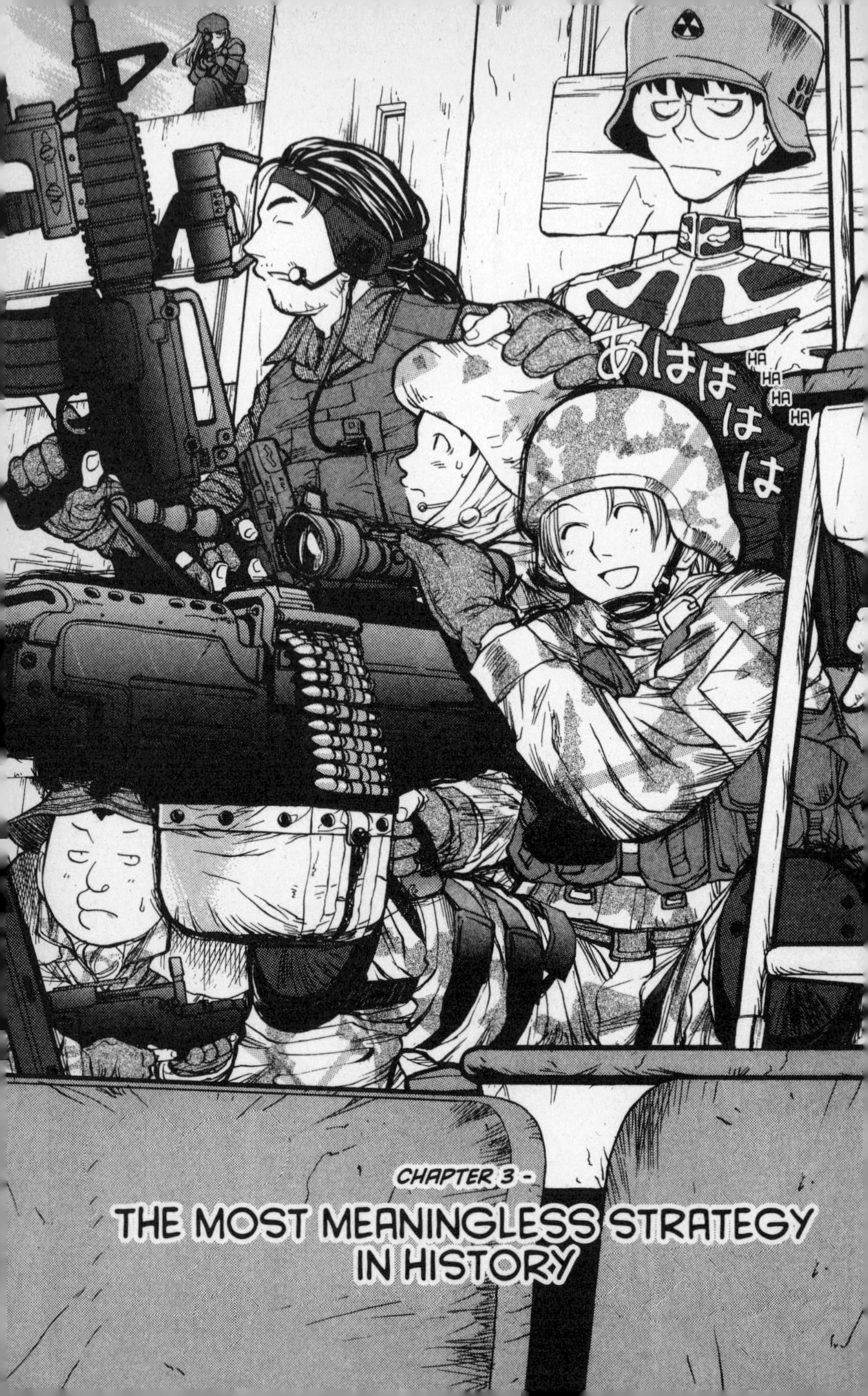
あはははは
HA HA HA HA
CHAPTER 3 -
THE MOST MEANINGLESS STRATEGY IN HISTORY

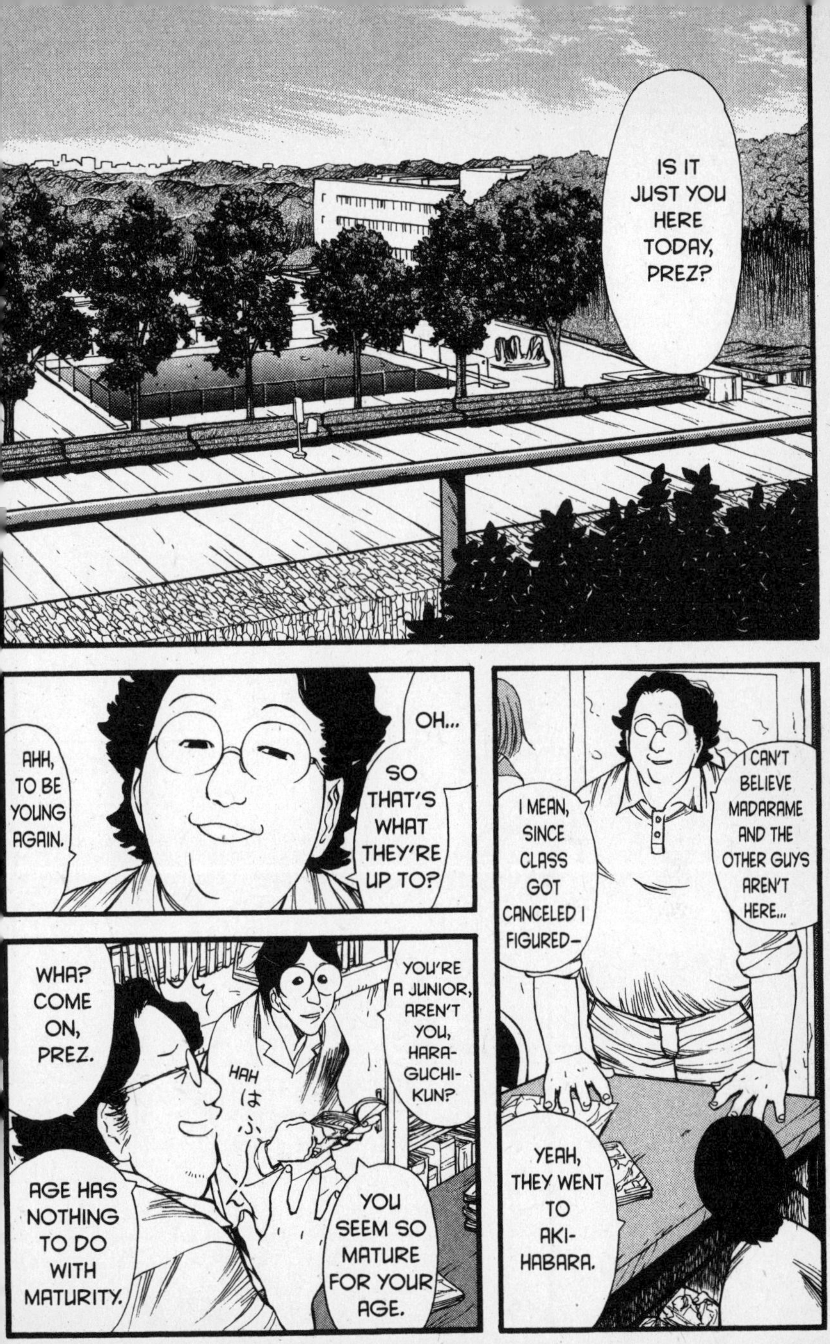

IS IT JUST YOU HERE TODAY, PREZ?
I CAN'T BELIEVE MADARAME AND THE OTHER GUYS AREN'T HERE...
I MEAN, SINCE CLASS GOT CANCELED I FIGURED—
YEAH, THEY WENT TO AKI-HABARA.
OH...
SO THAT'S WHAT THEY'RE UP TO?
AHH, TO BE YOUNG AGAIN.
YOU'RE A JUNIOR, AREN'T YOU, HARA-GUCHI-KUN?
WHA? COME ON, PREZ.
HAH はふ
YOU SEEM SO MATURE FOR YOUR AGE.
AGE HAS NOTHING TO DO WITH MATURITY.

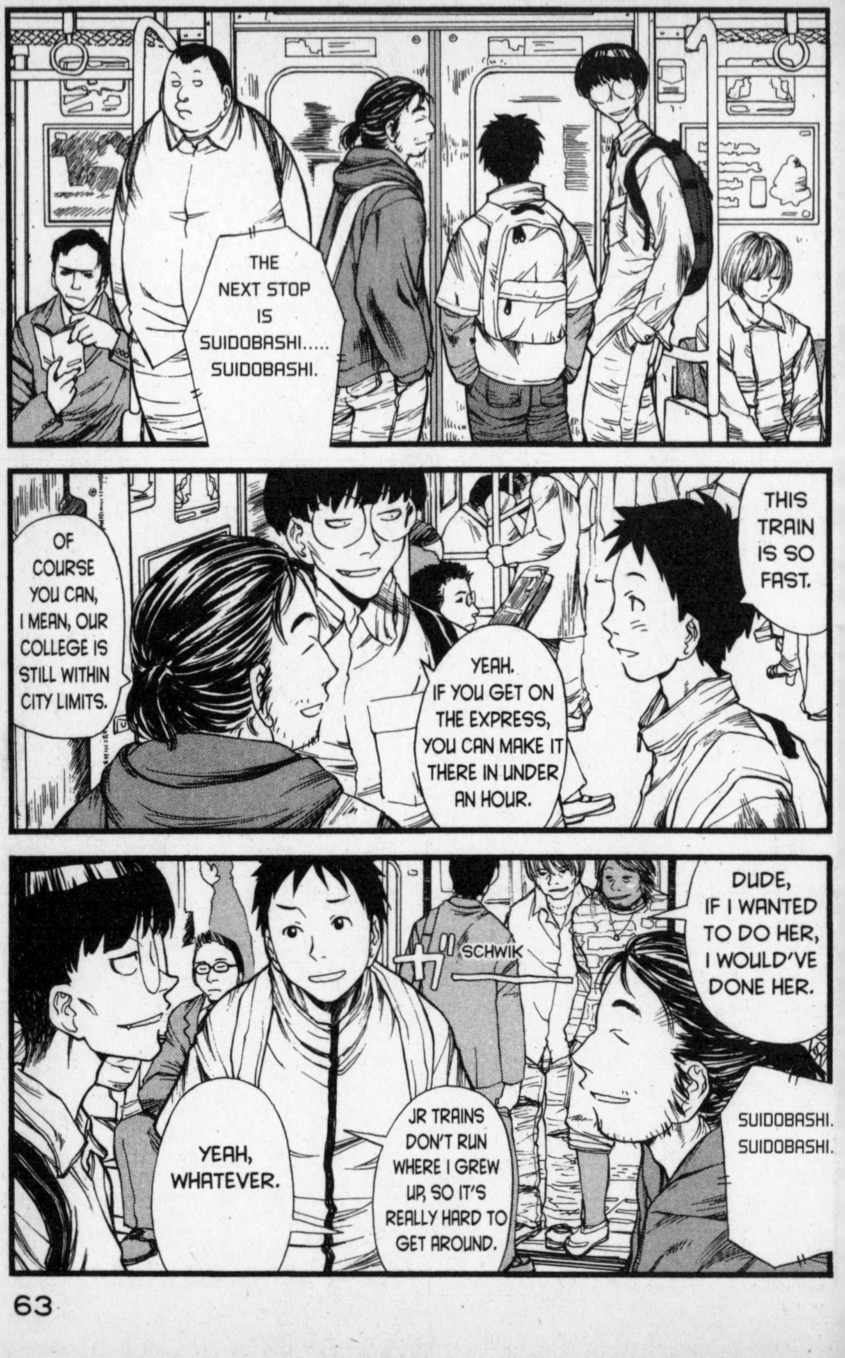
THE NEXT STOP IS SUIDOBASHI..... SUIDOBASHI.
THIS TRAIN IS SO FAST.
YEAH. IF YOU GET ON THE EXPRESS, YOU CAN MAKE IT THERE IN UNDER AN HOUR.
OF COURSE YOU CAN, I MEAN, OUR COLLEGE IS STILL WITHIN CITY LIMITS.
DUDE, IF I WANTED TO DO HER, I WOULD'VE DONE HER.
SUIDOBASHI. SUIDOBASHI.
SCHWIK
JR TRAINS DON'T RUN WHERE I GREW UP, SO IT'S REALLY HARD TO GET AROUND.
YEAH, WHATEVER.

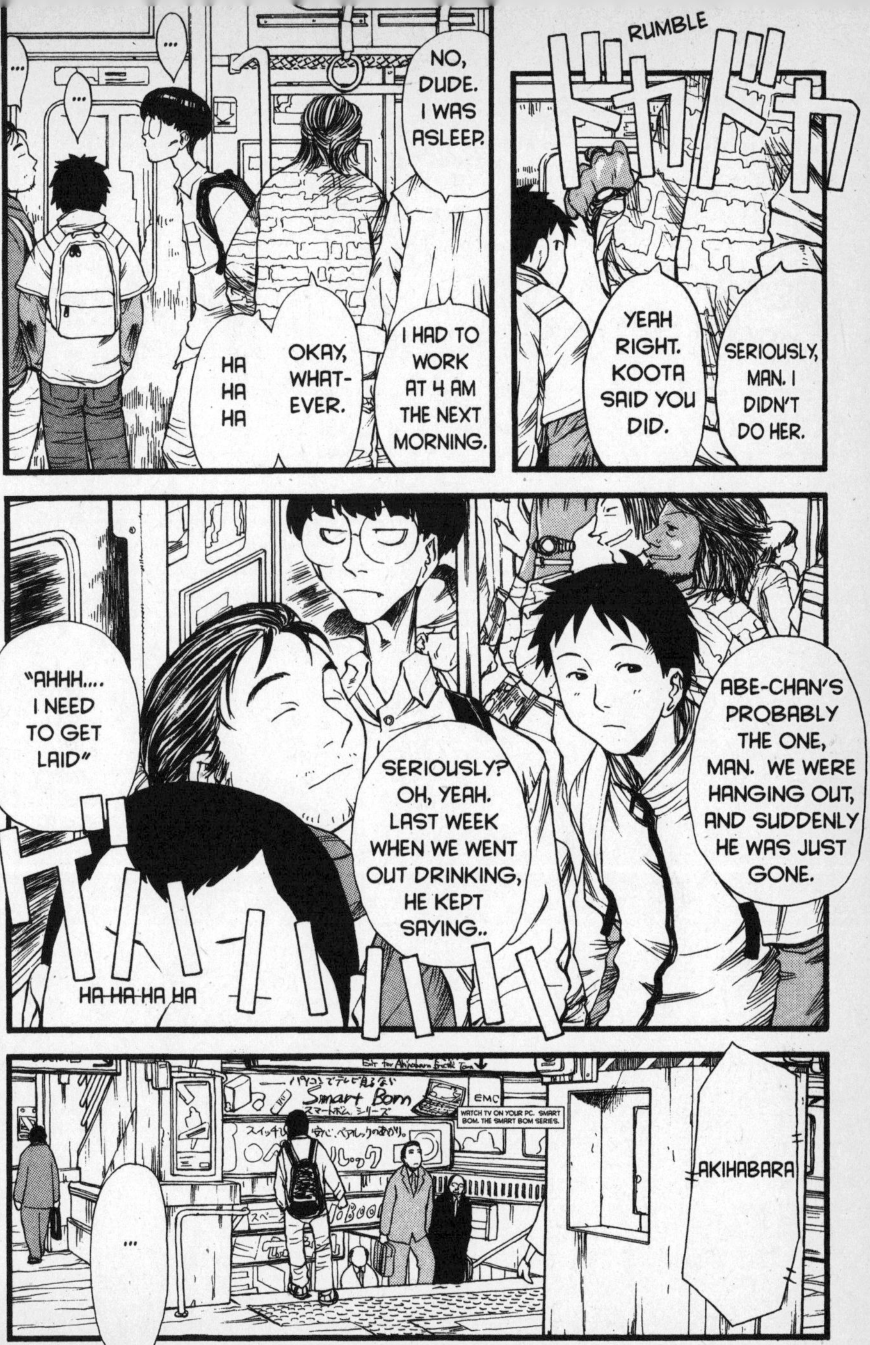
RUMBLE
SERIOUSLY, MAN. I DIDN'T DO HER.
YEAH RIGHT. KOOTA SAID YOU DID.
NO, DUDE. I WAS ASLEEP.
I HAD TO WORK AT 4 AM THE NEXT MORNING.
OKAY, WHAT-EVER.
HA HA HA
...
...
...
ABE-CHAN'S PROBABLY THE ONE, MAN. WE WERE HANGING OUT, AND SUDDENLY HE WAS JUST GONE.
SERIOUSLY? OH, YEAH. LAST WEEK WHEN WE WENT OUT DRINKING, HE KEPT SAYING..
"AHHH.... I NEED TO GET LAID"
HA HA HA HA
AKIHABARA
Smart Bom
WATCH TV ON YOUR PC. SMART BOM. THE SMART BOM SERIES.
...

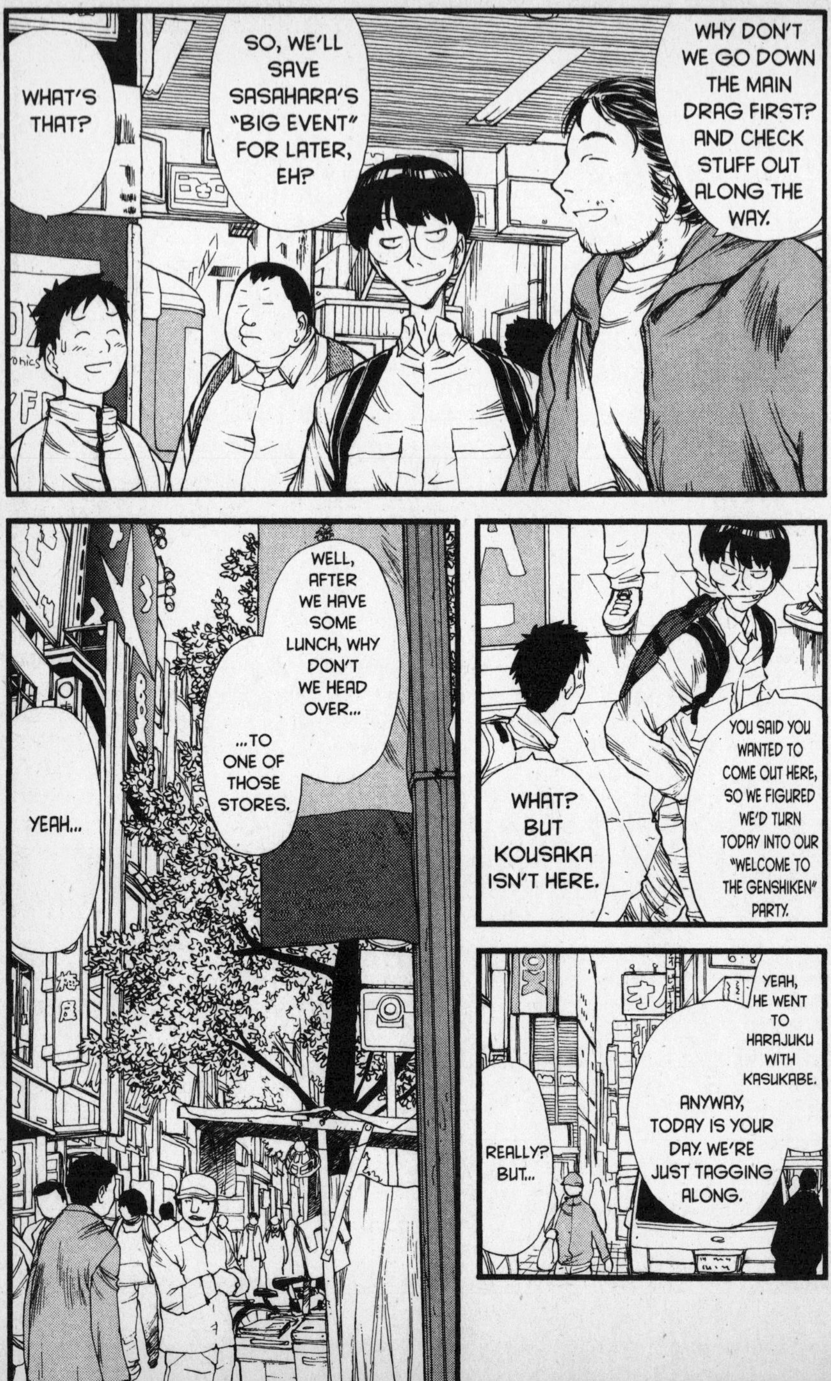
WHY DON'T WE GO DOWN THE MAIN DRAG FIRST? AND CHECK STUFF OUT ALONG THE WAY.
SO, WE'LL SAVE SASAHARA'S "BIG EVENT" FOR LATER, EH?
WHAT'S THAT?
YOU SAID YOU WANTED TO COME OUT HERE, SO WE FIGURED WE'D TURN TODAY INTO OUR "WELCOME TO THE GENSHIKEN" PARTY.
WHAT? BUT KOUSAKA ISN'T HERE.
YEAH, HE WENT TO HARAJUKU WITH KASUKABE.
ANYWAY, TODAY IS YOUR DAY. WE'RE JUST TAGGING ALONG.
REALLY? BUT...
WELL, AFTER WE HAVE SOME LUNCH, WHY DON'T WE HEAD OVER...
...TO ONE OF THOSE STORES.
YEAH...

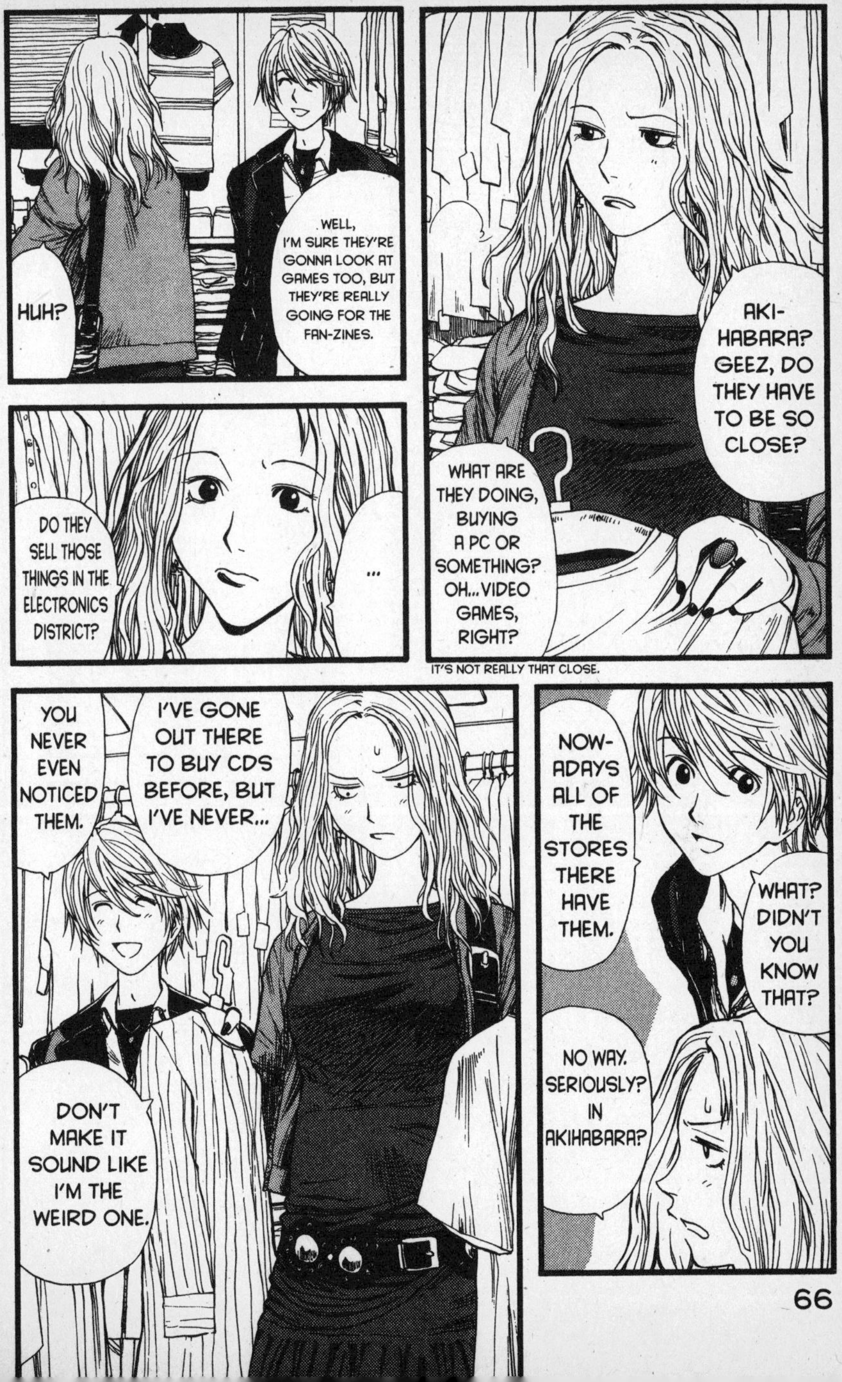
AKI-HABARA? GEEZ, DO THEY HAVE TO BE SO CLOSE?
WHAT ARE THEY DOING, BUYING A PC OR SOMETHING? OH...VIDEO GAMES, RIGHT?
IT'S NOT REALLY THAT CLOSE.
WELL, I'M SURE THEY'RE GONNA LOOK AT GAMES TOO, BUT THEY'RE REALLY GOING FOR THE FAN-ZINES.
HUH?
...
DO THEY SELL THOSE THINGS IN THE ELECTRONICS DISTRICT?
NOW-ADAYS ALL OF THE STORES THERE HAVE THEM.
WHAT? DIDN'T YOU KNOW THAT?
NO WAY. SERIOUSLY? IN AKIHABARA?
I'VE GONE OUT THERE TO BUY CDS BEFORE, BUT I'VE NEVER...
YOU NEVER EVEN NOTICED THEM.
DON'T MAKE IT SOUND LIKE I'M THE WEIRD ONE.

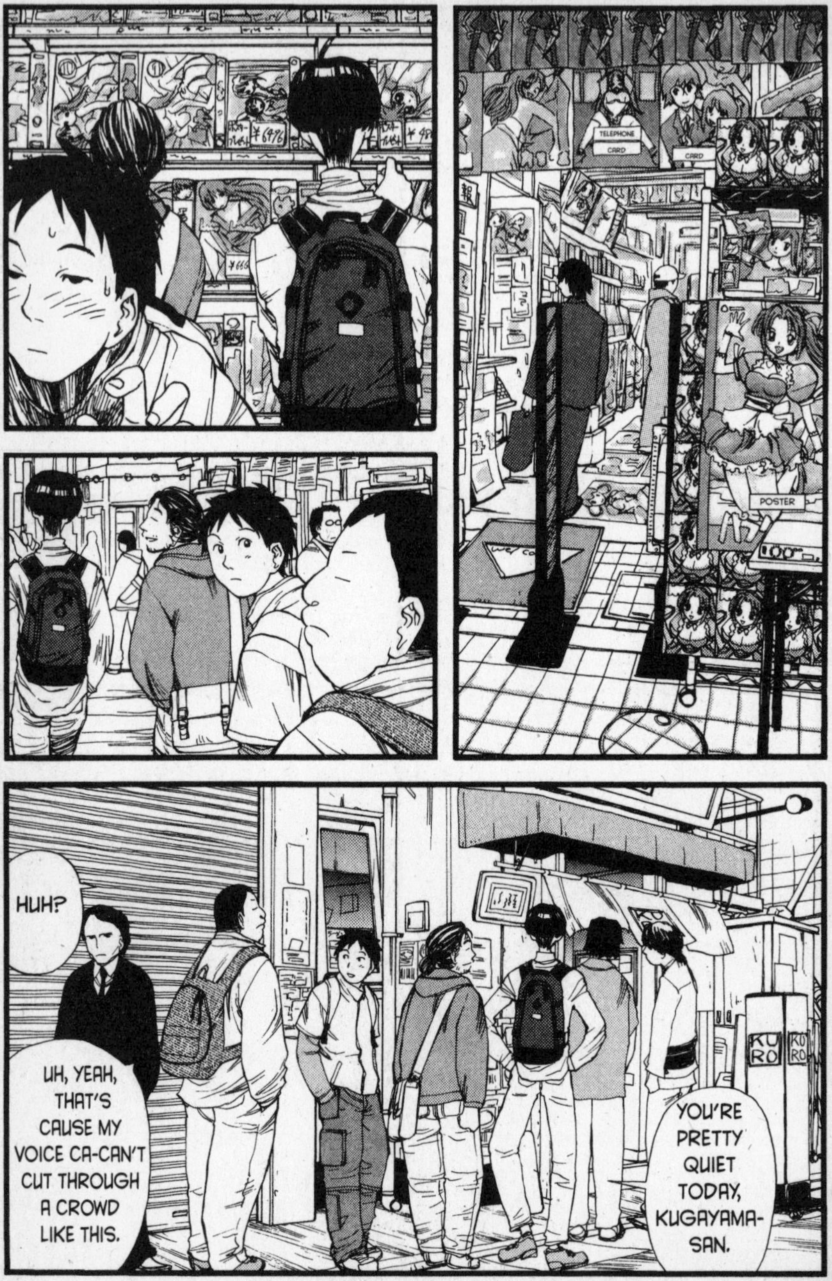
TELEPHONE
CARD
CARD
POSTER
YOU'RE PRETTY QUIET TODAY, KUGAYAMA-SAN.
HUH?
UH, YEAH, THAT'S CAUSE MY VOICE CA-CAN'T CUT THROUGH A CROWD LIKE THIS.

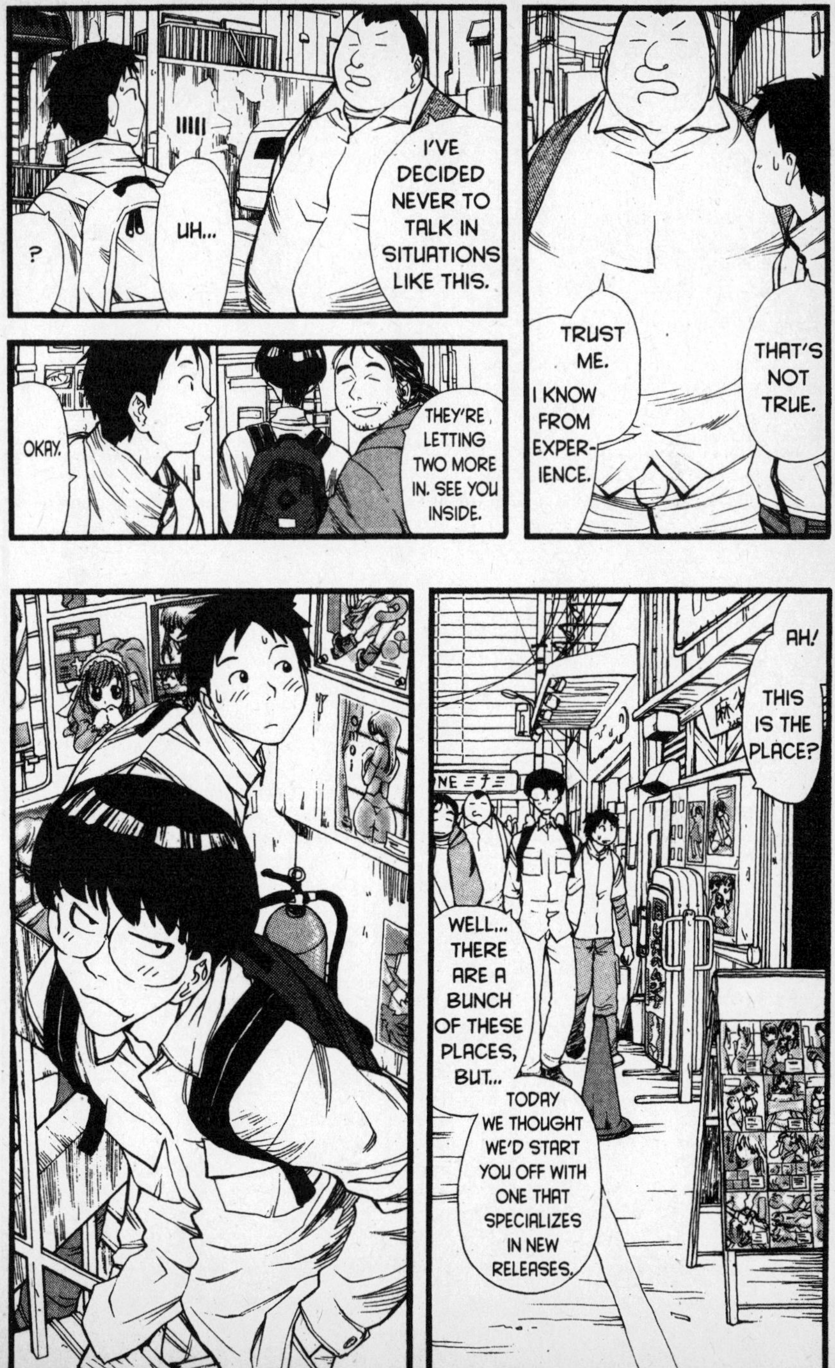
?
UH...
I'VE DECIDED NEVER TO TALK IN SITUATIONS LIKE THIS.
THAT'S NOT TRUE.
TRUST ME. I KNOW FROM EXPER-IENCE.
THEY'RE LETTING TWO MORE IN. SEE YOU INSIDE.
OKAY.
AH!
THIS IS THE PLACE?
WELL... THERE ARE A BUNCH OF THESE PLACES, BUT...
TODAY WE THOUGHT WE'D START YOU OFF WITH ONE THAT SPECIALIZES IN NEW RELEASES.

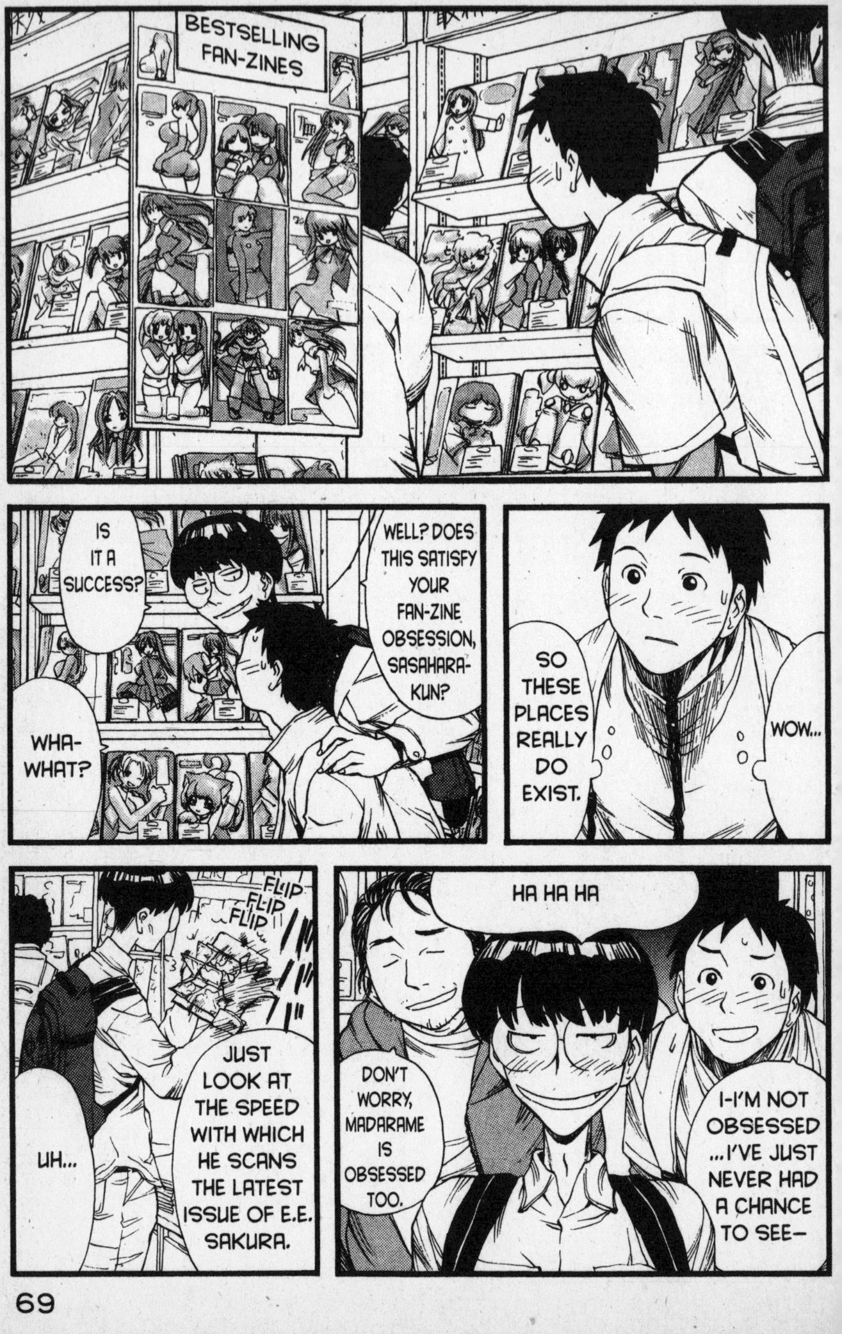
BESTSELLING FAN-ZINES
WOW...
SO THESE PLACES REALLY DO EXIST.
WELL? DOES THIS SATISFY YOUR FAN-ZINE OBSESSION, SASAHARA-KUN?
IS IT A SUCCESS?
WHA-WHAT?
HA HA HA
I-I'M NOT OBSESSED ...I'VE JUST NEVER HAD A CHANCE TO SEE—
DON'T WORRY, MADARAME IS OBSESSED TOO.
FLIP FLIP FLIP
JUST LOOK AT THE SPEED WITH WHICH HE SCANS THE LATEST ISSUE OF E.E. SAKURA.
UH...

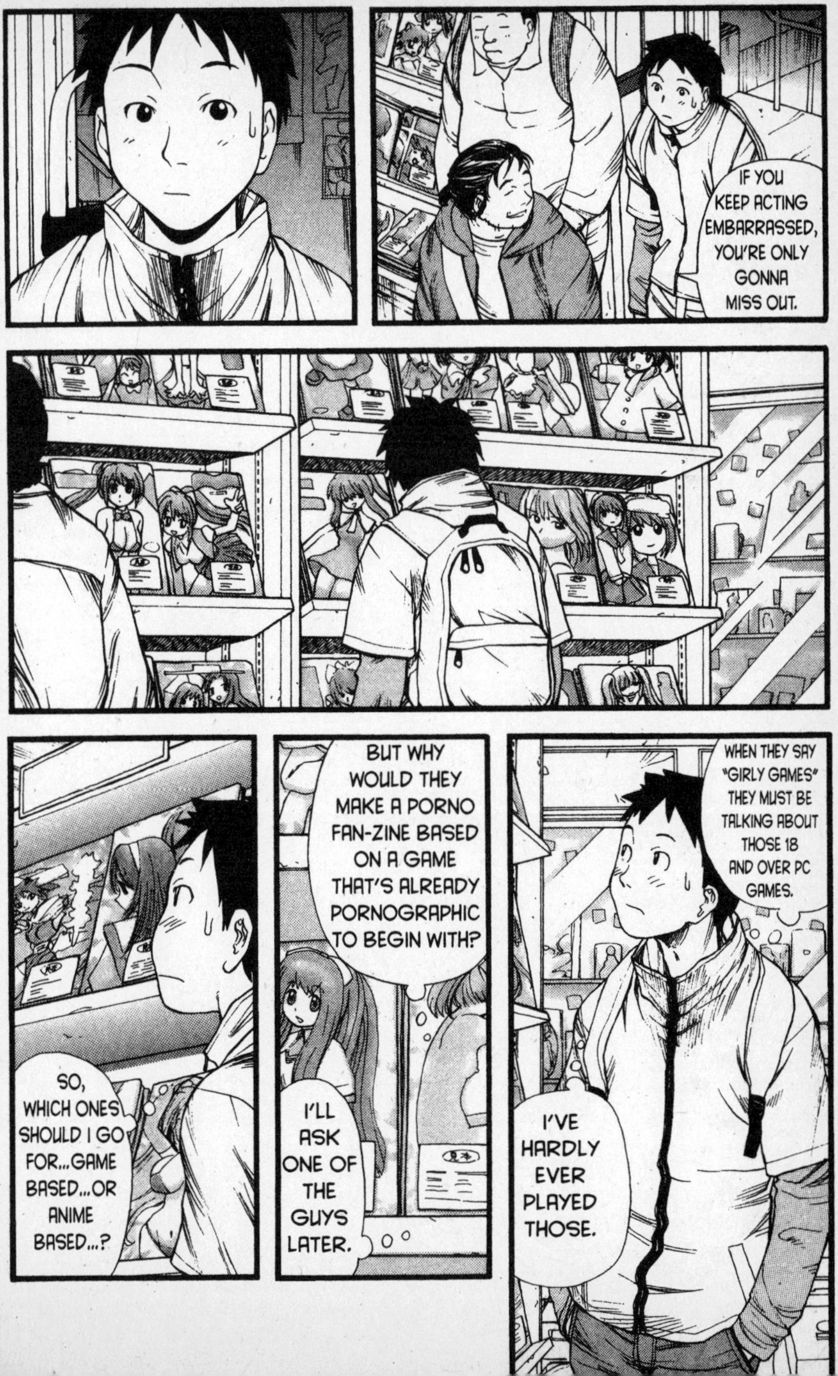
IF YOU KEEP ACTING EMBARRASSED, YOU'RE ONLY GONNA MISS OUT.
WHEN THEY SAY "GIRLY GAMES" THEY MUST BE TALKING ABOUT THOSE 18 AND OVER PC GAMES.
I'VE HARDLY EVER PLAYED THOSE.
BUT WHY WOULD THEY MAKE A PORNO FAN-ZINE BASED ON A GAME THAT'S ALREADY PORNOGRAPHIC TO BEGIN WITH?
I'LL ASK ONE OF THE GUYS LATER.
SO, WHICH ONES SHOULD I GO FOR...GAME BASED...OR ANIME BASED...?

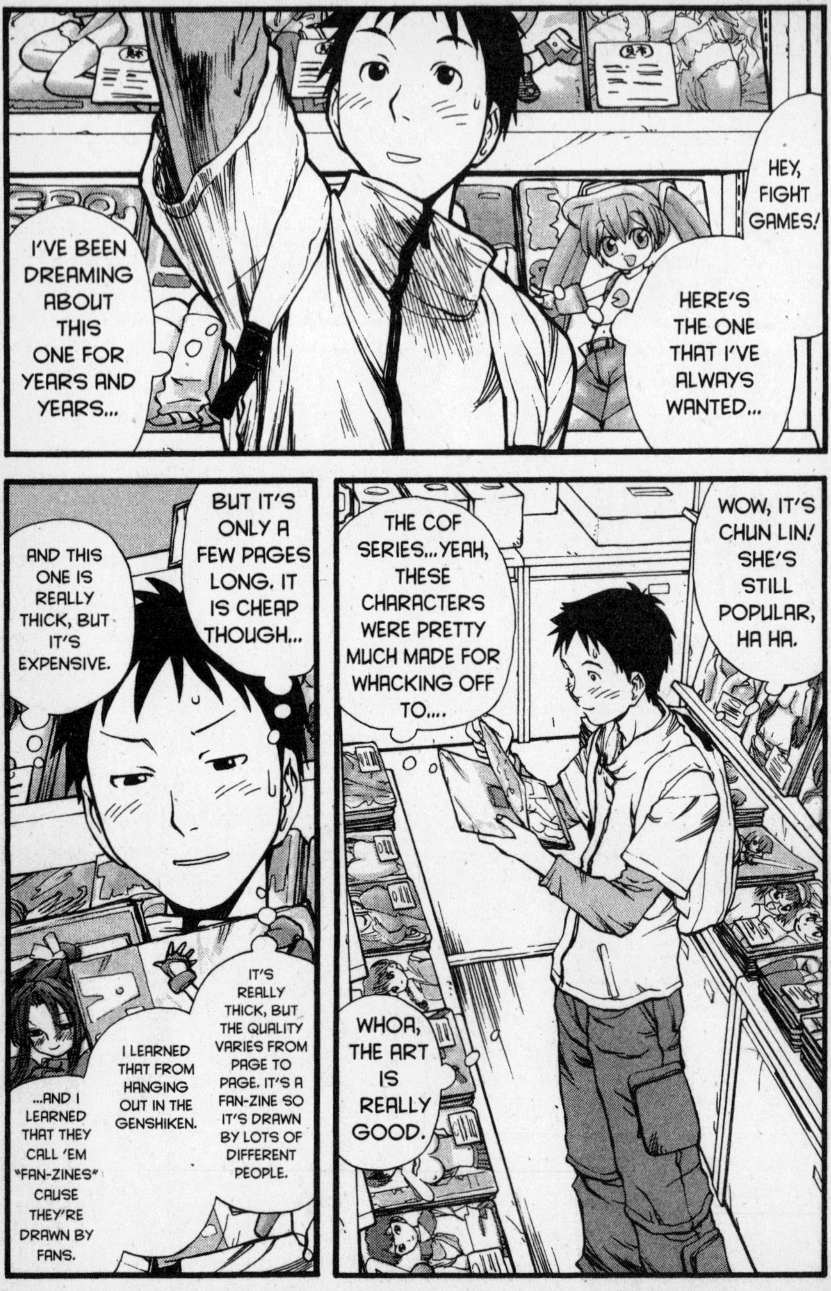
HEY, FIGHT GAMES!
HERE'S THE ONE THAT I'VE ALWAYS WANTED...
I'VE BEEN DREAMING ABOUT THIS ONE FOR YEARS AND YEARS...
WOW, IT'S CHUN LIN! SHE'S STILL POPULAR, HA HA.
THE COF SERIES...YEAH, THESE CHARACTERS WERE PRETTY MUCH MADE FOR WHACKING OFF TO....
WHOA, THE ART IS REALLY GOOD.
BUT IT'S ONLY A FEW PAGES LONG. IT IS CHEAP THOUGH...
AND THIS ONE IS REALLY THICK, BUT IT'S EXPENSIVE.
IT'S REALLY THICK, BUT THE QUALITY VARIES FROM PAGE TO PAGE. IT'S A FAN-ZINE SO IT'S DRAWN BY LOTS OF DIFFERENT PEOPLE.
I LEARNED THAT FROM HANGING OUT IN THE GENSHIKEN.
...AND I LEARNED THAT THEY CALL 'EM "FAN-ZINES" CAUSE THEY'RE DRAWN BY FANS.

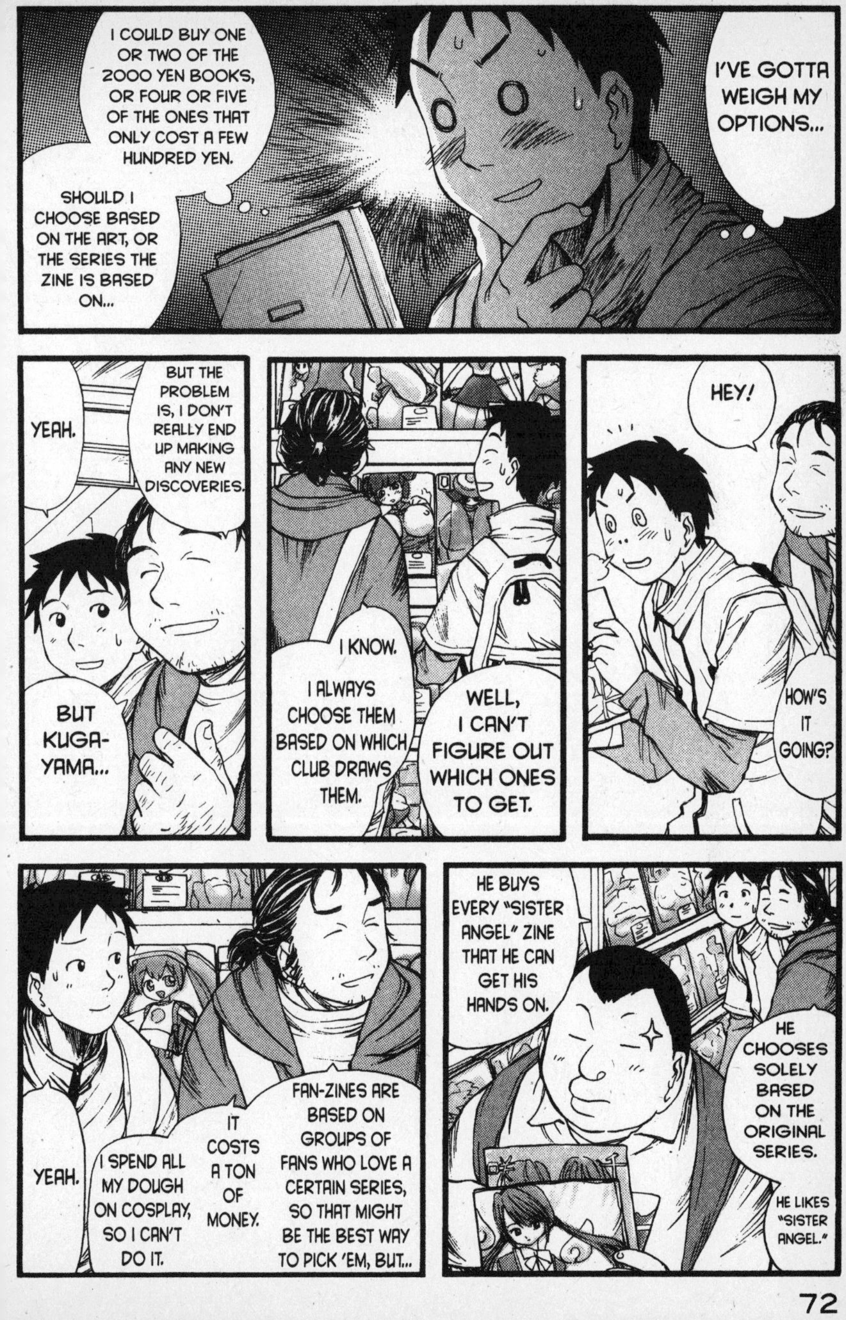
I'VE GOTTA WEIGH MY OPTIONS...
I COULD BUY ONE OR TWO OF THE 2000 YEN BOOKS, OR FOUR OR FIVE OF THE ONES THAT ONLY COST A FEW HUNDRED YEN.
SHOULD I CHOOSE BASED ON THE ART, OR THE SERIES THE ZINE IS BASED ON...
HEY!
HOW'S IT GOING?
WELL, I CAN'T FIGURE OUT WHICH ONES TO GET.
I KNOW.
I ALWAYS CHOOSE THEM BASED ON WHICH CLUB DRAWS THEM.
BUT THE PROBLEM IS, I DON'T REALLY END UP MAKING ANY NEW DISCOVERIES.
YEAH.
BUT KUGA-YAMA...
HE BUYS EVERY "SISTER ANGEL" ZINE THAT HE CAN GET HIS HANDS ON.
HE CHOOSES SOLELY BASED ON THE ORIGINAL SERIES.
HE LIKES "SISTER ANGEL."
FAN-ZINES ARE BASED ON GROUPS OF FANS WHO LOVE A CERTAIN SERIES, SO THAT MIGHT BE THE BEST WAY TO PICK 'EM, BUT...
IT COSTS A TON OF MONEY.
I SPEND ALL MY DOUGH ON COSPLAY, SO I CAN'T DO IT.
YEAH.

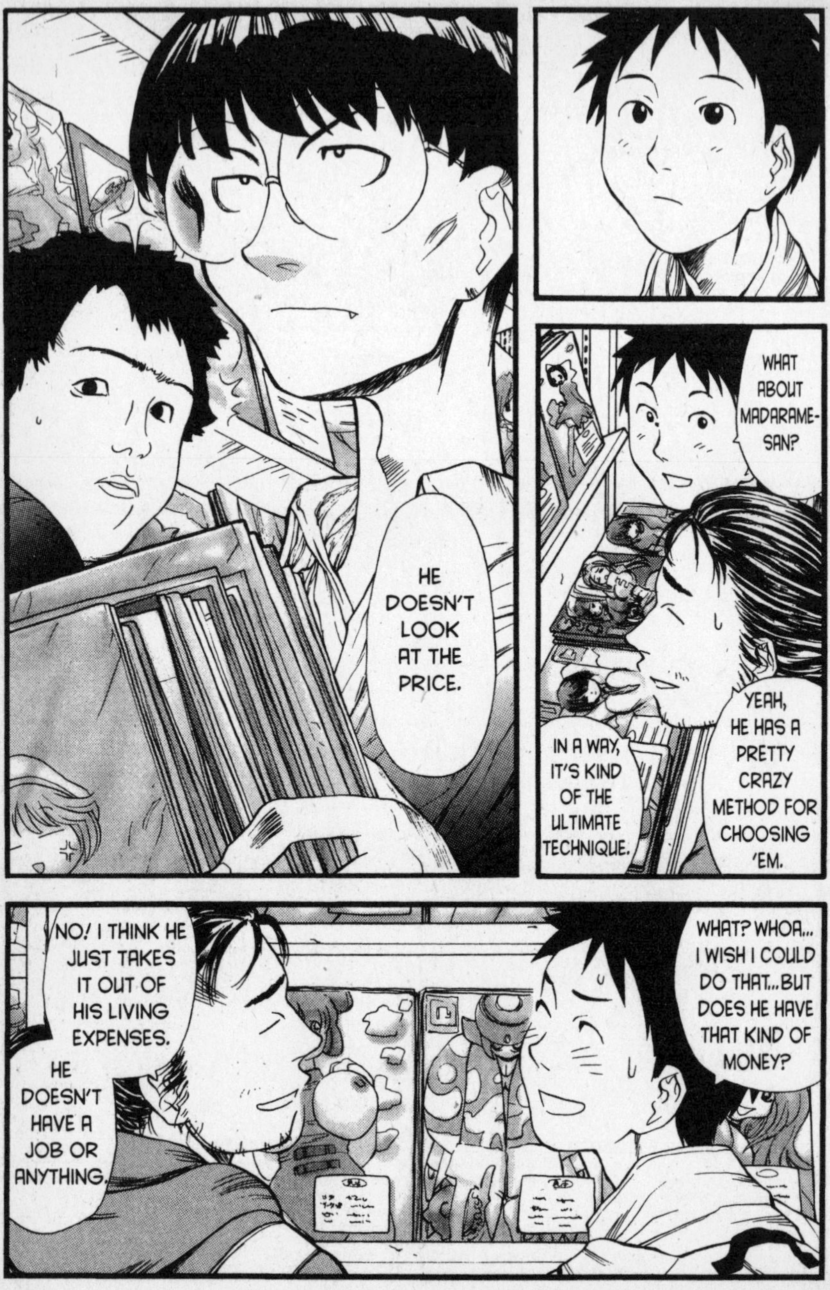
WHAT ABOUT MADARAME-SAN?
YEAH, HE HAS A PRETTY CRAZY METHOD FOR CHOOSING 'EM.
IN A WAY, IT'S KIND OF THE ULTIMATE TECHNIQUE.
HE DOESN'T LOOK AT THE PRICE.
WHAT? WHOA... I WISH I COULD DO THAT...BUT DOES HE HAVE THAT KIND OF MONEY?
NO! I THINK HE JUST TAKES IT OUT OF HIS LIVING EXPENSES.
HE DOESN'T HAVE A JOB OR ANYTHING.

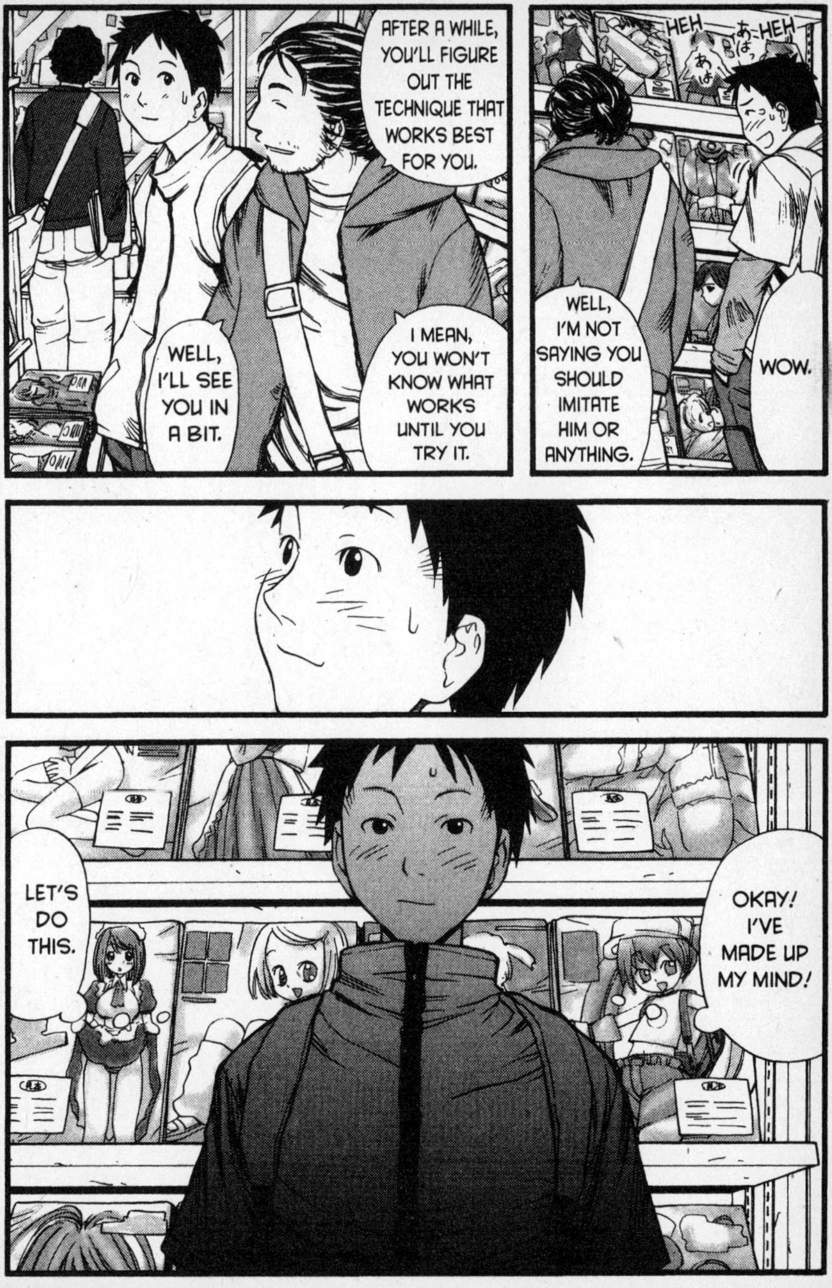
HEH HEH
WOW.
WELL, I'M NOT SAYING YOU SHOULD IMITATE HIM OR ANYTHING.
AFTER A WHILE, YOU'LL FIGURE OUT THE TECHNIQUE THAT WORKS BEST FOR YOU.
I MEAN, YOU WON'T KNOW WHAT WORKS UNTIL YOU TRY IT.
WELL, I'LL SEE YOU IN A BIT.
OKAY! I'VE MADE UP MY MIND!
LET'S DO THIS.

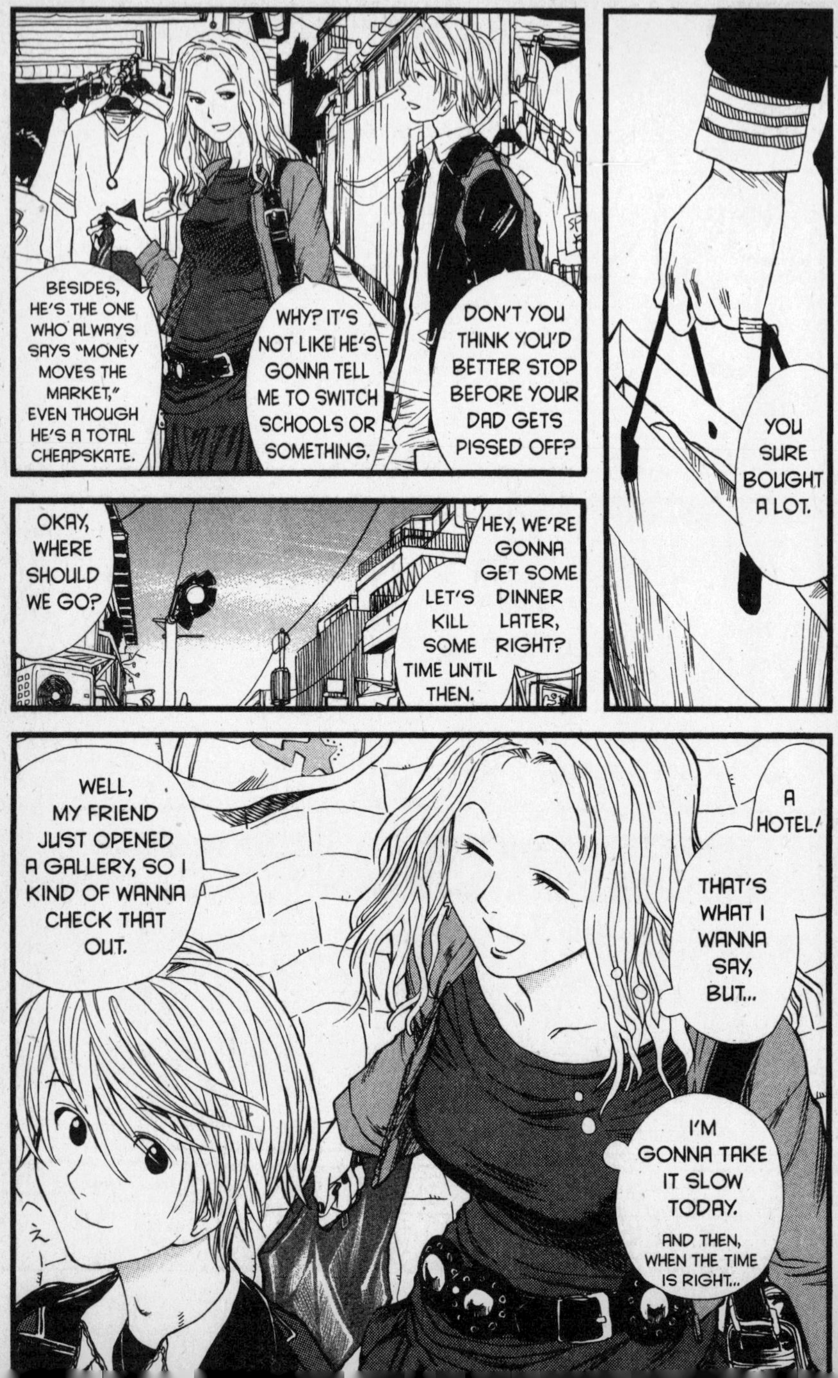
YOU SURE BOUGHT A LOT.
DON'T YOU THINK YOU'D BETTER STOP BEFORE YOUR DAD GETS PISSED OFF?
WHY? IT'S NOT LIKE HE'S GONNA TELL ME TO SWITCH SCHOOLS OR SOMETHING.
BESIDES, HE'S THE ONE WHO ALWAYS SAYS "MONEY MOVES THE MARKET," EVEN THOUGH HE'S A TOTAL CHEAPSKATE.
HEY, WE'RE GONNA GET SOME DINNER LATER, RIGHT?
LET'S KILL SOME TIME UNTIL THEN.
OKAY, WHERE SHOULD WE GO?
A HOTEL!
THAT'S WHAT I WANNA SAY, BUT...
WELL, MY FRIEND JUST OPENED A GALLERY, SO I KIND OF WANNA CHECK THAT OUT.
I'M GONNA TAKE IT SLOW TODAY.
AND THEN, WHEN THE TIME IS RIGHT...

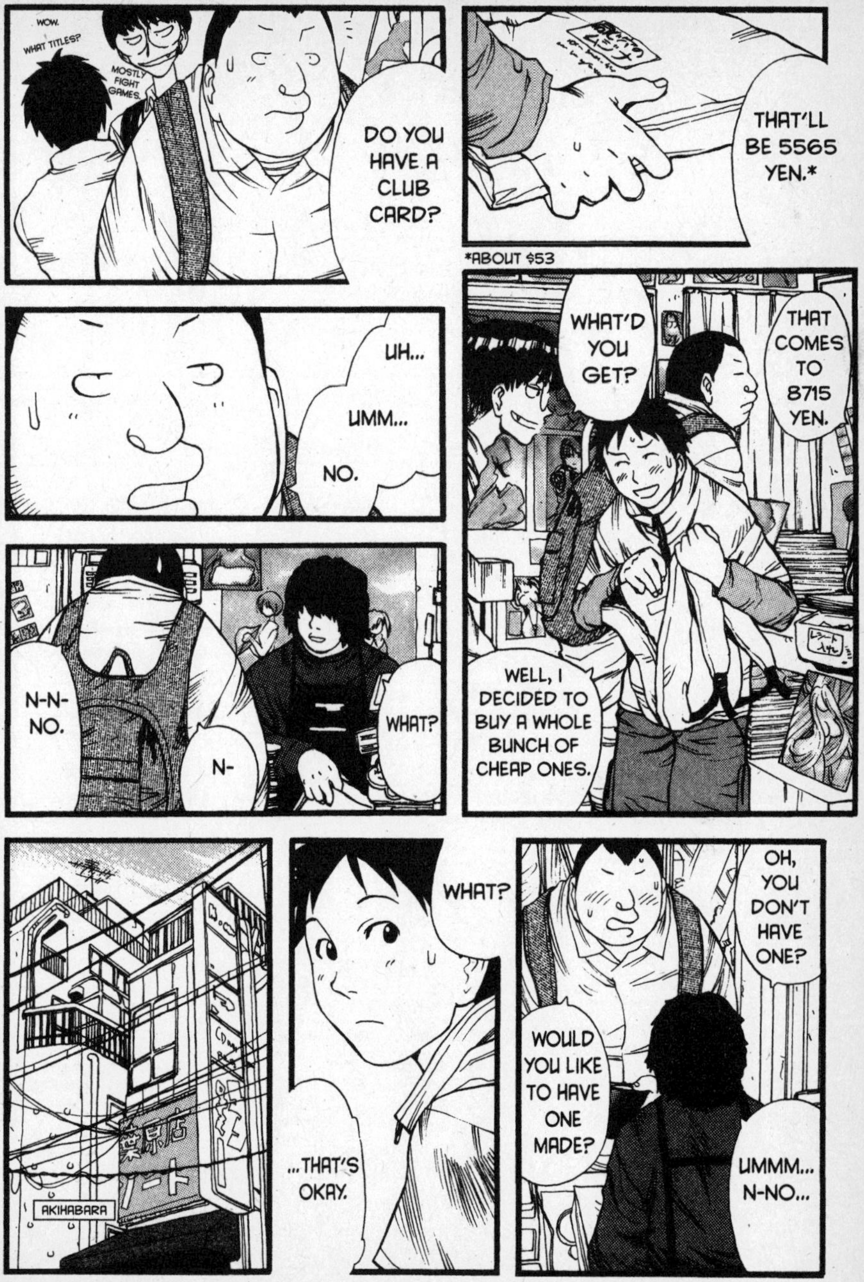
THAT'LL BE 5565 YEN.*
*ABOUT $53
DO YOU HAVE A CLUB CARD?
WOW.
WHAT TITLES?
MOSTLY FIGHT GAMES.
THAT COMES TO 8715 YEN.
WHAT'D YOU GET?
WELL, I DECIDED TO BUY A WHOLE BUNCH OF CHEAP ONES.
UH...
UMM...
NO.
WHAT?
N-
N-N-NO.
OH, YOU DON'T HAVE ONE?
WOULD YOU LIKE TO HAVE ONE MADE?
UMMM... N-NO...
WHAT?
...THAT'S OKAY.
AKIHABARA

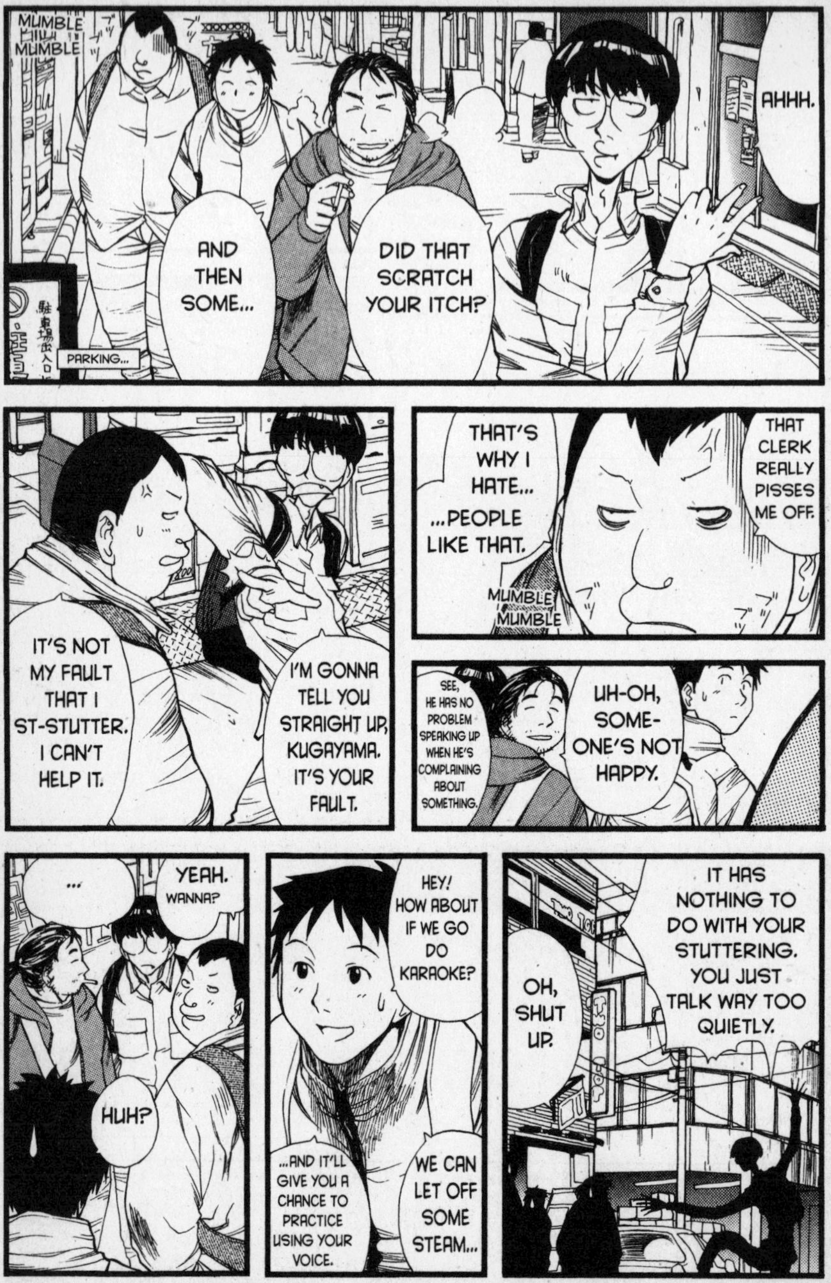
AHHH.
DID THAT SCRATCH YOUR ITCH?
AND THEN SOME...
MUMBLE MUMBLE
PARKING...
THAT CLERK REALLY PISSES ME OFF.
THAT'S WHY I HATE... ...PEOPLE LIKE THAT.
MUMBLE MUMBLE
UH-OH, SOME-ONE'S NOT HAPPY.
SEE, HE HAS NO PROBLEM SPEAKING UP WHEN HE'S COMPLAINING ABOUT SOMETHING.
I'M GONNA TELL YOU STRAIGHT UP, KUGAYAMA. IT'S YOUR FAULT.
IT'S NOT MY FAULT THAT I ST-STUTTER. I CAN'T HELP IT.
IT HAS NOTHING TO DO WITH YOUR STUTTERING. YOU JUST TALK WAY TOO QUIETLY.
OH, SHUT UP.
HEY! HOW ABOUT IF WE GO DO KARAOKE?
WE CAN LET OFF SOME STEAM...
...AND IT'LL GIVE YOU A CHANCE TO PRACTICE USING YOUR VOICE.
YEAH. WANNA?
...
HUH?

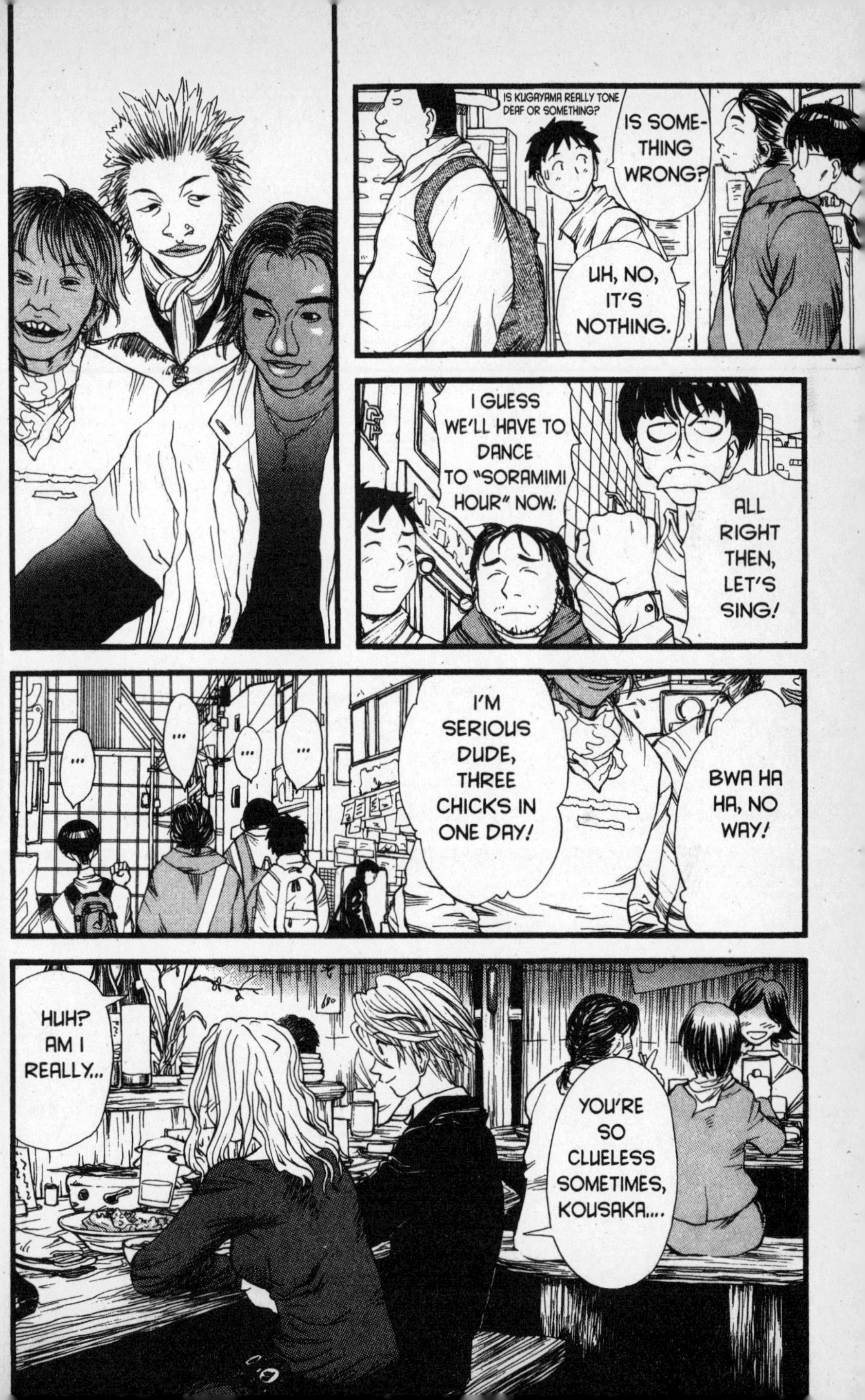
IS KUGAYAMA REALLY TONE DEAF OR SOMETHING?
IS SOMETHING WRONG?
UH, NO, IT'S NOTHING.
ALL RIGHT THEN, LET'S SING!
I GUESS WE'LL HAVE TO DANCE TO "SORAMIMI HOUR" NOW.
BWA HA HA, NO WAY!
I'M SERIOUS DUDE, THREE CHICKS IN ONE DAY!
...
...
...
...
YOU'RE SO CLUELESS SOMETIMES, KOUSAKA....
HUH? AM I REALLY...

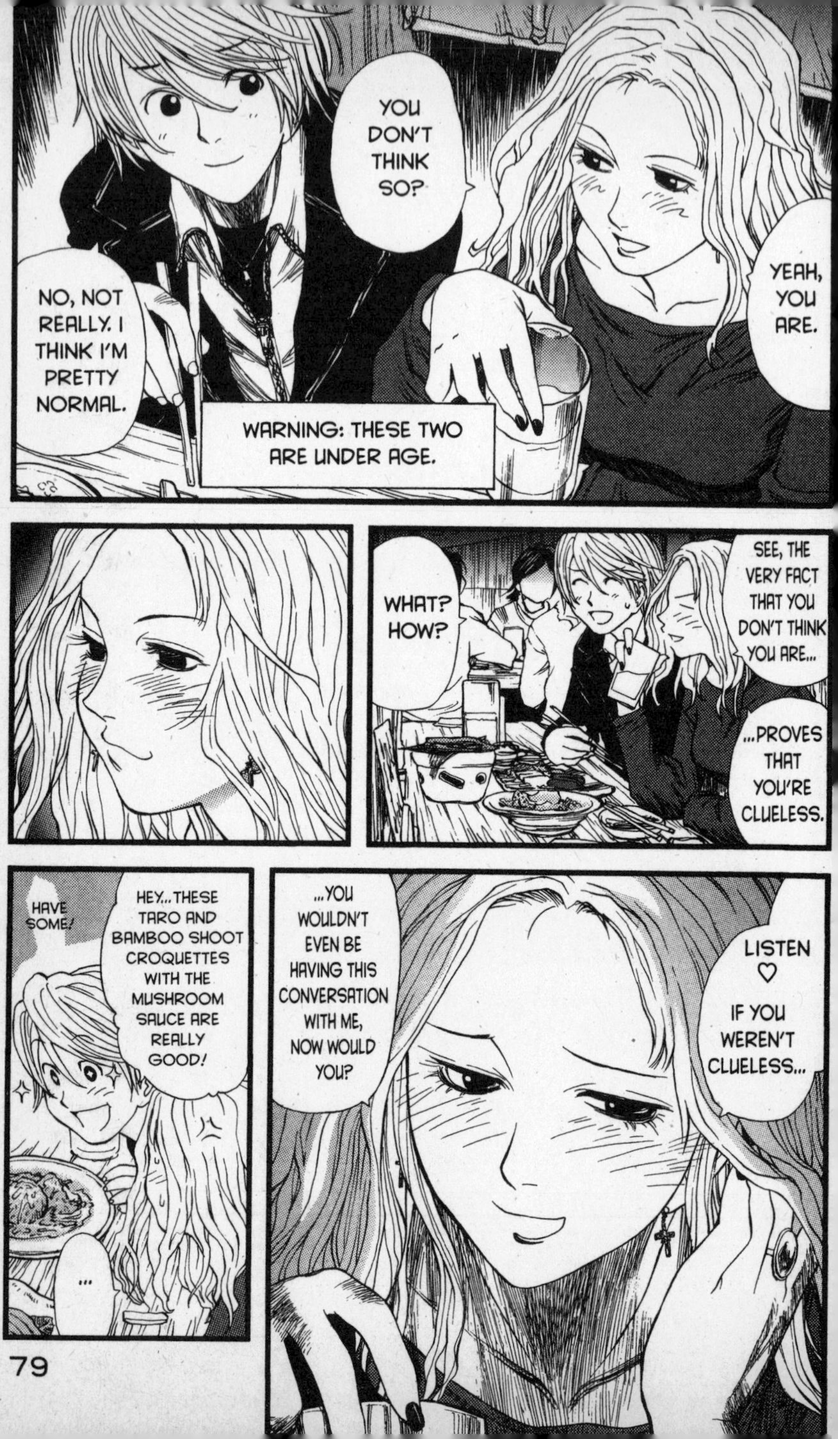
YOU DON'T THINK SO?
YEAH, YOU ARE.
NO, NOT REALLY. I THINK I'M PRETTY NORMAL.
WARNING: THESE TWO ARE UNDER AGE.
SEE, THE VERY FACT THAT YOU DON'T THINK YOU ARE...
...PROVES THAT YOU'RE CLUELESS.
WHAT? HOW?
LISTEN ♡ IF YOU WEREN'T CLUELESS...
...YOU WOULDN'T EVEN BE HAVING THIS CONVERSATION WITH ME, NOW WOULD YOU?
HEY... THESE TARO AND BAMBOO SHOOT CROQUETTES WITH THE MUSHROOM SAUCE ARE REALLY GOOD!
HAVE SOME!
...

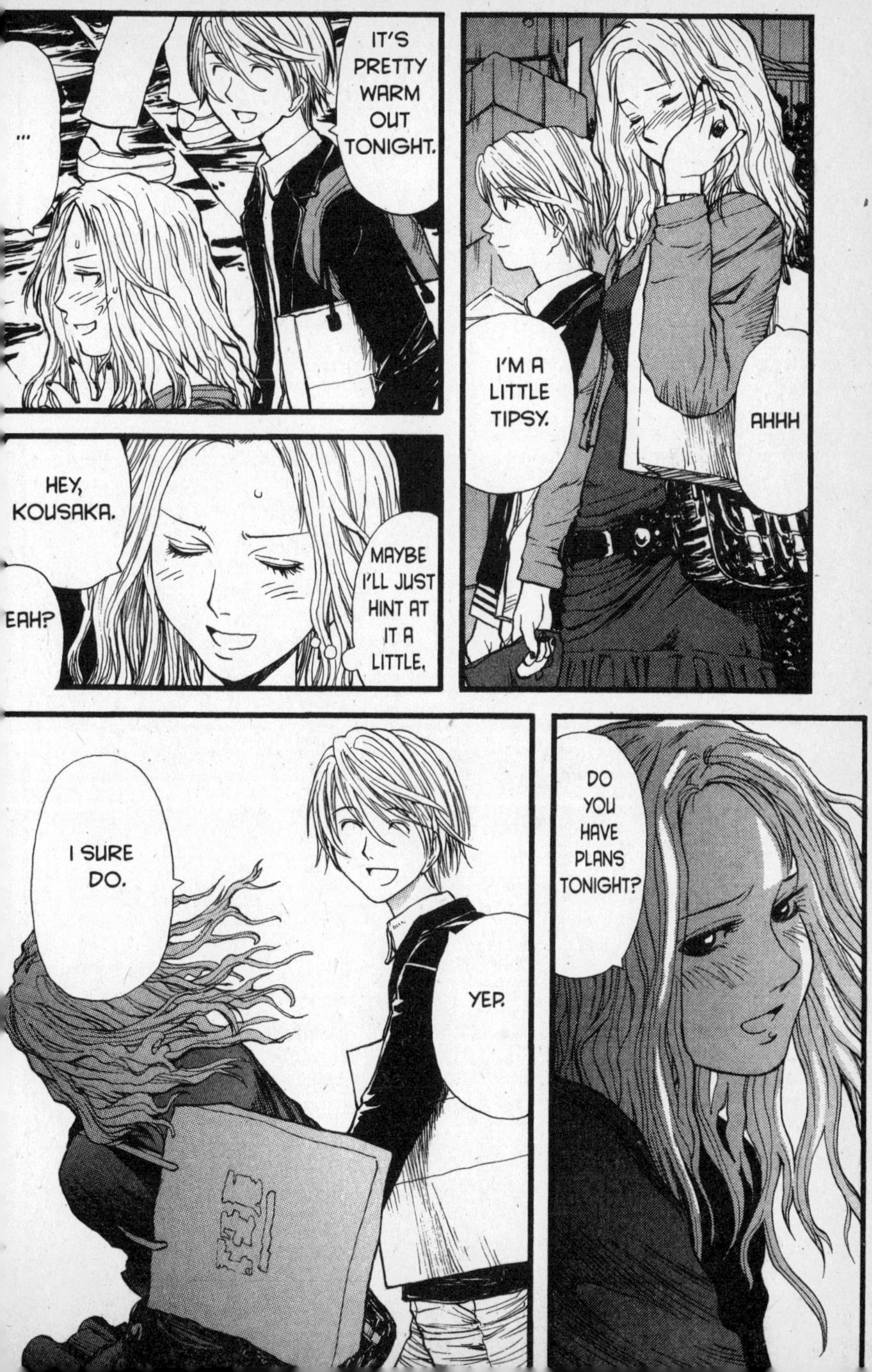
AHHH
I'M A LITTLE TIPSY.
IT'S PRETTY WARM OUT TONIGHT.
...
MAYBE I'LL JUST HINT AT IT A LITTLE.
HEY, KOUSAKA.
EAH?
DO YOU HAVE PLANS TONIGHT?
YEP.
I SURE DO.

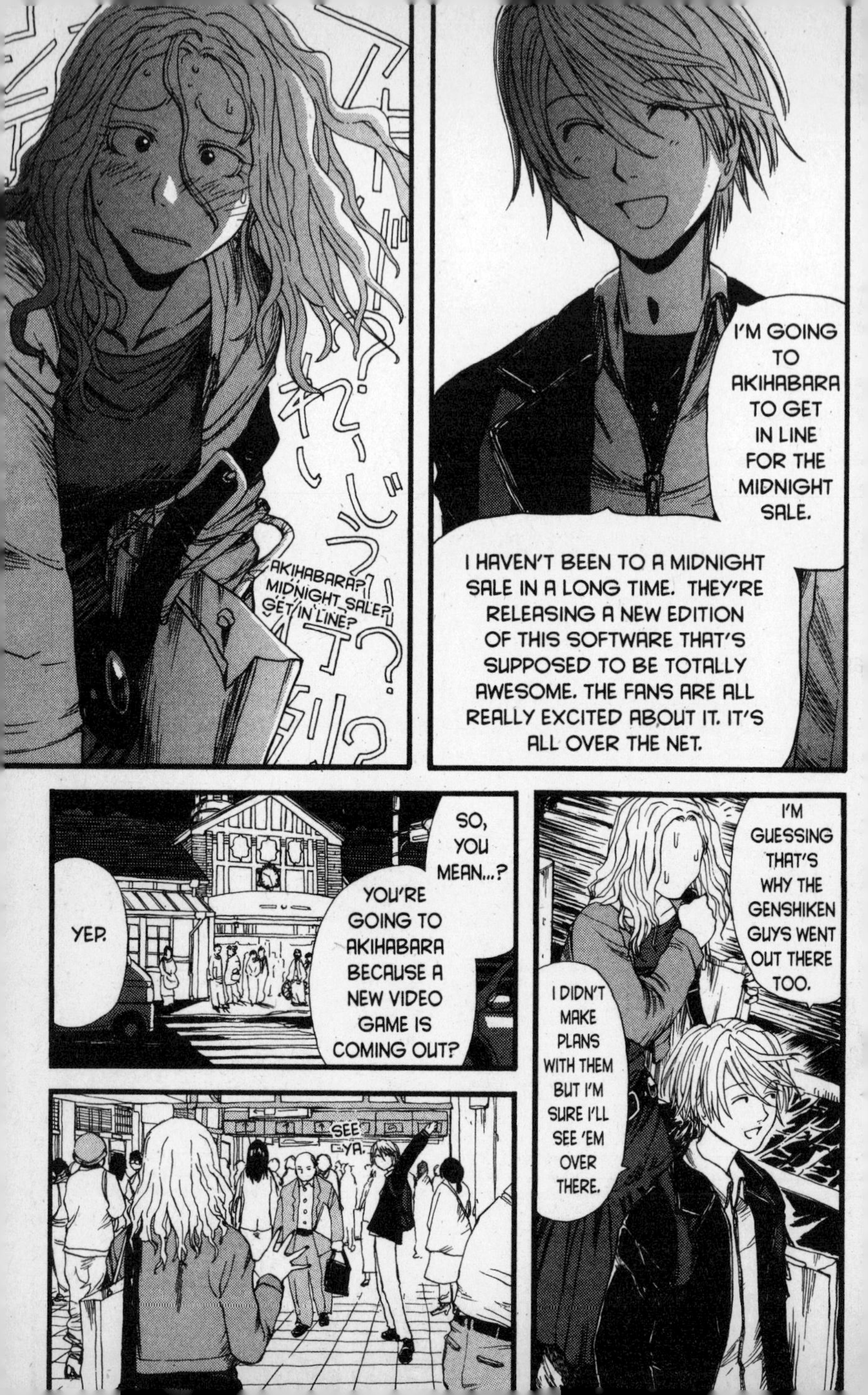
I'M GOING TO AKIHABARA TO GET IN LINE FOR THE MIDNIGHT SALE.
I HAVEN'T BEEN TO A MIDNIGHT SALE IN A LONG TIME. THEY'RE RELEASING A NEW EDITION OF THIS SOFTWARE THAT'S SUPPOSED TO BE TOTALLY AWESOME. THE FANS ARE ALL REALLY EXCITED ABOUT IT. IT'S ALL OVER THE NET.
AKIHABARA? MIDNIGHT SALE? GET IN LINE?
I'M GUESSING THAT'S WHY THE GENSHIKEN GUYS WENT OUT THERE TOO.
I DIDN'T MAKE PLANS WITH THEM BUT I'M SURE I'LL SEE 'EM OVER THERE.
SO, YOU MEAN...?
YOU'RE GOING TO AKIHABARA BECAUSE A NEW VIDEO GAME IS COMING OUT?
YEP.
SEE YA.

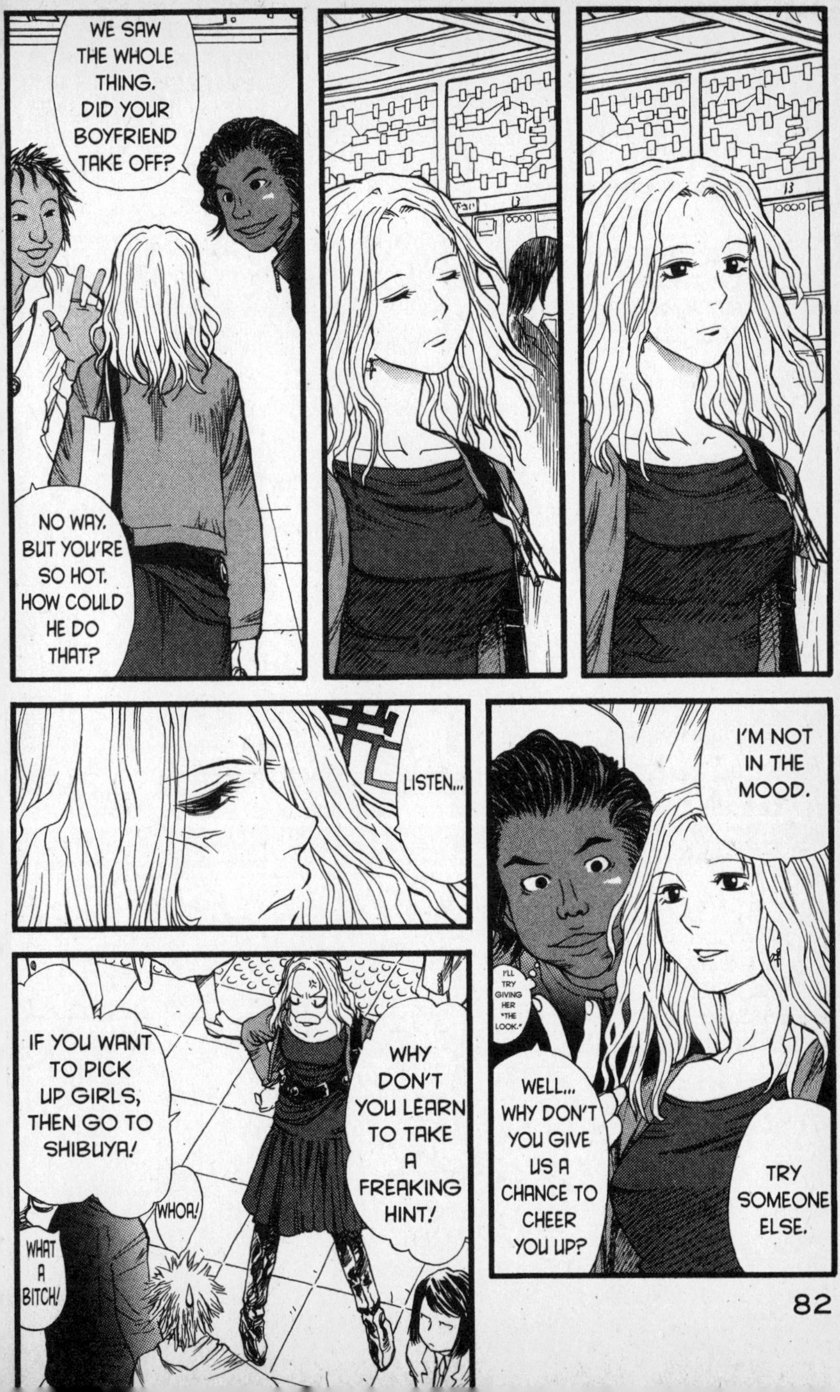
WE SAW THE WHOLE THING. DID YOUR BOYFRIEND TAKE OFF?
NO WAY. BUT YOU'RE SO HOT. HOW COULD HE DO THAT?
I'M NOT IN THE MOOD.
TRY SOMEONE ELSE.
I'LL TRY GIVING HER "THE LOOK."
WELL... WHY DON'T YOU GIVE US A CHANCE TO CHEER YOU UP?
LISTEN...
WHY DON'T YOU LEARN TO TAKE A FREAKING HINT!
IF YOU WANT TO PICK UP GIRLS, THEN GO TO SHIBUYA!
WHOA!
WHAT A BITCH!

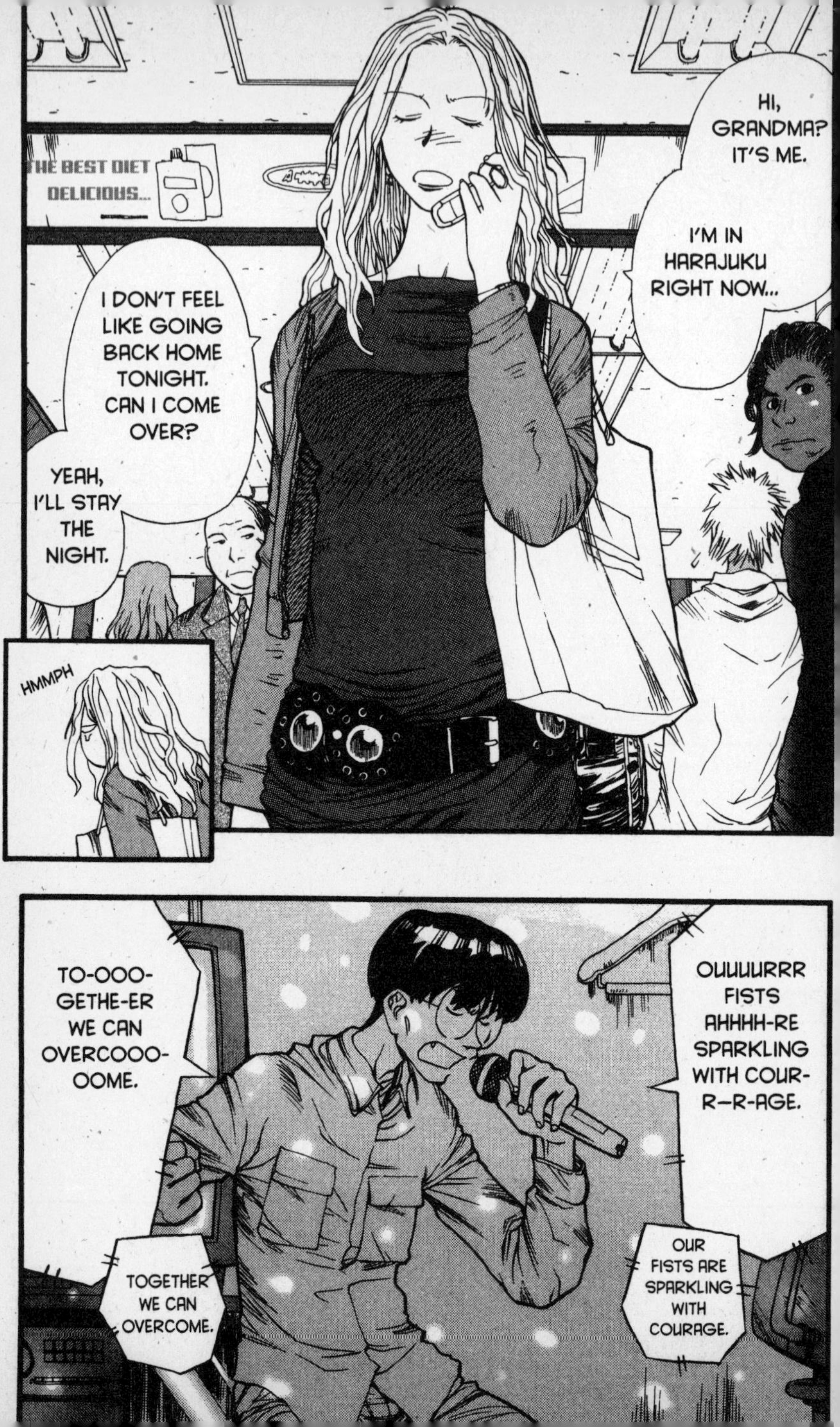
HI, GRANDMA? IT'S ME.
I'M IN HARAJUKU RIGHT NOW...
THE BEST DIET
DELICIOUS...
I DON'T FEEL LIKE GOING BACK HOME TONIGHT. CAN I COME OVER?
YEAH, I'LL STAY THE NIGHT.
HMMPH
OUUUURRR FISTS AHHHH-RE SPARKLING WITH COUR-R–R-AGE.
TO-OOO-GETHE-ER WE CAN OVERCOOO-OOME.
OUR FISTS ARE SPARKLING WITH COURAGE.
TOGETHER WE CAN OVERCOME.

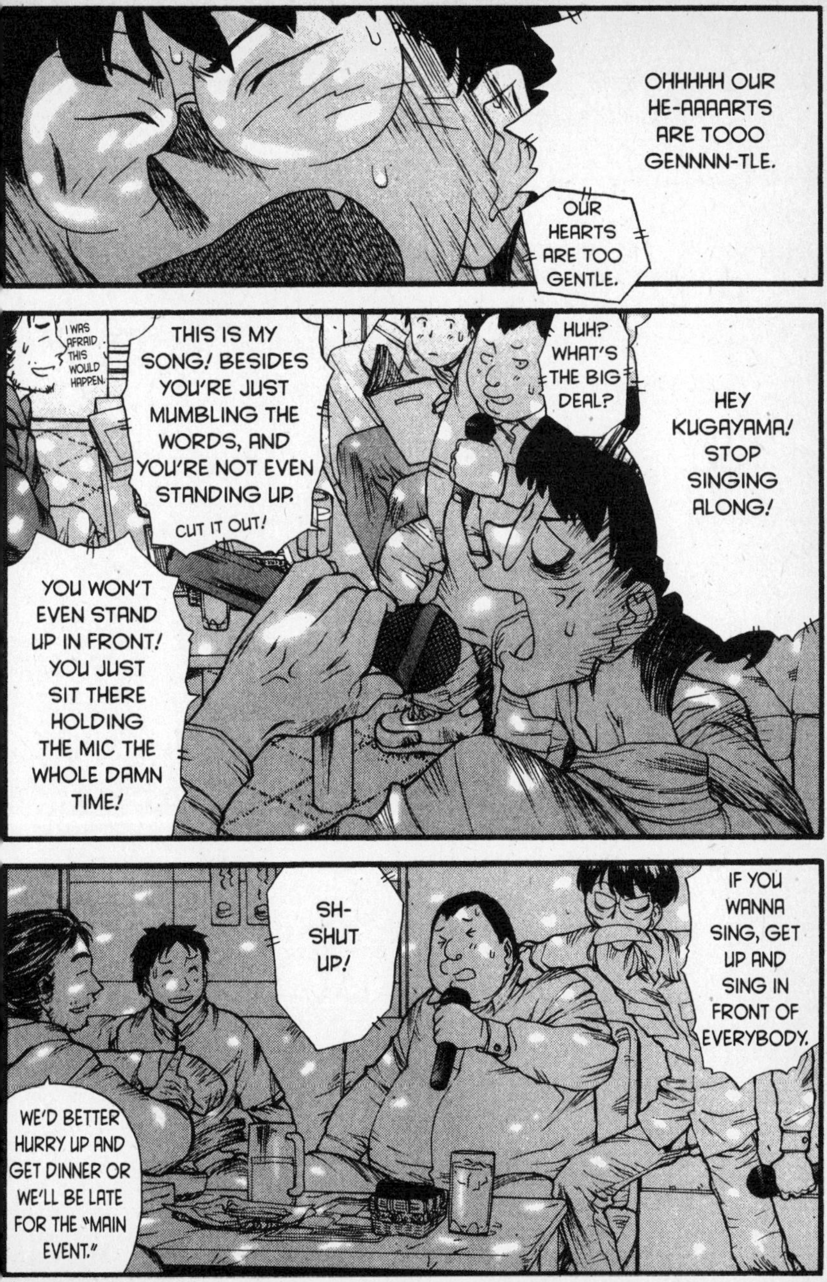
OHHHHH OUR HE-AAAARTS ARE TOOO GENNNN-TLE.
OUR HEARTS ARE TOO GENTLE.
HEY KUGAYAMA! STOP SINGING ALONG!
HUH? WHAT'S THE BIG DEAL?
THIS IS MY SONG! BESIDES YOU'RE JUST MUMBLING THE WORDS, AND YOU'RE NOT EVEN STANDING UP.
CUT IT OUT!
I WAS AFRAID THIS WOULD HAPPEN.
YOU WON'T EVEN STAND UP IN FRONT! YOU JUST SIT THERE HOLDING THE MIC THE WHOLE DAMN TIME!
IF YOU WANNA SING, GET UP AND SING IN FRONT OF EVERYBODY.
SH-SHUT UP!
WE'D BETTER HURRY UP AND GET DINNER OR WE'LL BE LATE FOR THE "MAIN EVENT."

END OF CHAPTER 3

MADARAME HARUNOBU

PROFILE

HARUNOBU MADARAME

BORN FEBRUARY 25TH
BLOOD TYPE O

FAVORITE MANGA
BE-BOP-HELL-SING
YOTAROO'S SAD SONG

FAVORITE ANIME
MOBILE SUITS T-GANGARU
DOREMI-CHAN
YUCKO!
THE ADVENTURES OF DORA THE SPACE PIRATE
SPIRITED AFAR

FAVORITE VIDEO GAMES
THE DIARY OF KAGERO
NINJA ADVENTURES
ENCHO
SHINOBI RETURNS
THE OUTLAW KANKIRO

FAVORITE FIGHT GAME CHARACTERS
KINAKO BERETTA
TARURUN

*THESE ARE THE CHARACTER'S CHOICES AND DO NOT NECESSARILY REFLECT THE AUTHOR'S TASTES.

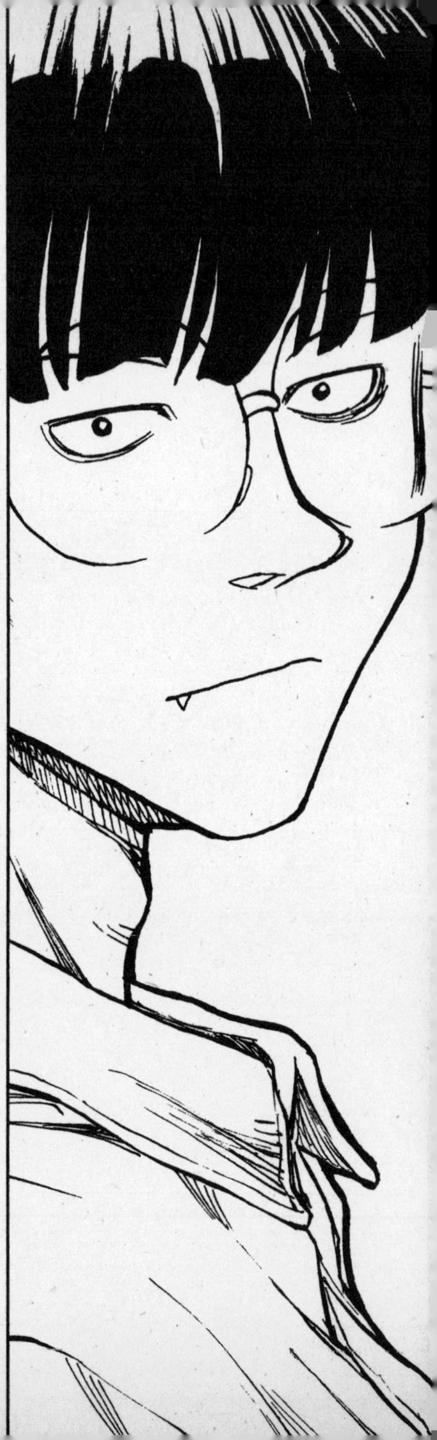

CAUSE VS EFFECT

I'M WAITING IN LINE TO BUY IT TOO, BUT...
I DON'T EVEN HAVE A PC.
PART OF IT IS THAT I FEEL OBLIGATED TO BUY IT SINCE IT'S A LIMITED EDITION.
BUT I MADE UP MY OWN MIND.
I'M BUYING IT FOR THE COMPUTER THAT I'M GONNA GET...
SOMEDAY.
KA KA KA
IDIOT-
IDIOT-

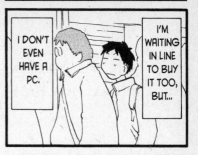

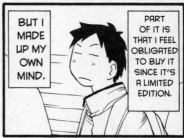

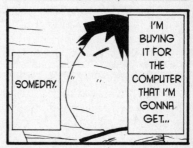

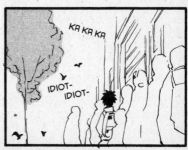

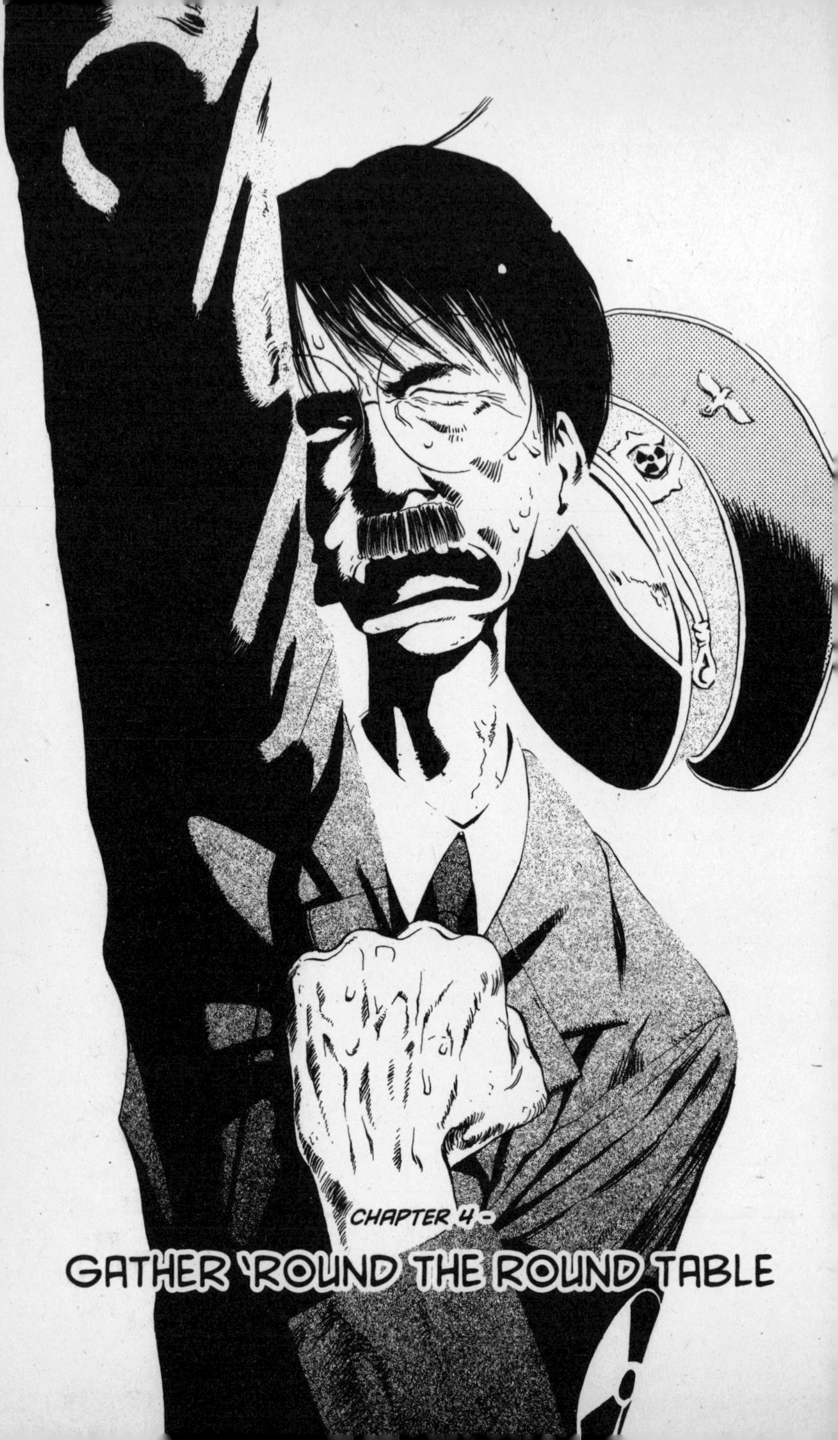
CHAPTER 4 -
GATHER 'ROUND THE ROUND TABLE

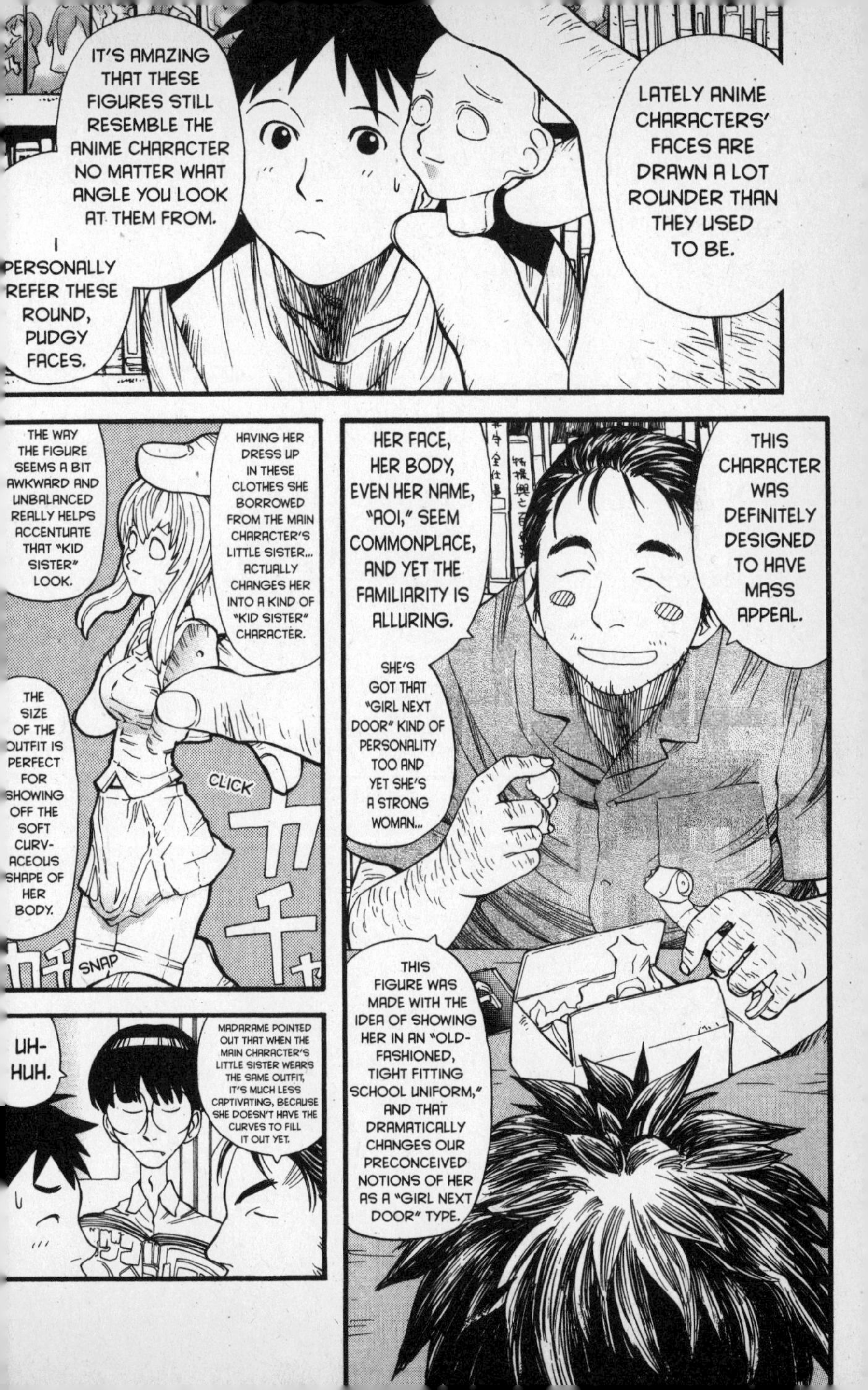
LATELY ANIME CHARACTERS' FACES ARE DRAWN A LOT ROUNDER THAN THEY USED TO BE.
IT'S AMAZING THAT THESE FIGURES STILL RESEMBLE THE ANIME CHARACTER NO MATTER WHAT ANGLE YOU LOOK AT THEM FROM.
I PERSONALLY REFER THESE ROUND, PUDGY FACES.
THIS CHARACTER WAS DEFINITELY DESIGNED TO HAVE MASS APPEAL.
HER FACE, HER BODY, EVEN HER NAME, "AOI," SEEM COMMONPLACE, AND YET THE FAMILIARITY IS ALLURING.
SHE'S GOT THAT "GIRL NEXT DOOR" KIND OF PERSONALITY TOO AND YET SHE'S A STRONG WOMAN...
HAVING HER DRESS UP IN THESE CLOTHES SHE BORROWED FROM THE MAIN CHARACTER'S LITTLE SISTER... ACTUALLY CHANGES HER INTO A KIND OF "KID SISTER" CHARACTER.
THE WAY THE FIGURE SEEMS A BIT AWKWARD AND UNBALANCED REALLY HELPS ACCENTUATE THAT "KID SISTER" LOOK.
THE SIZE OF THE OUTFIT IS PERFECT FOR SHOWING OFF THE SOFT CURV- ACEOUS SHAPE OF HER BODY.
CLICK
SNAP
THIS FIGURE WAS MADE WITH THE IDEA OF SHOWING HER IN AN "OLD-FASHIONED, TIGHT FITTING SCHOOL UNIFORM," AND THAT DRAMATICALLY CHANGES OUR PRECONCEIVED NOTIONS OF HER AS A "GIRL NEXT DOOR" TYPE.
MADARAME POINTED OUT THAT WHEN THE MAIN CHARACTER'S LITTLE SISTER WEARS THE SAME OUTFIT, IT'S MUCH LESS CAPTIVATING, BECAUSE SHE DOESN'T HAVE THE CURVES TO FILL IT OUT YET.
UH-HUH.

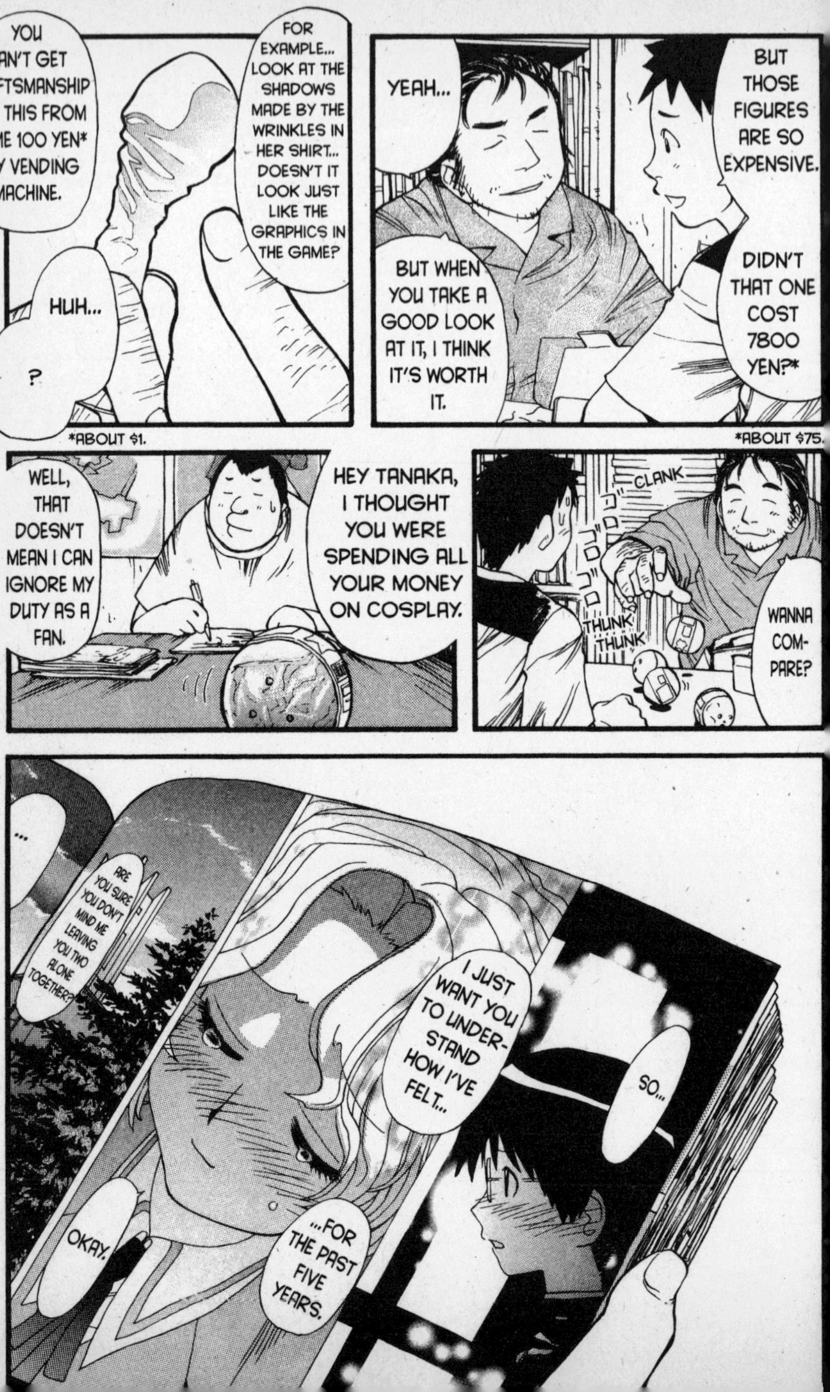
BUT THOSE FIGURES ARE SO EXPENSIVE.
YEAH...
DIDN'T THAT ONE COST 7800 YEN?*
BUT WHEN YOU TAKE A GOOD LOOK AT IT, I THINK IT'S WORTH IT.
*ABOUT $75.
FOR EXAMPLE... LOOK AT THE SHADOWS MADE BY THE WRINKLES IN HER SHIRT... DOESN'T IT LOOK JUST LIKE THE GRAPHICS IN THE GAME?
YOU CAN'T GET CRAFTSMANSHIP LIKE THIS FROM SOME 100 YEN* TOY VENDING MACHINE.
HUH...
?
*ABOUT $1.
CLANK
THUNK THUNK
WANNA COMPARE?
HEY TANAKA, I THOUGHT YOU WERE SPENDING ALL YOUR MONEY ON COSPLAY.
WELL, THAT DOESN'T MEAN I CAN IGNORE MY DUTY AS A FAN.
SO...
I JUST WANT YOU TO UNDERSTAND HOW I'VE FELT...
...FOR THE PAST FIVE YEARS.
...
ARE YOU SURE YOU DON'T MIND ME LEAVING YOU TWO ALONE TOGETHER?
OKAY.

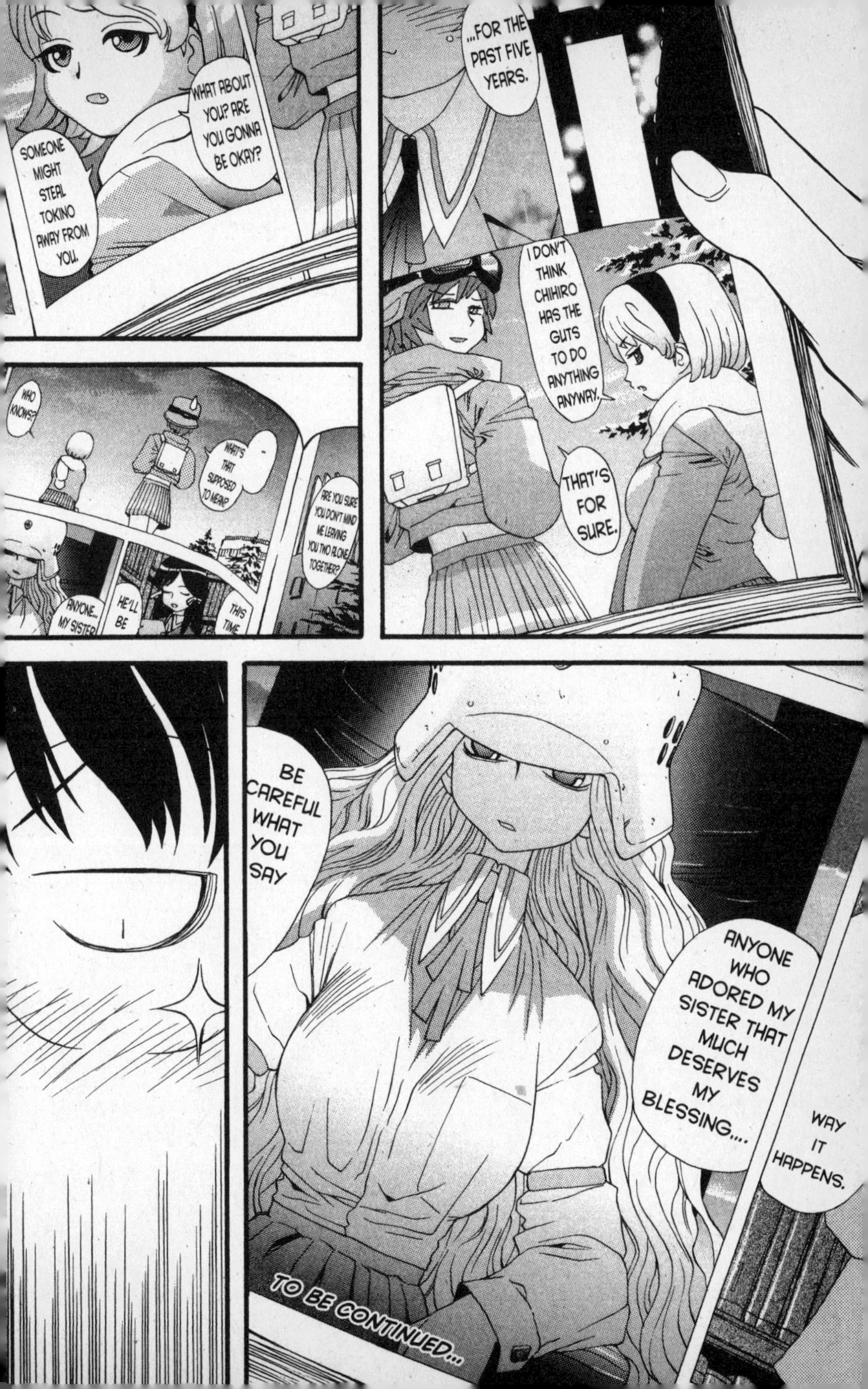
...FOR THE PAST FIVE YEARS.
I DON'T THINK CHIHIRO HAS THE GUTS TO DO ANYTHING ANYWAY.
THAT'S FOR SURE.
WHAT ABOUT YOU? ARE YOU GONNA BE OKAY?
SOMEONE MIGHT STEAL TOKINO AWAY FROM YOU.
ARE YOU SURE YOU DON'T MIND ME LEAVING YOU TWO ALONE TOGETHER?
WHAT'S THAT SUPPOSED TO MEAN?
WHO KNOWS?
THIS TIME
HE'LL BE
ANYONE... MY SISTER
ANYONE WHO ADORED MY SISTER THAT MUCH DESERVES MY BLESSING...
WAY IT HAPPENS.
BE CAREFUL WHAT YOU SAY
TO BE CONTINUED...

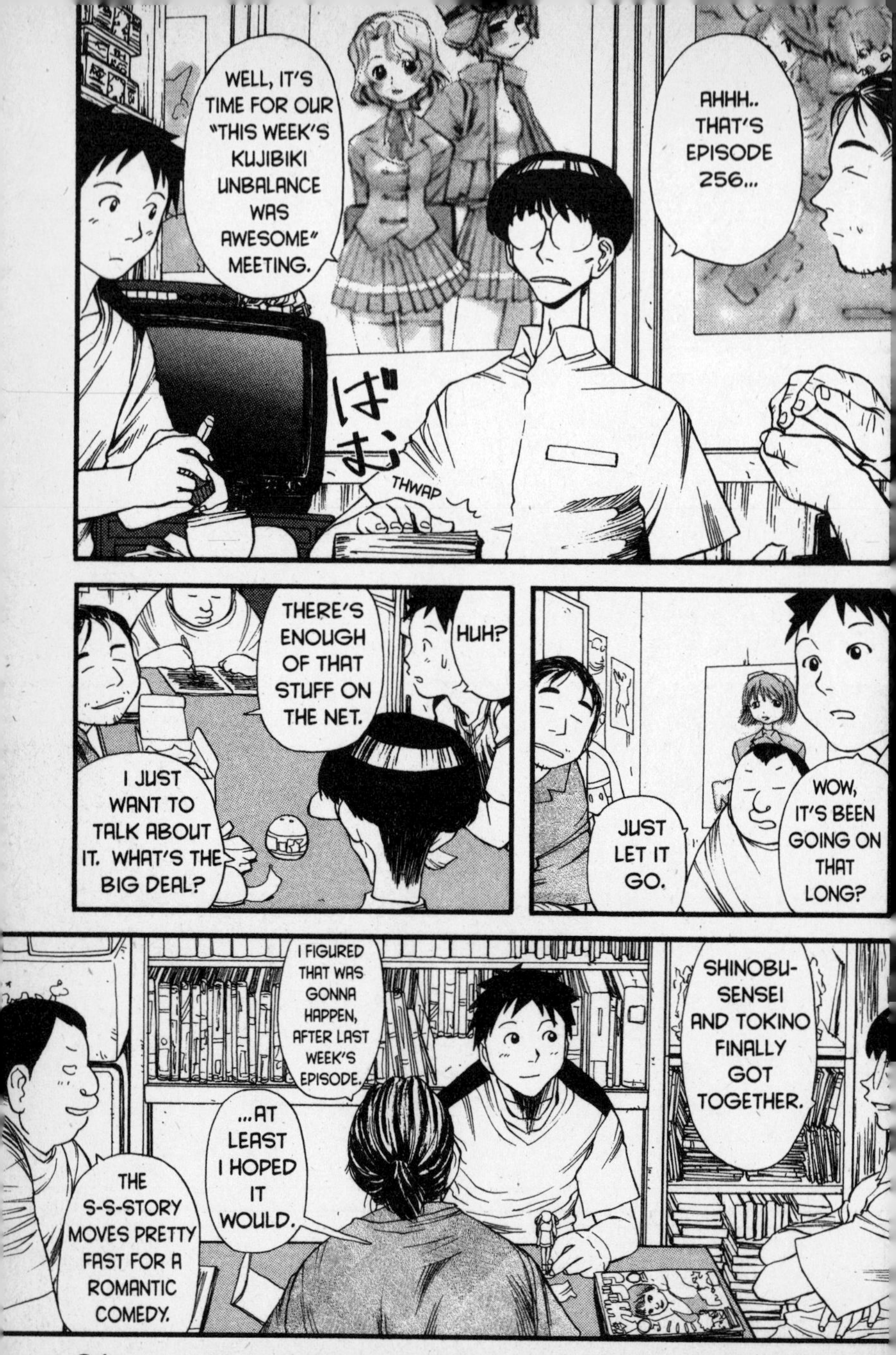
AHHH.. THAT'S EPISODE 256...
WELL, IT'S TIME FOR OUR "THIS WEEK'S KUJIBIKI UNBALANCE WAS AWESOME" MEETING.
ばむ
THWAP
WOW, IT'S BEEN GOING ON THAT LONG?
JUST LET IT GO.
HUH?
THERE'S ENOUGH OF THAT STUFF ON THE NET.
I JUST WANT TO TALK ABOUT IT. WHAT'S THE BIG DEAL?
SHINOBU-SENSEI AND TOKINO FINALLY GOT TOGETHER.
I FIGURED THAT WAS GONNA HAPPEN, AFTER LAST WEEK'S EPISODE.
...AT LEAST I HOPED IT WOULD.
THE S-S-STORY MOVES PRETTY FAST FOR A ROMANTIC COMEDY.

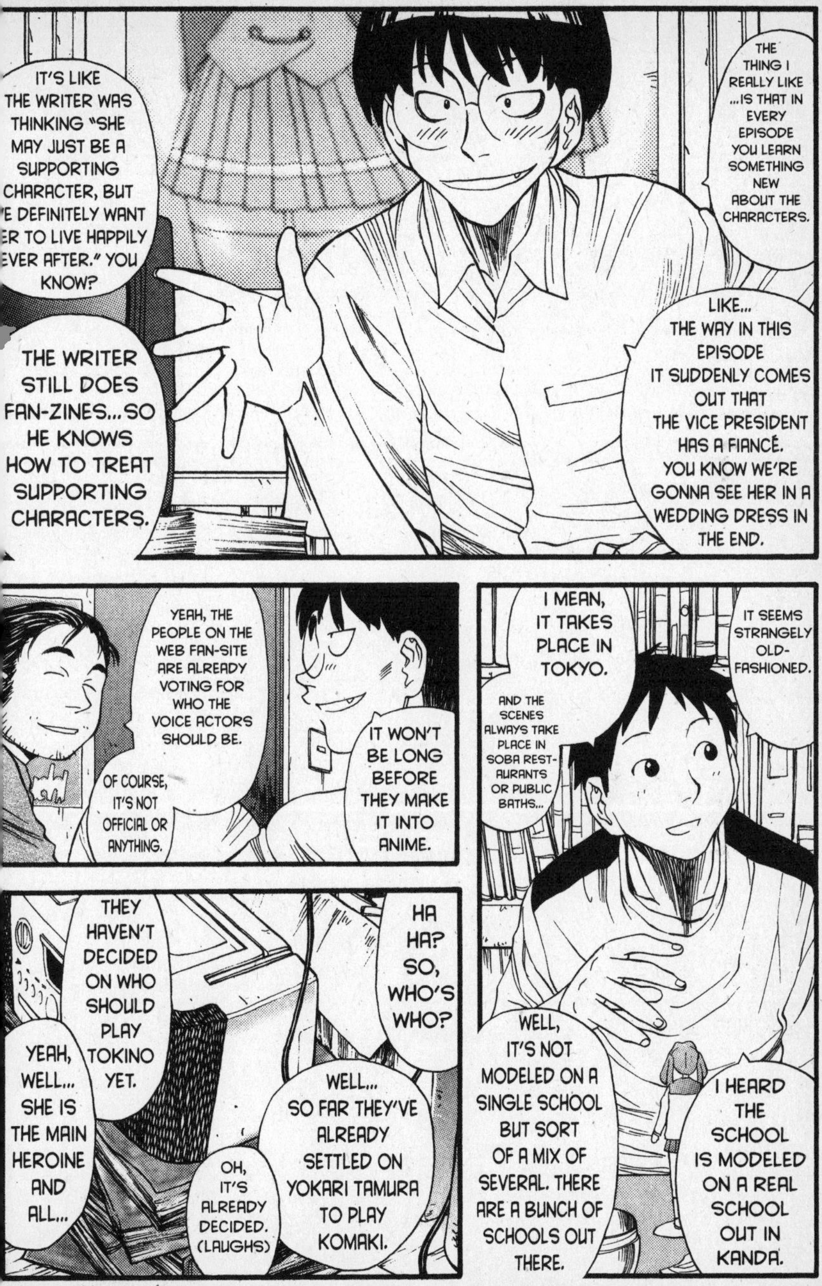
THE THING I REALLY LIKE ...IS THAT IN EVERY EPISODE YOU LEARN SOMETHING NEW ABOUT THE CHARACTERS.
LIKE... THE WAY IN THIS EPISODE IT SUDDENLY COMES OUT THAT THE VICE PRESIDENT HAS A FIANCÉ. YOU KNOW WE'RE GONNA SEE HER IN A WEDDING DRESS IN THE END.
IT'S LIKE THE WRITER WAS THINKING "SHE MAY JUST BE A SUPPORTING CHARACTER, BUT E DEFINITELY WANT ER TO LIVE HAPPILY EVER AFTER." YOU KNOW?
THE WRITER STILL DOES FAN-ZINES... SO HE KNOWS HOW TO TREAT SUPPORTING CHARACTERS.
IT SEEMS STRANGELY OLD-FASHIONED.
I MEAN, IT TAKES PLACE IN TOKYO.
AND THE SCENES ALWAYS TAKE PLACE IN SOBA REST-AURANTS OR PUBLIC BATHS...
I HEARD THE SCHOOL IS MODELED ON A REAL SCHOOL OUT IN KANDA.
WELL, IT'S NOT MODELED ON A SINGLE SCHOOL BUT SORT OF A MIX OF SEVERAL. THERE ARE A BUNCH OF SCHOOLS OUT THERE.
IT WON'T BE LONG BEFORE THEY MAKE IT INTO ANIME.
YEAH, THE PEOPLE ON THE WEB FAN-SITE ARE ALREADY VOTING FOR WHO THE VOICE ACTORS SHOULD BE.
OF COURSE, IT'S NOT OFFICIAL OR ANYTHING.
HA HA? SO, WHO'S WHO?
THEY HAVEN'T DECIDED ON WHO SHOULD PLAY TOKINO YET.
WELL... SO FAR THEY'VE ALREADY SETTLED ON YOKARI TAMURA TO PLAY KOMAKI.
OH, IT'S ALREADY DECIDED. (LAUGHS)
YEAH, WELL... SHE IS THE MAIN HEROINE AND ALL...

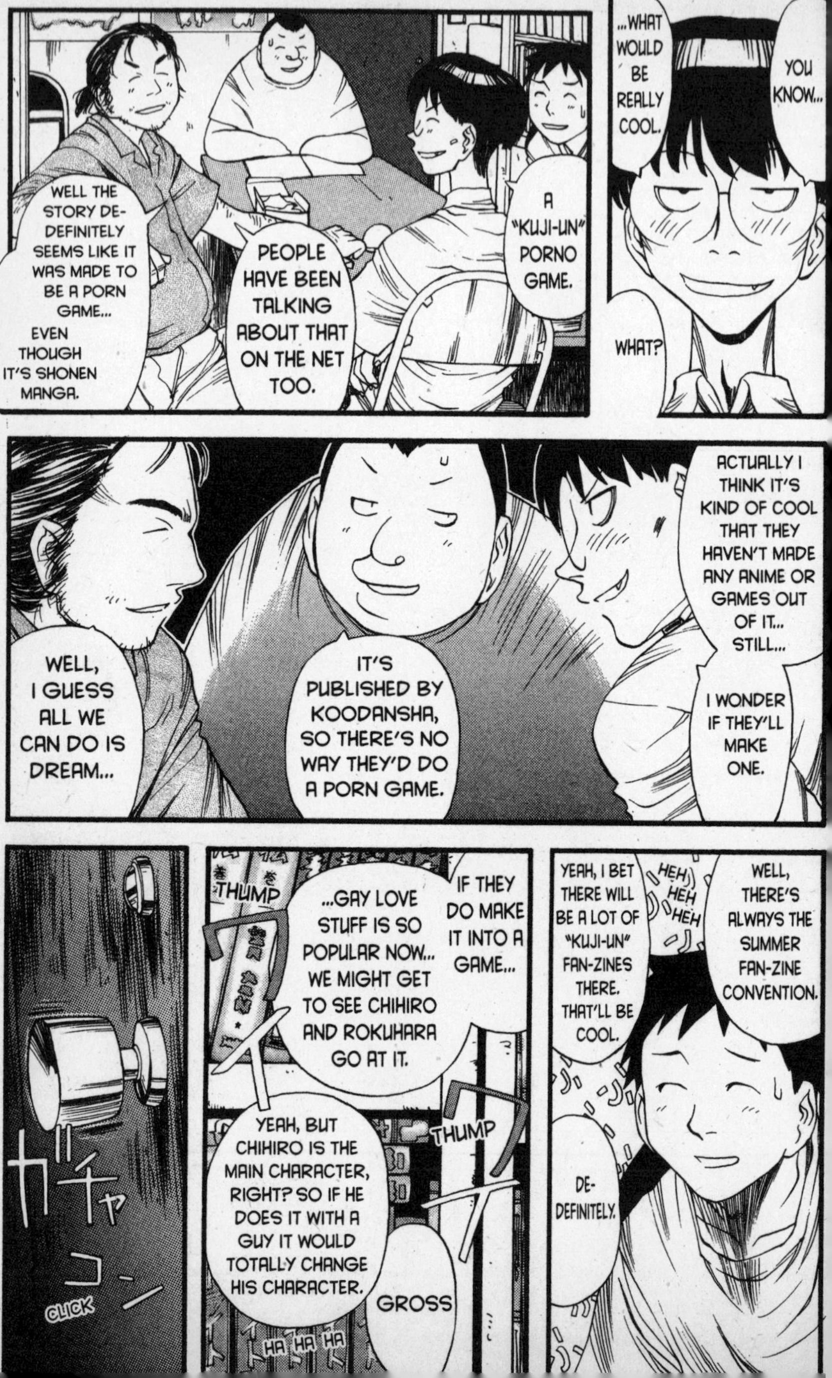
YOU KNOW...
...WHAT WOULD BE REALLY COOL.
WHAT?
A "KUJI-UN" PORNO GAME.
PEOPLE HAVE BEEN TALKING ABOUT THAT ON THE NET TOO.
WELL THE STORY DE-DEFINITELY SEEMS LIKE IT WAS MADE TO BE A PORN GAME... EVEN THOUGH IT'S SHONEN MANGA.
ACTUALLY I THINK IT'S KIND OF COOL THAT THEY HAVEN'T MADE ANY ANIME OR GAMES OUT OF IT... STILL...
I WONDER IF THEY'LL MAKE ONE.
IT'S PUBLISHED BY KOODANSHA, SO THERE'S NO WAY THEY'D DO A PORN GAME.
WELL, I GUESS ALL WE CAN DO IS DREAM...
WELL, THERE'S ALWAYS THE SUMMER FAN-ZINE CONVENTION.
HEH HEH HEH
YEAH, I BET THERE WILL BE A LOT OF "KUJI-UN" FAN-ZINES THERE. THAT'LL BE COOL.
DE-DEFINITELY.
IF THEY DO MAKE IT INTO A GAME...
THUMP
...GAY LOVE STUFF IS SO POPULAR NOW... WE MIGHT GET TO SEE CHIHIRO AND ROKUHARA GO AT IT.
THUMP
YEAH, BUT CHIHIRO IS THE MAIN CHARACTER, RIGHT? SO IF HE DOES IT WITH A GUY IT WOULD TOTALLY CHANGE HIS CHARACTER.
GROSS
HA HA HA
ガチャ
コン
CLICK

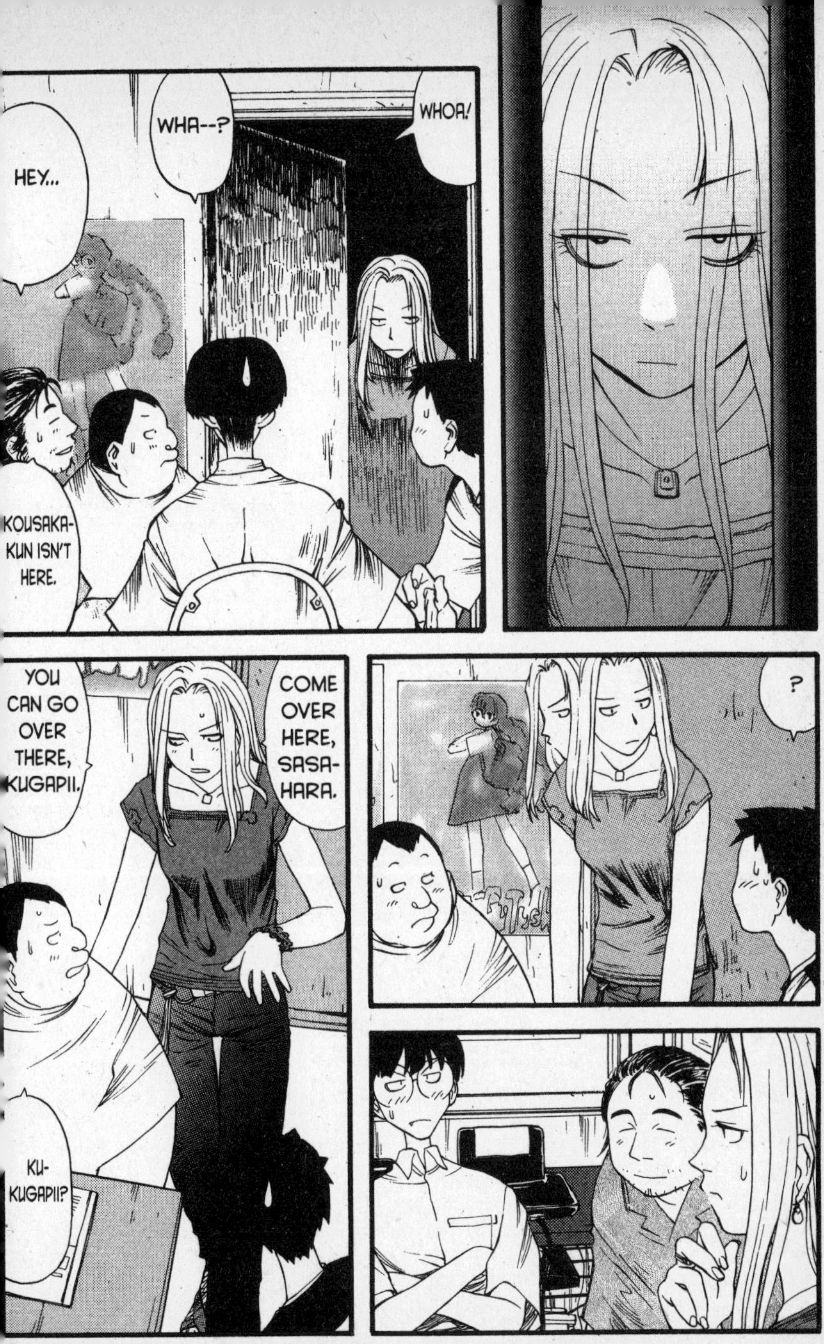
WHOA!
WHA--?
HEY...
KOUSAKA-KUN ISN'T HERE.
?
COME OVER HERE, SASA-HARA.
YOU CAN GO OVER THERE, KUGAPII.
KU-KUGAPII?

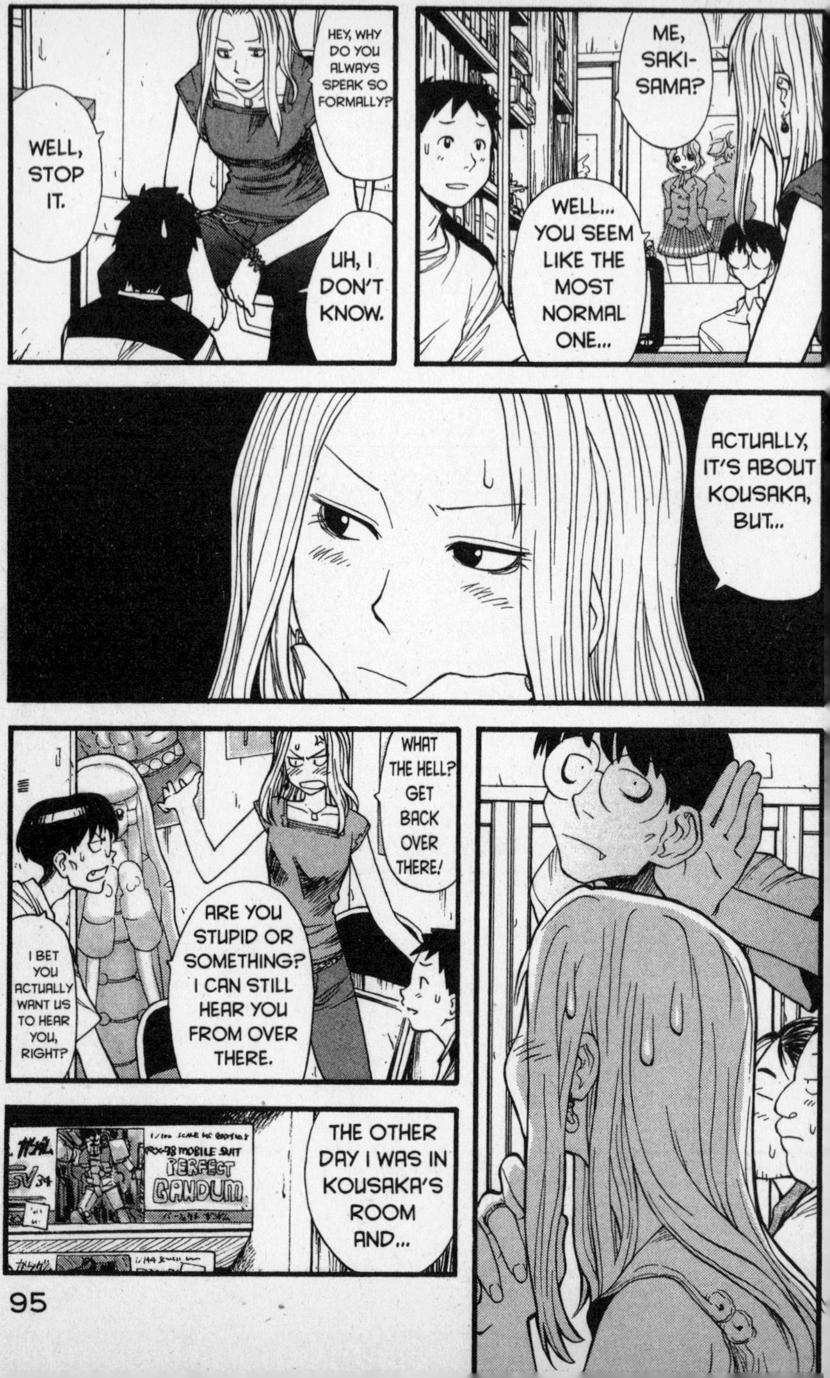
ME, SAKI-SAMA?
WELL... YOU SEEM LIKE THE MOST NORMAL ONE...
HEY, WHY DO YOU ALWAYS SPEAK SO FORMALLY?
UH, I DON'T KNOW.
WELL, STOP IT.
ACTUALLY, IT'S ABOUT KOUSAKA, BUT...
WHAT THE HELL? GET BACK OVER THERE!
ARE YOU STUPID OR SOMETHING? I CAN STILL HEAR YOU FROM OVER THERE.
I BET YOU ACTUALLY WANT US TO HEAR YOU, RIGHT?
THE OTHER DAY I WAS IN KOUSAKA'S ROOM AND...
RX-78 MOBILE SUIT
PERFECT GANDUM

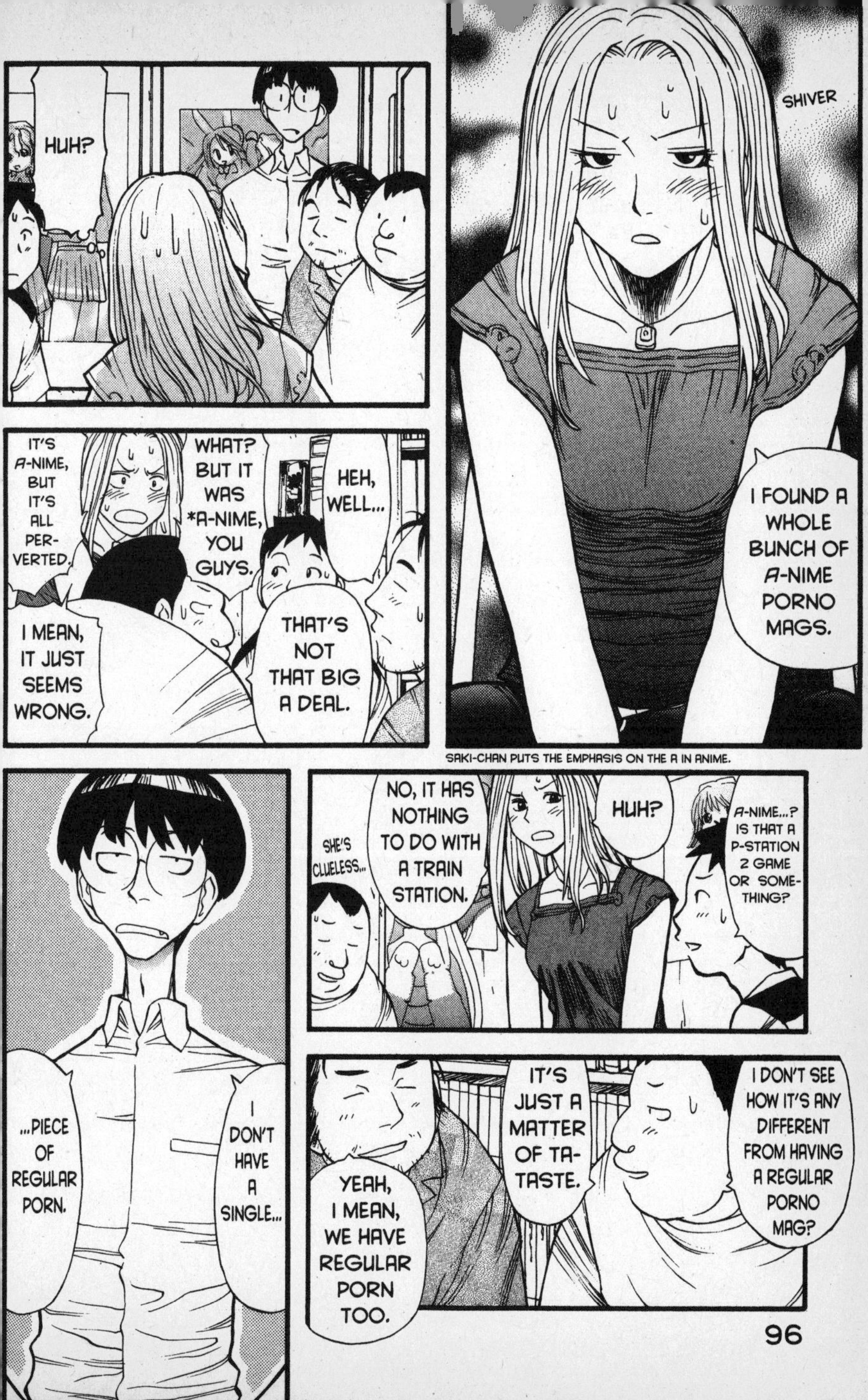
SHIVER
I FOUND A WHOLE BUNCH OF A-NIME PORNO MAGS.
HUH?
HEH, WELL...
WHAT? BUT IT WAS *A-NIME, YOU GUYS.
IT'S A-NIME, BUT IT'S ALL PER-VERTED.
THAT'S NOT THAT BIG A DEAL.
I MEAN, IT JUST SEEMS WRONG.
SAKI-CHAN PUTS THE EMPHASIS ON THE A IN ANIME.
A-NIME...? IS THAT A P-STATION 2 GAME OR SOME-THING?
HUH?
NO, IT HAS NOTHING TO DO WITH A TRAIN STATION.
SHE'S CLUELESS...
I DON'T SEE HOW IT'S ANY DIFFERENT FROM HAVING A REGULAR PORNO MAG?
IT'S JUST A MATTER OF TA-TASTE.
YEAH, I MEAN, WE HAVE REGULAR PORN TOO.
I DON'T HAVE A SINGLE...
...PIECE OF REGULAR PORN.

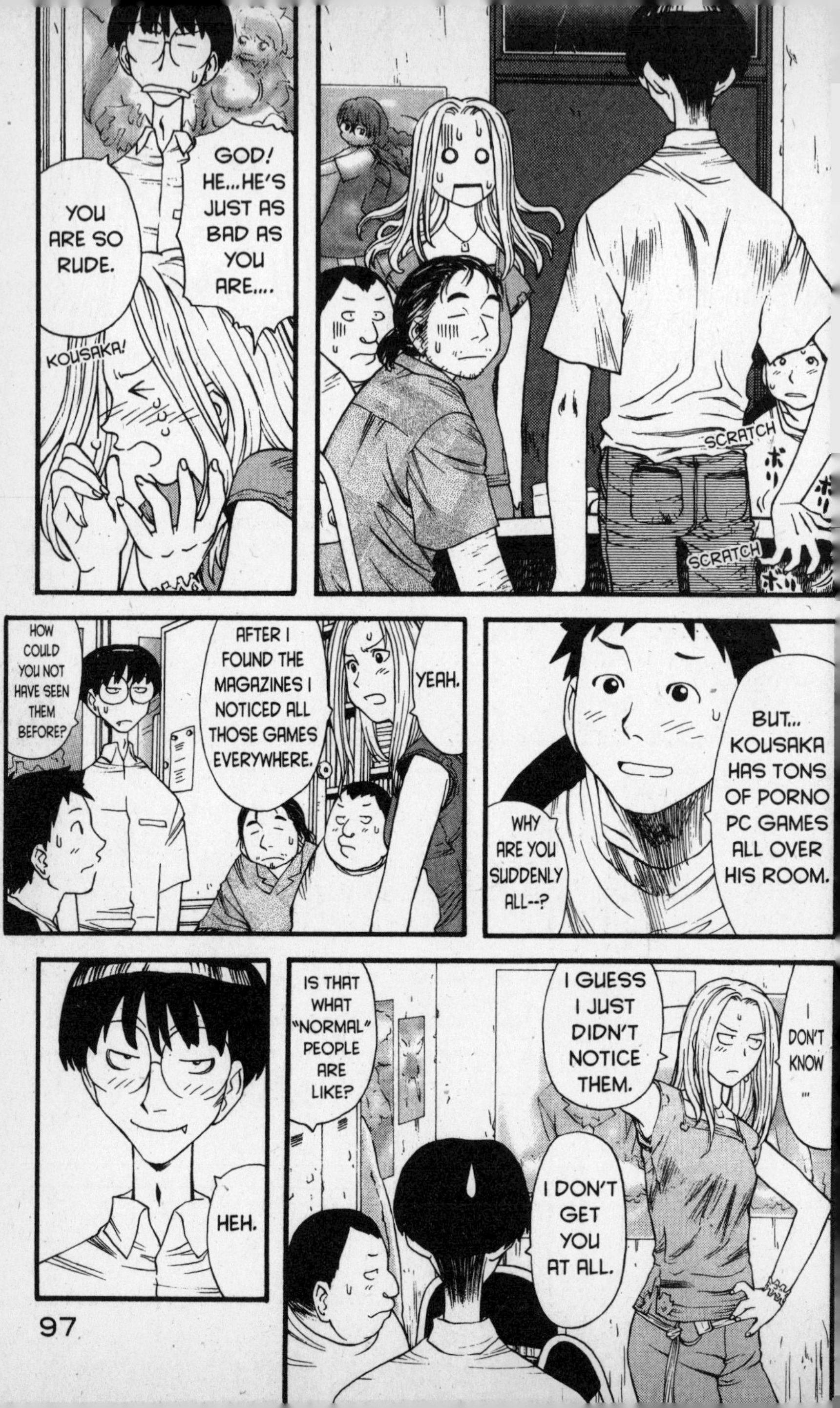
SCRATCH
ボリ
SCRATCH
GOD! HE...HE'S JUST AS BAD AS YOU ARE....
YOU ARE SO RUDE.
KOUSAKA!
BUT... KOUSAKA HAS TONS OF PORNO PC GAMES ALL OVER HIS ROOM.
WHY ARE YOU SUDDENLY ALL--?
YEAH.
AFTER I FOUND THE MAGAZINES I NOTICED ALL THOSE GAMES EVERYWHERE.
HOW COULD YOU NOT HAVE SEEN THEM BEFORE?
I DON'T KNOW ...
I GUESS I JUST DIDN'T NOTICE THEM.
IS THAT WHAT "NORMAL" PEOPLE ARE LIKE?
I DON'T GET YOU AT ALL.
HEH.

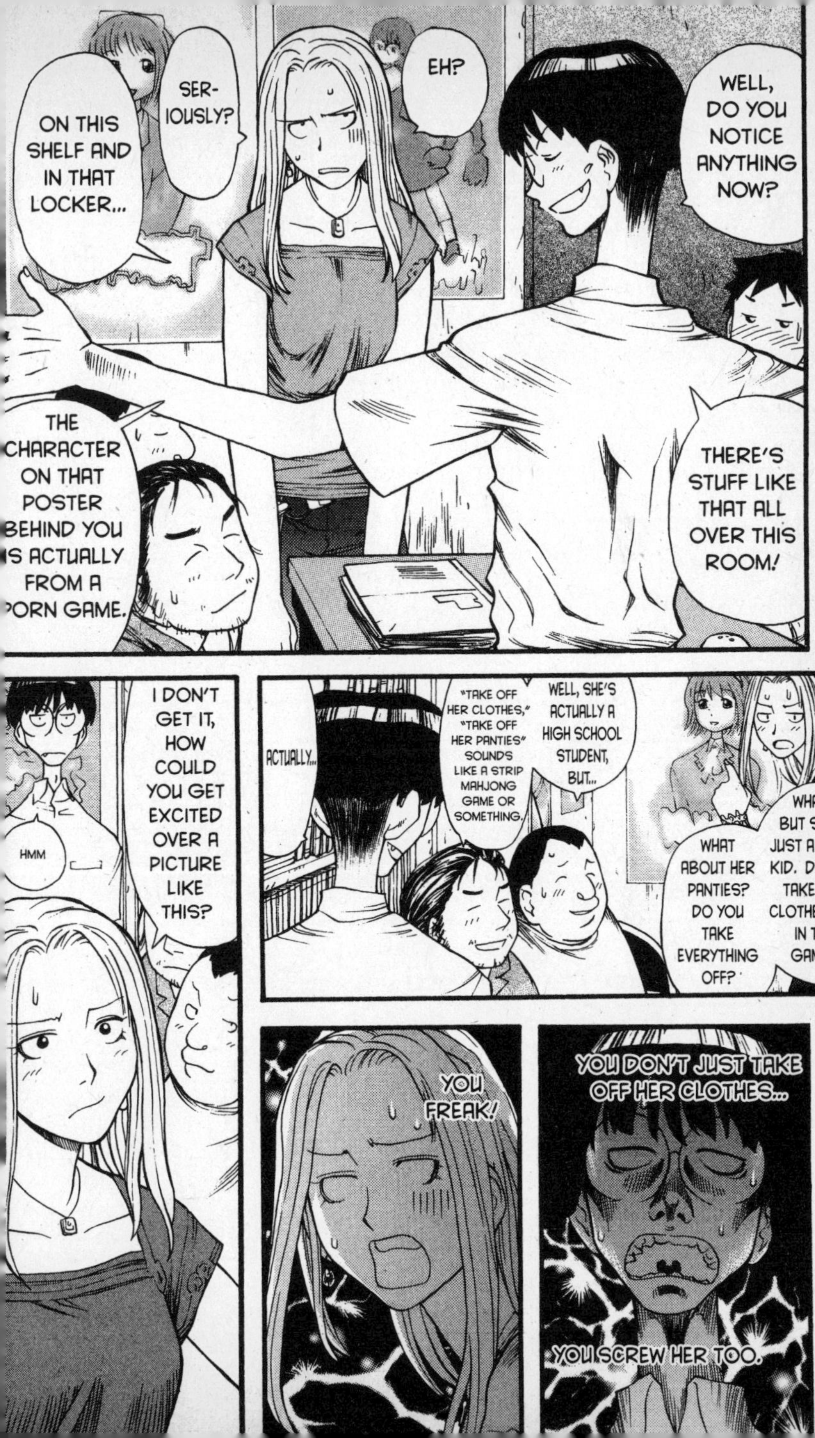
WELL, DO YOU NOTICE ANYTHING NOW?
EH?
SER-IOUSLY?
ON THIS SHELF AND IN THAT LOCKER...
THERE'S STUFF LIKE THAT ALL OVER THIS ROOM!
THE CHARACTER ON THAT POSTER BEHIND YOU IS ACTUALLY FROM A PORN GAME.
WHAT? BUT SHE'S JUST A LITTLE KID. DO YOU TAKE HER CLOTHES OFF IN THE GAME?
WHAT ABOUT HER PANTIES? DO YOU TAKE EVERYTHING OFF?
WELL, SHE'S ACTUALLY A HIGH SCHOOL STUDENT, BUT...
"TAKE OFF HER CLOTHES," "TAKE OFF HER PANTIES" SOUNDS LIKE A STRIP MAHJONG GAME OR SOMETHING.
ACTUALLY...
YOU DON'T JUST TAKE OFF HER CLOTHES...
YOU SCREW HER TOO.
YOU FREAK!
I DON'T GET IT, HOW COULD YOU GET EXCITED OVER A PICTURE LIKE THIS?
HMM

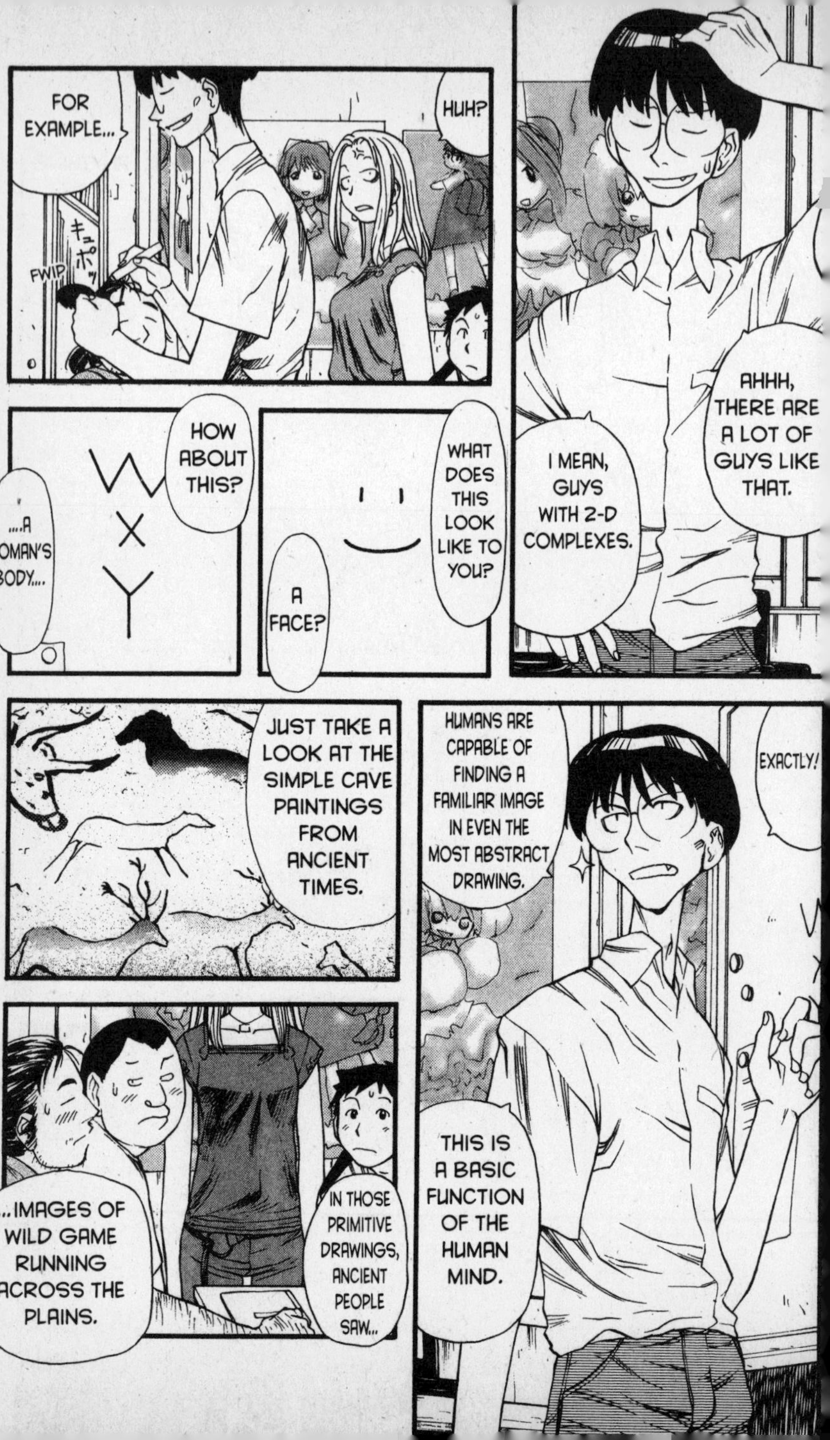
AHHH, THERE ARE A LOT OF GUYS LIKE THAT.
I MEAN, GUYS WITH 2-D COMPLEXES.
HUH?
FOR EXAMPLE...
キュポッ
FWIP
WHAT DOES THIS LOOK LIKE TO YOU?
A FACE?
HOW ABOUT THIS?
W
X
Y
...A WOMAN'S BODY...
EXACTLY!
HUMANS ARE CAPABLE OF FINDING A FAMILIAR IMAGE IN EVEN THE MOST ABSTRACT DRAWING.
THIS IS A BASIC FUNCTION OF THE HUMAN MIND.
JUST TAKE A LOOK AT THE SIMPLE CAVE PAINTINGS FROM ANCIENT TIMES.
IN THOSE PRIMITIVE DRAWINGS, ANCIENT PEOPLE SAW...
...IMAGES OF WILD GAME RUNNING ACROSS THE PLAINS.

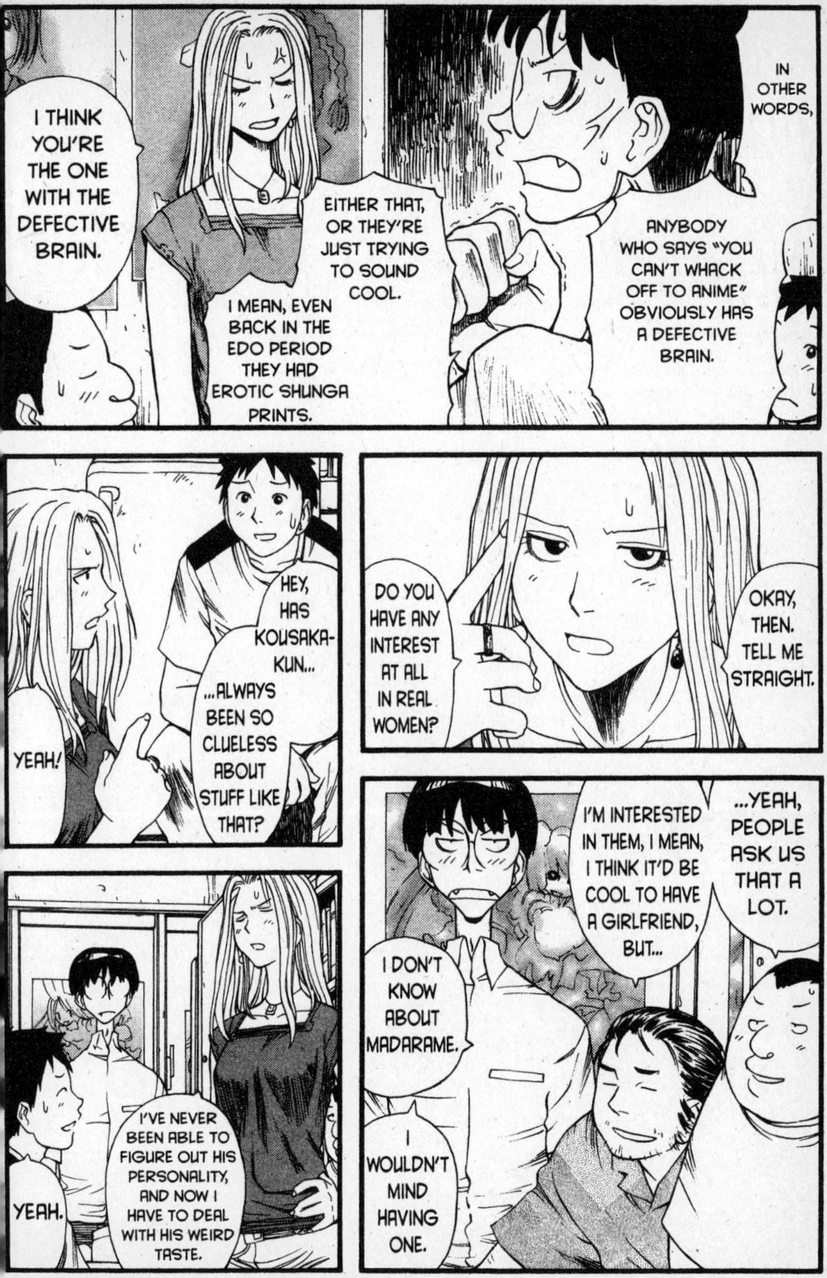
IN OTHER WORDS,
ANYBODY WHO SAYS "YOU CAN'T WHACK OFF TO ANIME" OBVIOUSLY HAS A DEFECTIVE BRAIN.
EITHER THAT, OR THEY'RE JUST TRYING TO SOUND COOL.
I MEAN, EVEN BACK IN THE EDO PERIOD THEY HAD EROTIC SHUNGA PRINTS.
I THINK YOU'RE THE ONE WITH THE DEFECTIVE BRAIN.
OKAY, THEN. TELL ME STRAIGHT.
DO YOU HAVE ANY INTEREST AT ALL IN REAL WOMEN?
HEY, HAS KOUSAKA-KUN...
...ALWAYS BEEN SO CLUELESS ABOUT STUFF LIKE THAT?
YEAH!
...YEAH, PEOPLE ASK US THAT A LOT.
I'M INTERESTED IN THEM, I MEAN, I THINK IT'D BE COOL TO HAVE A GIRLFRIEND, BUT...
I DON'T KNOW ABOUT MADARAME.
I WOULDN'T MIND HAVING ONE.
I'VE NEVER BEEN ABLE TO FIGURE OUT HIS PERSONALITY, AND NOW I HAVE TO DEAL WITH HIS WEIRD TASTE.
YEAH.

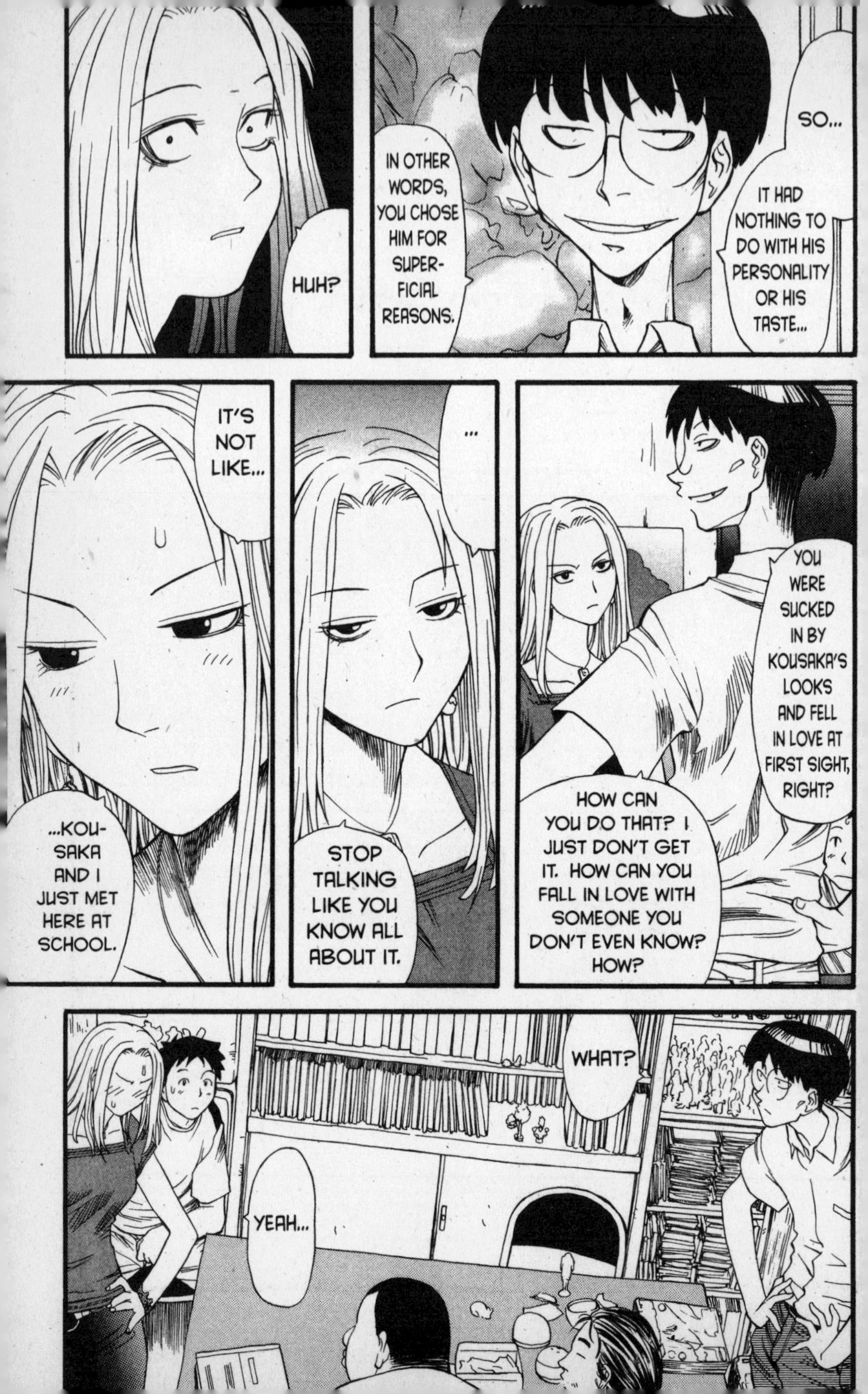
SO...
IT HAD NOTHING TO DO WITH HIS PERSONALITY OR HIS TASTE...
IN OTHER WORDS, YOU CHOSE HIM FOR SUPER-FICIAL REASONS.
HUH?
YOU WERE SUCKED IN BY KOUSAKA'S LOOKS AND FELL IN LOVE AT FIRST SIGHT, RIGHT?
HOW CAN YOU DO THAT? I JUST DON'T GET IT. HOW CAN YOU FALL IN LOVE WITH SOMEONE YOU DON'T EVEN KNOW? HOW?
...
STOP TALKING LIKE YOU KNOW ALL ABOUT IT.
IT'S NOT LIKE...
...KOU-SAKA AND I JUST MET HERE AT SCHOOL.
WHAT?
YEAH...

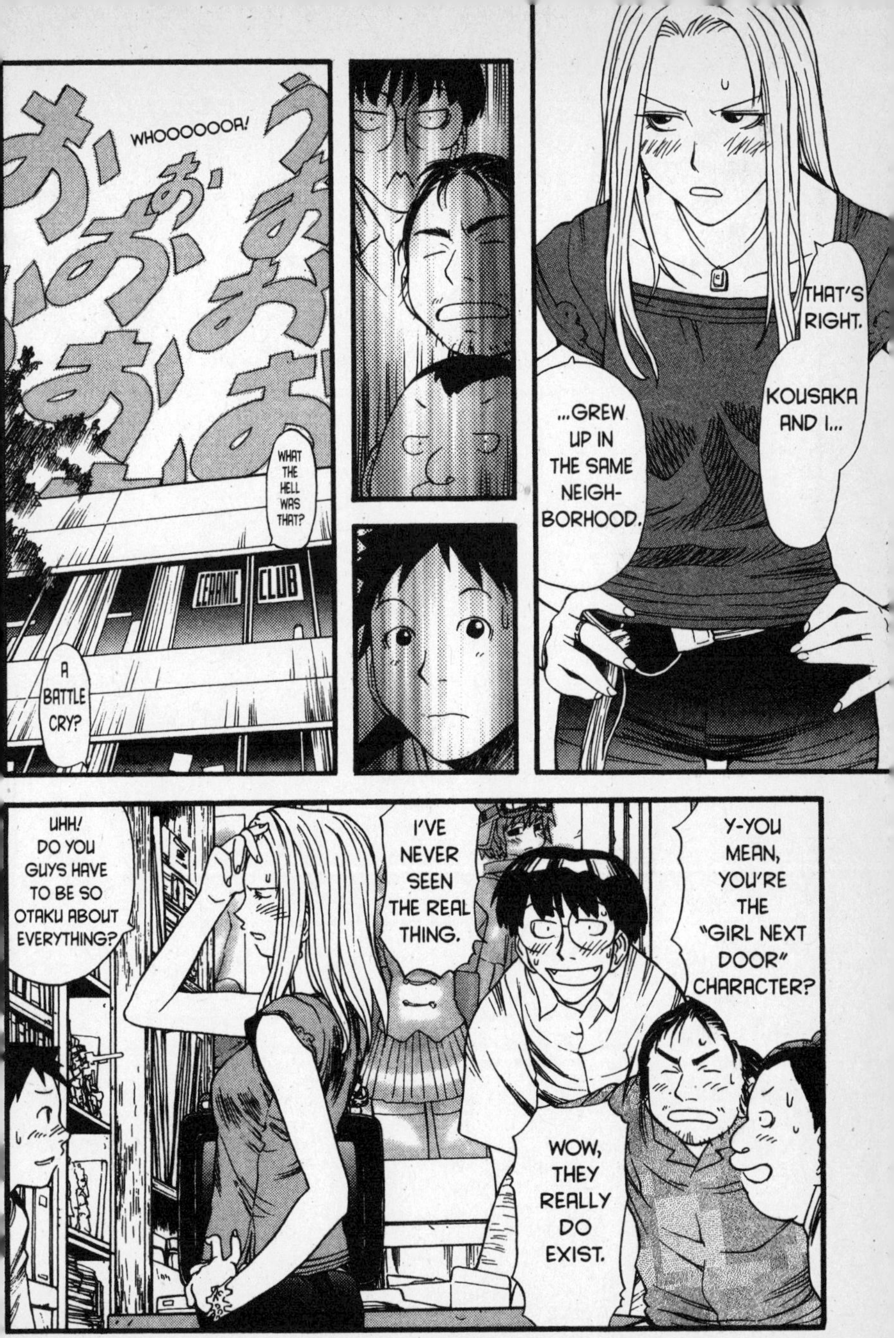
THAT'S RIGHT.
KOUSAKA AND I...
...GREW UP IN THE SAME NEIGH-BORHOOD.
WHOOOOOOR!
WHAT THE HELL WAS THAT?
CERAMIC CLUB
A BATTLE CRY?
Y-YOU MEAN, YOU'RE THE "GIRL NEXT DOOR" CHARACTER?
WOW, THEY REALLY DO EXIST.
I'VE NEVER SEEN THE REAL THING.
UHH! DO YOU GUYS HAVE TO BE SO OTAKU ABOUT EVERYTHING?

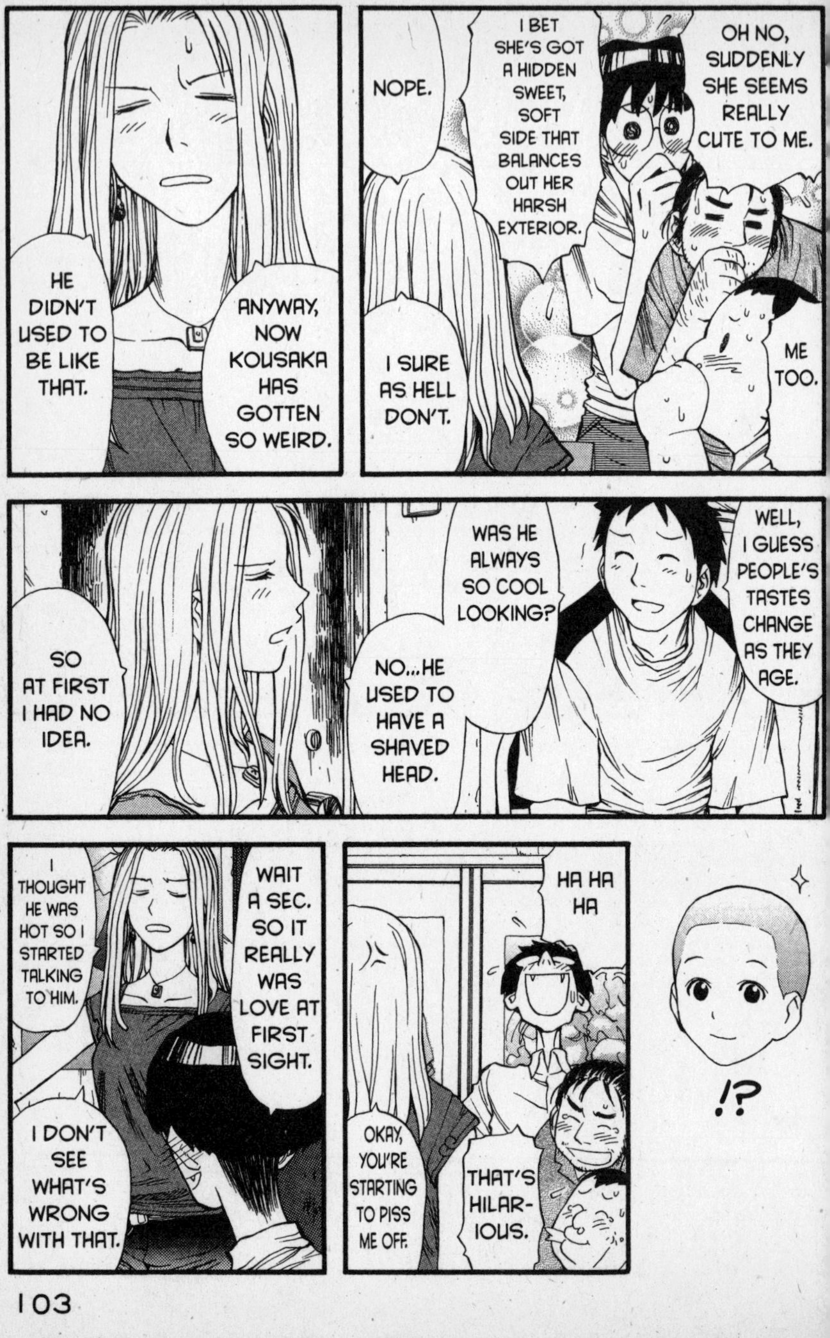
OH NO, SUDDENLY SHE SEEMS REALLY CUTE TO ME.
I BET SHE'S GOT A HIDDEN SWEET, SOFT SIDE THAT BALANCES OUT HER HARSH EXTERIOR.
NOPE.
ME TOO.
I SURE AS HELL DON'T.
ANYWAY, NOW KOUSAKA HAS GOTTEN SO WEIRD.
HE DIDN'T USED TO BE LIKE THAT.
WELL, I GUESS PEOPLE'S TASTES CHANGE AS THEY AGE.
WAS HE ALWAYS SO COOL LOOKING?
NO...HE USED TO HAVE A SHAVED HEAD.
SO AT FIRST I HAD NO IDEA.
!?
HA HA HA
THAT'S HILAR-IOUS.
OKAY, YOU'RE STARTING TO PISS ME OFF.
WAIT A SEC. SO IT REALLY WAS LOVE AT FIRST SIGHT.
I THOUGHT HE WAS HOT SO I STARTED TALKING TO HIM.
I DON'T SEE WHAT'S WRONG WITH THAT.

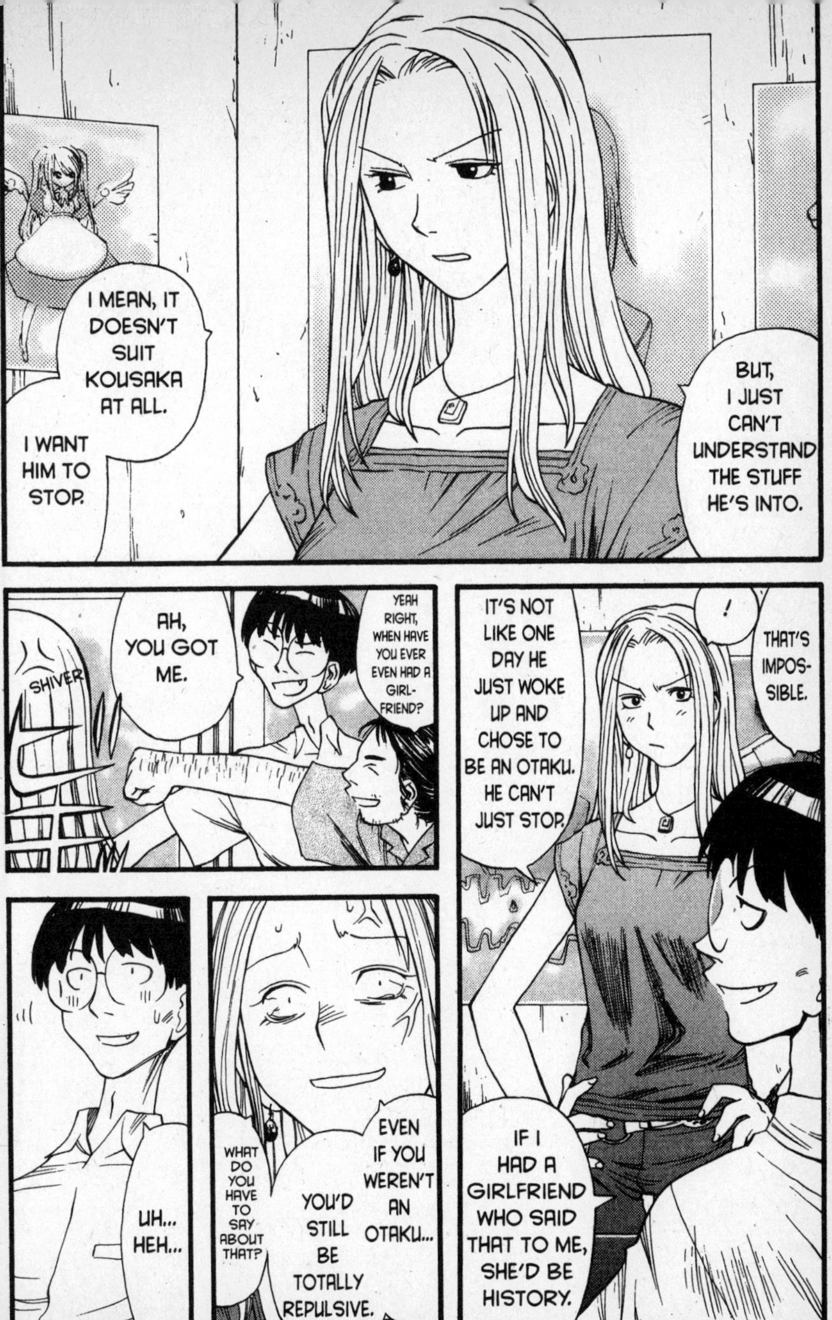
BUT, I JUST CAN'T UNDERSTAND THE STUFF HE'S INTO.
I MEAN, IT DOESN'T SUIT KOUSAKA AT ALL.
I WANT HIM TO STOP.
!
THAT'S IMPOS-SIBLE.
IT'S NOT LIKE ONE DAY HE JUST WOKE UP AND CHOSE TO BE AN OTAKU. HE CAN'T JUST STOP.
IF I HAD A GIRLFRIEND WHO SAID THAT TO ME, SHE'D BE HISTORY.
YEAH RIGHT, WHEN HAVE YOU EVER EVEN HAD A GIRL-FRIEND?
AH, YOU GOT ME.
SHIVER
EVEN IF YOU WEREN'T AN OTAKU...
YOU'D STILL BE TOTALLY REPULSIVE.
WHAT DO YOU HAVE TO SAY ABOUT THAT?
UH... HEH...

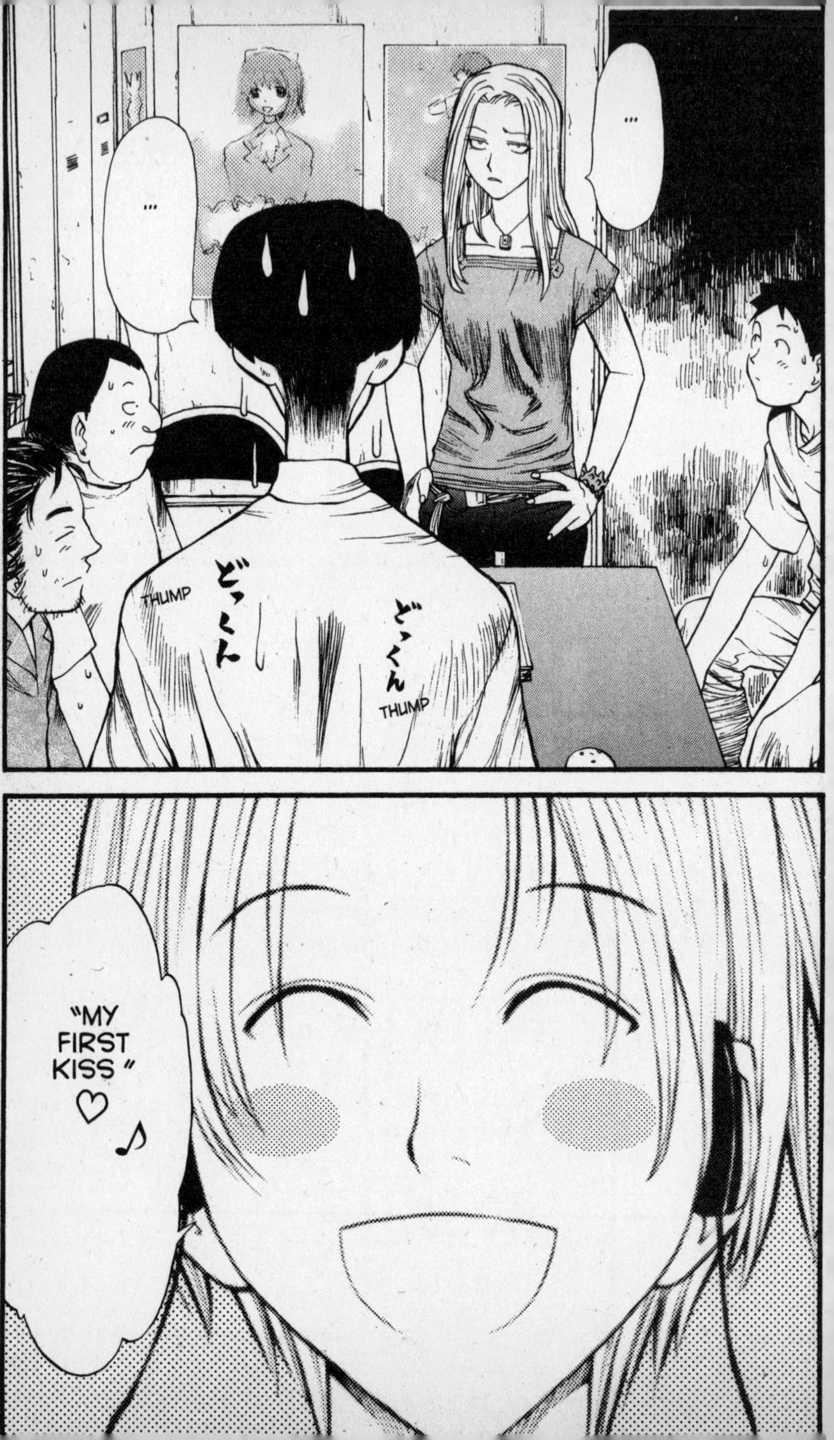
...
...
どっくん
THUMP
どっくん
THUMP
"MY FIRST KISS" ♡ ♪

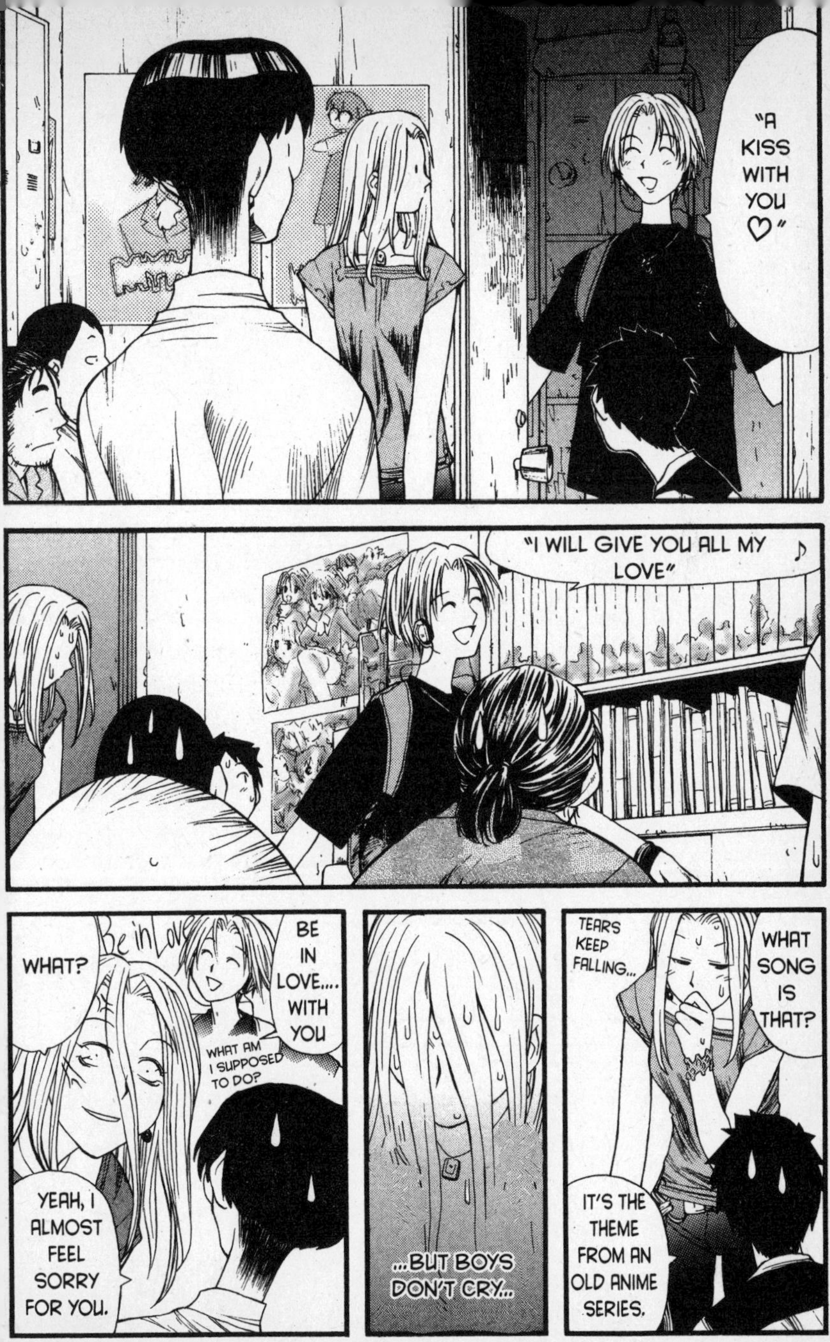
"A KISS WITH YOU ♡"
"I WILL GIVE YOU ALL MY LOVE" ♪
♪
WHAT SONG IS THAT?
TEARS KEEP FALLING...
IT'S THE THEME FROM AN OLD ANIME SERIES.
...BUT BOYS DON'T CRY...
BE IN LOVE.... WITH YOU
Be in Love
WHAT?
WHAT AM I SUPPOSED TO DO?
YEAH, I ALMOST FEEL SORRY FOR YOU.

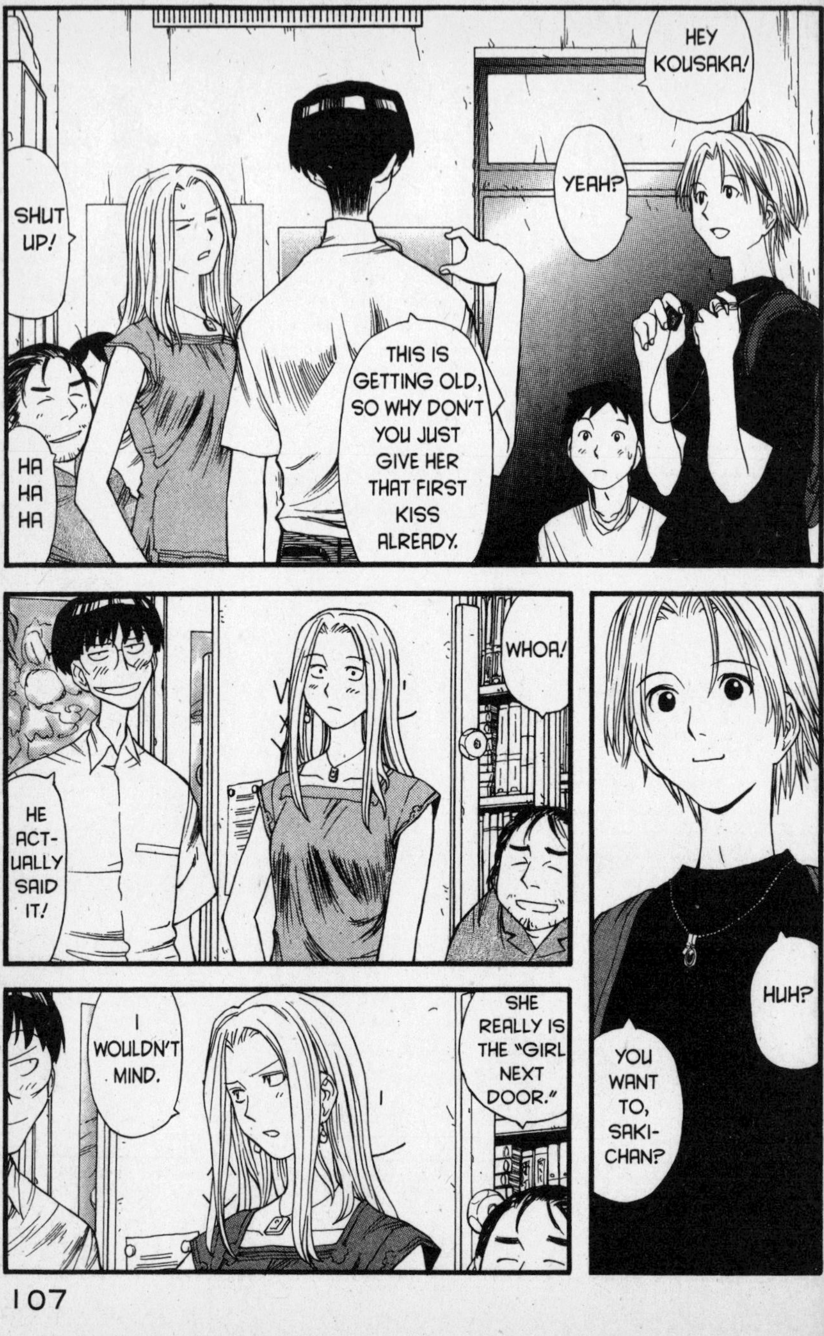
HEY KOUSAKA!
YEAH?
THIS IS GETTING OLD, SO WHY DON'T YOU JUST GIVE HER THAT FIRST KISS ALREADY.
SHUT UP!
HA HA HA
HUH?
YOU WANT TO, SAKI-CHAN?
WHOA!
HE ACT-UALLY SAID IT!
SHE REALLY IS THE "GIRL NEXT DOOR."
I WOULDN'T MIND.

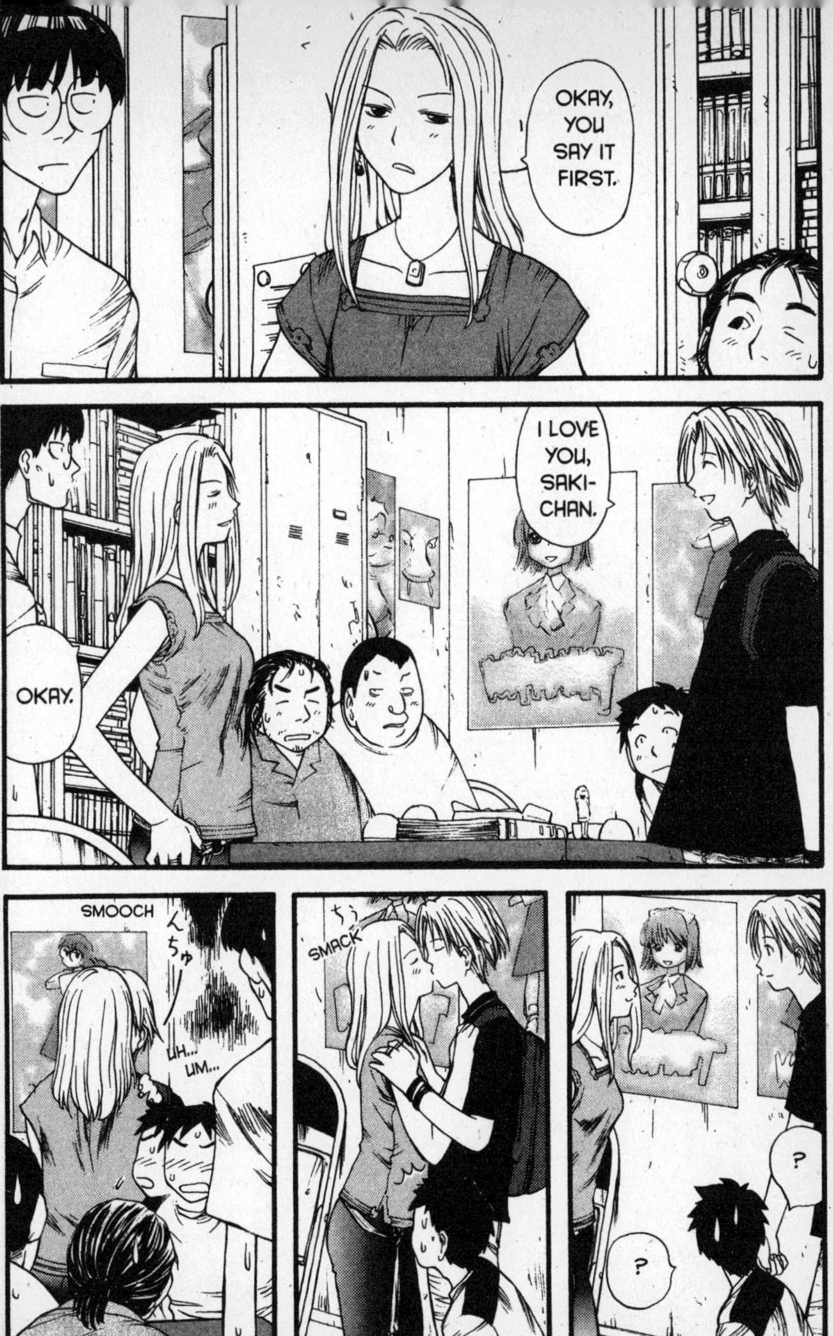
OKAY, YOU SAY IT FIRST.
I LOVE YOU, SAKI-CHAN.
OKAY.
?
?
ちう
SMACK
SMOOCH
んちゅ
UH... UM...

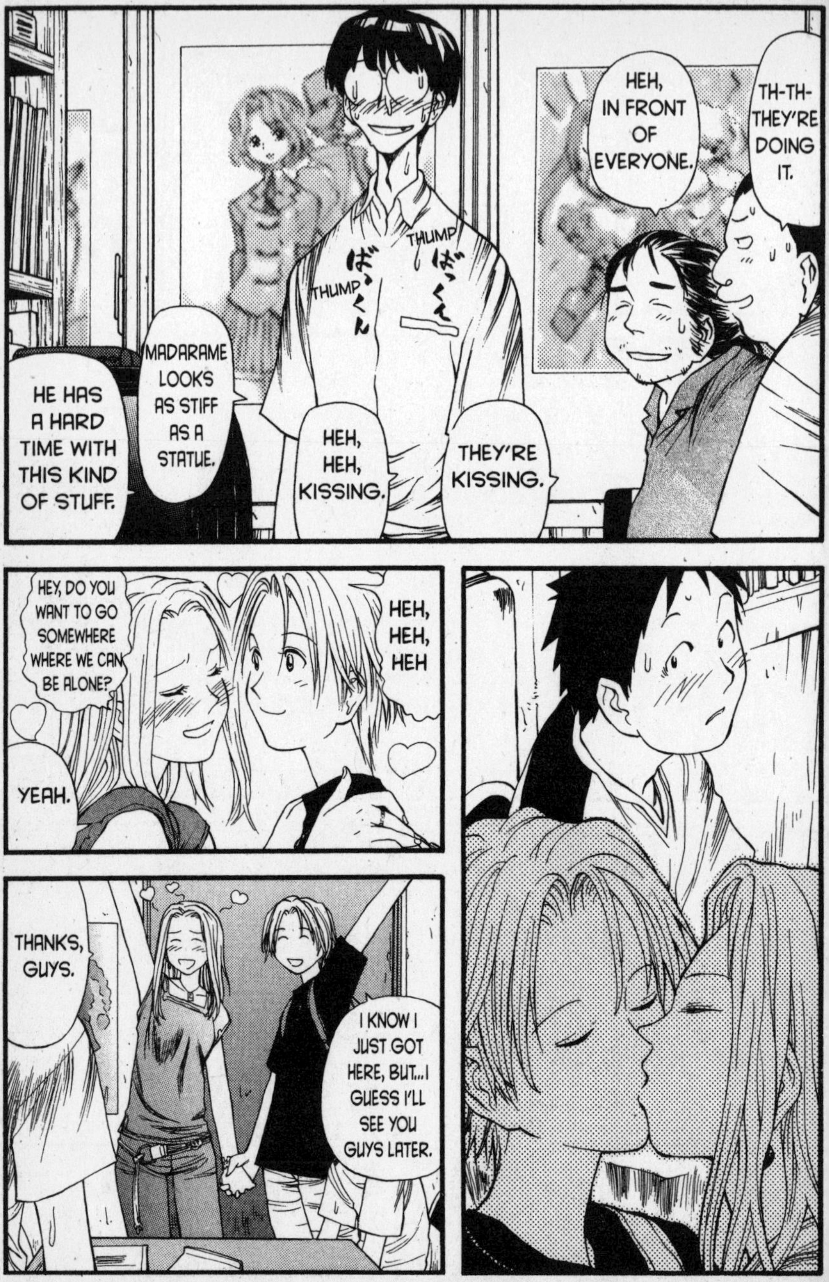
TH-TH-THEY'RE DOING IT.
HEH, IN FRONT OF EVERYONE.
THUMP
ばっくん
THUMP
ばっくん
THEY'RE KISSING.
HEH, HEH, KISSING.
MADARAME LOOKS AS STIFF AS A STATUE.
HE HAS A HARD TIME WITH THIS KIND OF STUFF.
HEH, HEH, HEH
HEY, DO YOU WANT TO GO SOMEWHERE WHERE WE CAN BE ALONE?
YEAH.
I KNOW I JUST GOT HERE, BUT...I GUESS I'LL SEE YOU GUYS LATER.
THANKS, GUYS.

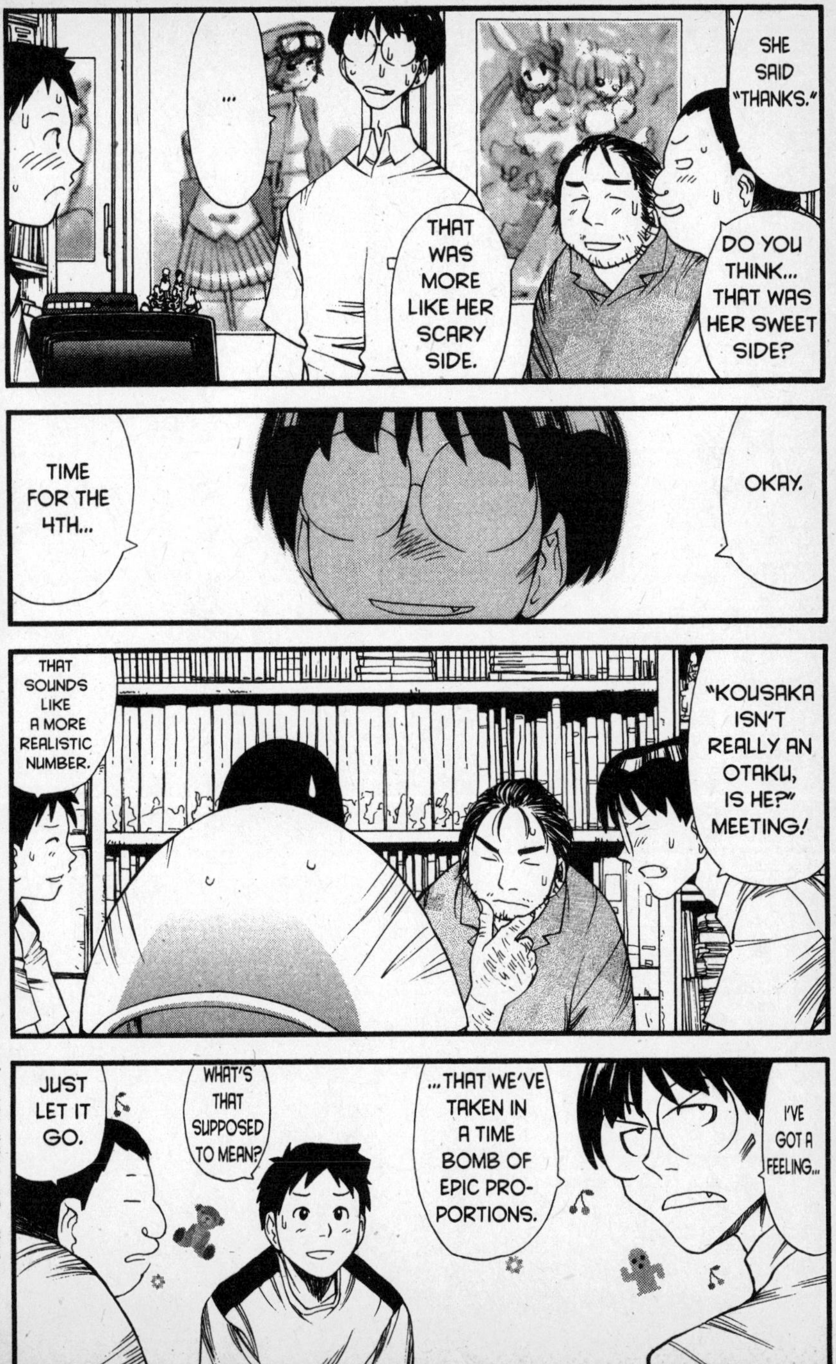
SHE SAID "THANKS."
DO YOU THINK... THAT WAS HER SWEET SIDE?
THAT WAS MORE LIKE HER SCARY SIDE.
...
OKAY.
TIME FOR THE 4TH...
"KOUSAKA ISN'T REALLY AN OTAKU, IS HE?" MEETING!
THAT SOUNDS LIKE A MORE REALISTIC NUMBER.
I'VE GOT A FEELING...
...THAT WE'VE TAKEN IN A TIME BOMB OF EPIC PRO-PORTIONS.
WHAT'S THAT SUPPOSED TO MEAN?
JUST LET IT GO.

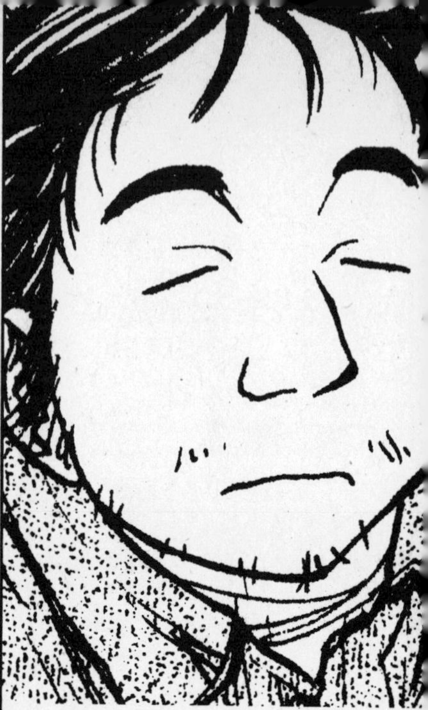

TANAKA SOUICHIRO

PROFILE

SOUICHIRO TANAKA

BIRTHDAY DECEMBER 22ND
BLOOD TYPE AB

FAVORITE MANGA
THE SEVEN STAR STORIES

FAVORITE ANIME
RYUNOS: THE CASTLE IN THE SKY
CONAN THE BOY FROM THE FUTURE

FAVORITE VIDEO GAMES
YUUJIRO TACTIC
THE STORY OF MR. STUPID

FAVORITE FIGHT GAME CHARACTERS
DR. HAYWOOD

KUGAYAMA MITSUNORI

PROFILE

MITSUNORI KUGAYAMA

BIRTHDAY JUNE 29TH
BLOOD TYPE A

FAVORITE MANGA
ANMAN BALL

FAVORITE ANIME
FUN WITH THE TARURUN FAMILY (BEFORE THE THEME SONG CHANGED)

FAVORITE VIDEO GAMES
EXITGE

FAVORITE FIGHT GAME CHARACTERS
THE LOVELY YOOGA TISETTE

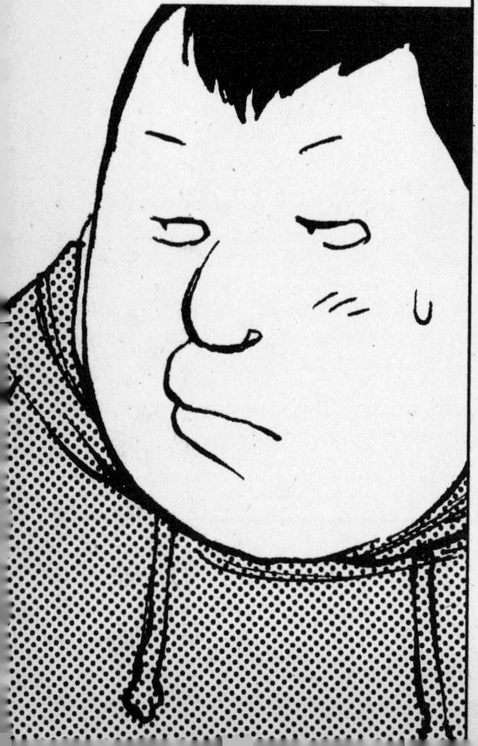

NICKNAMES

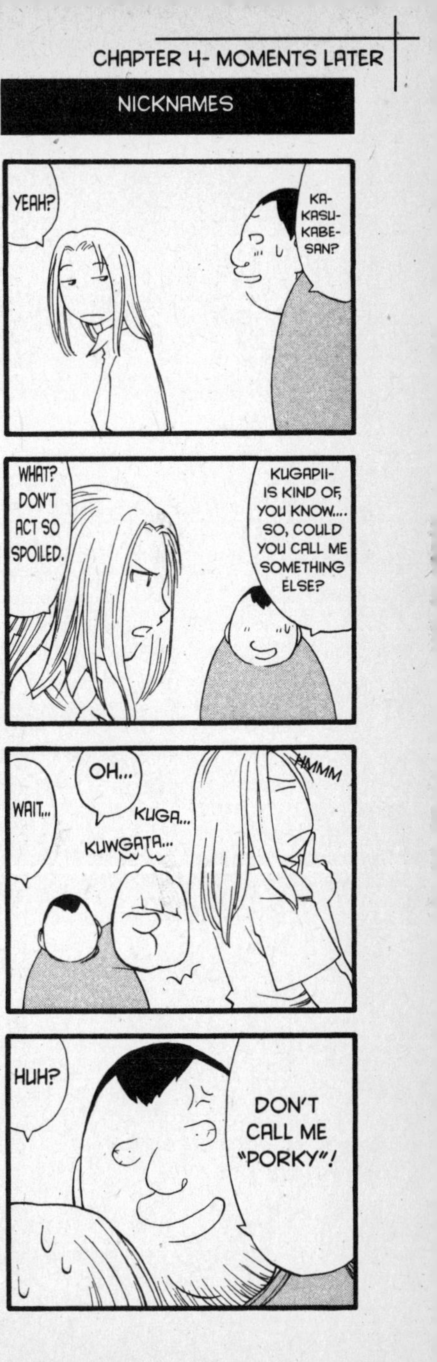
KA-KASU-KABE-SAN?
YEAH?
KUGAPII- IS KIND OF, YOU KNOW.... SO, COULD YOU CALL ME SOMETHING ELSE?
WHAT? DON'T ACT SO SPOILED.
HMMM
OH...
KUGA...
WAIT...
KUWGATA...
DON'T CALL ME "PORKY"!
HUH?

A NEW NAME

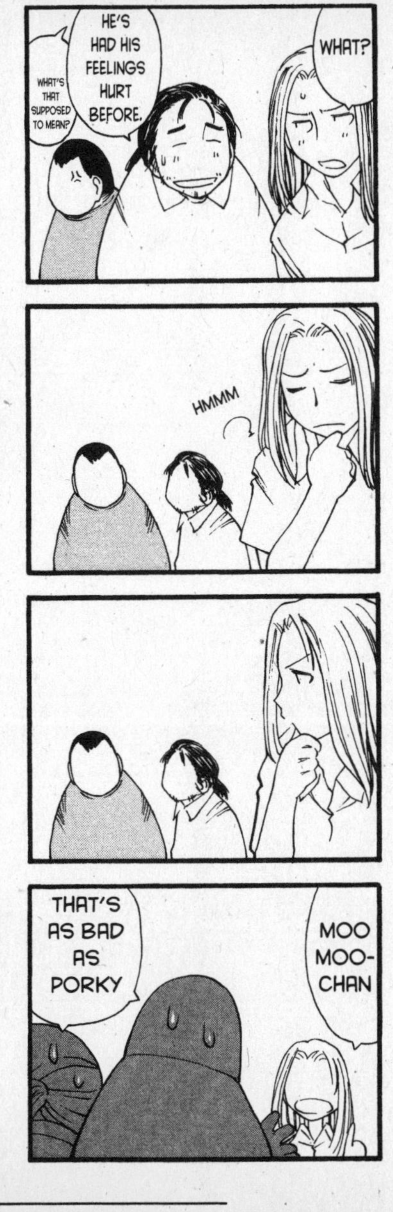
WHAT?
HE'S HAD HIS FEELINGS HURT BEFORE.
WHAT'S THAT SUPPOSED TO MEAN?
HMMM
MOO MOO-CHAN
THAT'S AS BAD AS PORKY

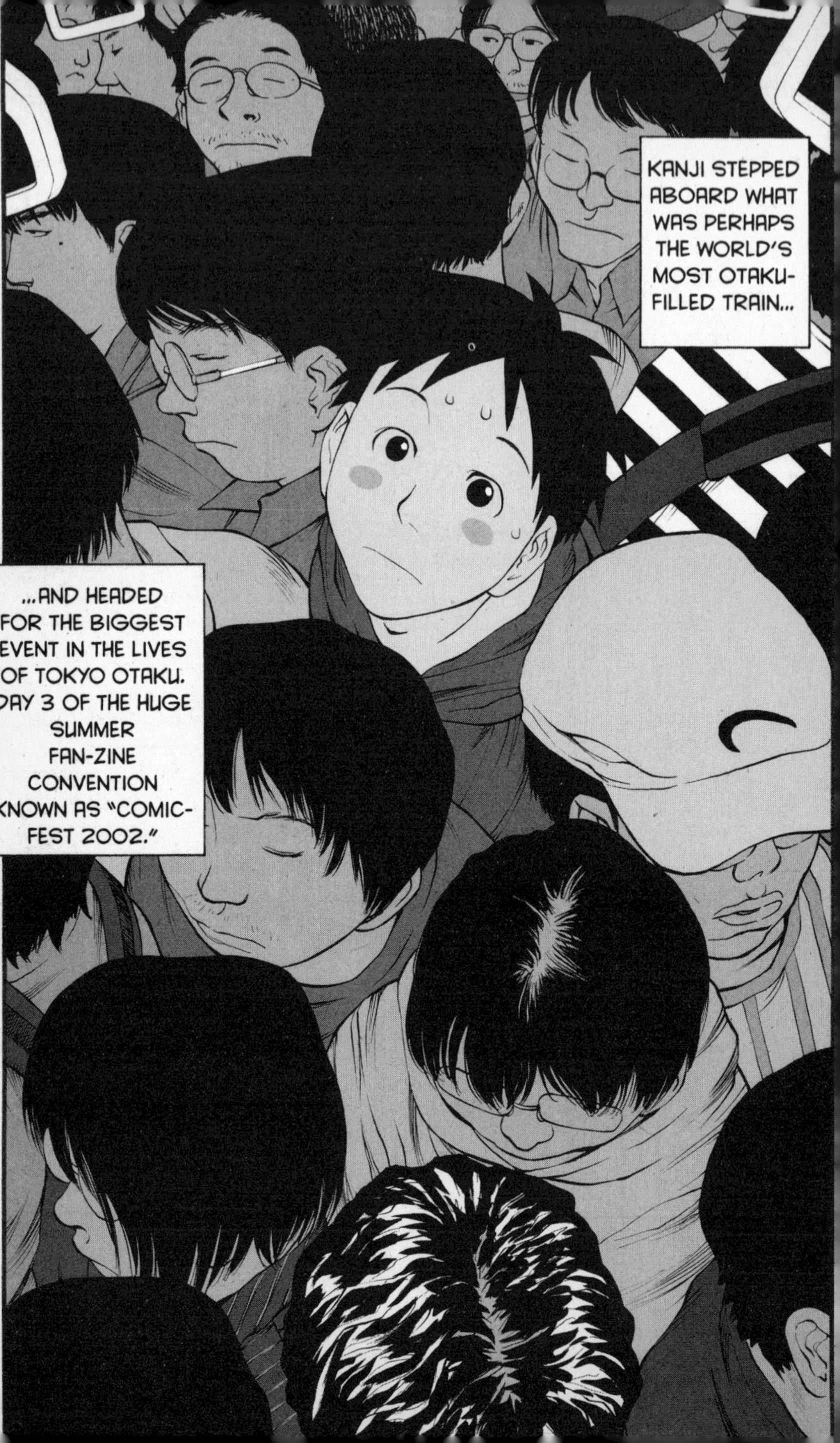
KANJI STEPPED ABOARD WHAT WAS PERHAPS THE WORLD'S MOST OTAKU-FILLED TRAIN...
...AND HEADED FOR THE BIGGEST EVENT IN THE LIVES OF TOKYO OTAKU. DAY 3 OF THE HUGE SUMMER FAN-ZINE CONVENTION KNOWN AS "COMIC-FEST 2002."

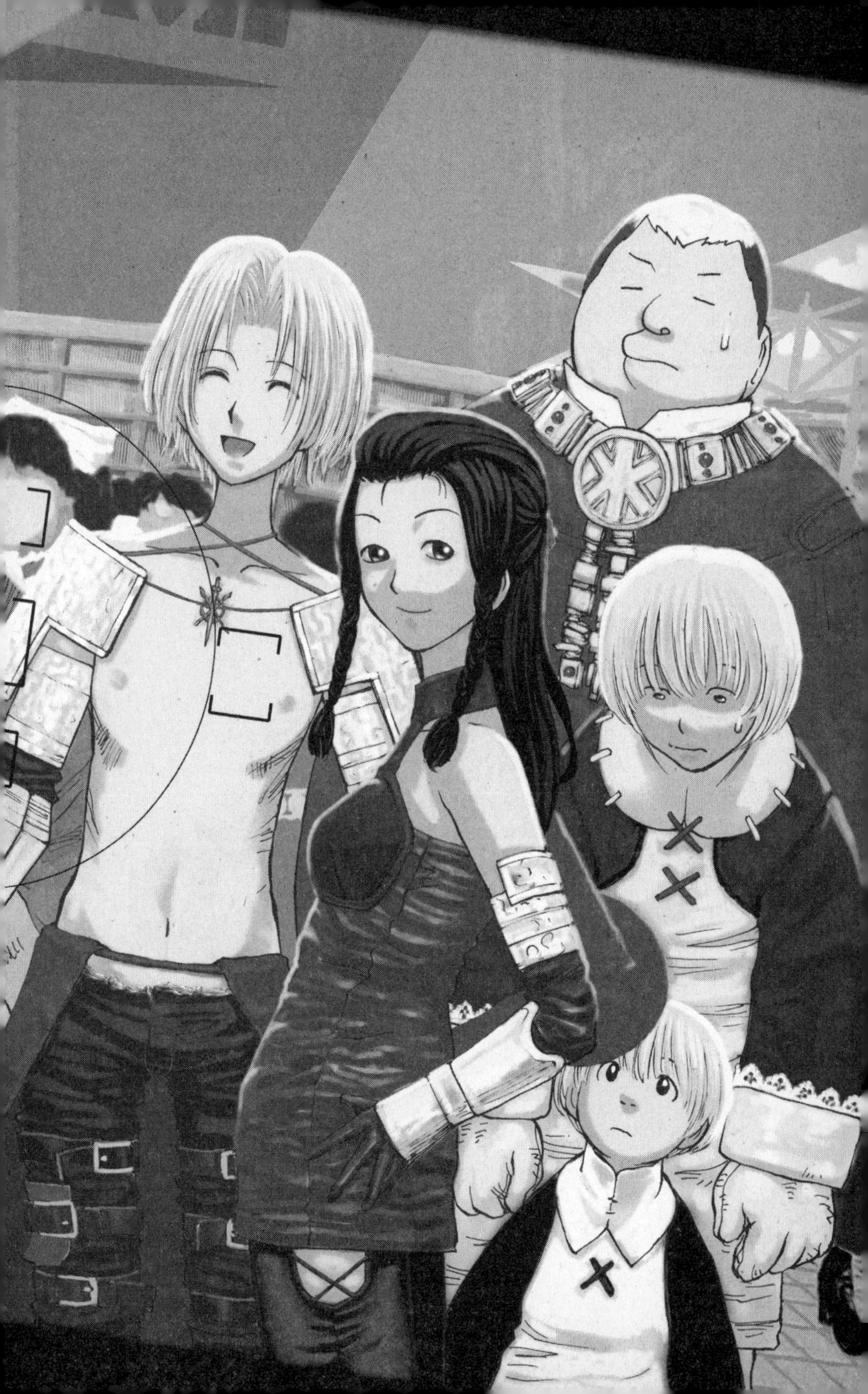

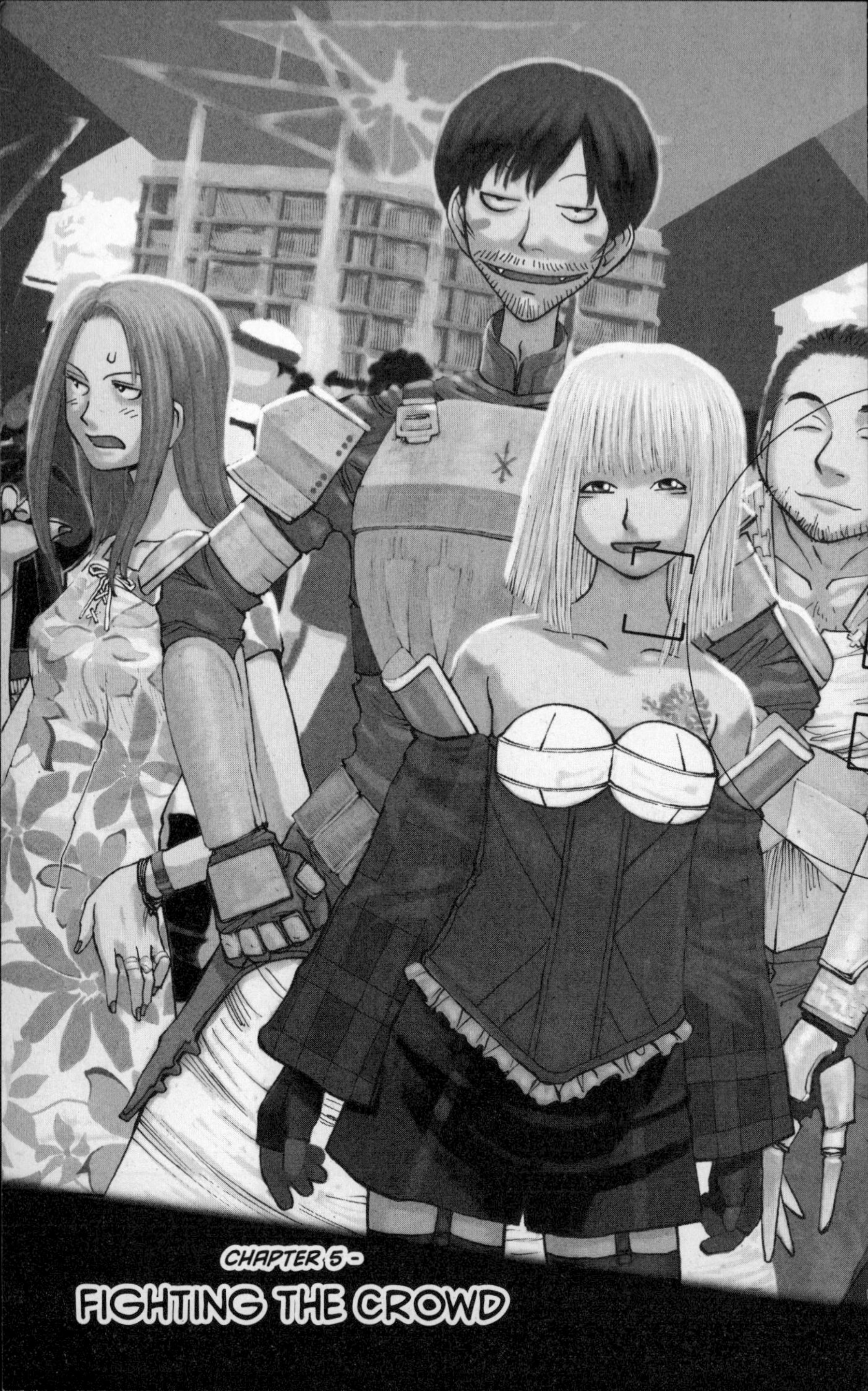
CHAPTER 5 -
FIGHTING THE CROWD

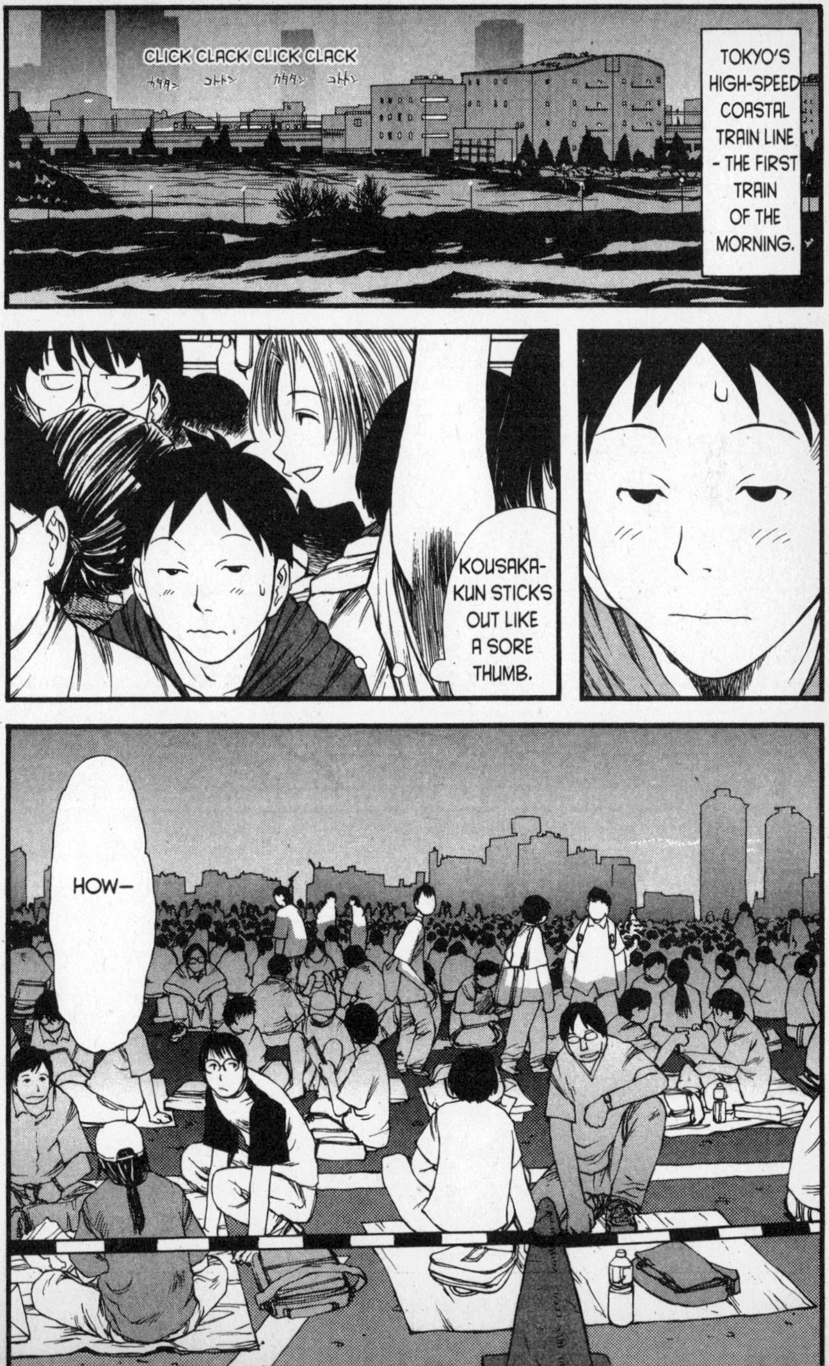
CLICK CLACK CLICK CLACK
TOKYO'S HIGH-SPEED COASTAL TRAIN LINE - THE FIRST TRAIN OF THE MORNING.
KOUSAKA-KUN STICKS OUT LIKE A SORE THUMB.
HOW—

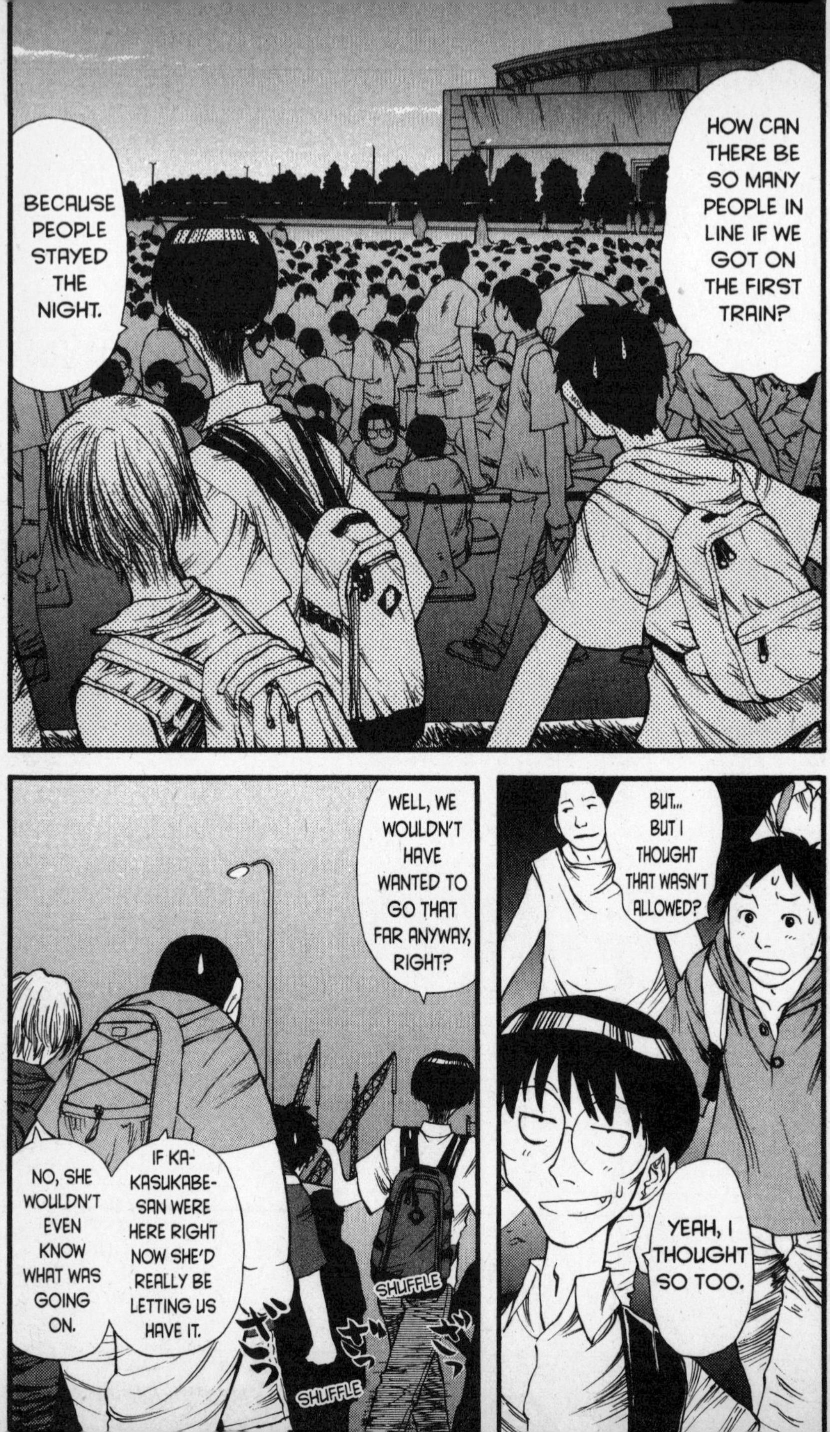
HOW CAN THERE BE SO MANY PEOPLE IN LINE IF WE GOT ON THE FIRST TRAIN?
BECAUSE PEOPLE STAYED THE NIGHT.
BUT... BUT I THOUGHT THAT WASN'T ALLOWED?
YEAH, I THOUGHT SO TOO.
WELL, WE WOULDN'T HAVE WANTED TO GO THAT FAR ANYWAY, RIGHT?
IF KA-KASUKABE-SAN WERE HERE RIGHT NOW SHE'D REALLY BE LETTING US HAVE IT.
NO, SHE WOULDN'T EVEN KNOW WHAT WAS GOING ON.
SHUFFLE
SHUFFLE

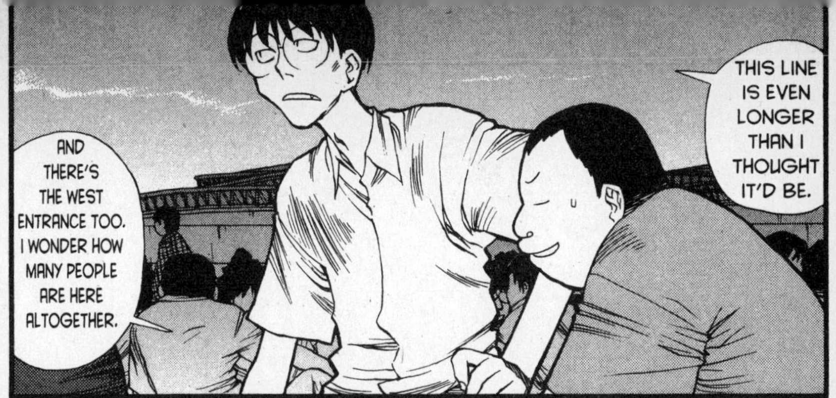
THIS LINE IS EVEN LONGER THAN I THOUGHT IT'D BE.
AND THERE'S THE WEST ENTRANCE TOO. I WONDER HOW MANY PEOPLE ARE HERE ALTOGETHER.

TANAKA IS WAITING AT THE WEST ENTRANCE, WHICH IS CLOSER TO THE COSPLAY SECTION.

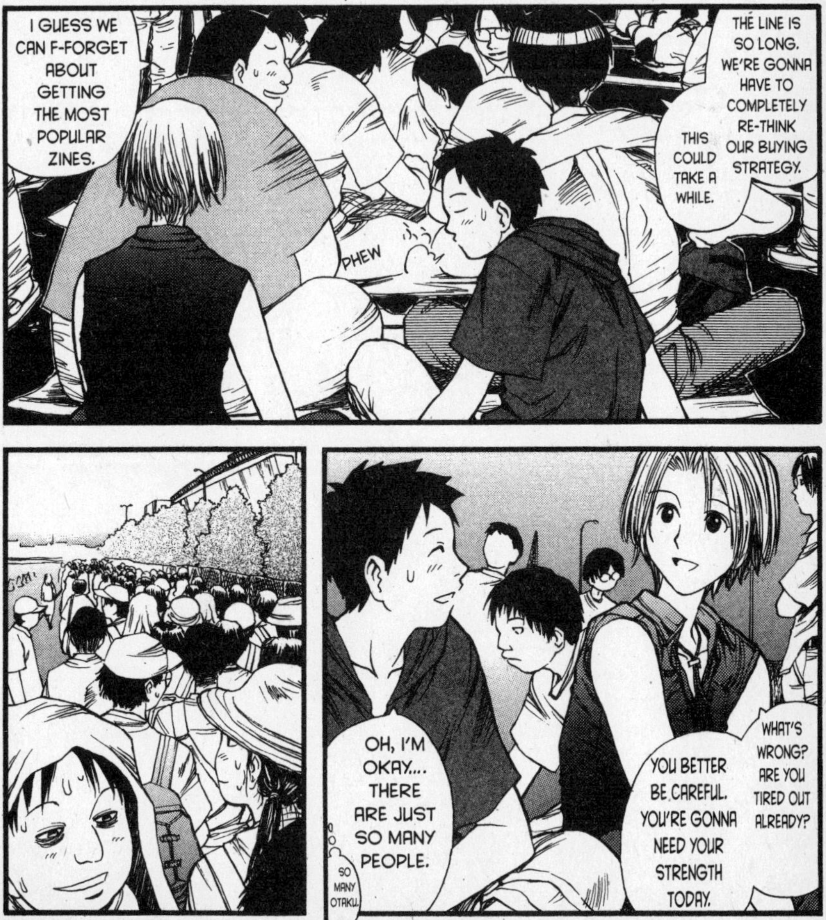
THE LINE IS SO LONG. WE'RE GONNA HAVE TO COMPLETELY RE-THINK OUR BUYING STRATEGY.
THIS COULD TAKE A WHILE.
I GUESS WE CAN F-FORGET ABOUT GETTING THE MOST POPULAR ZINES.
PHEW
WHAT'S WRONG? ARE YOU TIRED OUT ALREADY?
OH, I'M OKAY.... THERE ARE JUST SO MANY PEOPLE.
SO MANY OTAKU.
YOU BETTER BE CAREFUL. YOU'RE GONNA NEED YOUR STRENGTH TODAY.

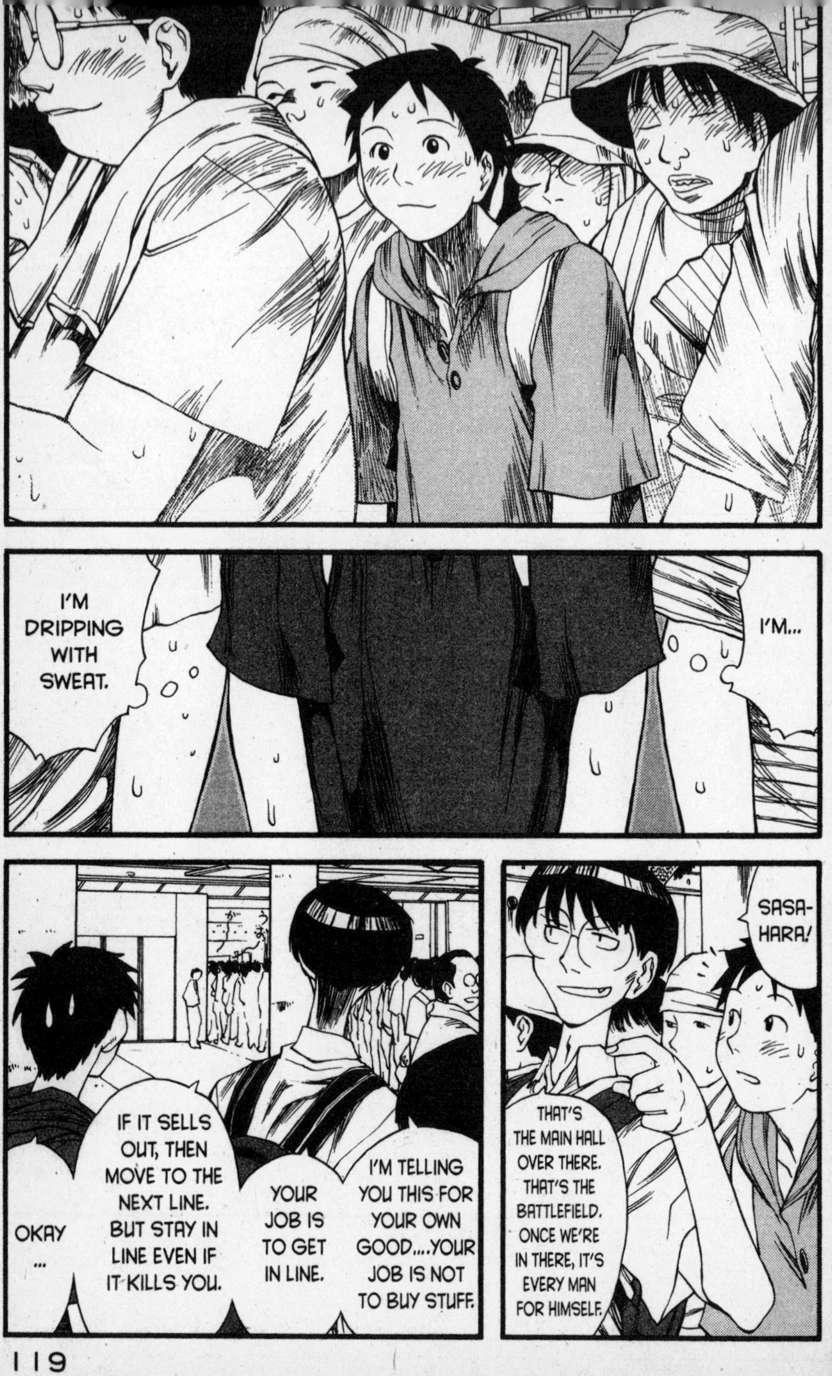
I'M...
I'M DRIPPING WITH SWEAT.
SASA-HARA!
THAT'S THE MAIN HALL OVER THERE. THAT'S THE BATTLEFIELD. ONCE WE'RE IN THERE, IT'S EVERY MAN FOR HIMSELF.
I'M TELLING YOU THIS FOR YOUR OWN GOOD....YOUR JOB IS NOT TO BUY STUFF.
YOUR JOB IS TO GET IN LINE.
IF IT SELLS OUT, THEN MOVE TO THE NEXT LINE. BUT STAY IN LINE EVEN IF IT KILLS YOU.
OKAY ...

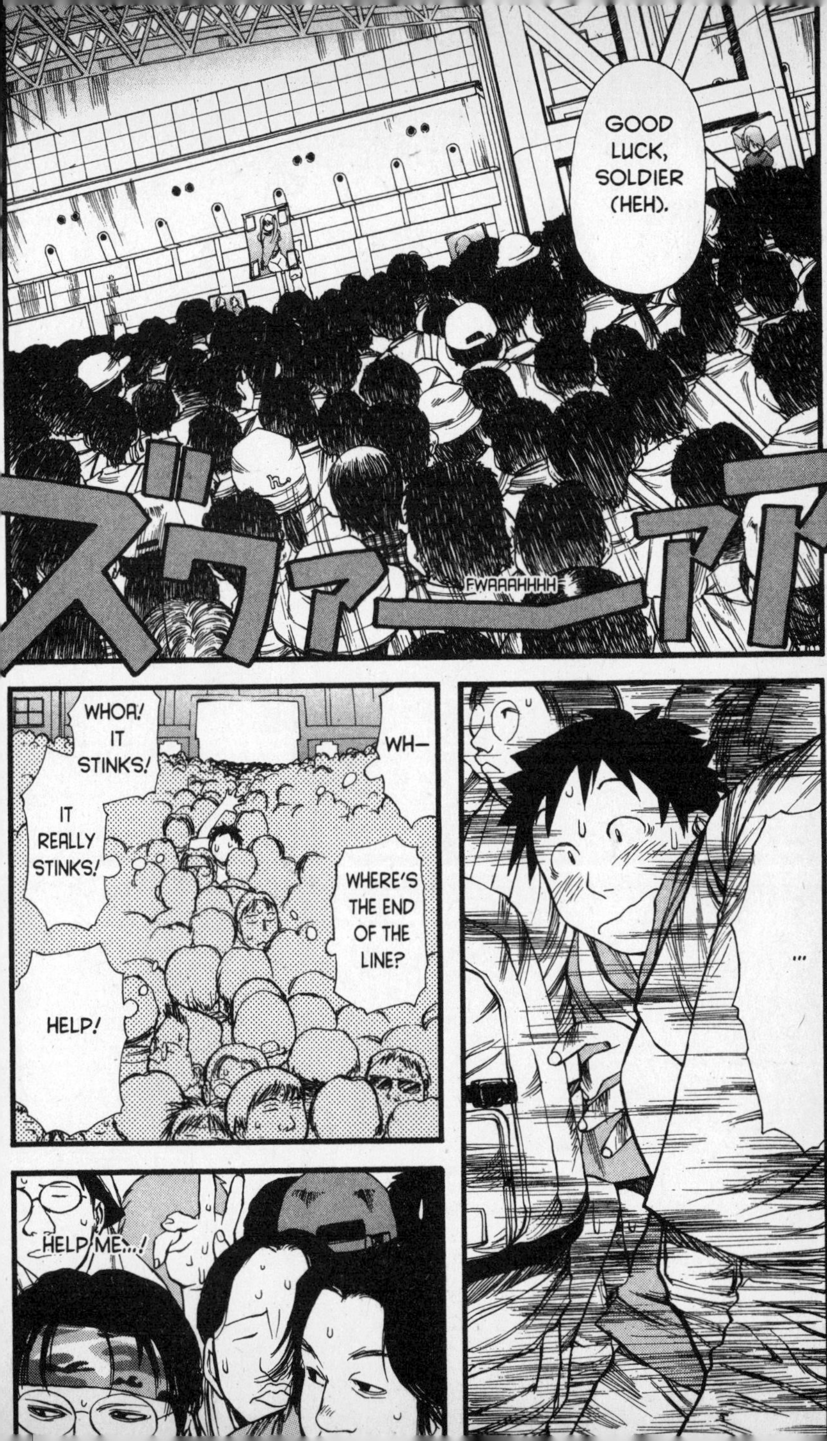
GOOD LUCK, SOLDIER (HEH).
FWAAAHHHH
...
WH—
WHERE'S THE END OF THE LINE?
WHOA! IT STINKS!
IT REALLY STINKS!
HELP!
HELP ME...!

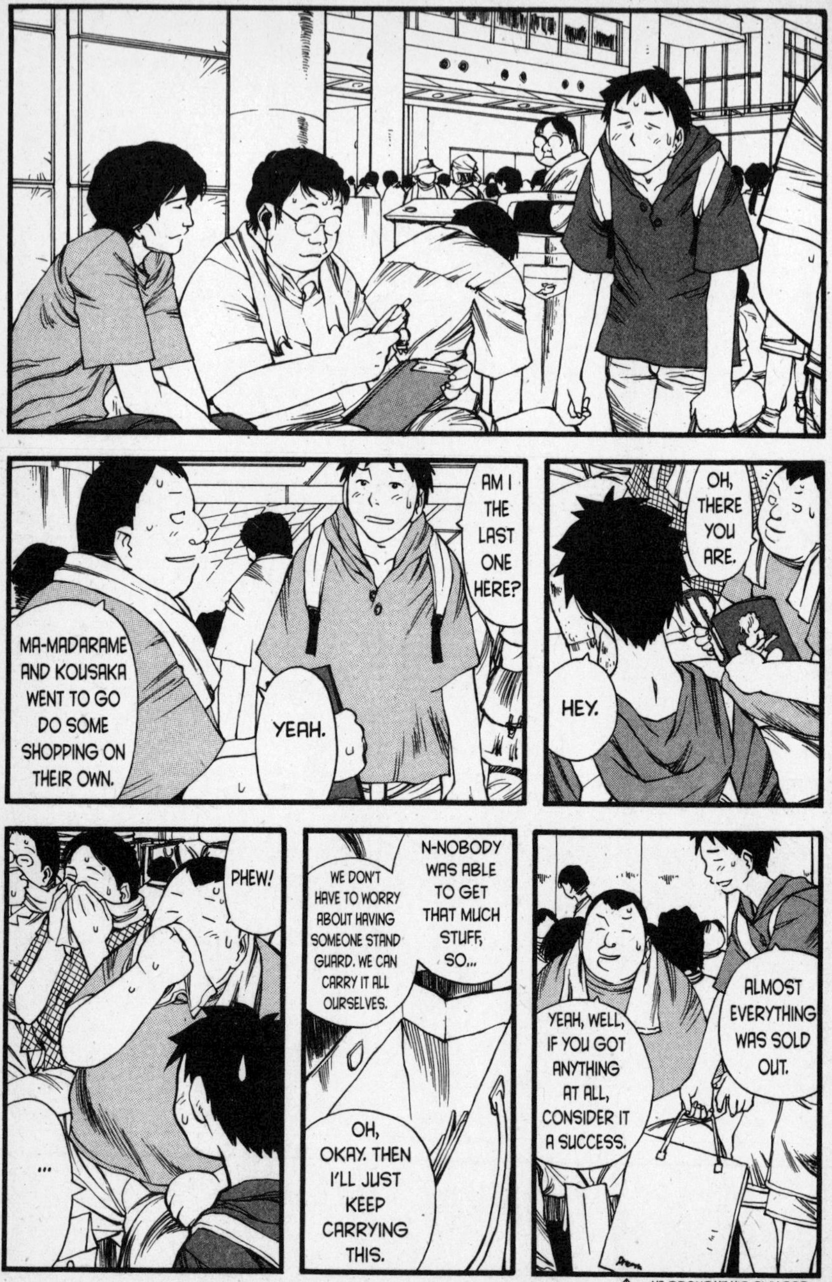
OH, THERE YOU ARE.
HEY.
AM I THE LAST ONE HERE?
YEAH.
MA-MADARAME AND KOUSAKA WENT TO GO DO SOME SHOPPING ON THEIR OWN.
ALMOST EVERYTHING WAS SOLD OUT.
YEAH, WELL, IF YOU GOT ANYTHING AT ALL, CONSIDER IT A SUCCESS.
N-NOBODY WAS ABLE TO GET THAT MUCH STUFF, SO...
WE DON'T HAVE TO WORRY ABOUT HAVING SOMEONE STAND GUARD. WE CAN CARRY IT ALL OURSELVES.
OH, OKAY. THEN I'LL JUST KEEP CARRYING THIS.
PHEW!
...

↖ HE BROUGHT HIS OWN BAG.

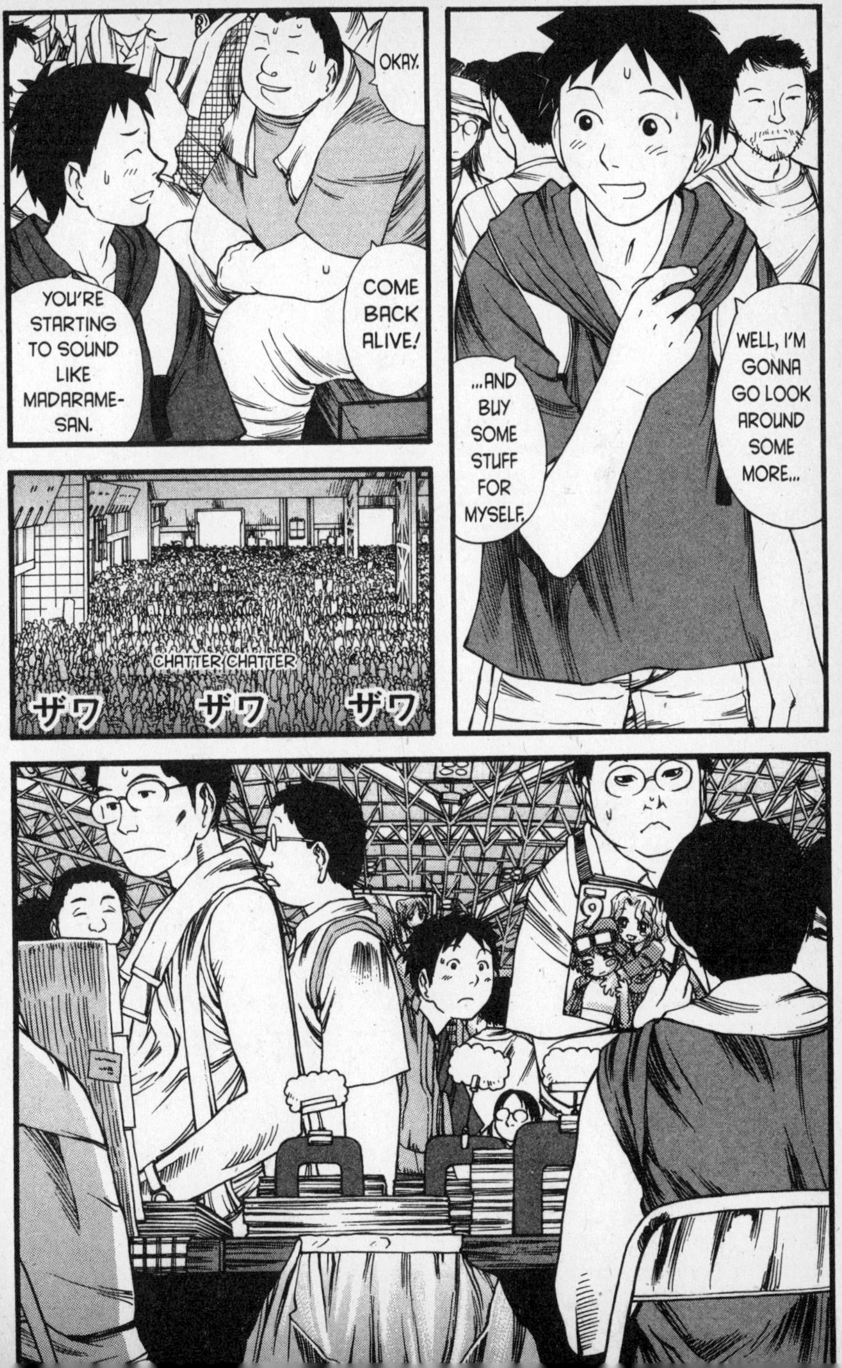
WELL, I'M GONNA GO LOOK AROUND SOME MORE...
...AND BUY SOME STUFF FOR MYSELF.
OKAY.
COME BACK ALIVE!
YOU'RE STARTING TO SOUND LIKE MADARAME-SAN.
ザワ ザワ ザワ
CHATTER CHATTER

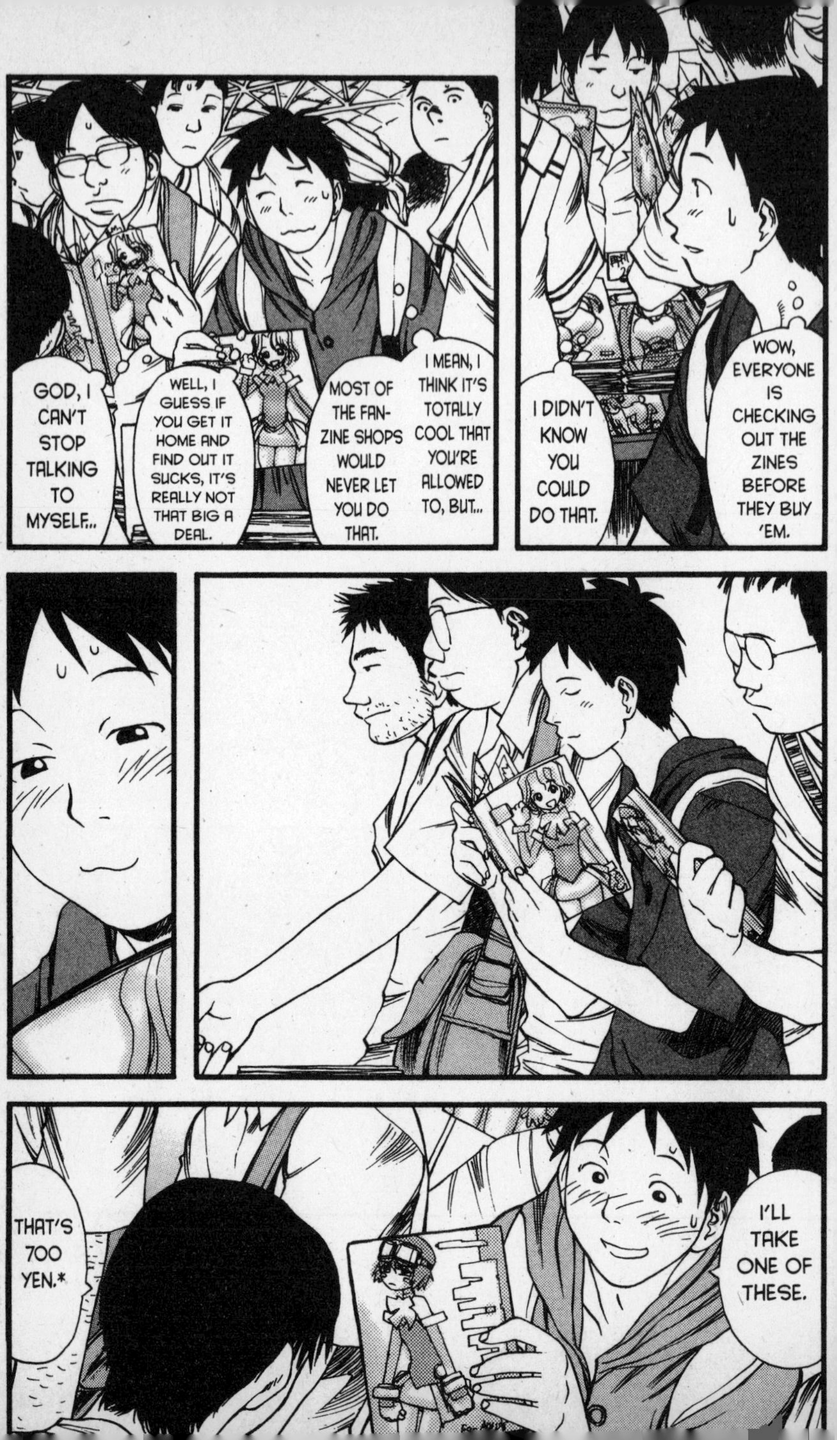
WOW, EVERYONE IS CHECKING OUT THE ZINES BEFORE THEY BUY 'EM.
I DIDN'T KNOW YOU COULD DO THAT.
I MEAN, I THINK IT'S TOTALLY COOL THAT YOU'RE ALLOWED TO, BUT...
MOST OF THE FAN-ZINE SHOPS WOULD NEVER LET YOU DO THAT.
WELL, I GUESS IF YOU GET IT HOME AND FIND OUT IT SUCKS, IT'S REALLY NOT THAT BIG A DEAL.
GOD, I CAN'T STOP TALKING TO MYSELF...
I'LL TAKE ONE OF THESE.
THAT'S 700 YEN.*

*ABOUT $6.70

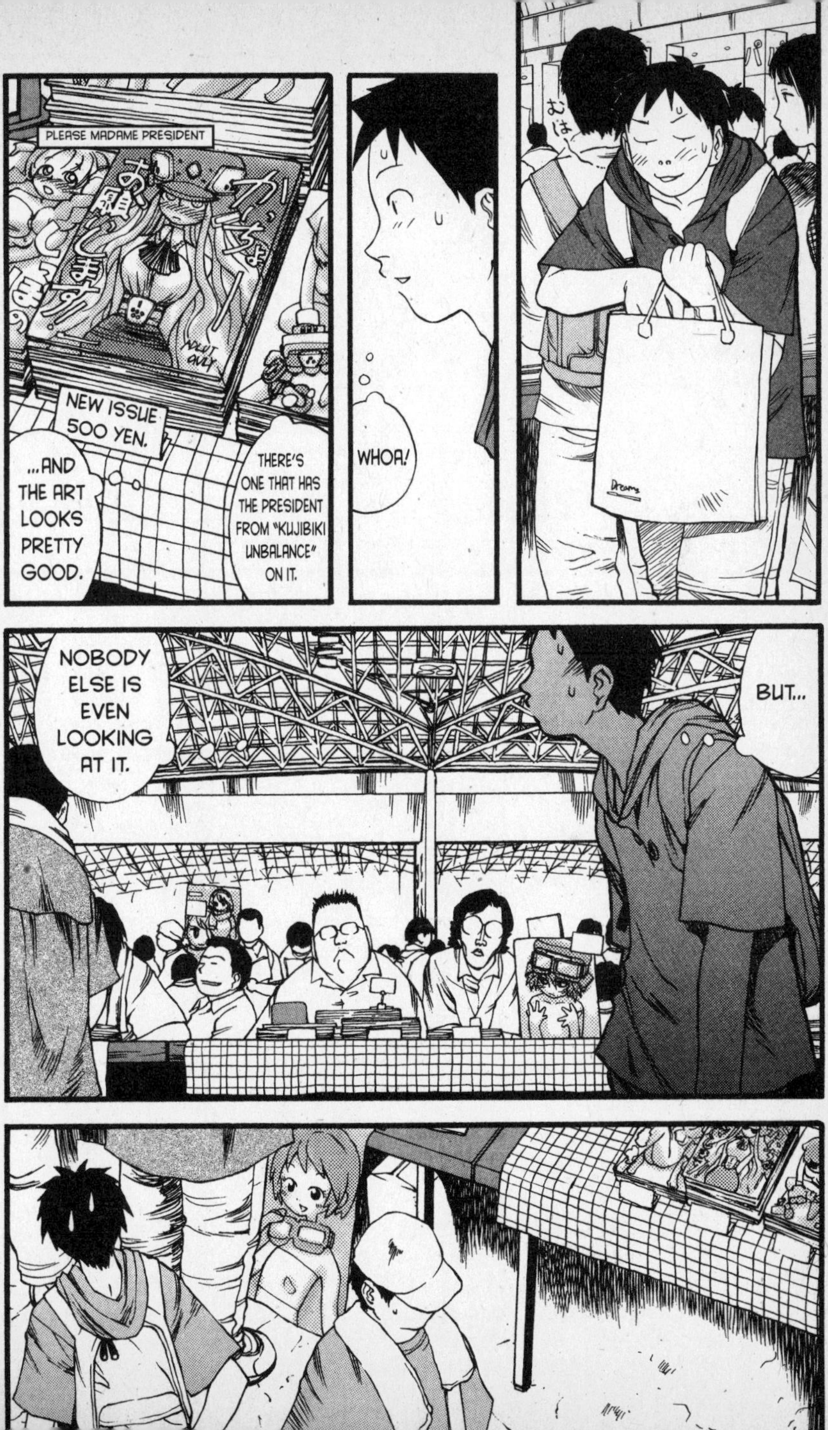
むは
WHOA!
PLEASE MADAME PRESIDENT
ADULT ONLY
NEW ISSUE 500 YEN.
THERE'S ONE THAT HAS THE PRESIDENT FROM "KUJIBIKI UNBALANCE" ON IT.
...AND THE ART LOOKS PRETTY GOOD.
BUT...
NOBODY ELSE IS EVEN LOOKING AT IT.

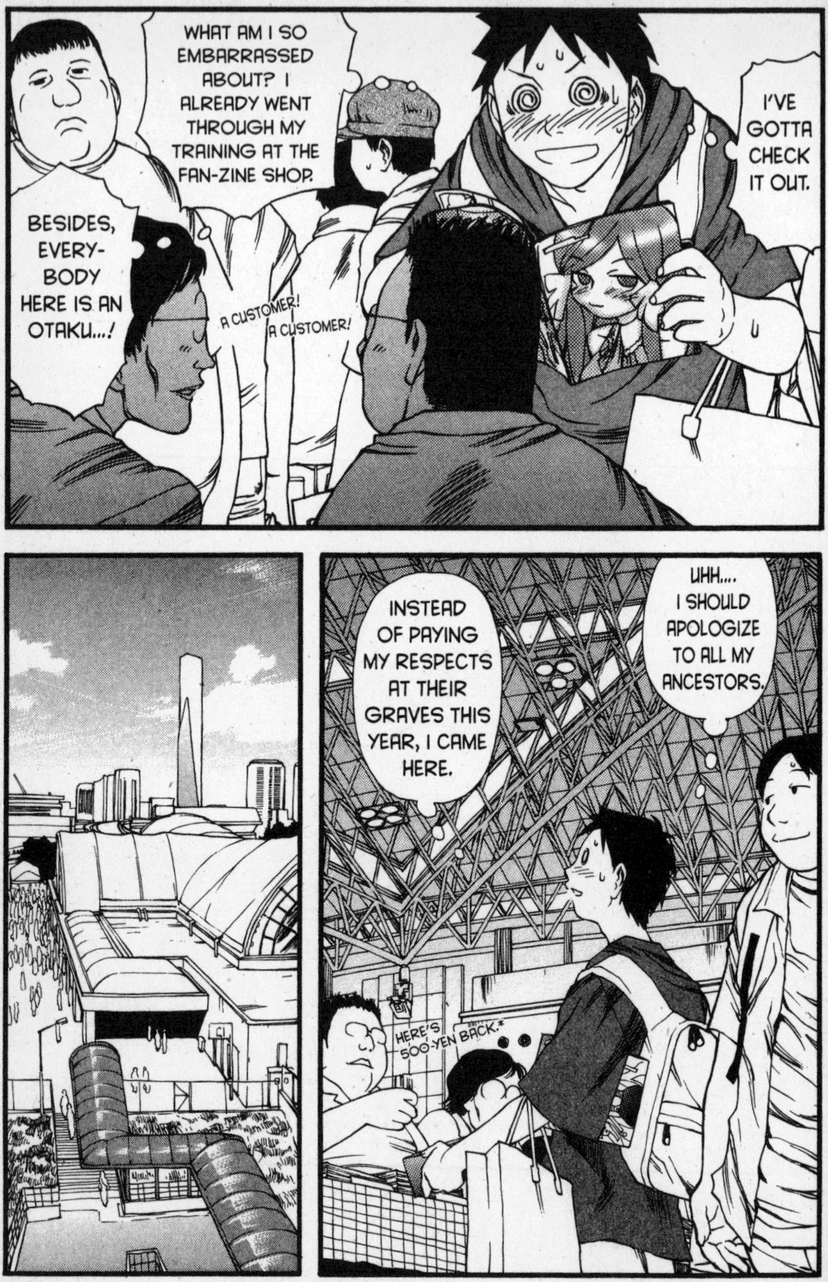
I'VE GOTTA CHECK IT OUT.
WHAT AM I SO EMBARRASSED ABOUT? I ALREADY WENT THROUGH MY TRAINING AT THE FAN-ZINE SHOP.
BESIDES, EVERYBODY HERE IS AN OTAKU...!
A CUSTOMER! A CUSTOMER!
UHH.... I SHOULD APOLOGIZE TO ALL MY ANCESTORS.
INSTEAD OF PAYING MY RESPECTS AT THEIR GRAVES THIS YEAR, I CAME HERE.
HERE'S 500-YEN BACK.*

*ABOUT $5.

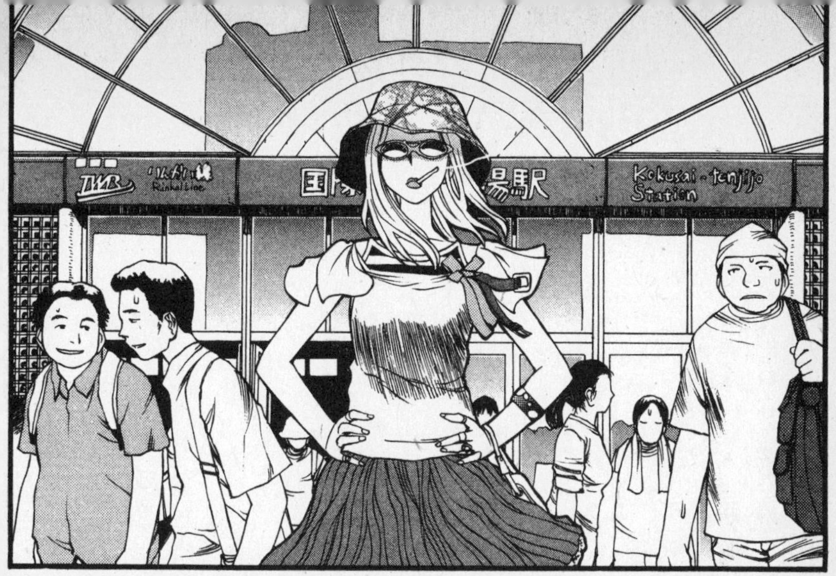
Rinkai Line
Kokusai - tenjijo Station

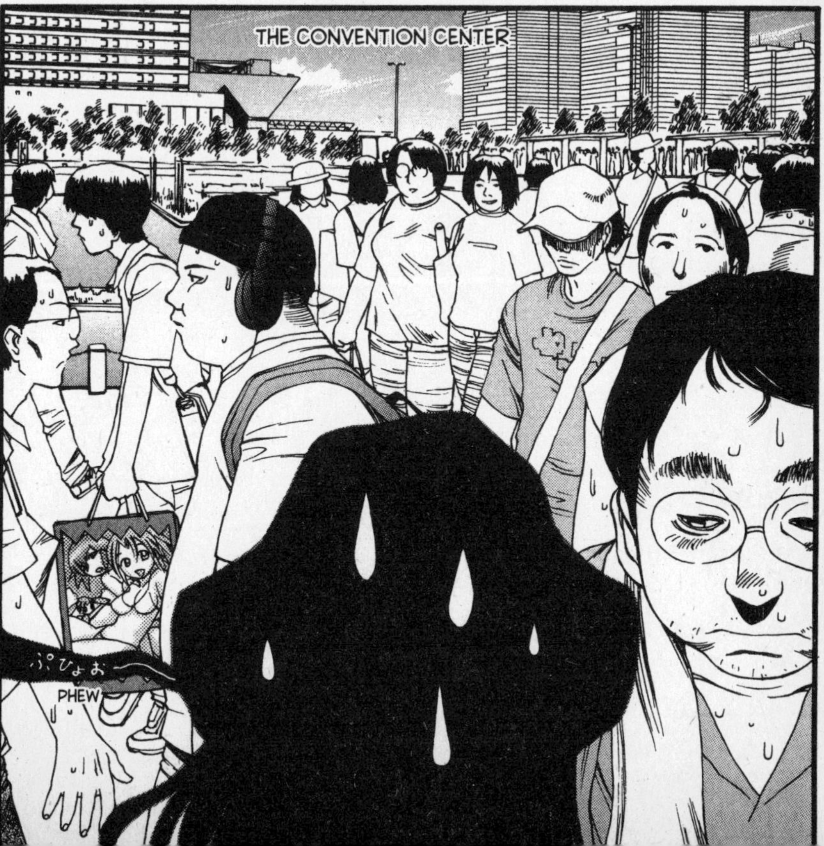
THE CONVENTION CENTER
ぷひょお〜
PHEW

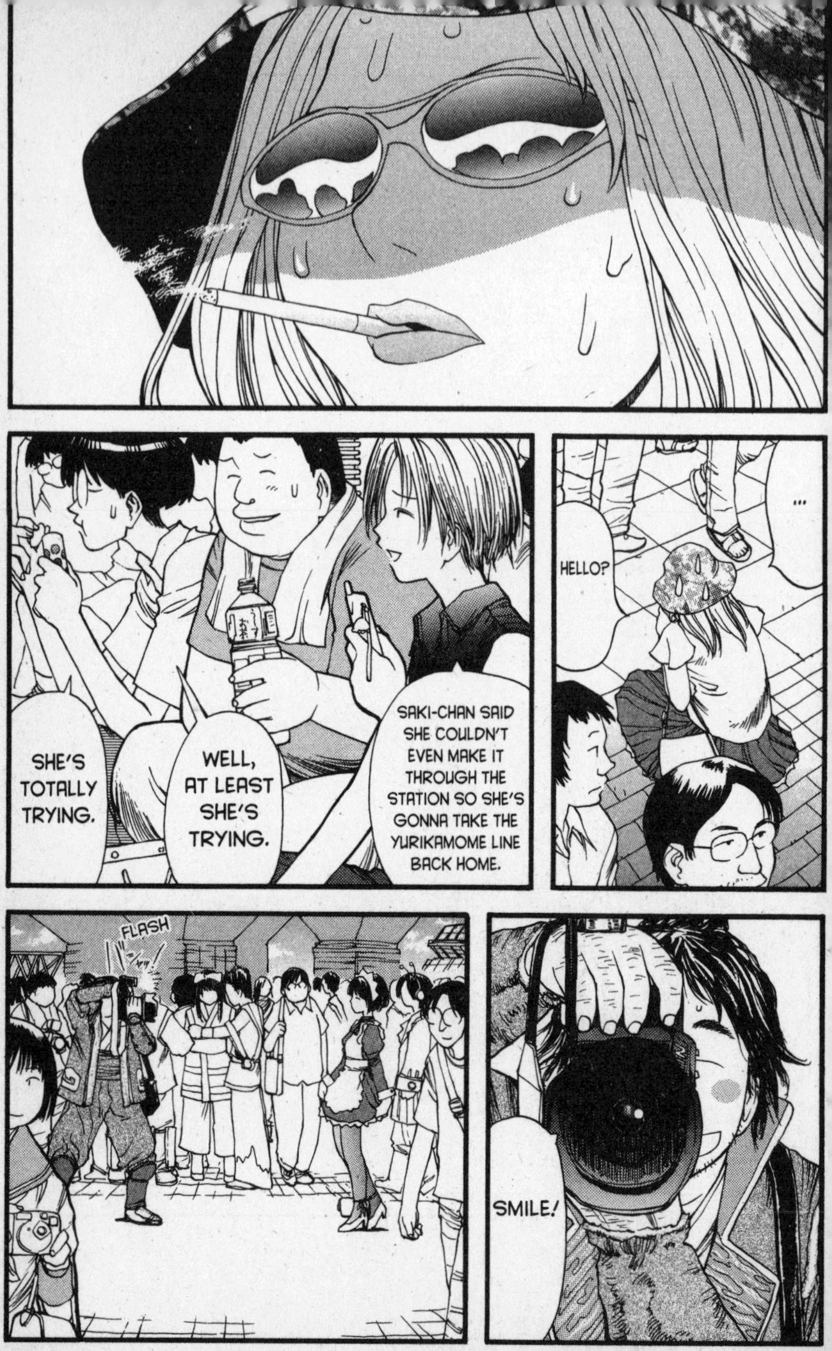
...
HELLO?
SAKI-CHAN SAID SHE COULDN'T EVEN MAKE IT THROUGH THE STATION SO SHE'S GONNA TAKE THE YURIKAMOME LINE BACK HOME.
WELL, AT LEAST SHE'S TRYING.
SHE'S TOTALLY TRYING.
SMILE!
FLASH

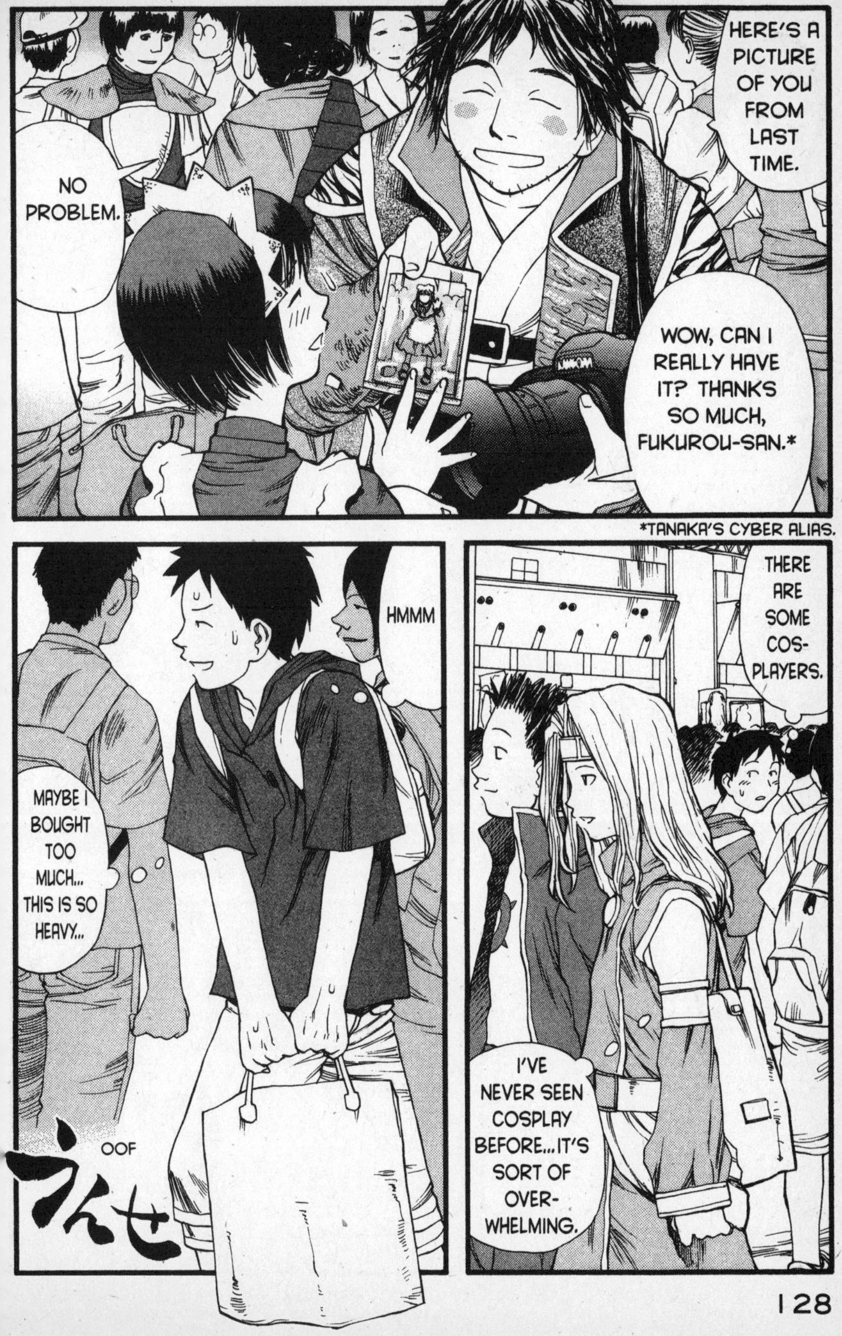
HERE'S A PICTURE OF YOU FROM LAST TIME.
WOW, CAN I REALLY HAVE IT? THANKS SO MUCH, FUKUROU-SAN.*
NO PROBLEM.
*TANAKA'S CYBER ALIAS.
THERE ARE SOME COS-PLAYERS.
I'VE NEVER SEEN COSPLAY BEFORE...IT'S SORT OF OVER-WHELMING.
HMMM
MAYBE I BOUGHT TOO MUCH... THIS IS SO HEAVY...
うんせ
OOF

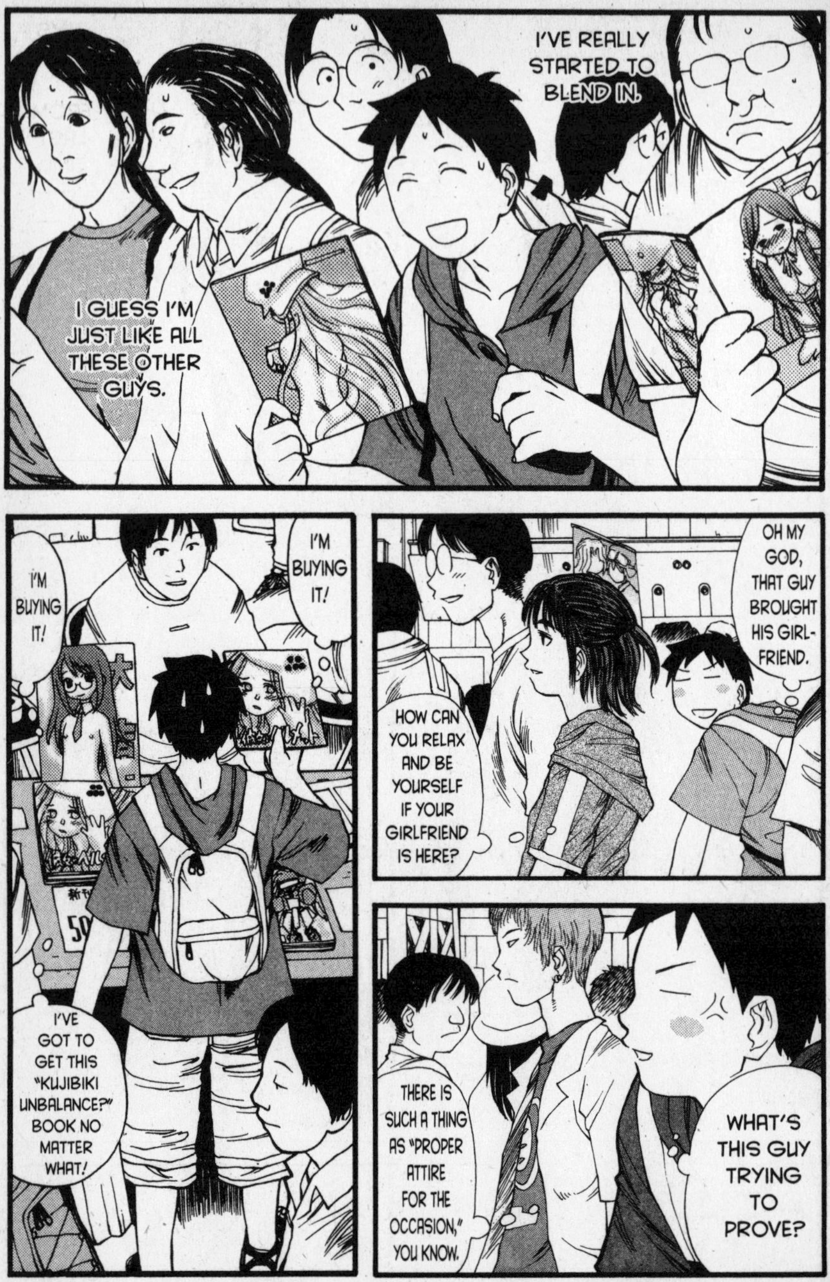

I'VE REALLY STARTED TO BLEND IN.
I GUESS I'M JUST LIKE ALL THESE OTHER GUYS.
OH MY GOD, THAT GUY BROUGHT HIS GIRL-FRIEND.
HOW CAN YOU RELAX AND BE YOURSELF IF YOUR GIRLFRIEND IS HERE?
WHAT'S THIS GUY TRYING TO PROVE?
THERE IS SUCH A THING AS "PROPER ATTIRE FOR THE OCCASION," YOU KNOW.
I'M BUYING IT!
I'M BUYING IT!
I'VE GOT TO GET THIS "KUJIBIKI UNBALANCE?" BOOK NO MATTER WHAT!

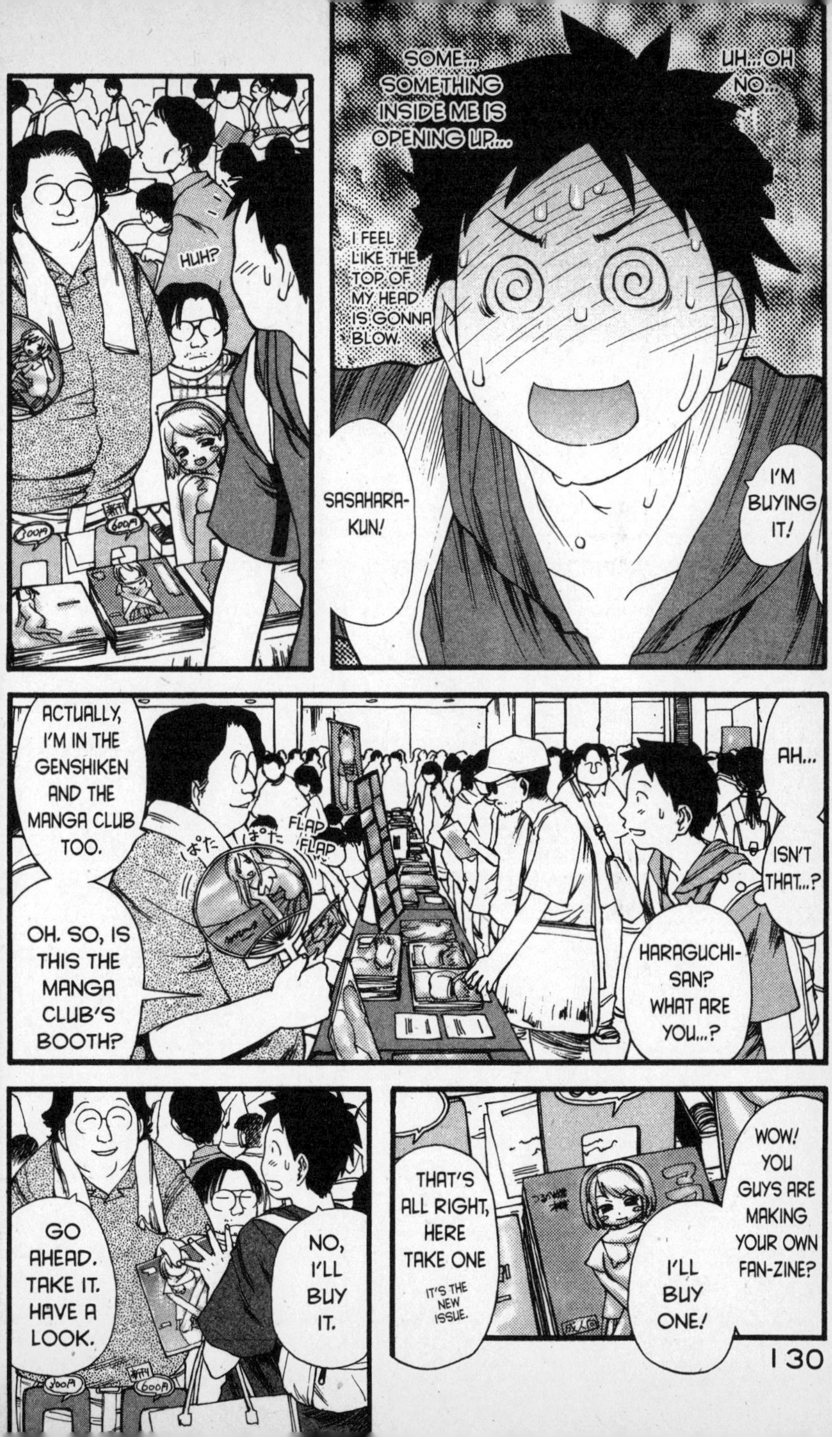
UH...OH NO...
SOME... SOMETHING INSIDE ME IS OPENING UP...
I FEEL LIKE THE TOP OF MY HEAD IS GONNA BLOW.
I'M BUYING IT!
SASAHARA-KUN!
HUH?
AH...
ISN'T THAT...?
HARAGUCHI-SAN? WHAT ARE YOU...?
ACTUALLY, I'M IN THE GENSHIKEN AND THE MANGA CLUB TOO.
FLAP FLAP
OH. SO, IS THIS THE MANGA CLUB'S BOOTH?
WOW! YOU GUYS ARE MAKING YOUR OWN FAN-ZINE?
I'LL BUY ONE!
THAT'S ALL RIGHT, HERE TAKE ONE
IT'S THE NEW ISSUE.
NO, I'LL BUY IT.
GO AHEAD. TAKE IT. HAVE A LOOK.

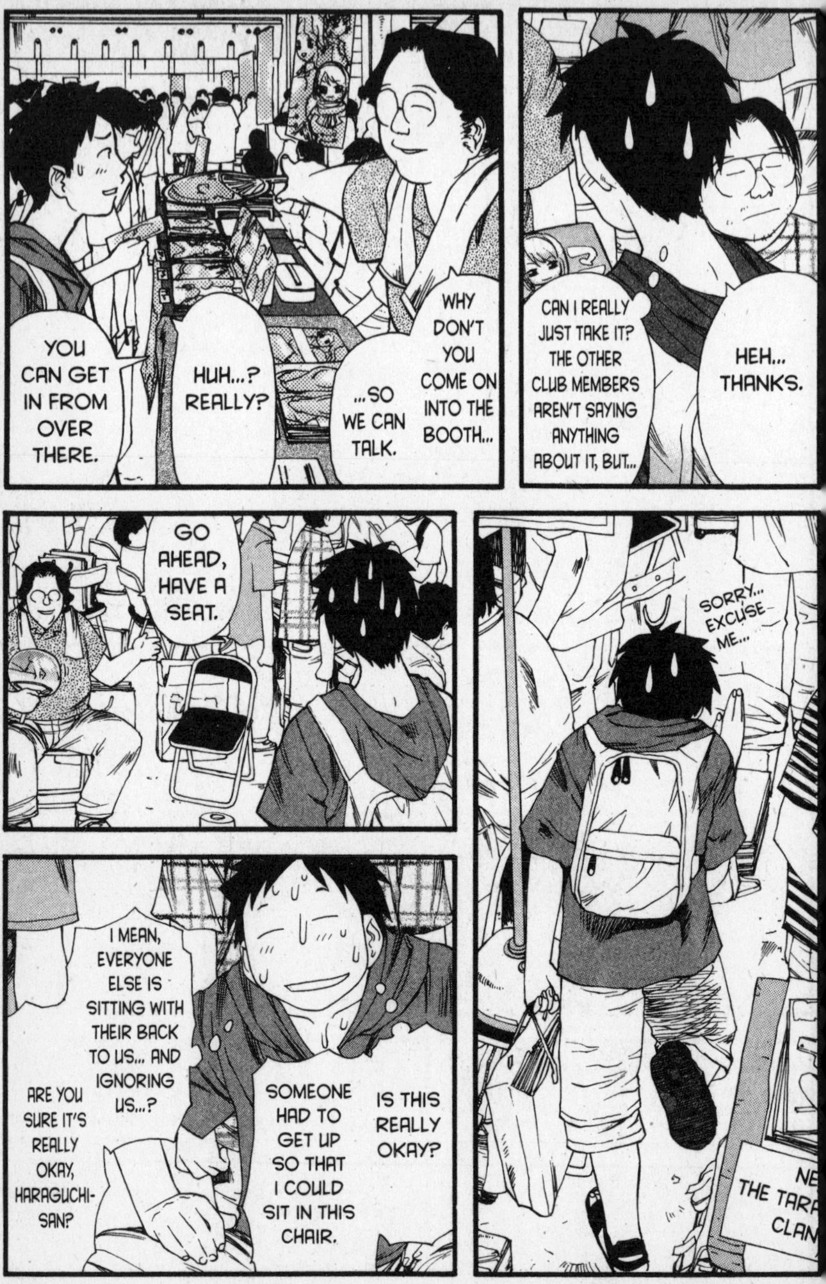
HEH... THANKS.
CAN I REALLY JUST TAKE IT? THE OTHER CLUB MEMBERS AREN'T SAYING ANYTHING ABOUT IT, BUT...
WHY DON'T YOU COME ON INTO THE BOOTH...
...SO WE CAN TALK.
HUH...? REALLY?
YOU CAN GET IN FROM OVER THERE.
SORRY... EXCUSE ME...
GO AHEAD, HAVE A SEAT.
IS THIS REALLY OKAY?
SOMEONE HAD TO GET UP SO THAT I COULD SIT IN THIS CHAIR.
I MEAN, EVERYONE ELSE IS SITTING WITH THEIR BACK TO US... AND IGNORING US...?
ARE YOU SURE IT'S REALLY OKAY, HARAGUCHI-SAN?

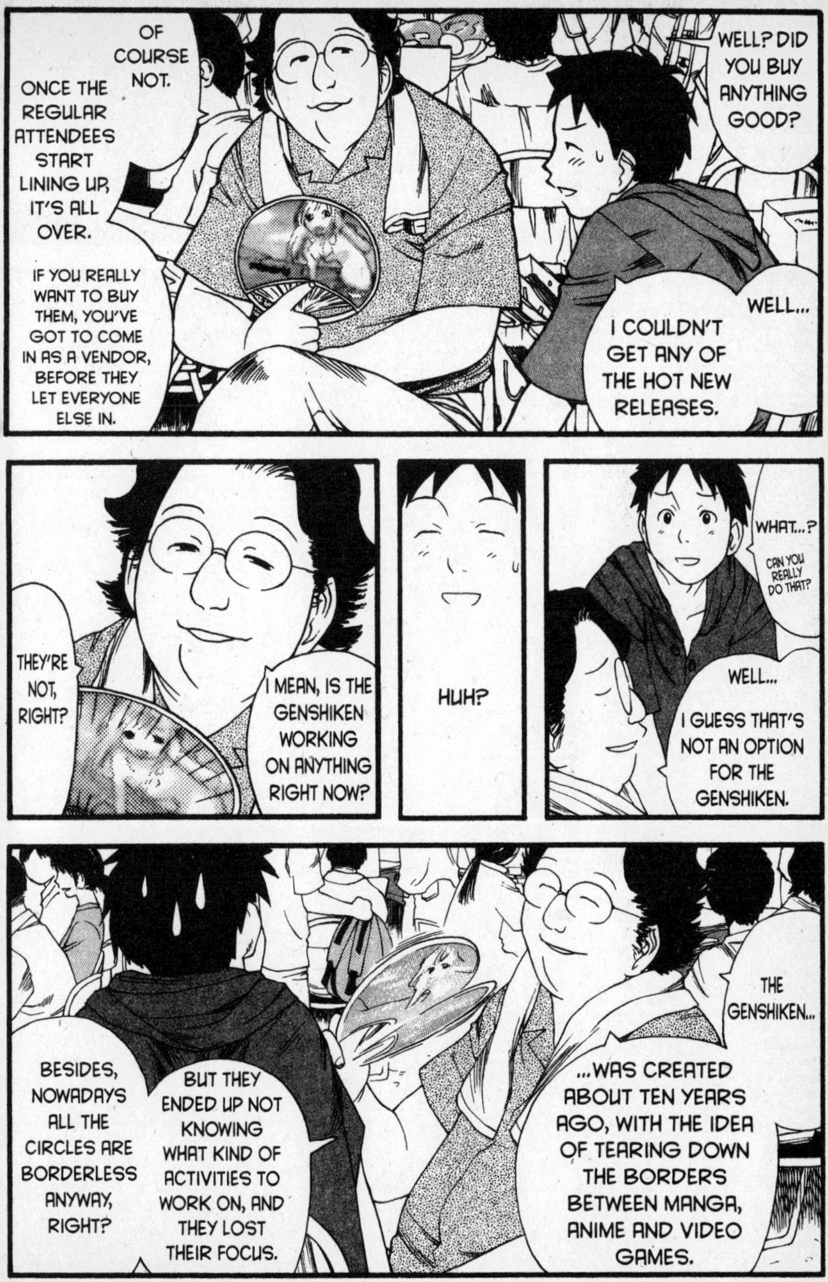
WELL? DID YOU BUY ANYTHING GOOD?
WELL...
I COULDN'T GET ANY OF THE HOT NEW RELEASES.
OF COURSE NOT.
ONCE THE REGULAR ATTENDEES START LINING UP, IT'S ALL OVER.
IF YOU REALLY WANT TO BUY THEM, YOU'VE GOT TO COME IN AS A VENDOR, BEFORE THEY LET EVERYONE ELSE IN.
WHAT...?
CAN YOU REALLY DO THAT?
WELL...
I GUESS THAT'S NOT AN OPTION FOR THE GENSHIKEN.
HUH?
I MEAN, IS THE GENSHIKEN WORKING ON ANYTHING RIGHT NOW?
THEY'RE NOT, RIGHT?
THE GENSHIKEN...
...WAS CREATED ABOUT TEN YEARS AGO, WITH THE IDEA OF TEARING DOWN THE BORDERS BETWEEN MANGA, ANIME AND VIDEO GAMES.
BUT THEY ENDED UP NOT KNOWING WHAT KIND OF ACTIVITIES TO WORK ON, AND THEY LOST THEIR FOCUS.
BESIDES, NOWADAYS ALL THE CIRCLES ARE BORDERLESS ANYWAY, RIGHT?

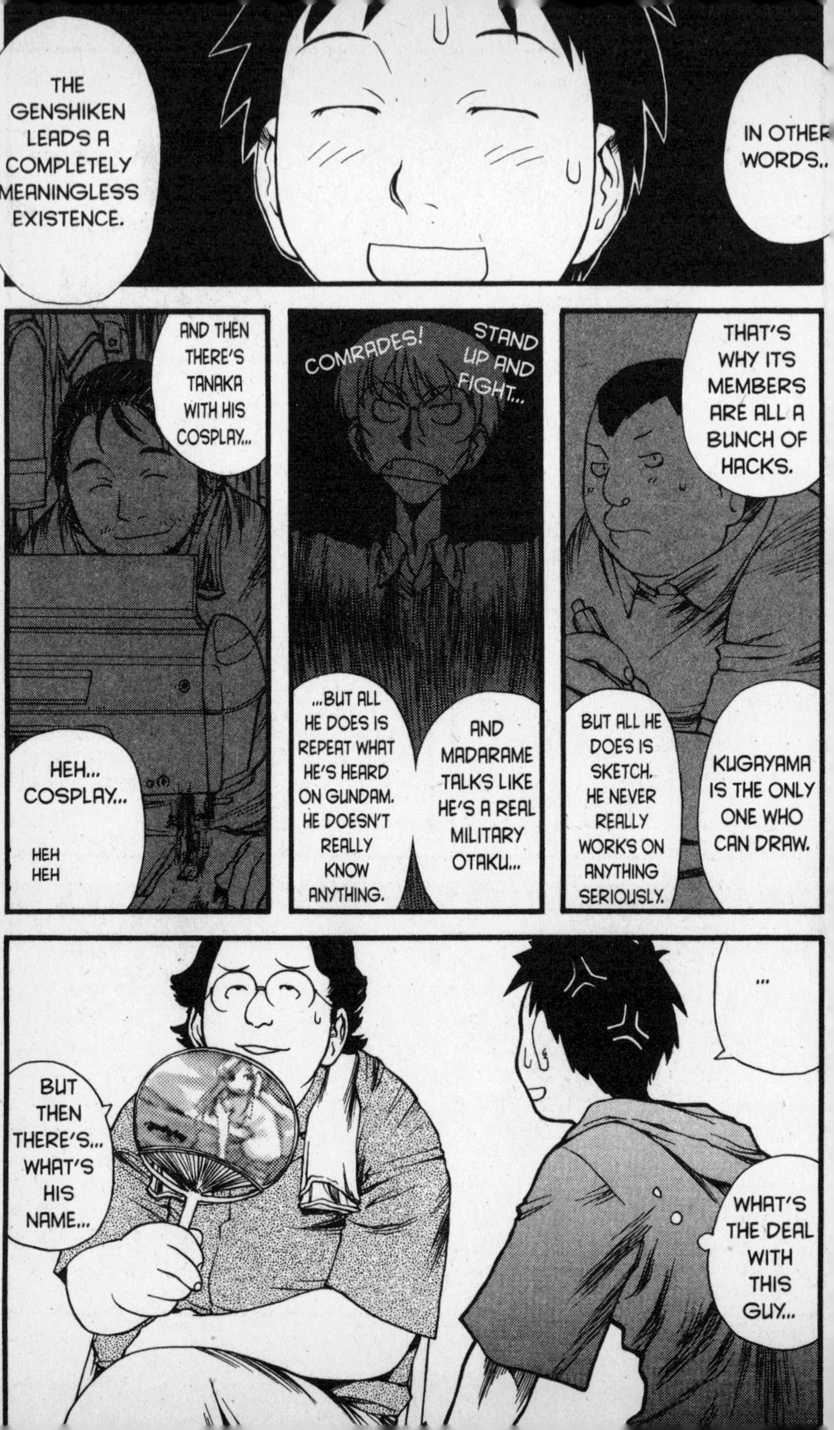
IN OTHER WORDS..
THE GENSHIKEN LEADS A COMPLETELY MEANINGLESS EXISTENCE.
THAT'S WHY ITS MEMBERS ARE ALL A BUNCH OF HACKS.
KUGAYAMA IS THE ONLY ONE WHO CAN DRAW.
BUT ALL HE DOES IS SKETCH. HE NEVER REALLY WORKS ON ANYTHING SERIOUSLY.
COMRADES!
STAND UP AND FIGHT...
AND MADARAME TALKS LIKE HE'S A REAL MILITARY OTAKU...
...BUT ALL HE DOES IS REPEAT WHAT HE'S HEARD ON GUNDAM. HE DOESN'T REALLY KNOW ANYTHING.
AND THEN THERE'S TANAKA WITH HIS COSPLAY...
HEH... COSPLAY...
HEH HEH
...
WHAT'S THE DEAL WITH THIS GUY...
BUT THEN THERE'S... WHAT'S HIS NAME...

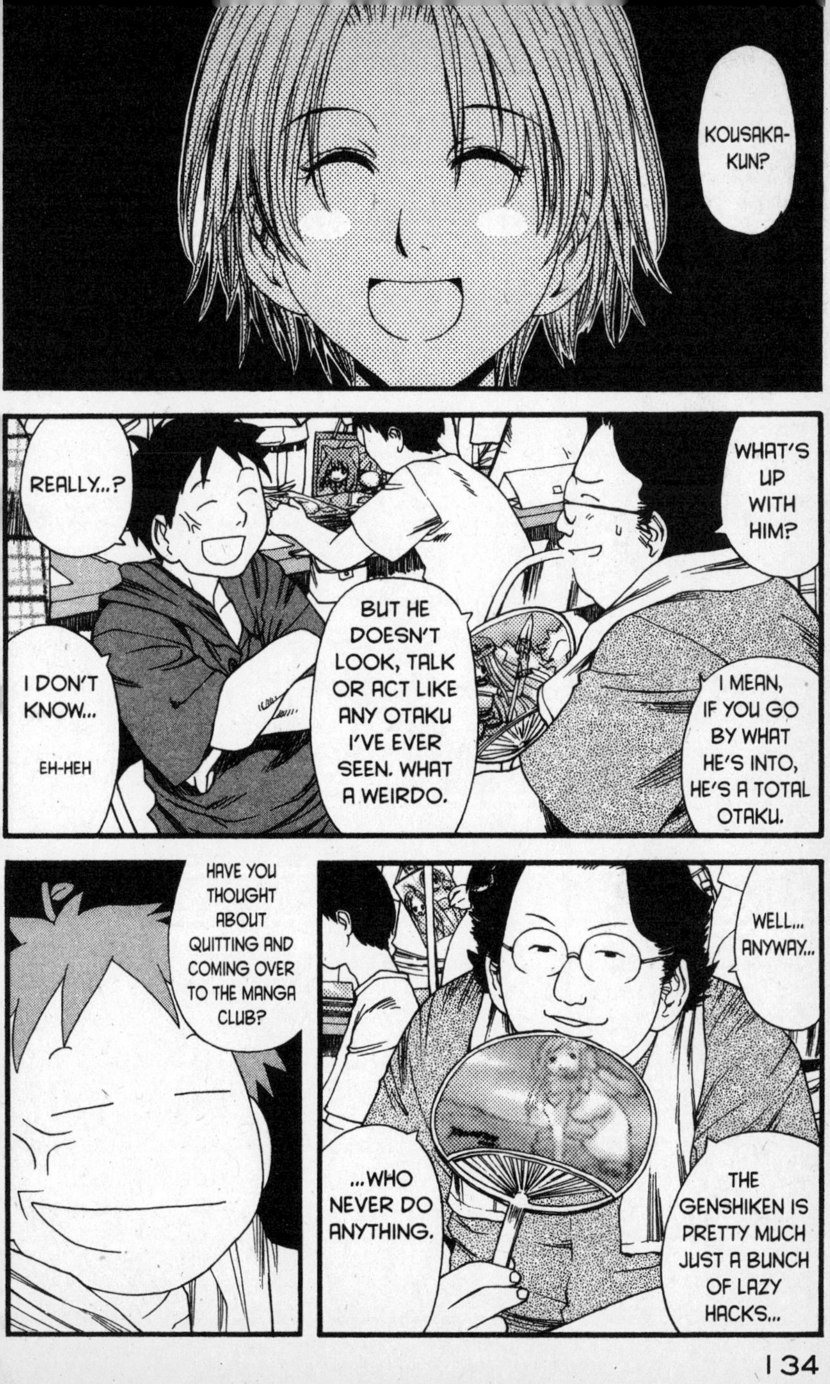
KOUSAKA-KUN?
WHAT'S UP WITH HIM?
REALLY...?
I MEAN, IF YOU GO BY WHAT HE'S INTO, HE'S A TOTAL OTAKU.
BUT HE DOESN'T LOOK, TALK OR ACT LIKE ANY OTAKU I'VE EVER SEEN. WHAT A WEIRDO.
I DON'T KNOW...
EH-HEH
WELL... ANYWAY...
THE GENSHIKEN IS PRETTY MUCH JUST A BUNCH OF LAZY HACKS...
...WHO NEVER DO ANYTHING.
HAVE YOU THOUGHT ABOUT QUITTING AND COMING OVER TO THE MANGA CLUB?

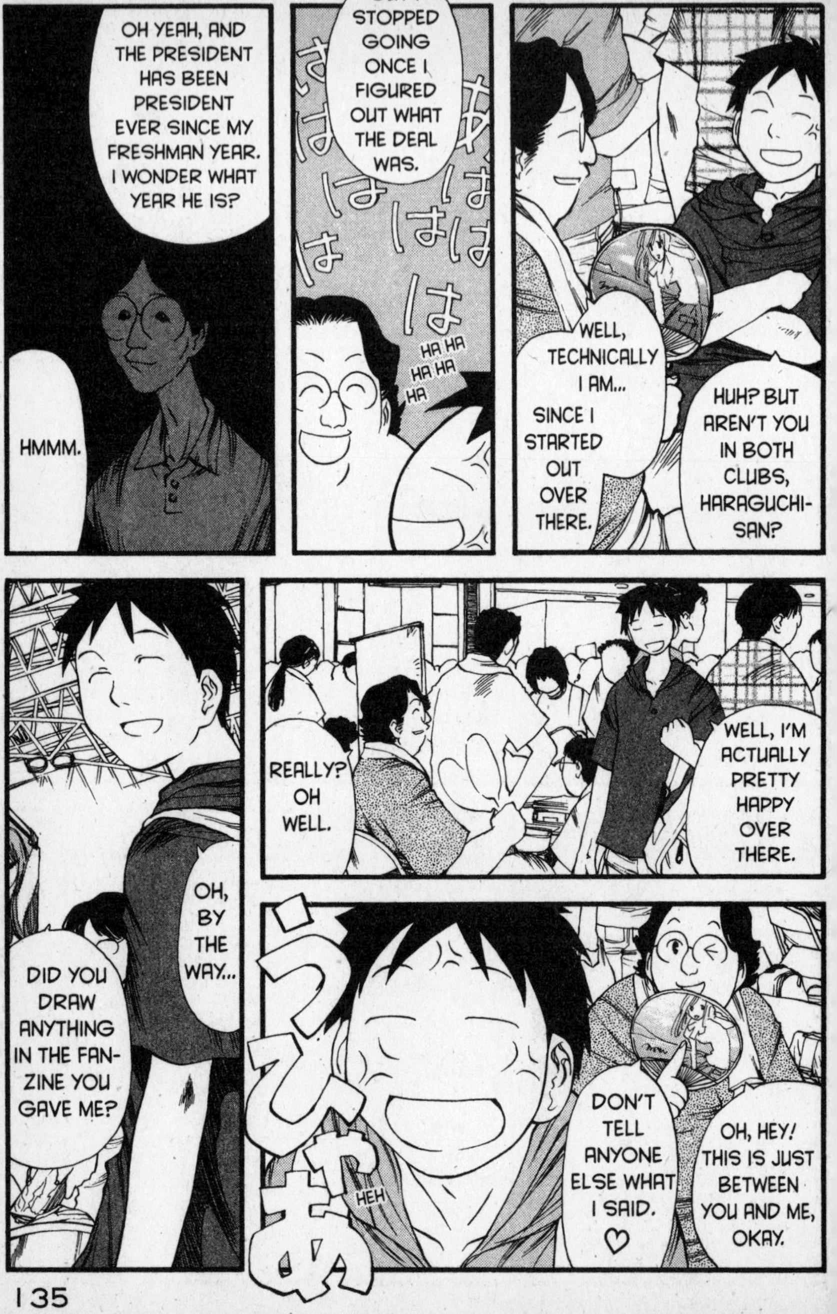
HUH? BUT AREN'T YOU IN BOTH CLUBS, HARAGUCHI-SAN?
WELL, TECHNICALLY I AM... SINCE I STARTED OUT OVER THERE.
BUT I STOPPED GOING ONCE I FIGURED OUT WHAT THE DEAL WAS.
あははははは
HA HA HA HA HA
OH YEAH, AND THE PRESIDENT HAS BEEN PRESIDENT EVER SINCE MY FRESHMAN YEAR. I WONDER WHAT YEAR HE IS?
HMMM.
WELL, I'M ACTUALLY PRETTY HAPPY OVER THERE.
REALLY? OH WELL.
OH, HEY! THIS IS JUST BETWEEN YOU AND ME, OKAY.
DON'T TELL ANYONE ELSE WHAT I SAID. ♡
うひゃあ
HEH
OH, BY THE WAY...
DID YOU DRAW ANYTHING IN THE FANZINE YOU GAVE ME?

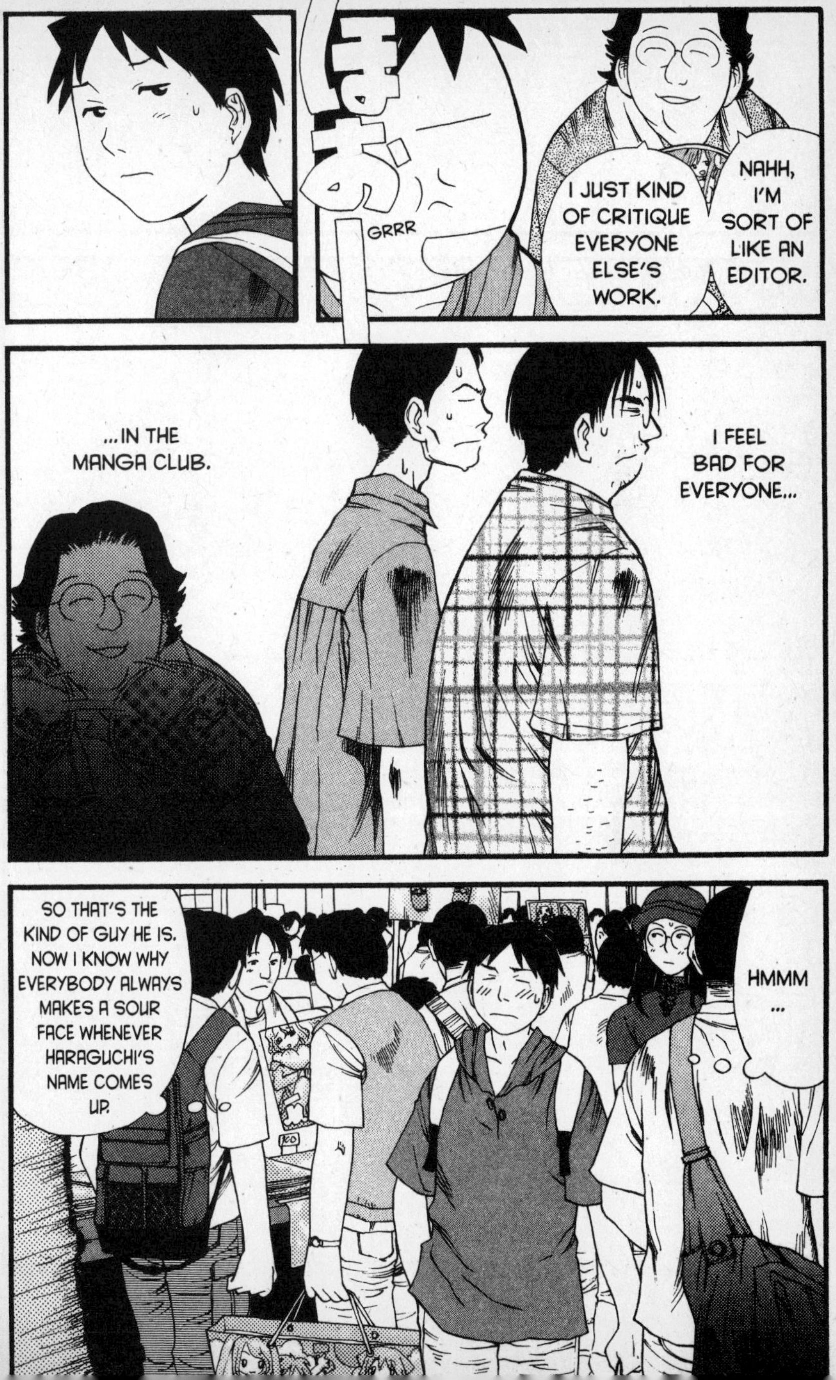
NAHH, I'M SORT OF LIKE AN EDITOR.
I JUST KIND OF CRITIQUE EVERYONE ELSE'S WORK.
GRRR
I FEEL BAD FOR EVERYONE...
...IN THE MANGA CLUB.
HMMM ...
SO THAT'S THE KIND OF GUY HE IS. NOW I KNOW WHY EVERYBODY ALWAYS MAKES A SOUR FACE WHENEVER HARAGUCHI'S NAME COMES UP.

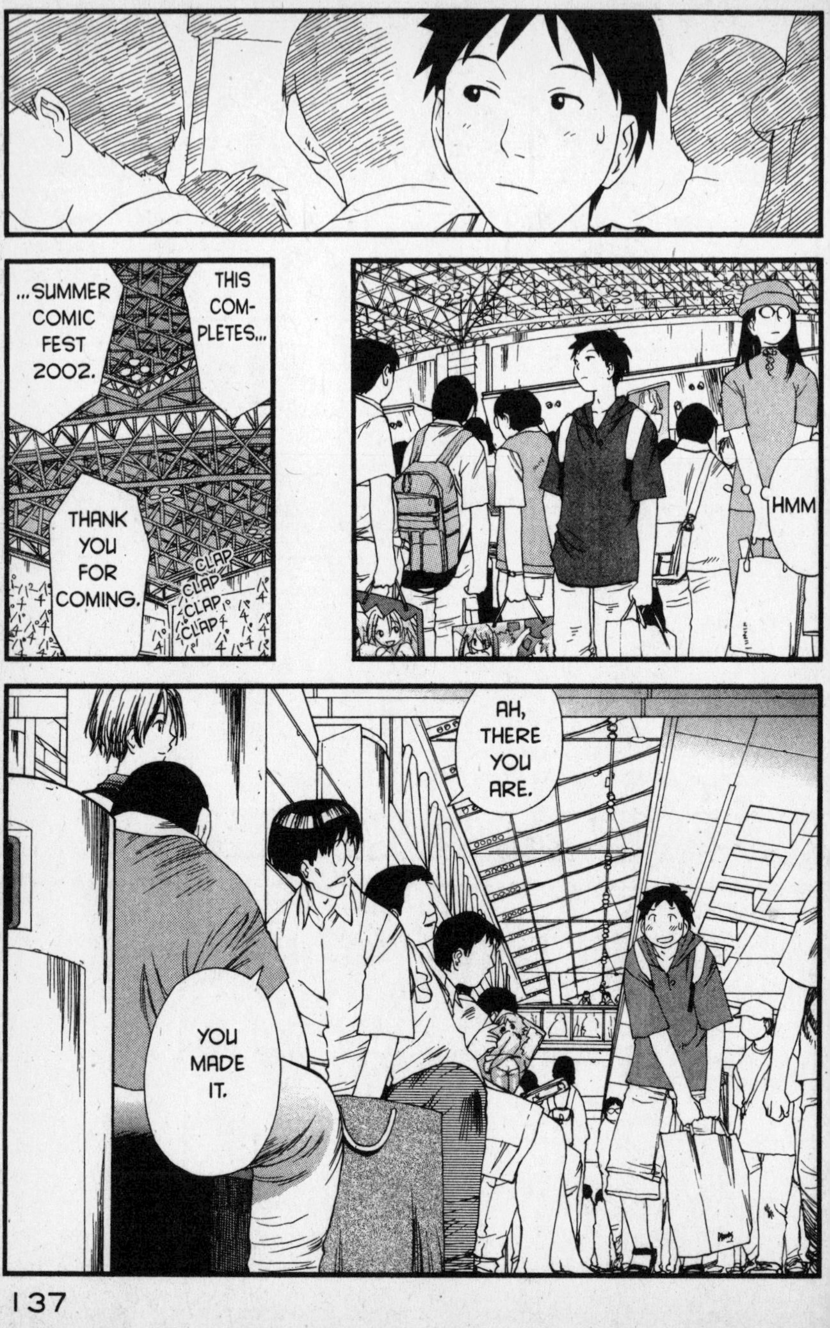
HMM
THIS COMPLETES...
...SUMMER COMIC FEST 2002.
THANK YOU FOR COMING.
CLAP CLAP CLAP CLAP
AH, THERE YOU ARE.
YOU MADE IT.

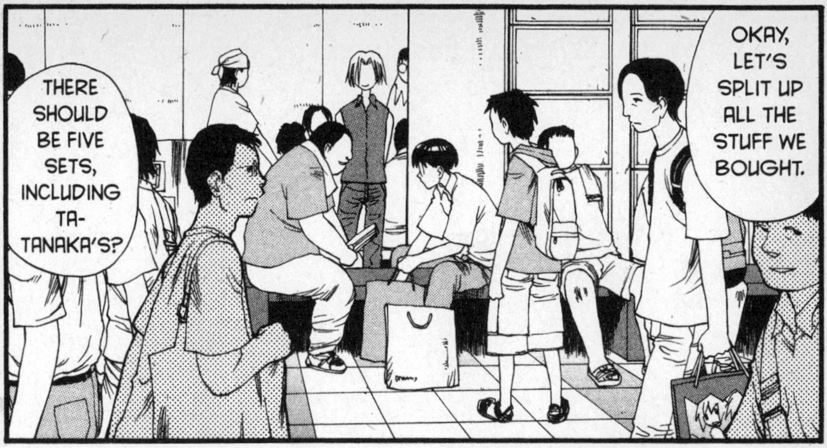
OKAY, LET'S SPLIT UP ALL THE STUFF WE BOUGHT.
THERE SHOULD BE FIVE SETS, INCLUDING TA-TANAKA'S?

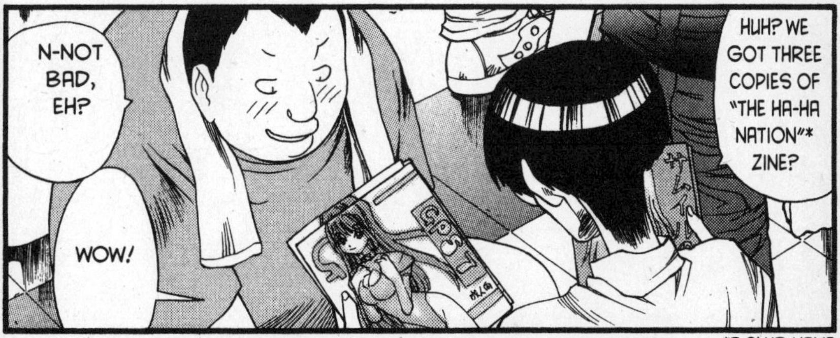
HUH? WE GOT THREE COPIES OF "THE HA-HA NATION"* ZINE?
N-NOT BAD, EH?
WOW!

*A CLUB NAME.

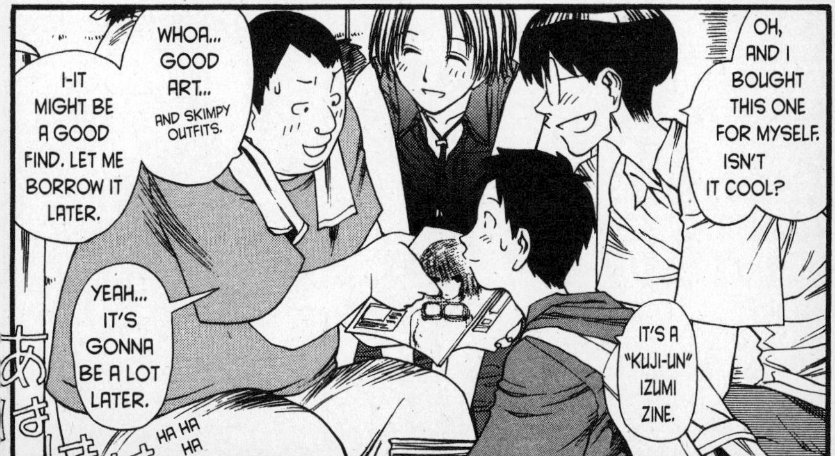
OH, AND I BOUGHT THIS ONE FOR MYSELF. ISN'T IT COOL?
IT'S A "KUJI-UN" IZUMI ZINE.
WHOA... GOOD ART... AND SKIMPY OUTFITS.
I-IT MIGHT BE A GOOD FIND. LET ME BORROW IT LATER.
YEAH... IT'S GONNA BE A LOT LATER.
HA HA HA
あははは

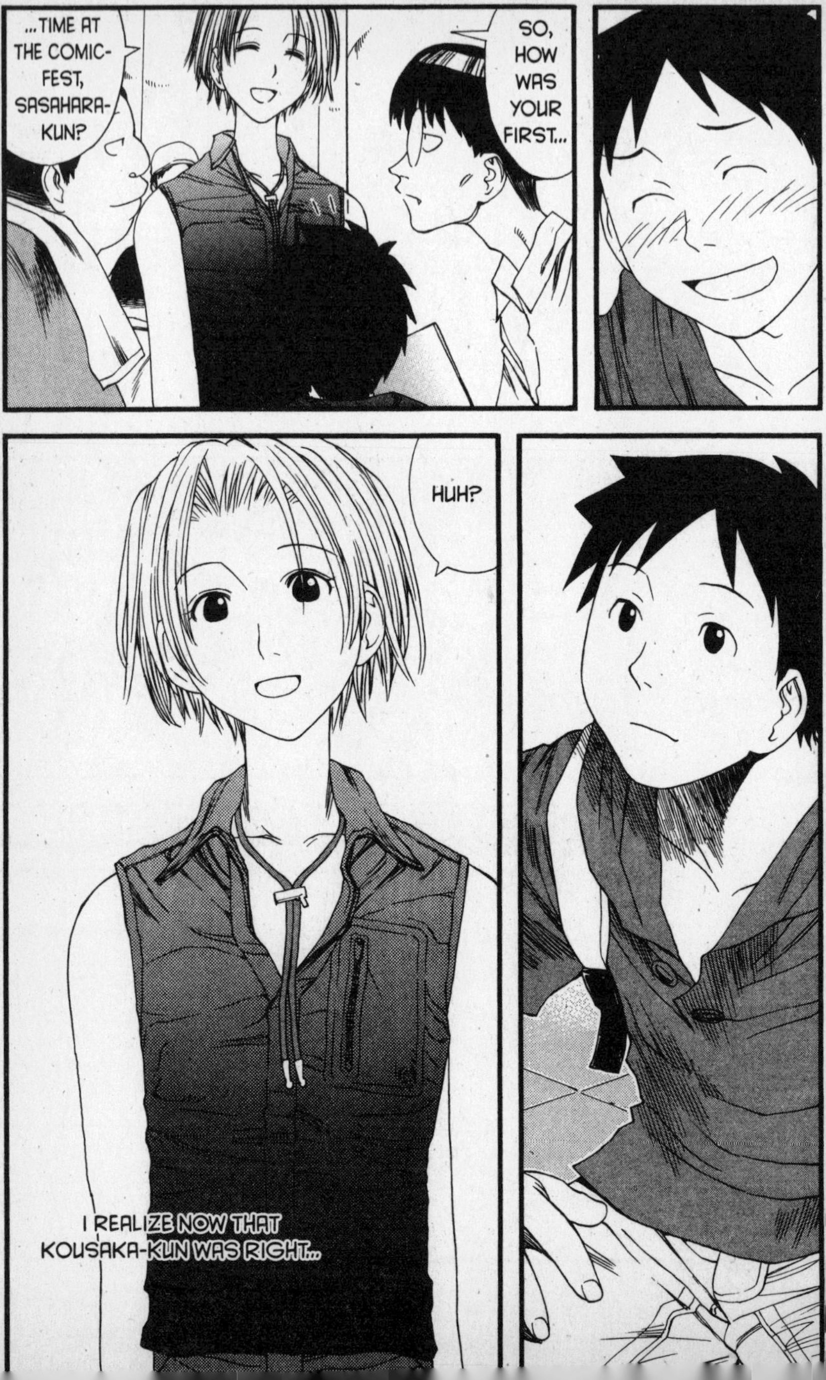
SO, HOW WAS YOUR FIRST...
...TIME AT THE COMIC-FEST, SASAHARA-KUN?
HUH?
I REALIZE NOW THAT KOUSAKA-KUN WAS RIGHT...

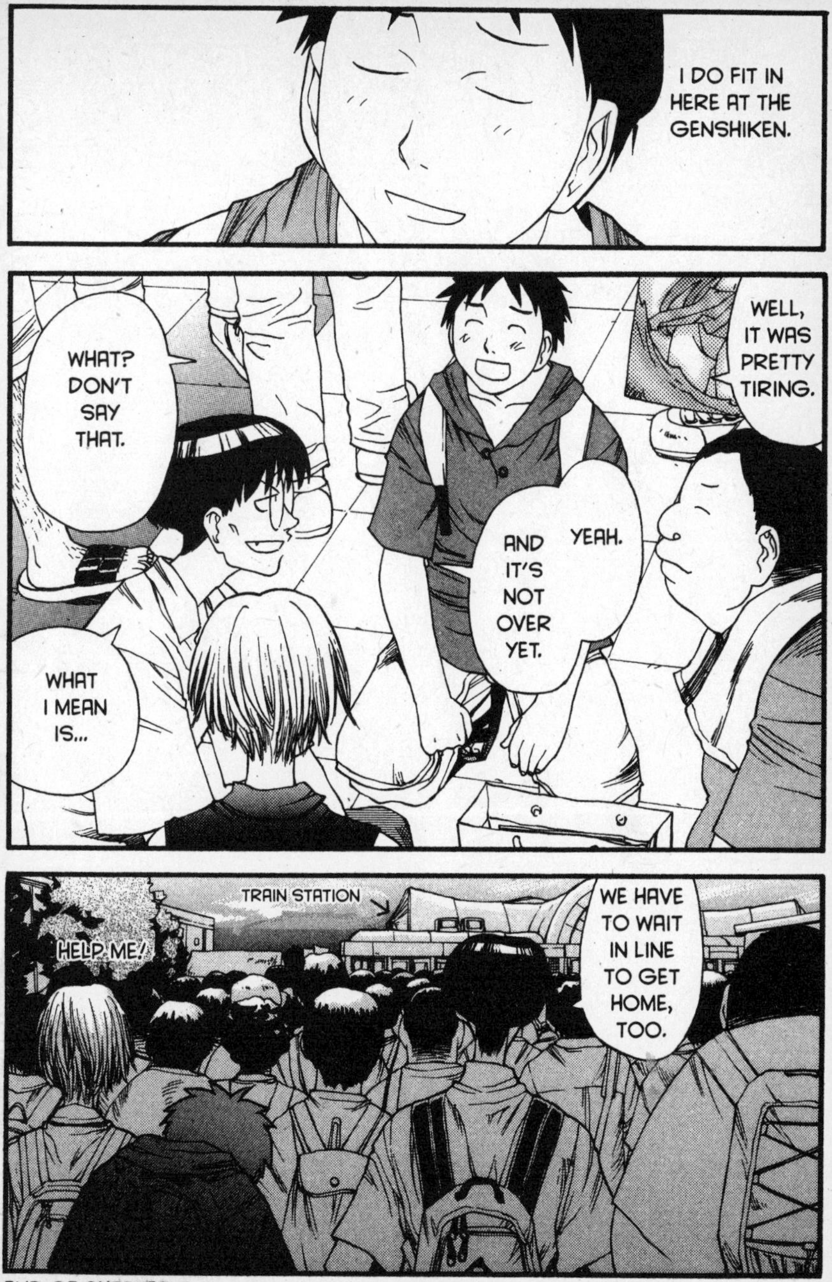
I DO FIT IN HERE AT THE GENSHIKEN.
WELL, IT WAS PRETTY TIRING.
YEAH.
AND IT'S NOT OVER YET.
WHAT? DON'T SAY THAT.
WHAT I MEAN IS...
WE HAVE TO WAIT IN LINE TO GET HOME, TOO.
TRAIN STATION
HELP ME!

END OF CHAPTER 5

KASUKABE SAKI

PROFILE

SAKI KASUKABE

BIRTHDAY JULY 19TH
BLOOD TYPE AB

FAVORITE MANGA
"LET'S GO" RAI
JUNIOR HIGH
ROYALTY IN MOTION

FAVORITE ANIME
NONE

FAVORITE GAME
"LIFE" (THE BOARD GAME)

FAVORITE FIGHT GAME CHARACTER
WHY ARE YOU ASKING ME THAT?

*THESE ARE THE CHARACTER'S CHOICES AND DO NOT NECESSARILY REFLECT THE AUTHOR'S TASTES.

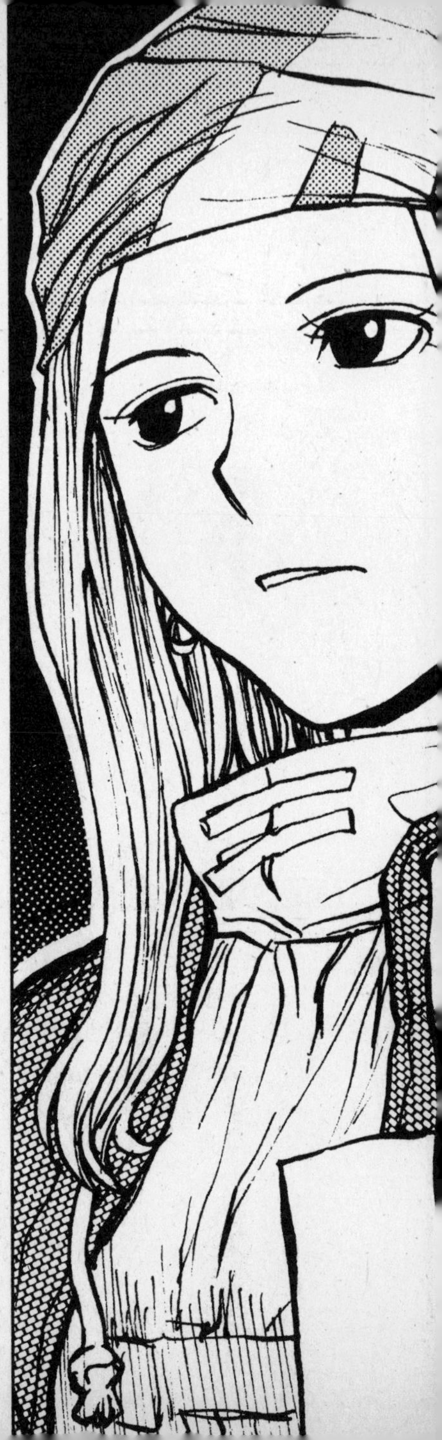

THEN AGAIN...

MADARAME-SAN.
YEAH?
WILL THE GEN-SHIKEN...
...EVER MAKE A FAN-ZINE?
HMMM
MUST BE A TABOO TOPIC.

DIFFERENT STROKES

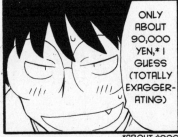

SO, HOW MUCH DID YOU SPEND AT THE COMIC-WHATEVER YOU CALL IT?
OH, NOT THAT MUCH...
ONLY ABOUT 90,000 YEN,* I GUESS (TOTALLY EXAGGER-ATING)
HMM... YEAH, I GUESS THAT SOUNDS ABOUT RIGHT.
...
SHE SPENDS HUNDREDS OF THOUSANDS OF YEN WHEN SHE SHOPS.

*ABOUT $900

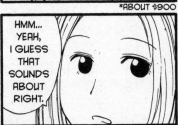

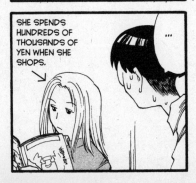

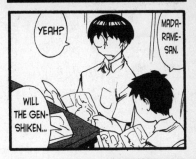

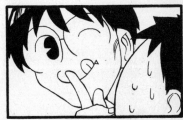

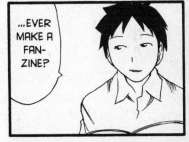

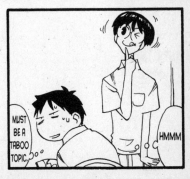

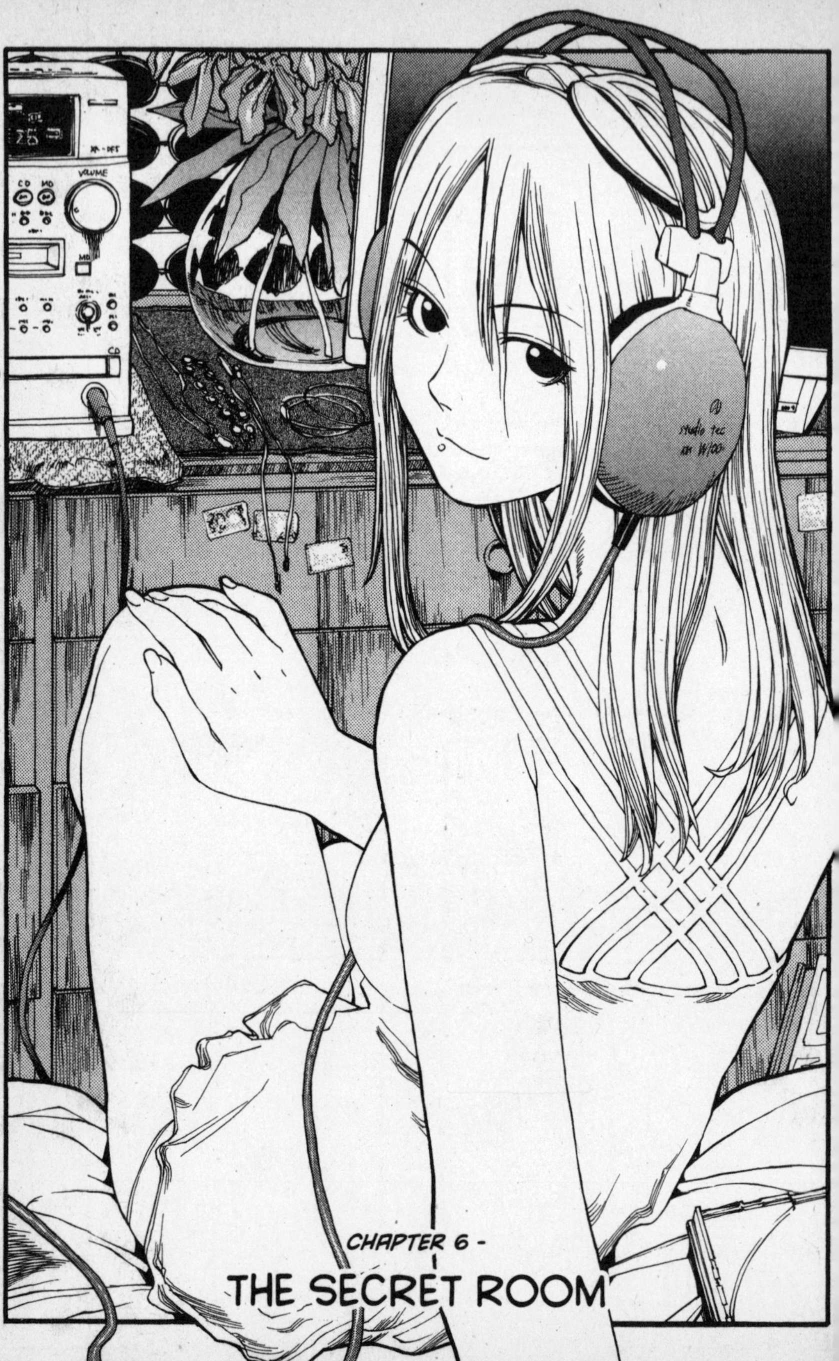
CHAPTER 6 -
THE SECRET ROOM

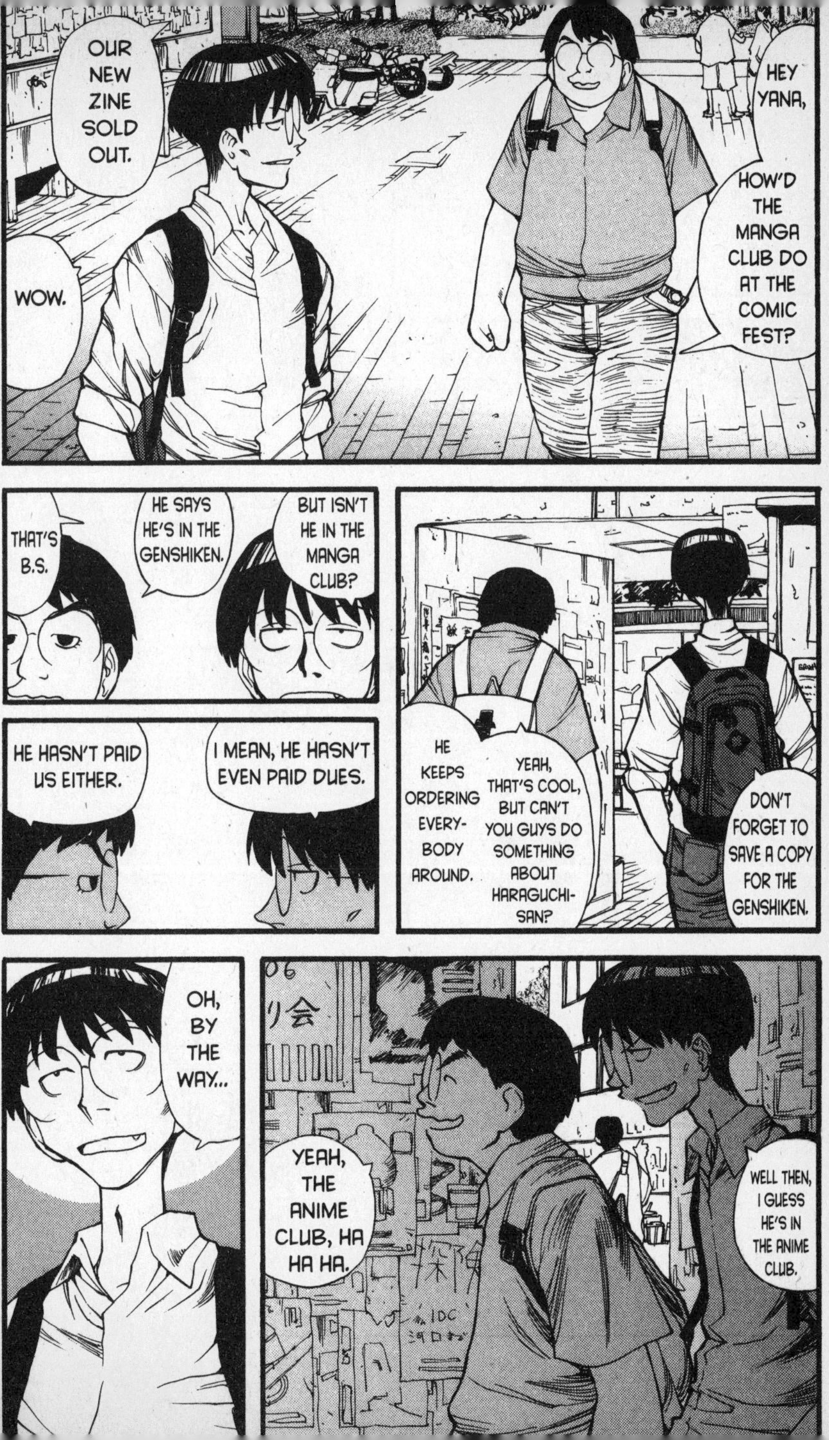
HEY YANA, HOW'D THE MANGA CLUB DO AT THE COMIC FEST?
OUR NEW ZINE SOLD OUT.
WOW.
DON'T FORGET TO SAVE A COPY FOR THE GENSHIKEN.
YEAH, THAT'S COOL, BUT CAN'T YOU GUYS DO SOMETHING ABOUT HARAGUCHI-SAN?
HE KEEPS ORDERING EVERY-BODY AROUND.
BUT ISN'T HE IN THE MANGA CLUB?
HE SAYS HE'S IN THE GENSHIKEN.
THAT'S B.S.
I MEAN, HE HASN'T EVEN PAID DUES.
HE HASN'T PAID US EITHER.
WELL THEN, I GUESS HE'S IN THE ANIME CLUB.
YEAH, THE ANIME CLUB, HA HA HA.
OH, BY THE WAY...

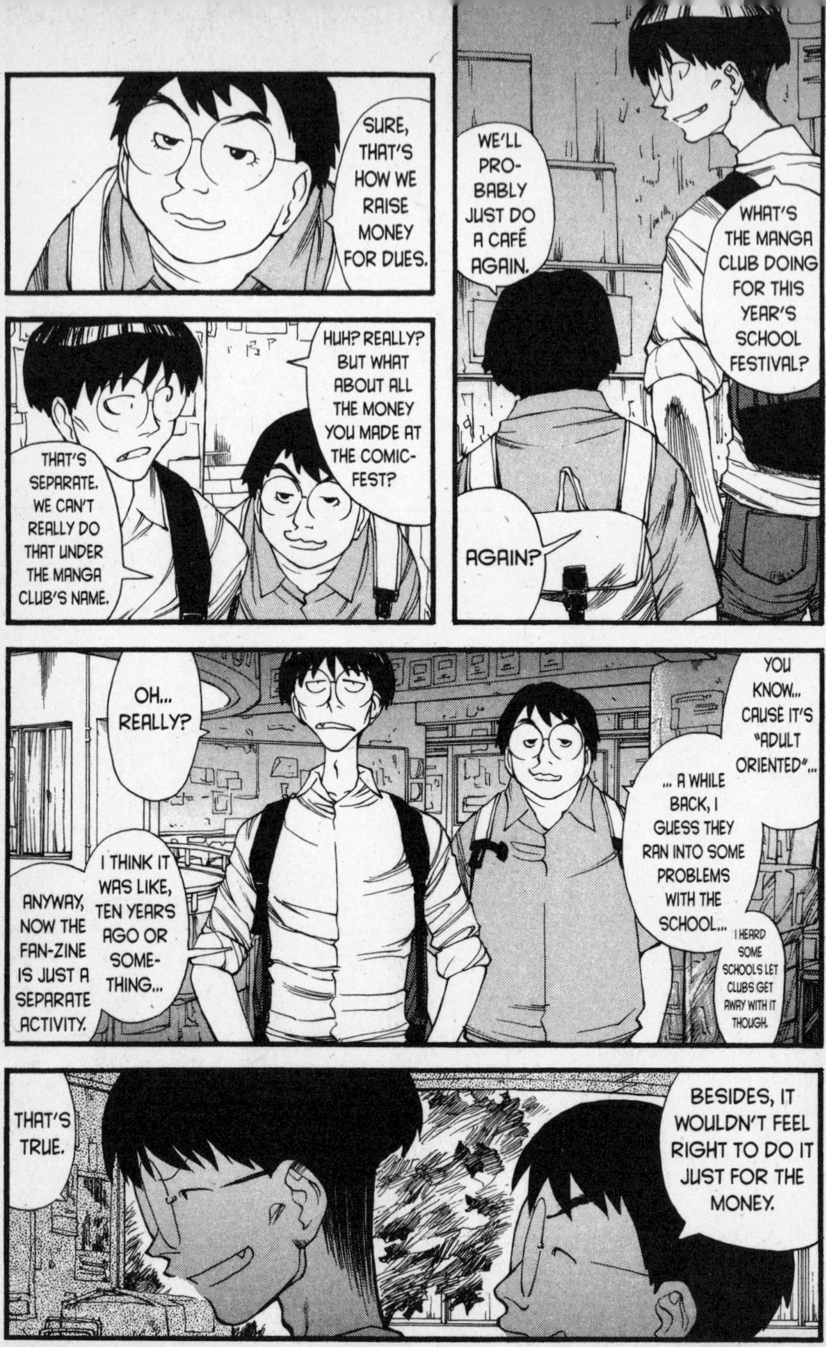
WHAT'S THE MANGA CLUB DOING FOR THIS YEAR'S SCHOOL FESTIVAL?
WE'LL PRO-BABLY JUST DO A CAFÉ AGAIN.
AGAIN?
SURE, THAT'S HOW WE RAISE MONEY FOR DUES.
HUH? REALLY? BUT WHAT ABOUT ALL THE MONEY YOU MADE AT THE COMIC-FEST?
THAT'S SEPARATE. WE CAN'T REALLY DO THAT UNDER THE MANGA CLUB'S NAME.
YOU KNOW... CAUSE IT'S "ADULT ORIENTED"...
... A WHILE BACK, I GUESS THEY RAN INTO SOME PROBLEMS WITH THE SCHOOL...
I HEARD SOME SCHOOLS LET CLUBS GET AWAY WITH IT THOUGH.
OH... REALLY?
I THINK IT WAS LIKE, TEN YEARS AGO OR SOME-THING...
ANYWAY, NOW THE FAN-ZINE IS JUST A SEPARATE ACTIVITY.
BESIDES, IT WOULDN'T FEEL RIGHT TO DO IT JUST FOR THE MONEY.
THAT'S TRUE.

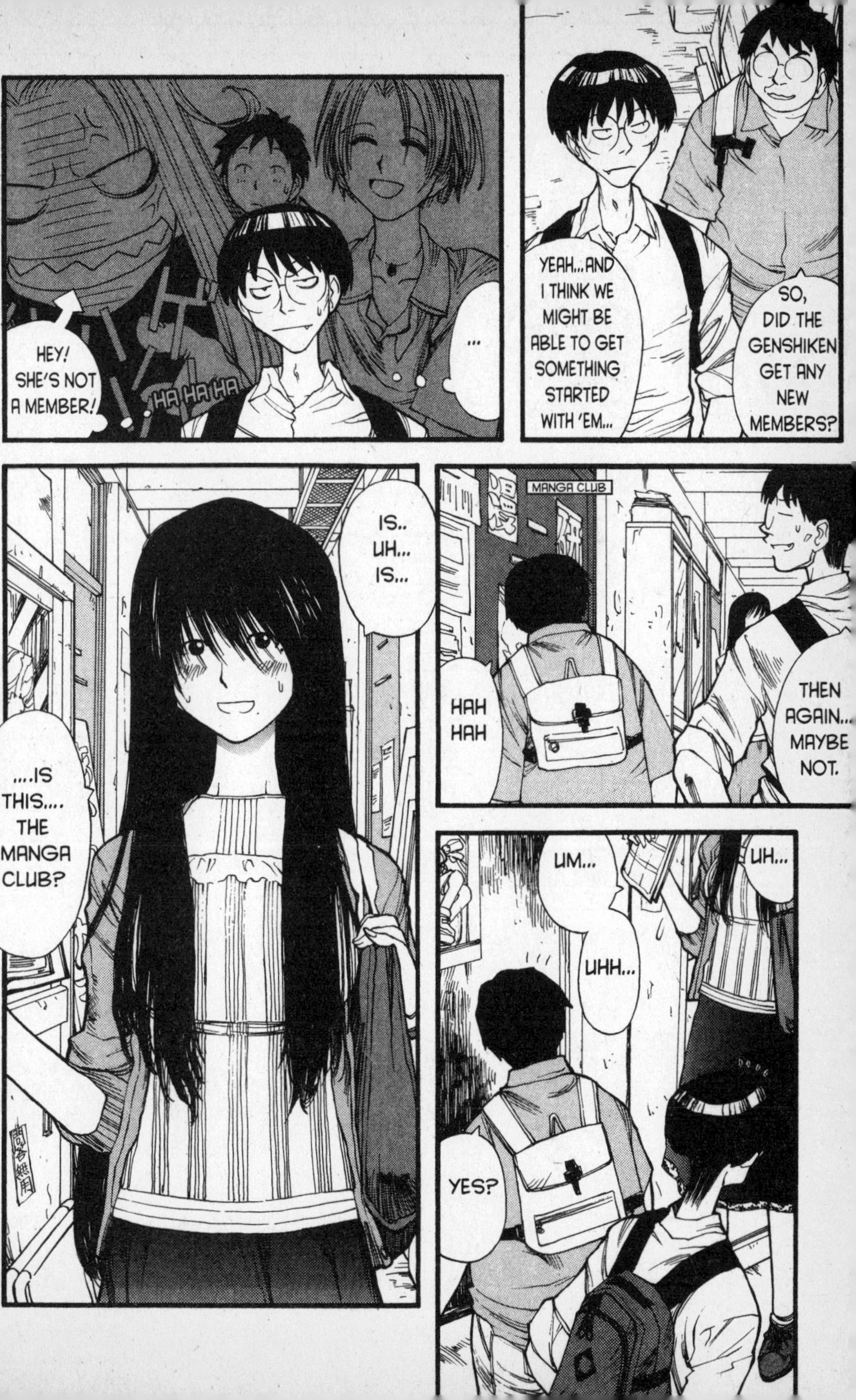
SO, DID THE GENSHIKEN GET ANY NEW MEMBERS?
YEAH...AND I THINK WE MIGHT BE ABLE TO GET SOMETHING STARTED WITH 'EM...
...
HEY! SHE'S NOT A MEMBER!
HA HA HA
MANGA CLUB
THEN AGAIN... MAYBE NOT.
HAH HAH
UH...
UM...
UHH...
YES?
IS.. UH... IS...
....IS THIS.... THE MANGA CLUB?
問答無用

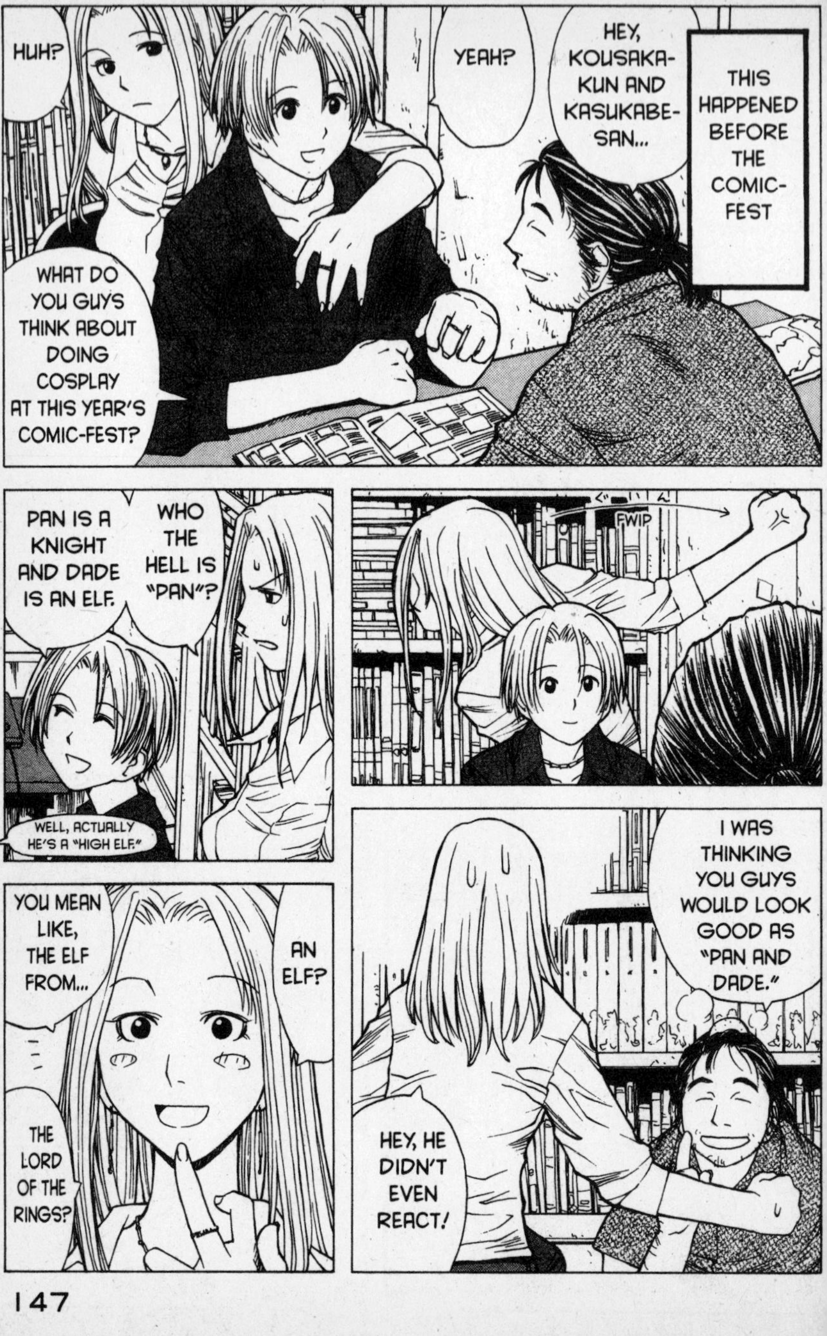
THIS HAPPENED BEFORE THE COMIC-FEST
HEY, KOUSAKA-KUN AND KASUKABE-SAN...
YEAH?
HUH?
WHAT DO YOU GUYS THINK ABOUT DOING COSPLAY AT THIS YEAR'S COMIC-FEST?
FWIP
WHO THE HELL IS "PAN"?
PAN IS A KNIGHT AND DADE IS AN ELF.
WELL, ACTUALLY HE'S A "HIGH ELF."
I WAS THINKING YOU GUYS WOULD LOOK GOOD AS "PAN AND DADE."
HEY, HE DIDN'T EVEN REACT!
AN ELF?
YOU MEAN LIKE, THE ELF FROM...
THE LORD OF THE RINGS?

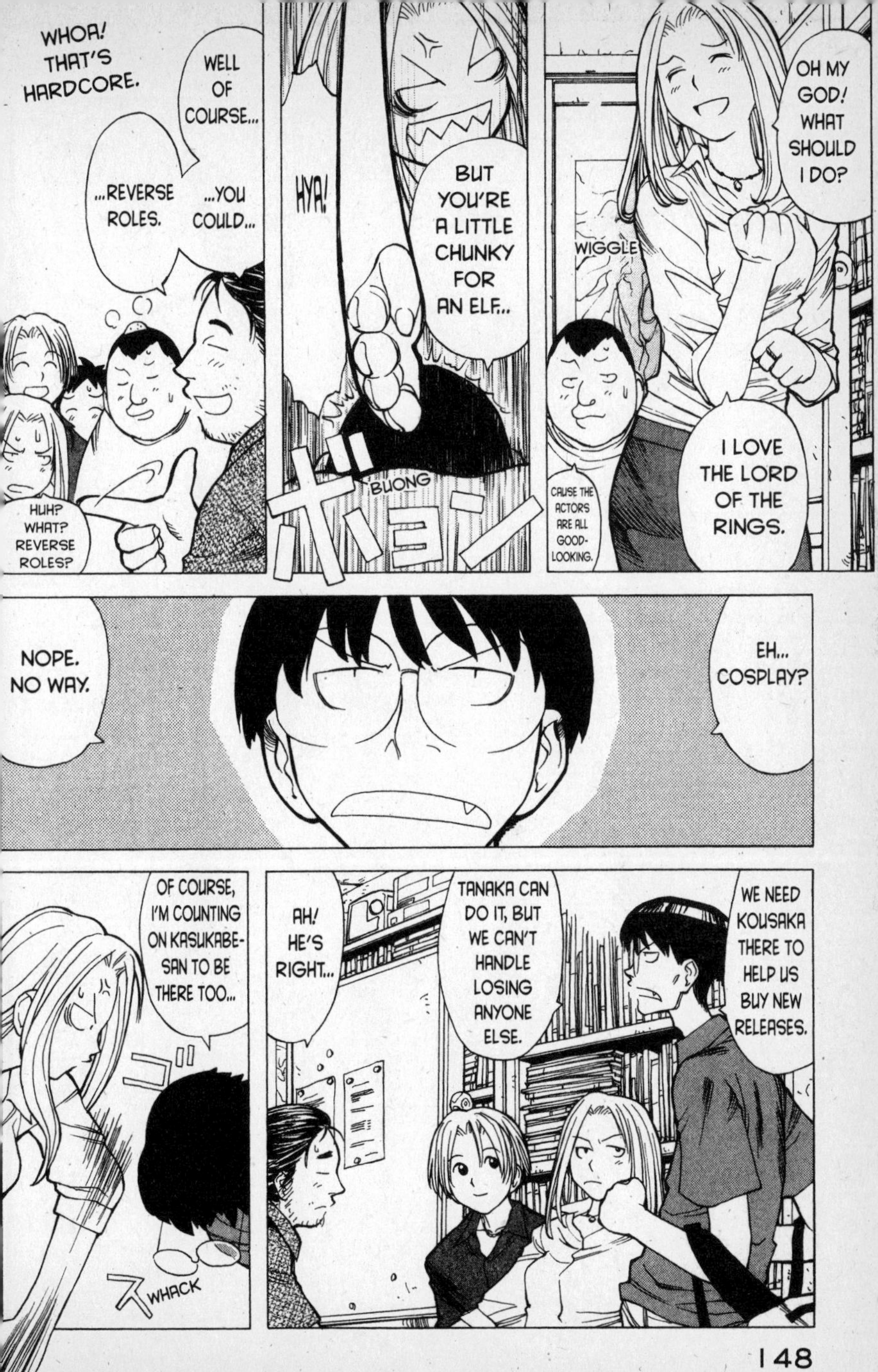
OH MY GOD! WHAT SHOULD I DO?
WIGGLE
I LOVE THE LORD OF THE RINGS.
CAUSE THE ACTORS ARE ALL GOOD-LOOKING.
HYA!
BUT YOU'RE A LITTLE CHUNKY FOR AN ELF...
BUONG
WELL OF COURSE...
WHOA! THAT'S HARDCORE.
...YOU COULD...
...REVERSE ROLES.
HUH? WHAT? REVERSE ROLES?
EH... COSPLAY?
NOPE. NO WAY.
WE NEED KOUSAKA THERE TO HELP US BUY NEW RELEASES.
TANAKA CAN DO IT, BUT WE CAN'T HANDLE LOSING ANYONE ELSE.
AH! HE'S RIGHT...
OF COURSE, I'M COUNTING ON KASUKABE-SAN TO BE THERE TOO...
WHACK

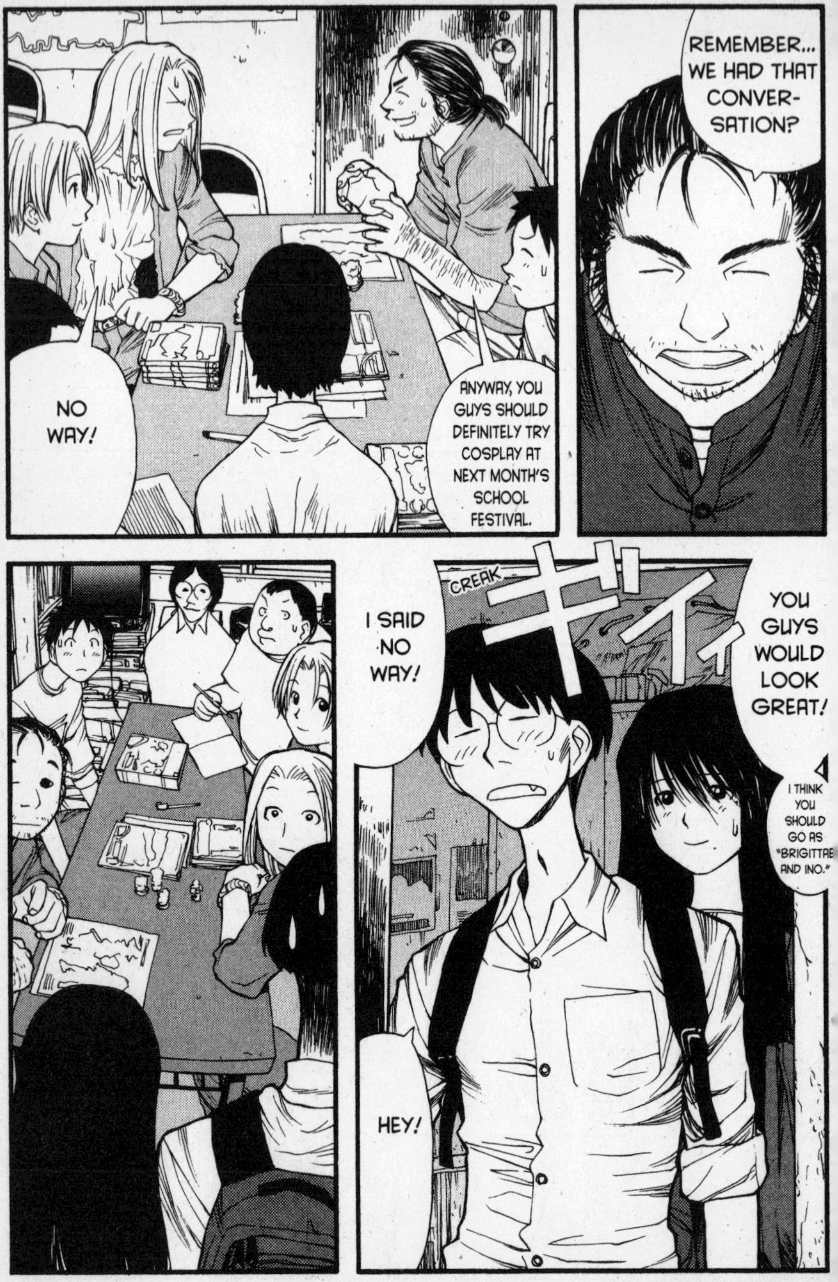
REMEMBER... WE HAD THAT CONVER- SATION?
ANYWAY, YOU GUYS SHOULD DEFINITELY TRY COSPLAY AT NEXT MONTH'S SCHOOL FESTIVAL.
NO WAY!
ギィ
CREAK
YOU GUYS WOULD LOOK GREAT!
I THINK YOU SHOULD GO AS "BRIGITTAE AND INO."
I SAID NO WAY!
HEY!

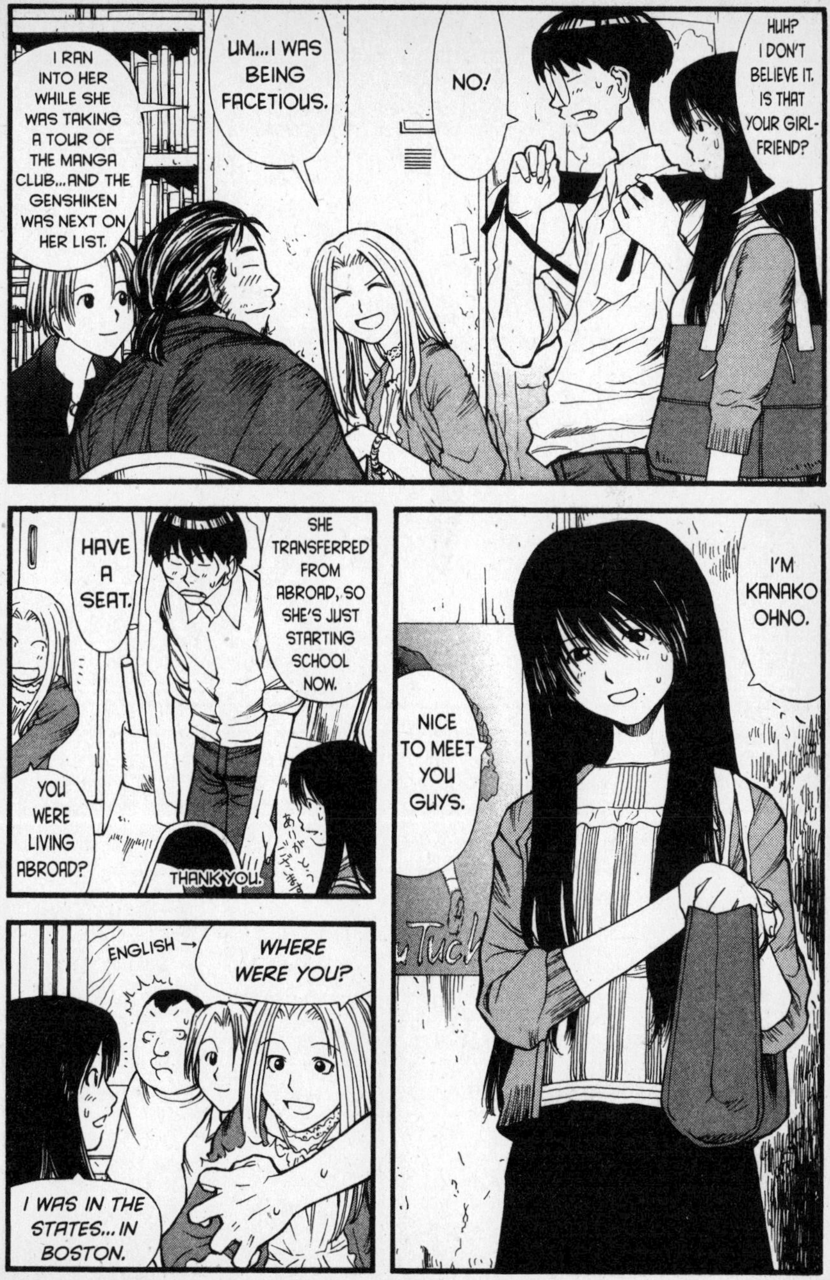
HUH? I DON'T BELIEVE IT. IS THAT YOUR GIRLFRIEND?
NO!
UM...I WAS BEING FACETIOUS.
I RAN INTO HER WHILE SHE WAS TAKING A TOUR OF THE MANGA CLUB...AND THE GENSHIKEN WAS NEXT ON HER LIST.
I'M KANAKO OHNO.
NICE TO MEET YOU GUYS.
SHE TRANSFERRED FROM ABROAD, SO SHE'S JUST STARTING SCHOOL NOW.
HAVE A SEAT.
ありがとうございます
THANK YOU.
YOU WERE LIVING ABROAD?
ENGLISH →
WHERE WERE YOU?
I WAS IN THE STATES... IN BOSTON.

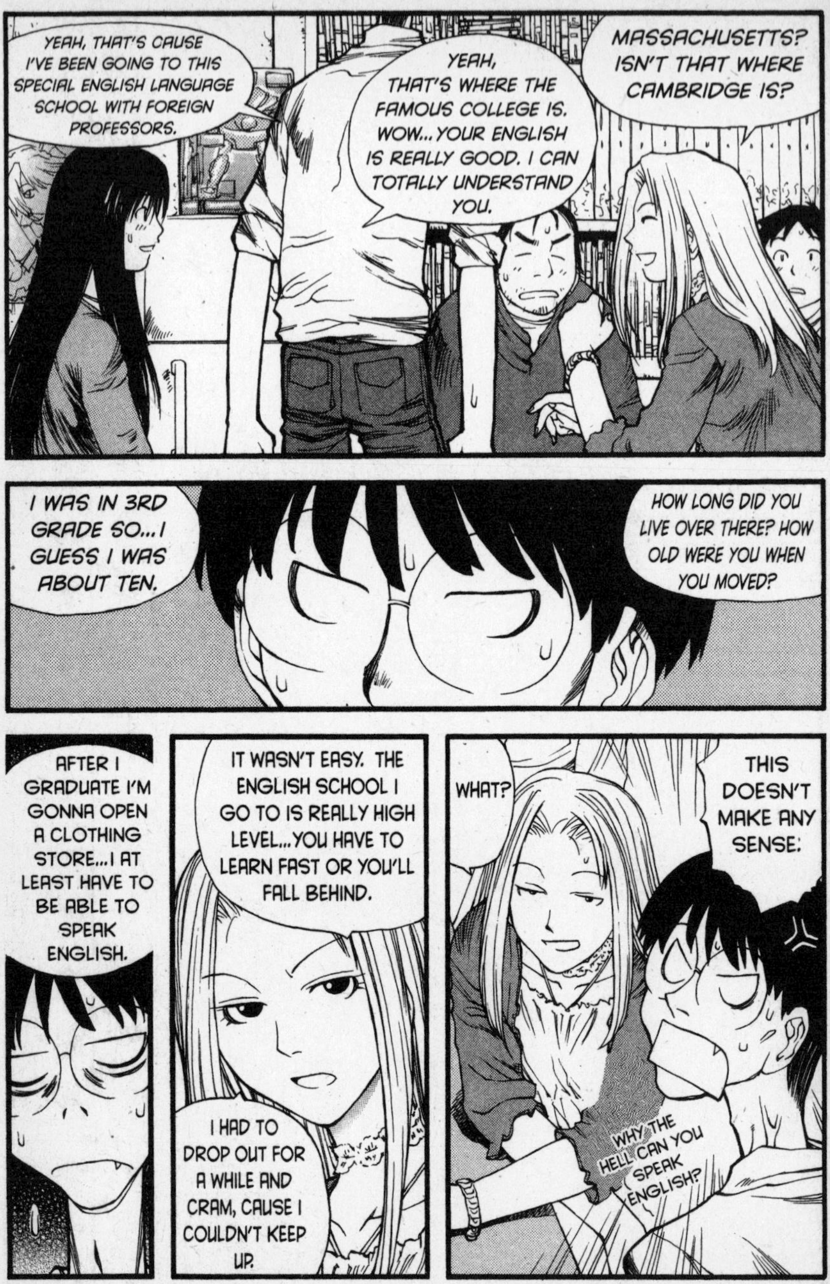
MASSACHUSETTS? ISN'T THAT WHERE CAMBRIDGE IS?
YEAH, THAT'S WHERE THE FAMOUS COLLEGE IS. WOW...YOUR ENGLISH IS REALLY GOOD. I CAN TOTALLY UNDERSTAND YOU.
YEAH, THAT'S CAUSE I'VE BEEN GOING TO THIS SPECIAL ENGLISH LANGUAGE SCHOOL WITH FOREIGN PROFESSORS.
HOW LONG DID YOU LIVE OVER THERE? HOW OLD WERE YOU WHEN YOU MOVED?
I WAS IN 3RD GRADE SO...I GUESS I WAS ABOUT TEN.
THIS DOESN'T MAKE ANY SENSE:
WHAT?
WHY THE HELL CAN YOU SPEAK ENGLISH?
IT WASN'T EASY. THE ENGLISH SCHOOL I GO TO IS REALLY HIGH LEVEL...YOU HAVE TO LEARN FAST OR YOU'LL FALL BEHIND.
I HAD TO DROP OUT FOR A WHILE AND CRAM, CAUSE I COULDN'T KEEP UP.
AFTER I GRADUATE I'M GONNA OPEN A CLOTHING STORE...I AT LEAST HAVE TO BE ABLE TO SPEAK ENGLISH.

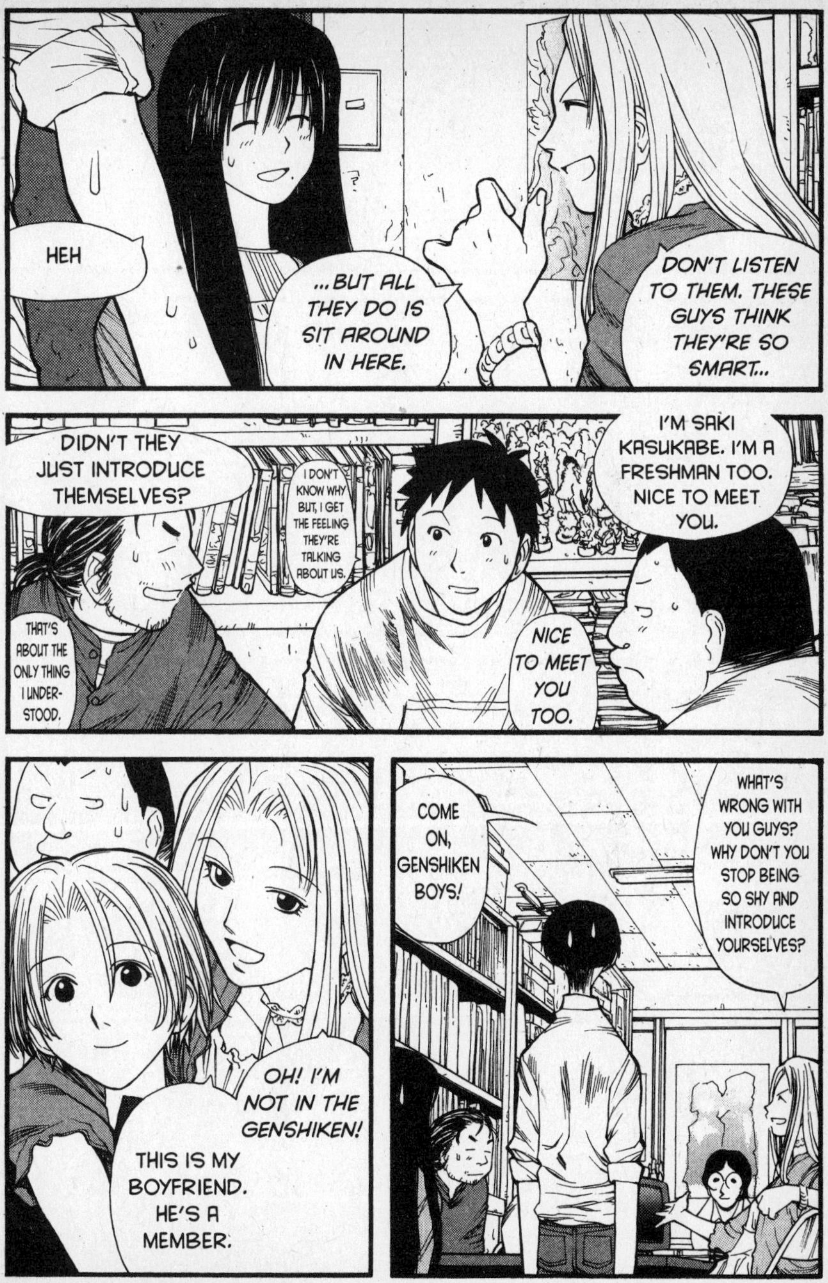
DON'T LISTEN TO THEM. THESE GUYS THINK THEY'RE SO SMART...
...BUT ALL THEY DO IS SIT AROUND IN HERE.
HEH
I'M SAKI KASUKABE. I'M A FRESHMAN TOO. NICE TO MEET YOU.
NICE TO MEET YOU TOO.
I DON'T KNOW WHY BUT, I GET THE FEELING THEY'RE TALKING ABOUT US.
DIDN'T THEY JUST INTRODUCE THEMSELVES?
THAT'S ABOUT THE ONLY THING I UNDER-STOOD.
WHAT'S WRONG WITH YOU GUYS? WHY DON'T YOU STOP BEING SO SHY AND INTRODUCE YOURSELVES?
COME ON, GENSHIKEN BOYS!
OH! I'M NOT IN THE GENSHIKEN!
THIS IS MY BOYFRIEND. HE'S A MEMBER.

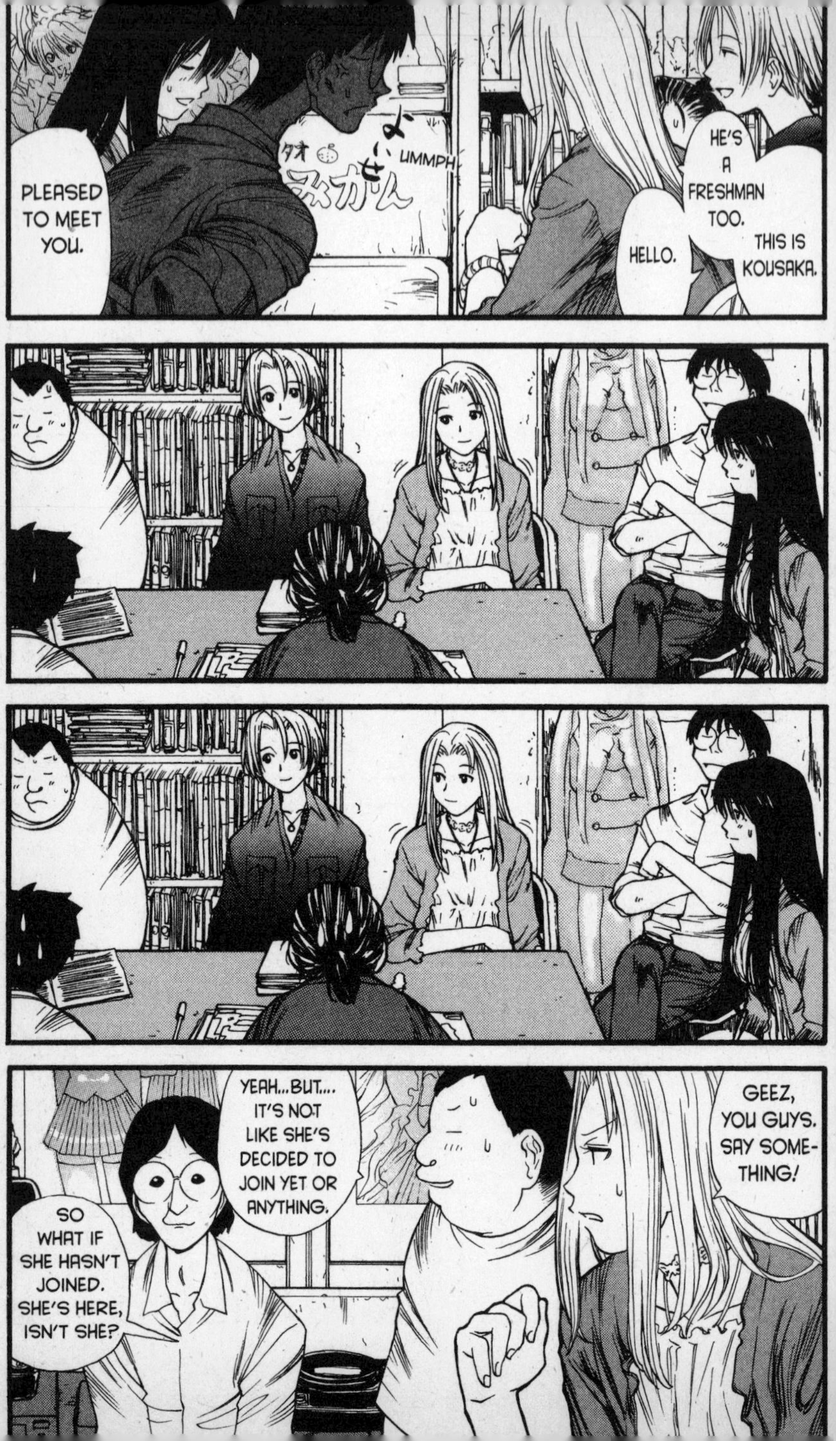
HE'S A FRESHMAN TOO. THIS IS KOUSAKA.
HELLO.
よいせ
UMMPH
みかん
PLEASED TO MEET YOU.
GEEZ, YOU GUYS. SAY SOME-THING!
YEAH...BUT.... IT'S NOT LIKE SHE'S DECIDED TO JOIN YET OR ANYTHING.
SO WHAT IF SHE HASN'T JOINED. SHE'S HERE, ISN'T SHE?

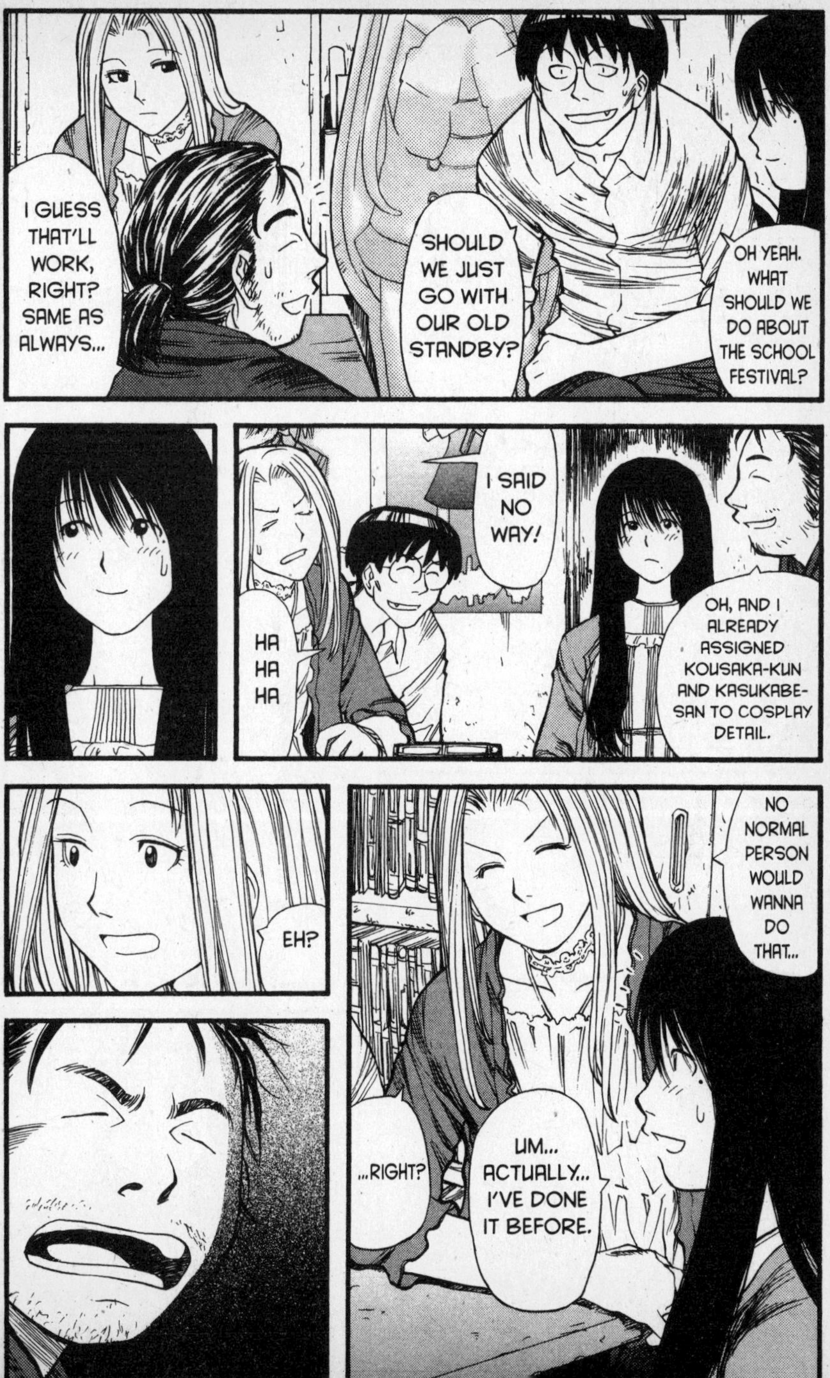

OH YEAH. WHAT SHOULD WE DO ABOUT THE SCHOOL FESTIVAL?
SHOULD WE JUST GO WITH OUR OLD STANDBY?
I GUESS THAT'LL WORK, RIGHT? SAME AS ALWAYS...
OH, AND I ALREADY ASSIGNED KOUSAKA-KUN AND KASUKABE-SAN TO COSPLAY DETAIL.
I SAID NO WAY!
HA HA HA
NO NORMAL PERSON WOULD WANNA DO THAT...
...RIGHT?
UM... ACTUALLY... I'VE DONE IT BEFORE.
EH?

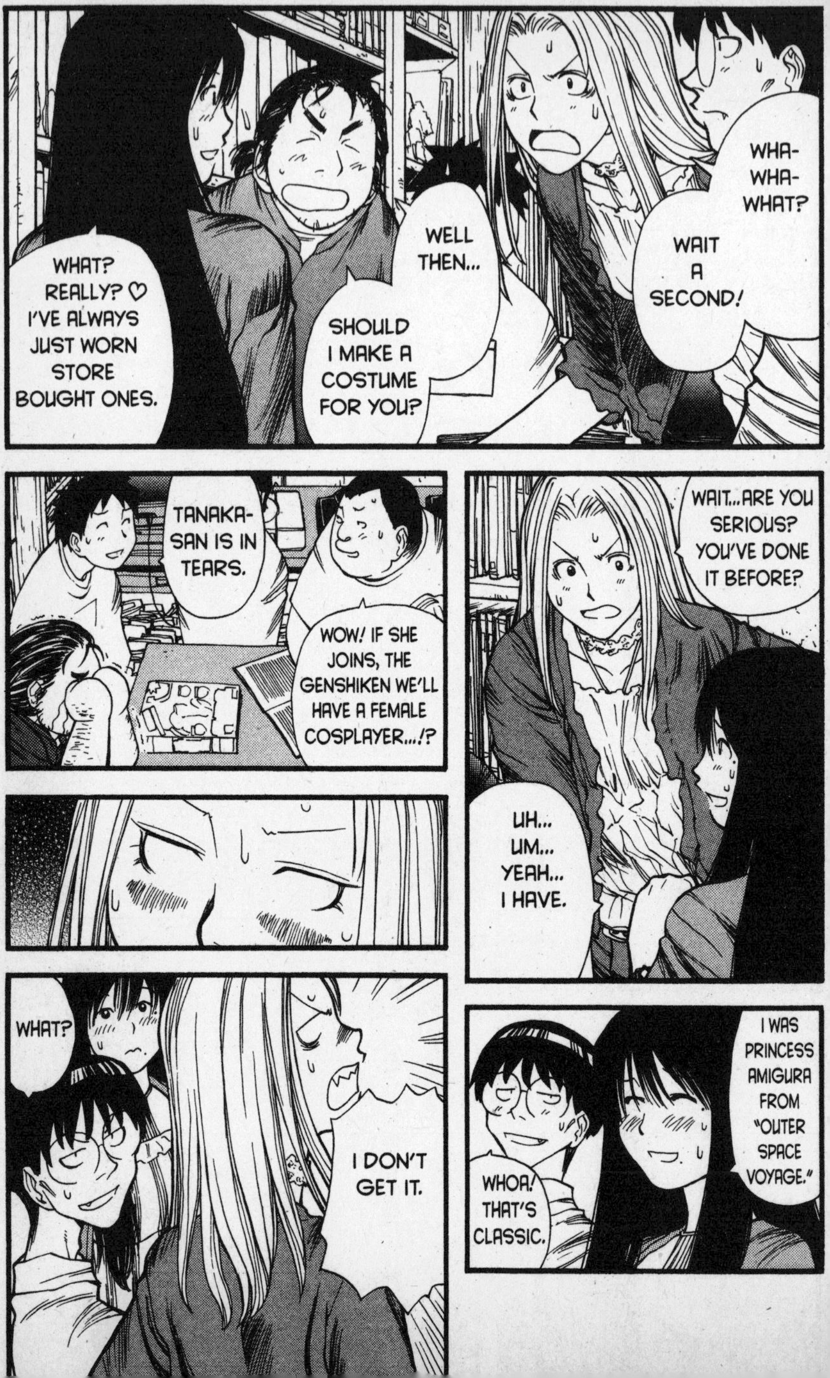
WHA-WHA-WHAT?
WAIT A SECOND!
WELL THEN...
SHOULD I MAKE A COSTUME FOR YOU?
WHAT? REALLY? ♡ I'VE ALWAYS JUST WORN STORE BOUGHT ONES.
WAIT...ARE YOU SERIOUS? YOU'VE DONE IT BEFORE?
UH... UM... YEAH... I HAVE.
TANAKA-SAN IS IN TEARS.
WOW! IF SHE JOINS, THE GENSHIKEN WE'LL HAVE A FEMALE COSPLAYER...!?
I WAS PRINCESS AMIGURA FROM "OUTER SPACE VOYAGE."
WHOA! THAT'S CLASSIC.
I DON'T GET IT.
WHAT?

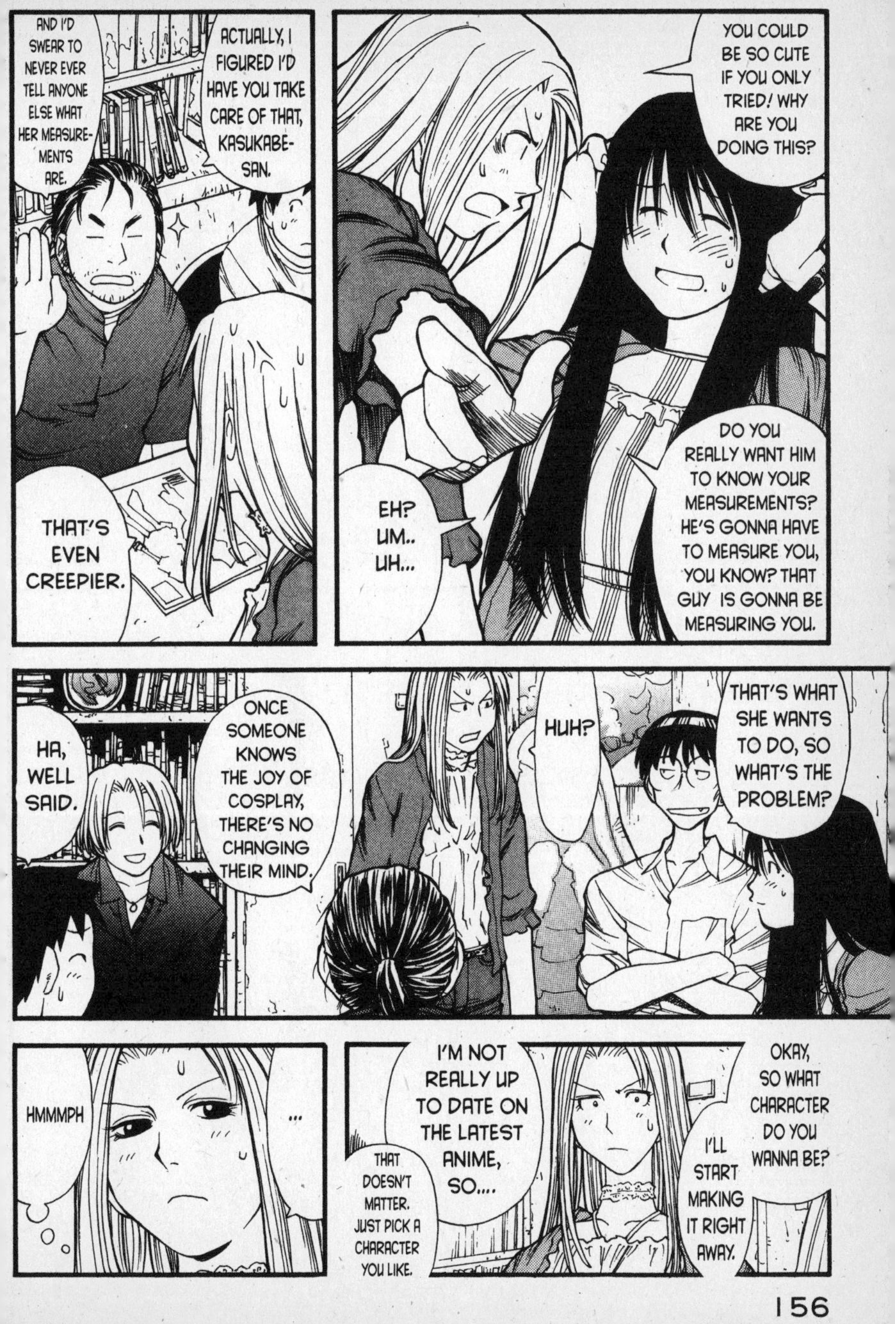
YOU COULD BE SO CUTE IF YOU ONLY TRIED! WHY ARE YOU DOING THIS?
DO YOU REALLY WANT HIM TO KNOW YOUR MEASUREMENTS? HE'S GONNA HAVE TO MEASURE YOU, YOU KNOW? THAT GUY IS GONNA BE MEASURING YOU.
EH? UM.. UH...
ACTUALLY, I FIGURED I'D HAVE YOU TAKE CARE OF THAT, KASUKABE-SAN.
AND I'D SWEAR TO NEVER EVER TELL ANYONE ELSE WHAT HER MEASUREMENTS ARE.
THAT'S EVEN CREEPIER.
THAT'S WHAT SHE WANTS TO DO, SO WHAT'S THE PROBLEM?
HUH?
ONCE SOMEONE KNOWS THE JOY OF COSPLAY, THERE'S NO CHANGING THEIR MIND.
HA, WELL SAID.
OKAY, SO WHAT CHARACTER DO YOU WANNA BE?
I'LL START MAKING IT RIGHT AWAY.
I'M NOT REALLY UP TO DATE ON THE LATEST ANIME, SO....
THAT DOESN'T MATTER. JUST PICK A CHARACTER YOU LIKE.
...
HMMMPH

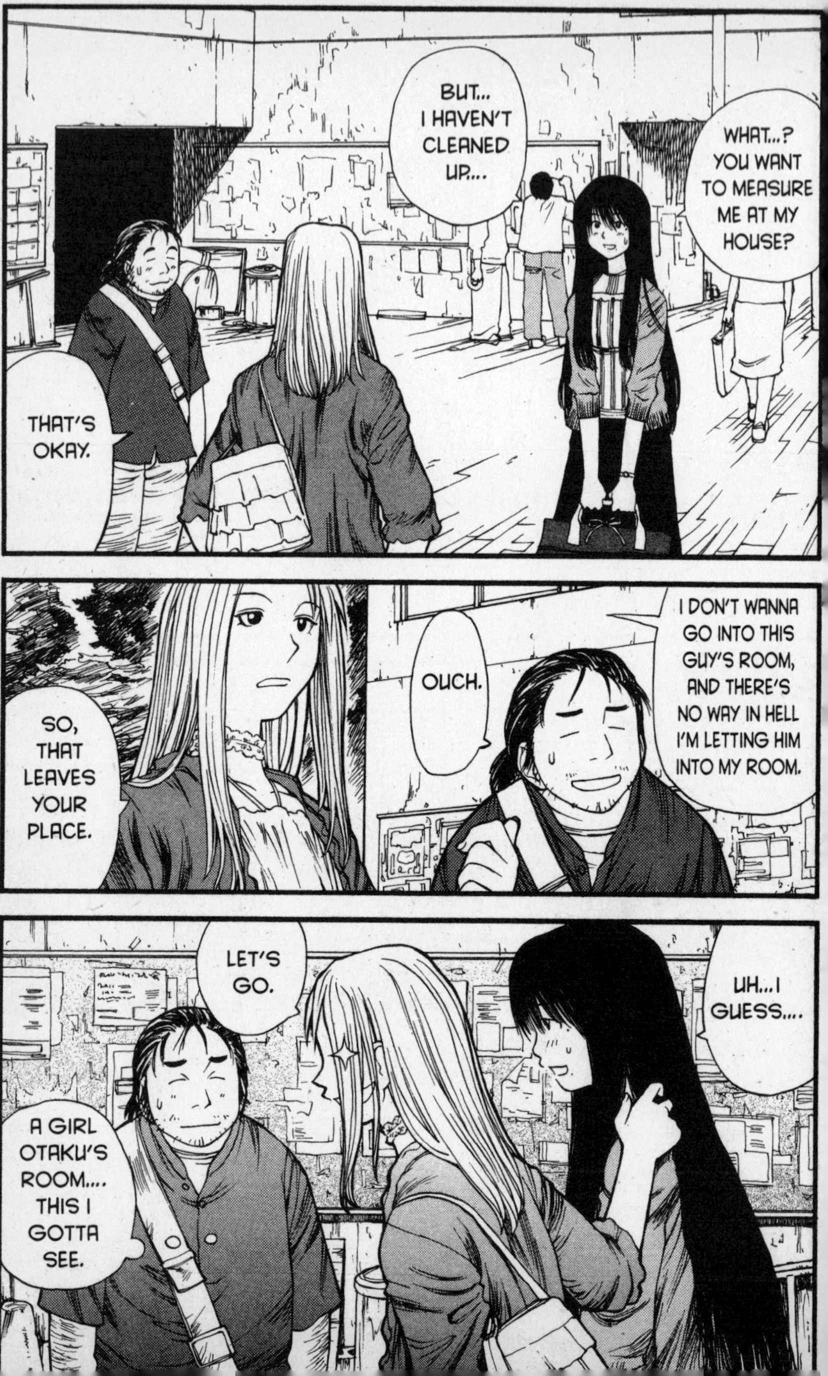
WHAT...? YOU WANT TO MEASURE ME AT MY HOUSE?
BUT... I HAVEN'T CLEANED UP...
THAT'S OKAY.
I DON'T WANNA GO INTO THIS GUY'S ROOM, AND THERE'S NO WAY IN HELL I'M LETTING HIM INTO MY ROOM.
OUCH.
SO, THAT LEAVES YOUR PLACE.
UH...I GUESS....
LET'S GO.
A GIRL OTAKU'S ROOM.... THIS I GOTTA SEE.

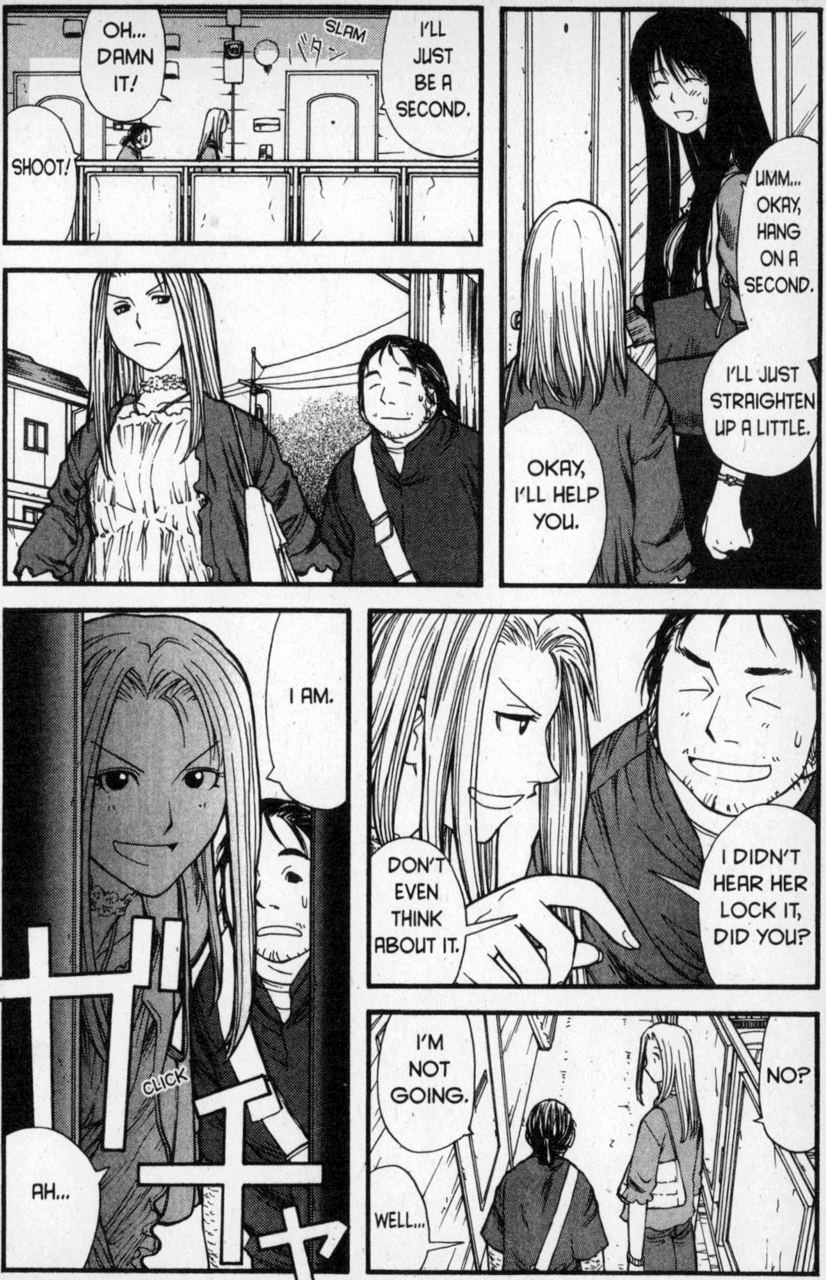
UMM... OKAY, HANG ON A SECOND.
I'LL JUST STRAIGHTEN UP A LITTLE.
OKAY, I'LL HELP YOU.
I'LL JUST BE A SECOND.
SLAM
OH... DAMN IT!
SHOOT!
I DIDN'T HEAR HER LOCK IT, DID YOU?
DON'T EVEN THINK ABOUT IT.
NO?
I'M NOT GOING.
WELL...
I AM.
CLICK
ガチャ
AH...

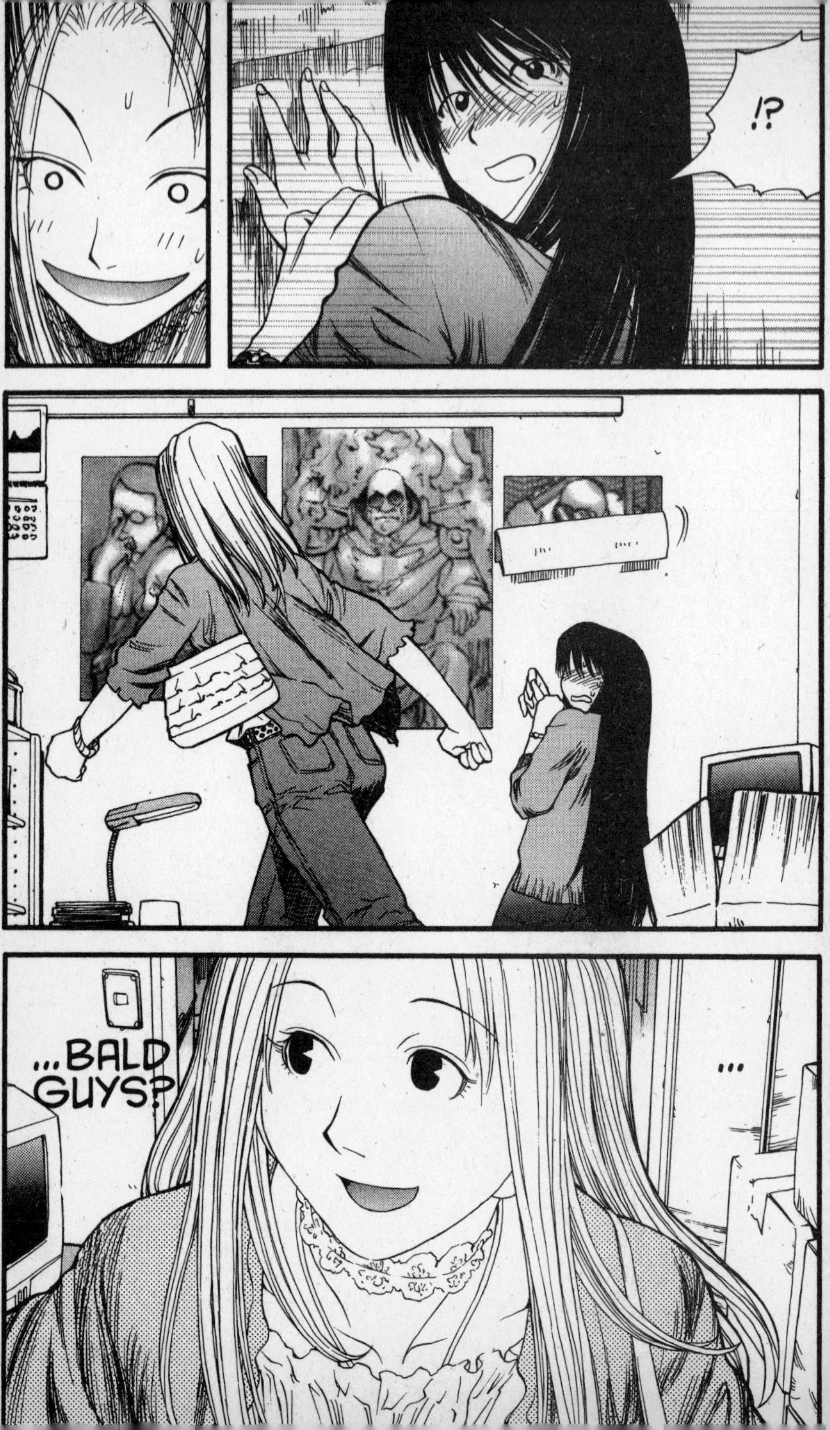
!?
...
...BALD GUYS?

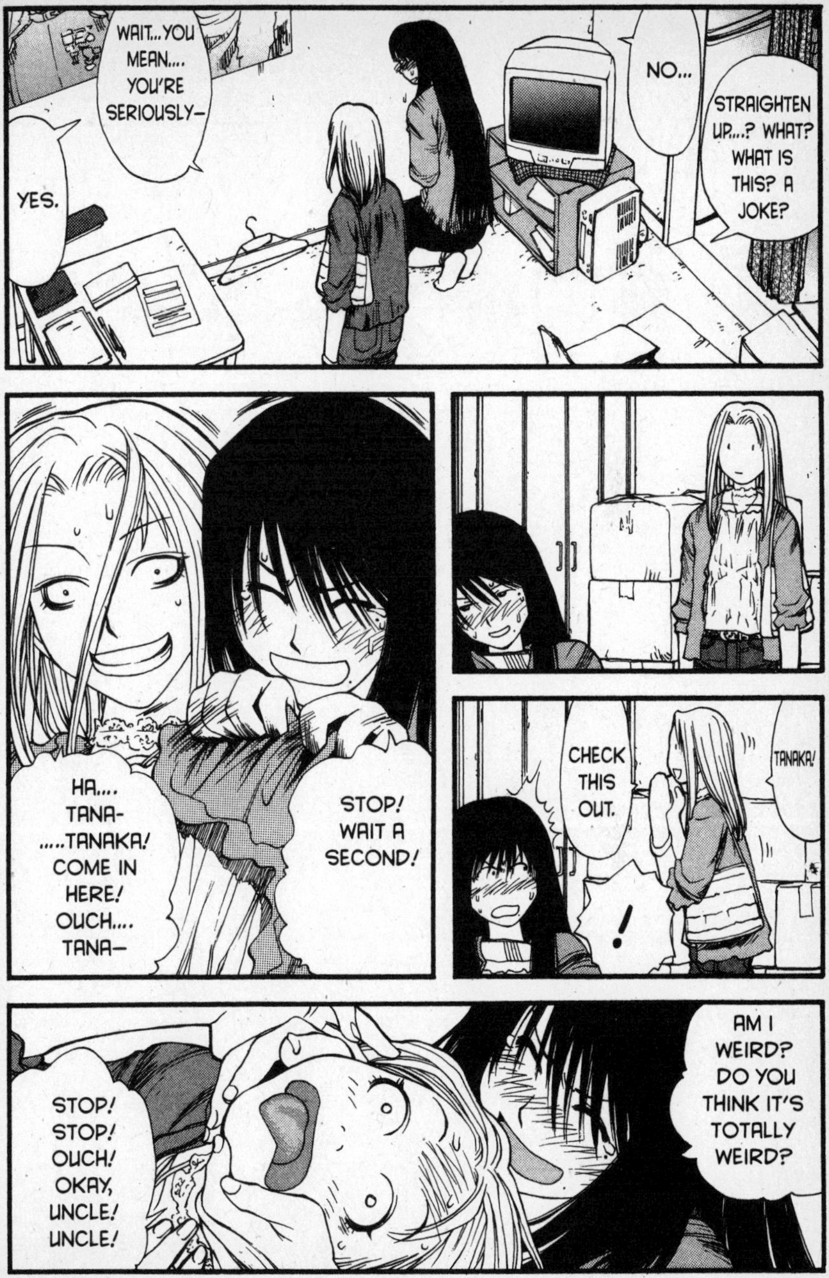
NO...
STRAIGHTEN UP...? WHAT? WHAT IS THIS? A JOKE?
WAIT...YOU MEAN.... YOU'RE SERIOUSLY—
YES.
TANAKA!
CHECK THIS OUT.
!
STOP! WAIT A SECOND!
HA.... TANA- .....TANAKA! COME IN HERE! OUCH.... TANA—
AM I WEIRD? DO YOU THINK IT'S TOTALLY WEIRD?
STOP! STOP! OUCH! OKAY, UNCLE! UNCLE!

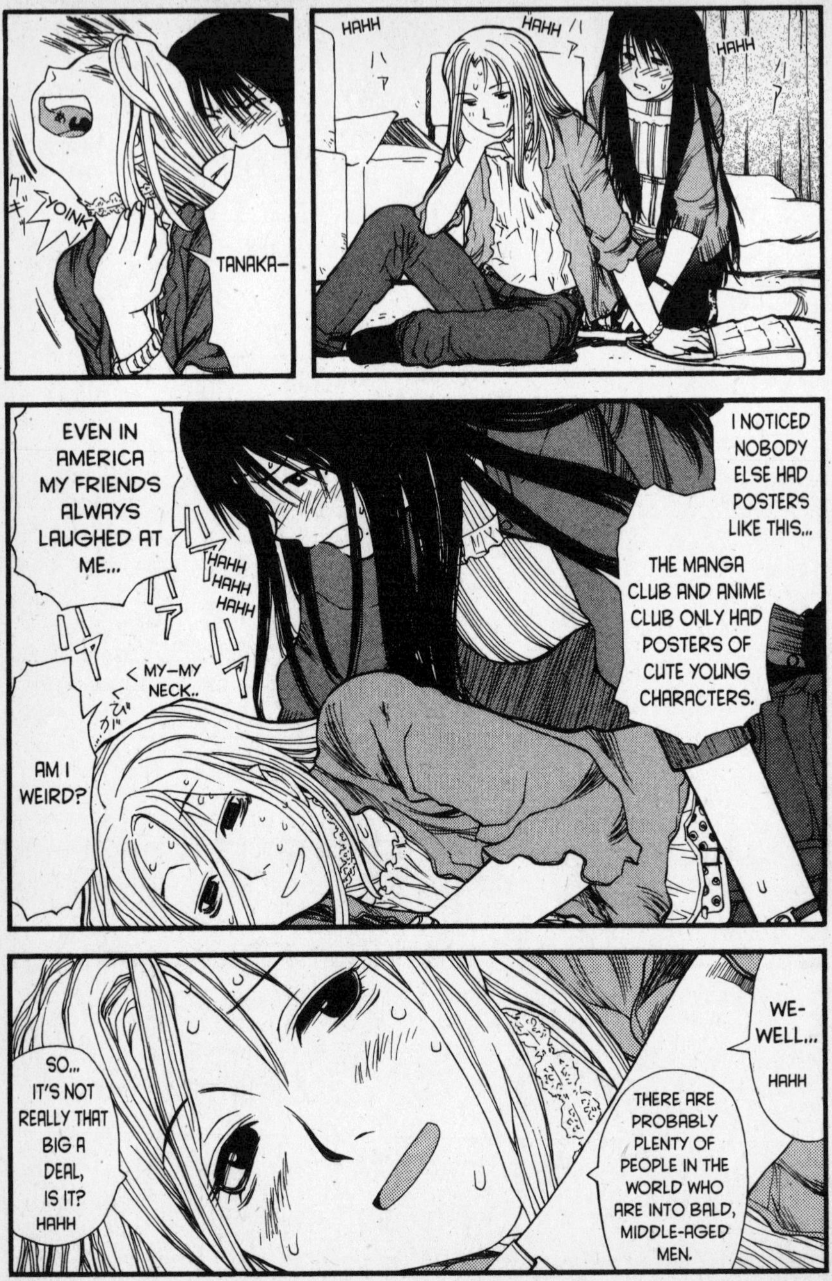
HAHH
HAHH
HAHH
YOINK
TANAKA—
I NOTICED NOBODY ELSE HAD POSTERS LIKE THIS...
THE MANGA CLUB AND ANIME CLUB ONLY HAD POSTERS OF CUTE YOUNG CHARACTERS.
EVEN IN AMERICA MY FRIENDS ALWAYS LAUGHED AT ME...
HAHH HAHH HAHH
MY—MY NECK..
AM I WEIRD?
WE-WELL...
HAHH
THERE ARE PROBABLY PLENTY OF PEOPLE IN THE WORLD WHO ARE INTO BALD, MIDDLE-AGED MEN.
SO... IT'S NOT REALLY THAT BIG A DEAL, IS IT?
HAHH

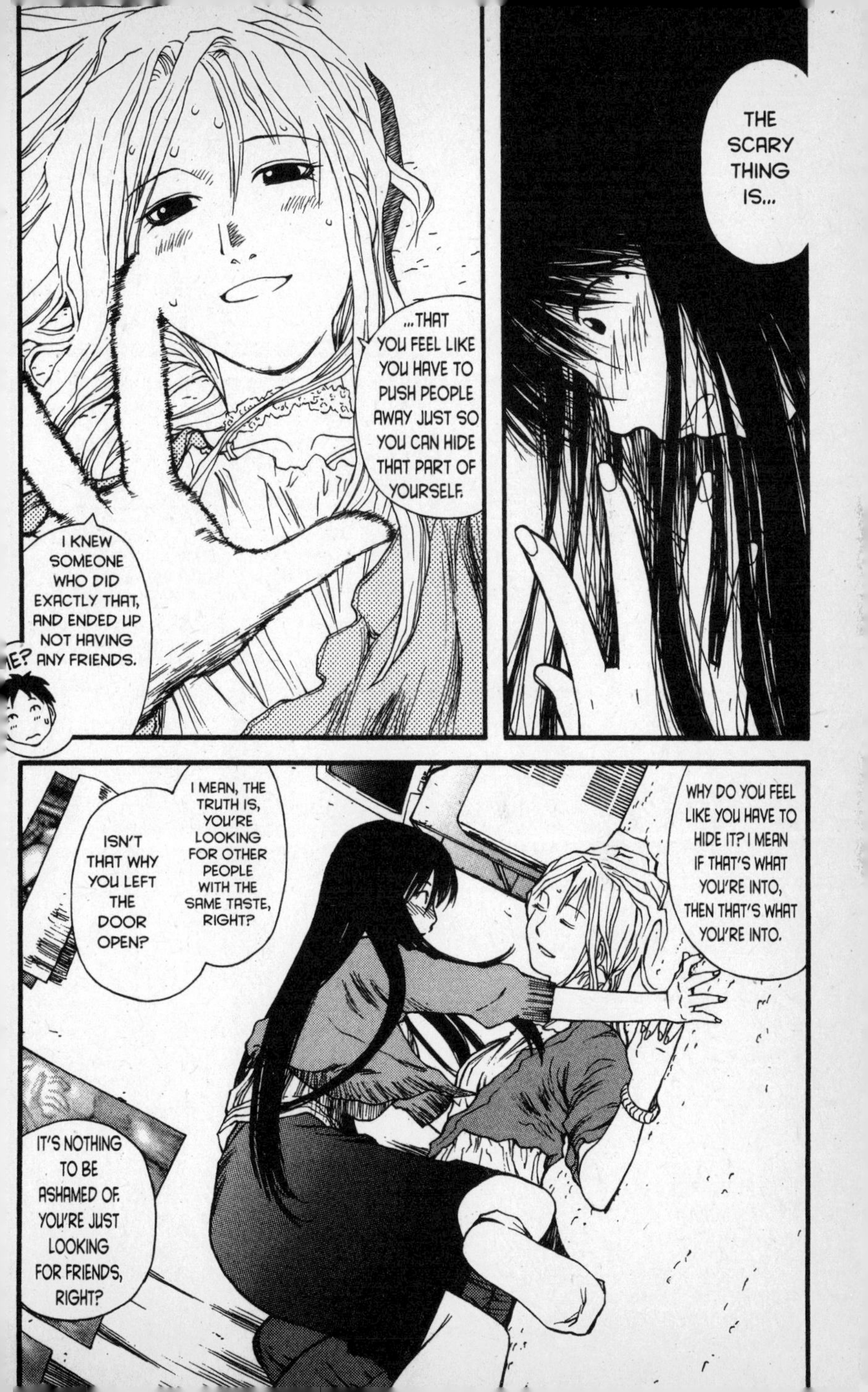
THE SCARY THING IS...
...THAT YOU FEEL LIKE YOU HAVE TO PUSH PEOPLE AWAY JUST SO YOU CAN HIDE THAT PART OF YOURSELF.
I KNEW SOMEONE WHO DID EXACTLY THAT, AND ENDED UP NOT HAVING ANY FRIENDS.
WHY DO YOU FEEL LIKE YOU HAVE TO HIDE IT? I MEAN IF THAT'S WHAT YOU'RE INTO, THEN THAT'S WHAT YOU'RE INTO.
I MEAN, THE TRUTH IS, YOU'RE LOOKING FOR OTHER PEOPLE WITH THE SAME TASTE, RIGHT?
ISN'T THAT WHY YOU LEFT THE DOOR OPEN?
IT'S NOTHING TO BE ASHAMED OF. YOU'RE JUST LOOKING FOR FRIENDS, RIGHT?

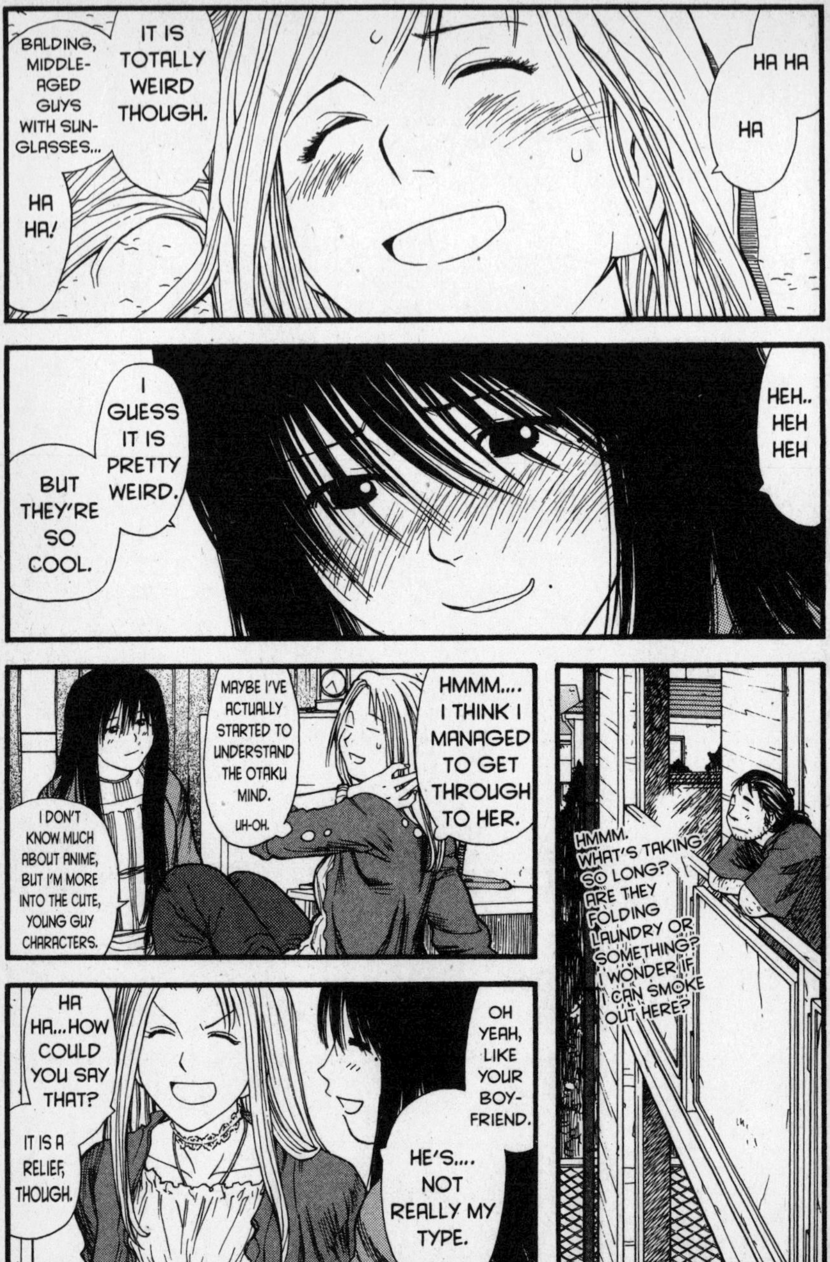
HA HA HA
IT IS TOTALLY WEIRD THOUGH.
BALDING, MIDDLE-AGED GUYS WITH SUNGLASSES...
HA HA!
HEH.. HEH HEH
I GUESS IT IS PRETTY WEIRD.
BUT THEY'RE SO COOL.
HMMM. WHAT'S TAKING SO LONG? ARE THEY FOLDING LAUNDRY OR SOMETHING? I WONDER IF I CAN SMOKE OUT HERE?
HMMM.... I THINK I MANAGED TO GET THROUGH TO HER.
MAYBE I'VE ACTUALLY STARTED TO UNDERSTAND THE OTAKU MIND.
UH-OH.
I DON'T KNOW MUCH ABOUT ANIME, BUT I'M MORE INTO THE CUTE, YOUNG GUY CHARACTERS.
OH YEAH, LIKE YOUR BOY-FRIEND.
HE'S.... NOT REALLY MY TYPE.
HA HA...HOW COULD YOU SAY THAT?
IT IS A RELIEF, THOUGH.

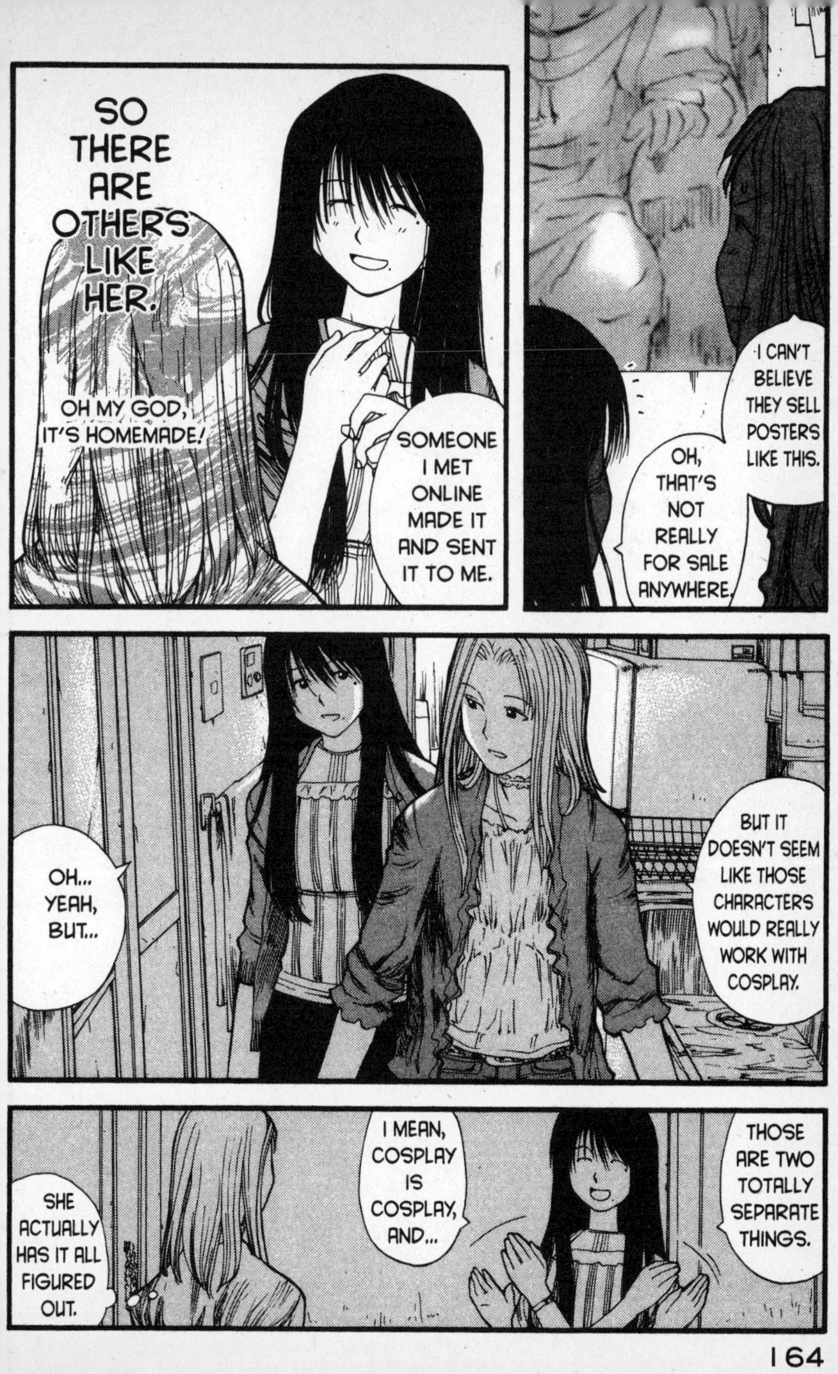
I CAN'T BELIEVE THEY SELL POSTERS LIKE THIS.
OH, THAT'S NOT REALLY FOR SALE ANYWHERE.
OH MY GOD, IT'S HOMEMADE!
SOMEONE I MET ONLINE MADE IT AND SENT IT TO ME.
SO THERE ARE OTHERS LIKE HER.
BUT IT DOESN'T SEEM LIKE THOSE CHARACTERS WOULD REALLY WORK WITH COSPLAY.
OH... YEAH, BUT...
I MEAN, COSPLAY IS COSPLAY, AND...
THOSE ARE TWO TOTALLY SEPARATE THINGS.
SHE ACTUALLY HAS IT ALL FIGURED OUT.

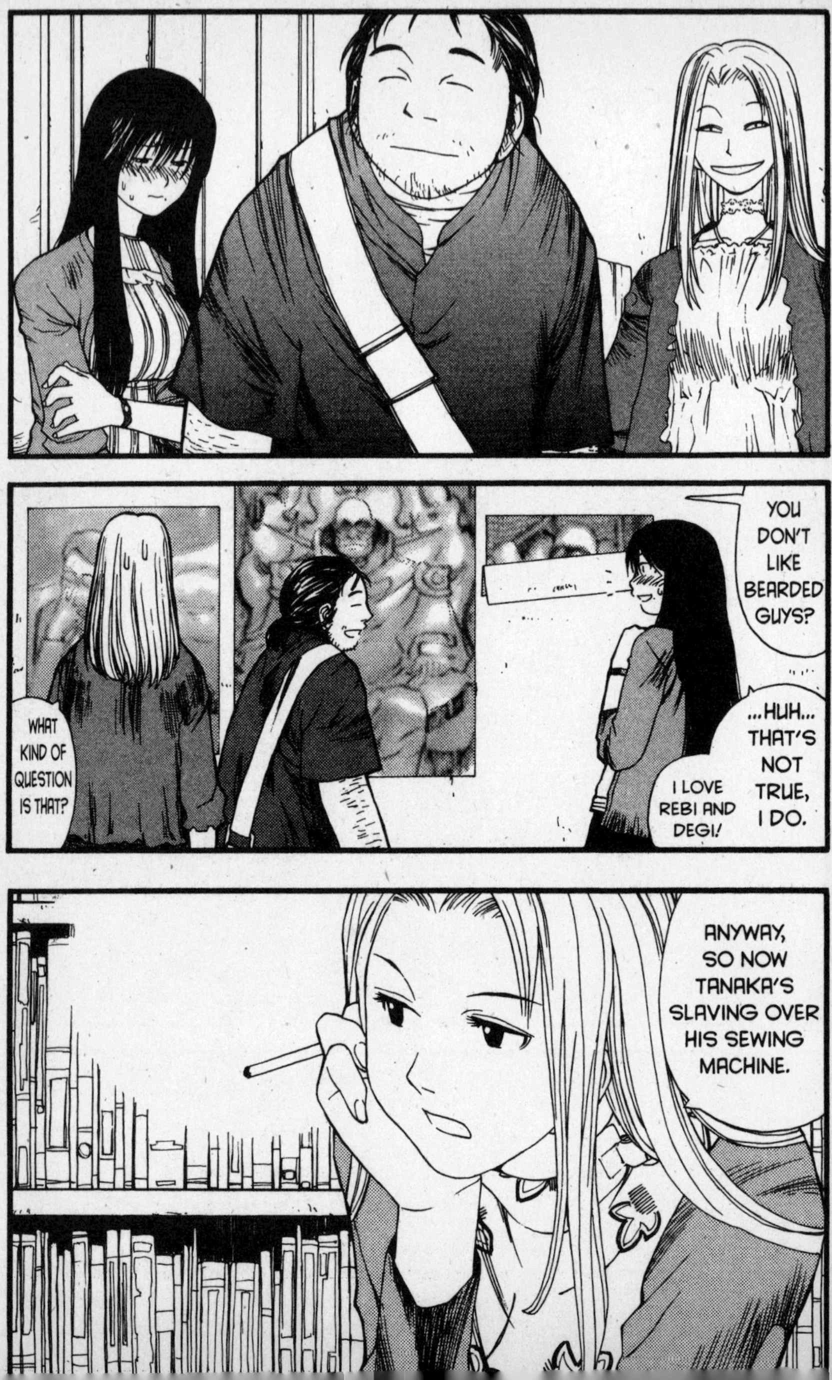
YOU DON'T LIKE BEARDED GUYS?
...HUH... THAT'S NOT TRUE, I DO.
I LOVE REBI AND DEGI!
WHAT KIND OF QUESTION IS THAT?
ANYWAY, SO NOW TANAKA'S SLAVING OVER HIS SEWING MACHINE.

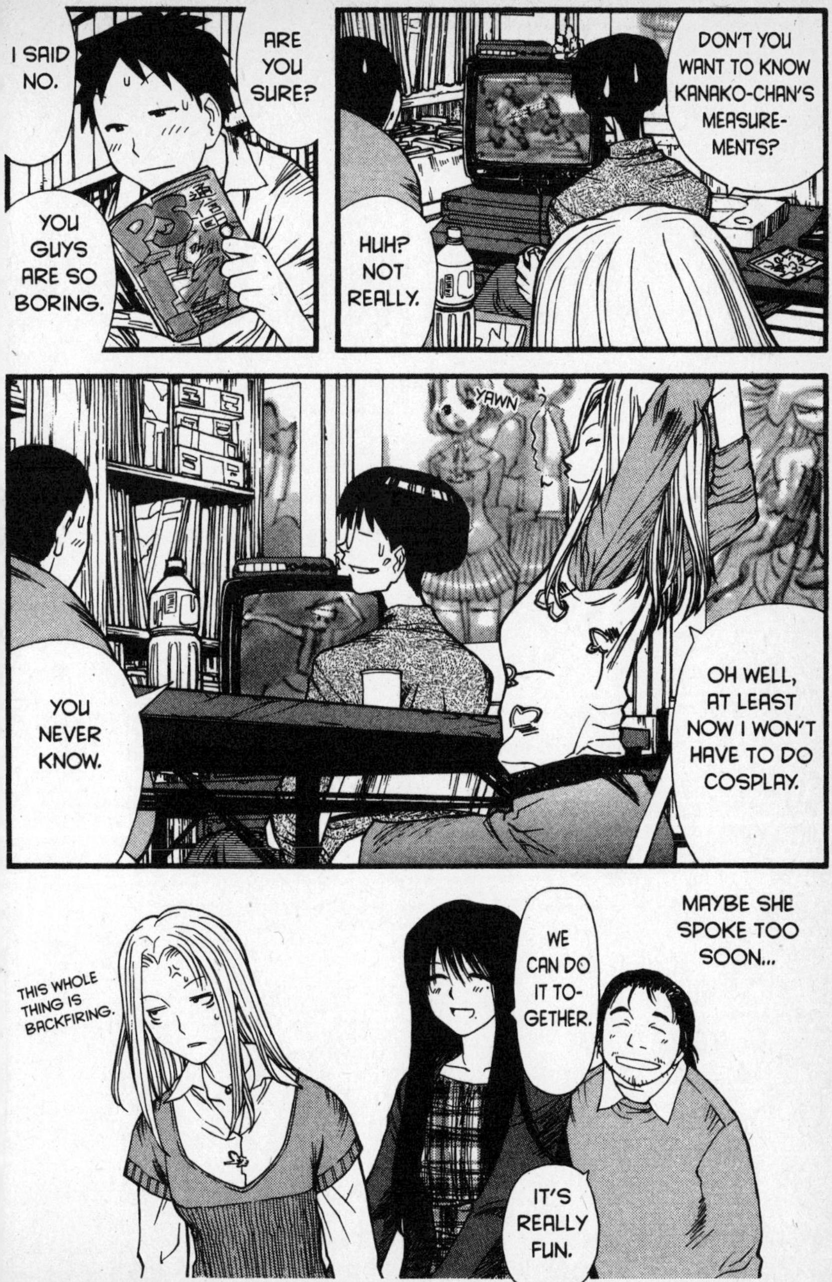
DON'T YOU WANT TO KNOW KANAKO-CHAN'S MEASURE-MENTS?
HUH? NOT REALLY.
ARE YOU SURE?
I SAID NO.
YOU GUYS ARE SO BORING.
YAWN
OH WELL, AT LEAST NOW I WON'T HAVE TO DO COSPLAY.
YOU NEVER KNOW.
MAYBE SHE SPOKE TOO SOON...
WE CAN DO IT TO-GETHER.
IT'S REALLY FUN.
THIS WHOLE THING IS BACKFIRING.

END OF CHAPTER 6

KANAKO OHNO

PROFILE

KANAKO OHNO

BIRTHDAY JULY 14TH
BLOOD TYPE O

FAVORITE MANGA
THE SILENT MASS

FAVORITE ANIME
MOBILE SUITS A GANGARU

FAVORITE VIDEO GAME
SAMURAI SPIRIT (ORIGINAL VERSION)

MEASUREMENTS
WHY AM I THE ONLY ONE WHO HAS TO WRITE THIS?

FAVORITE FIGHT GAME CHARACTERS
JUPPEI-CHAN
KENNY HISTEIGA
EARTHQUAKE NINJA
ZANGULA

*THESE ARE THE CHARACTER'S CHOICES AND DO NOT NECESSARILY REFLECT THE AUTHOR'S TASTES.

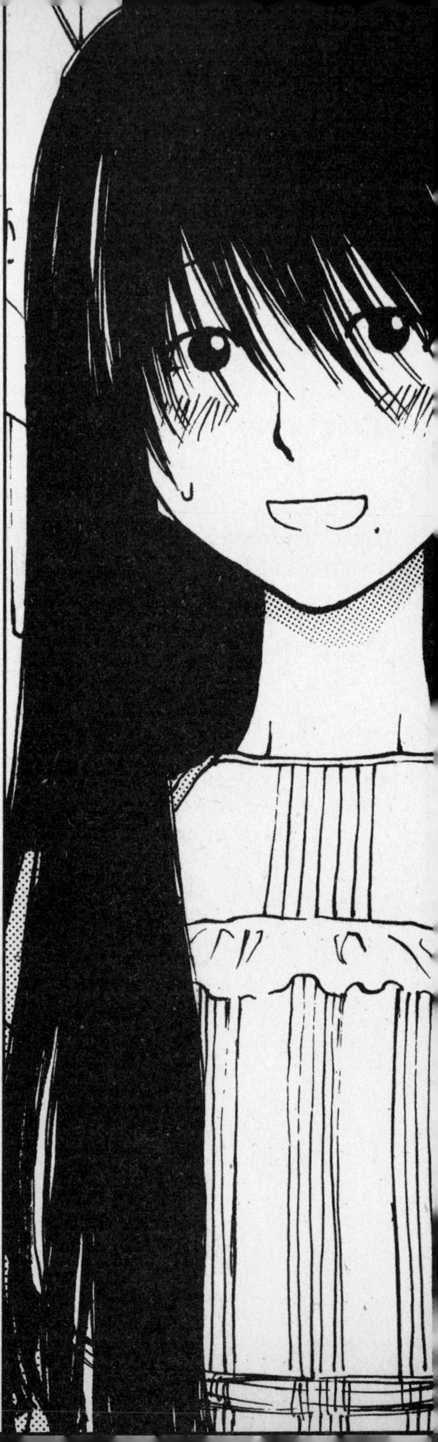

CHAPTER 6- MOMENTS LATER

SELF DESTRUCTION

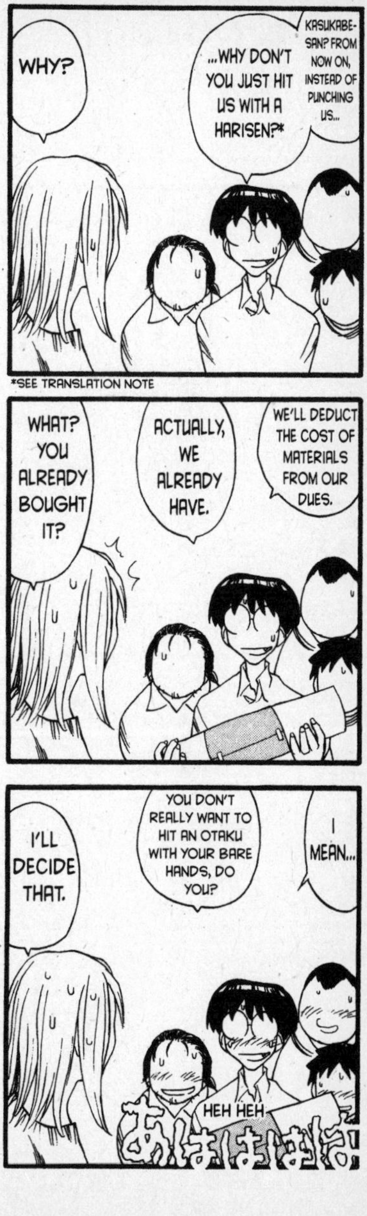
KASUKABE-SAN? FROM NOW ON, INSTEAD OF PUNCHING US...
...WHY DON'T YOU JUST HIT US WITH A HARISEN?*
WHY?
WE'LL DEDUCT THE COST OF MATERIALS FROM OUR DUES.
ACTUALLY, WE ALREADY HAVE.
WHAT? YOU ALREADY BOUGHT IT?
I MEAN...
YOU DON'T REALLY WANT TO HIT AN OTAKU WITH YOUR BARE HANDS, DO YOU?
I'LL DECIDE THAT.
HEH HEH

*SEE TRANSLATION NOTE

SPOILED

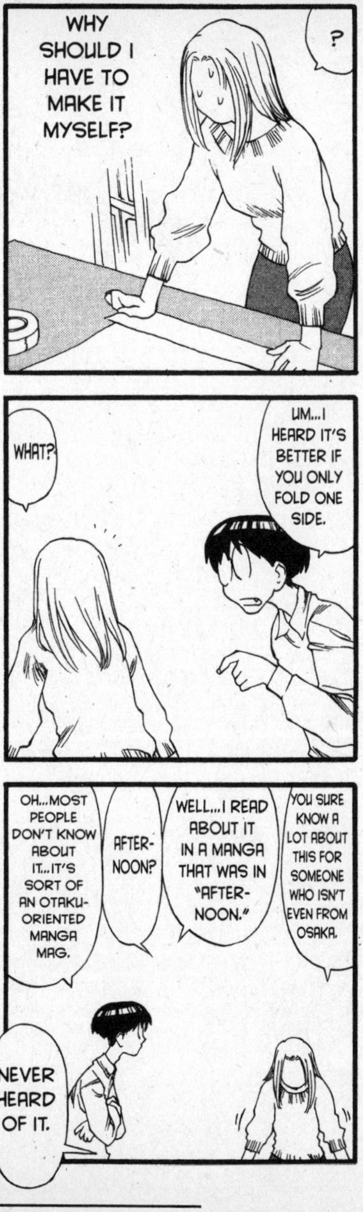
?
WHY SHOULD I HAVE TO MAKE IT MYSELF?
UM...I HEARD IT'S BETTER IF YOU ONLY FOLD ONE SIDE.
WHAT?
YOU SURE KNOW A LOT ABOUT THIS FOR SOMEONE WHO ISN'T EVEN FROM OSAKA.
WELL...I READ ABOUT IT IN A MANGA THAT WAS IN "AFTER-NOON."
AFTER-NOON?
OH...MOST PEOPLE DON'T KNOW ABOUT IT...IT'S SORT OF AN OTAKU-ORIENTED MANGA MAG.
NEVER HEARD OF IT.

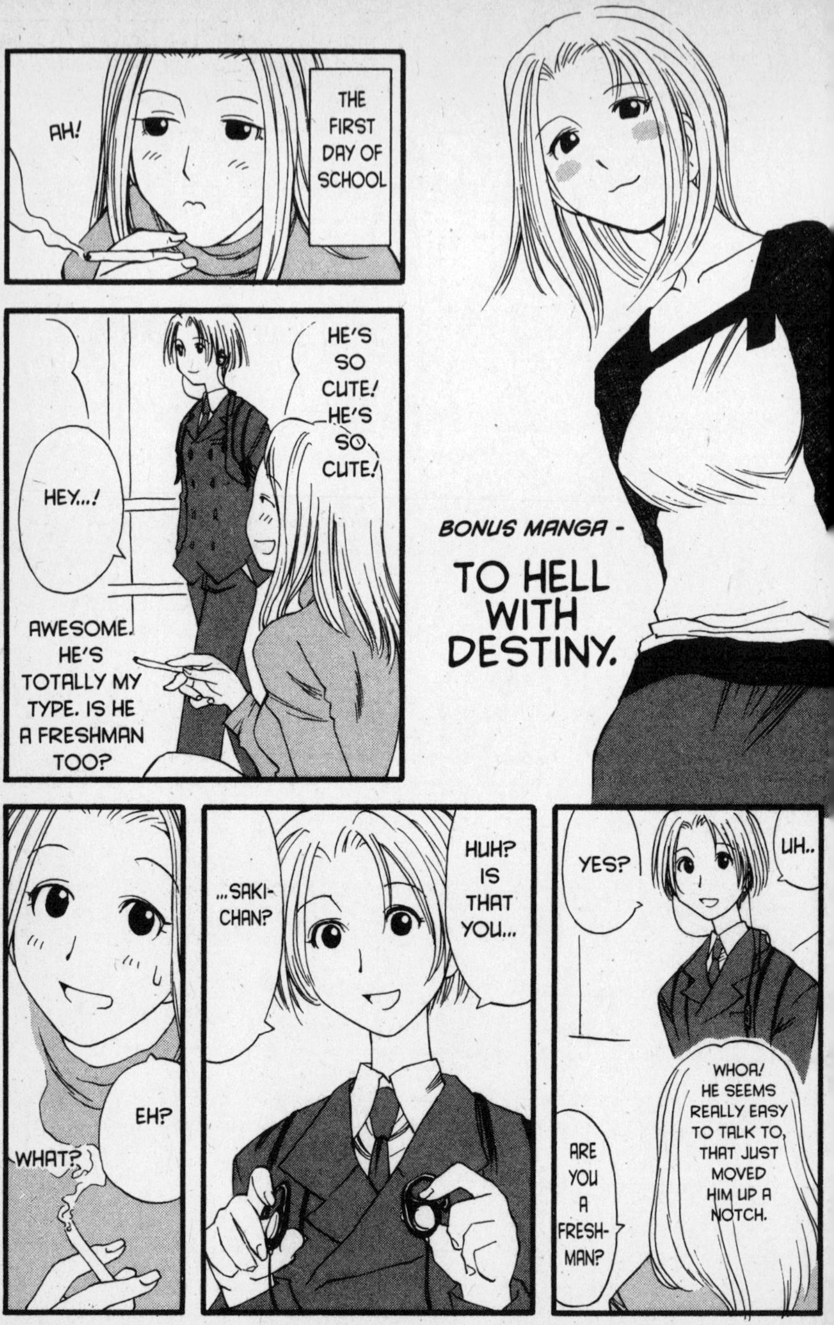
BONUS MANGA -
TO HELL WITH DESTINY.
THE FIRST DAY OF SCHOOL
AH!
HE'S SO CUTE! HE'S SO CUTE!
HEY...!
AWESOME. HE'S TOTALLY MY TYPE. IS HE A FRESHMAN TOO?
UH..
YES?
WHOA! HE SEEMS REALLY EASY TO TALK TO, THAT JUST MOVED HIM UP A NOTCH.
ARE YOU A FRESH-MAN?
HUH? IS THAT YOU...
...SAKI-CHAN?
EH?
WHAT?

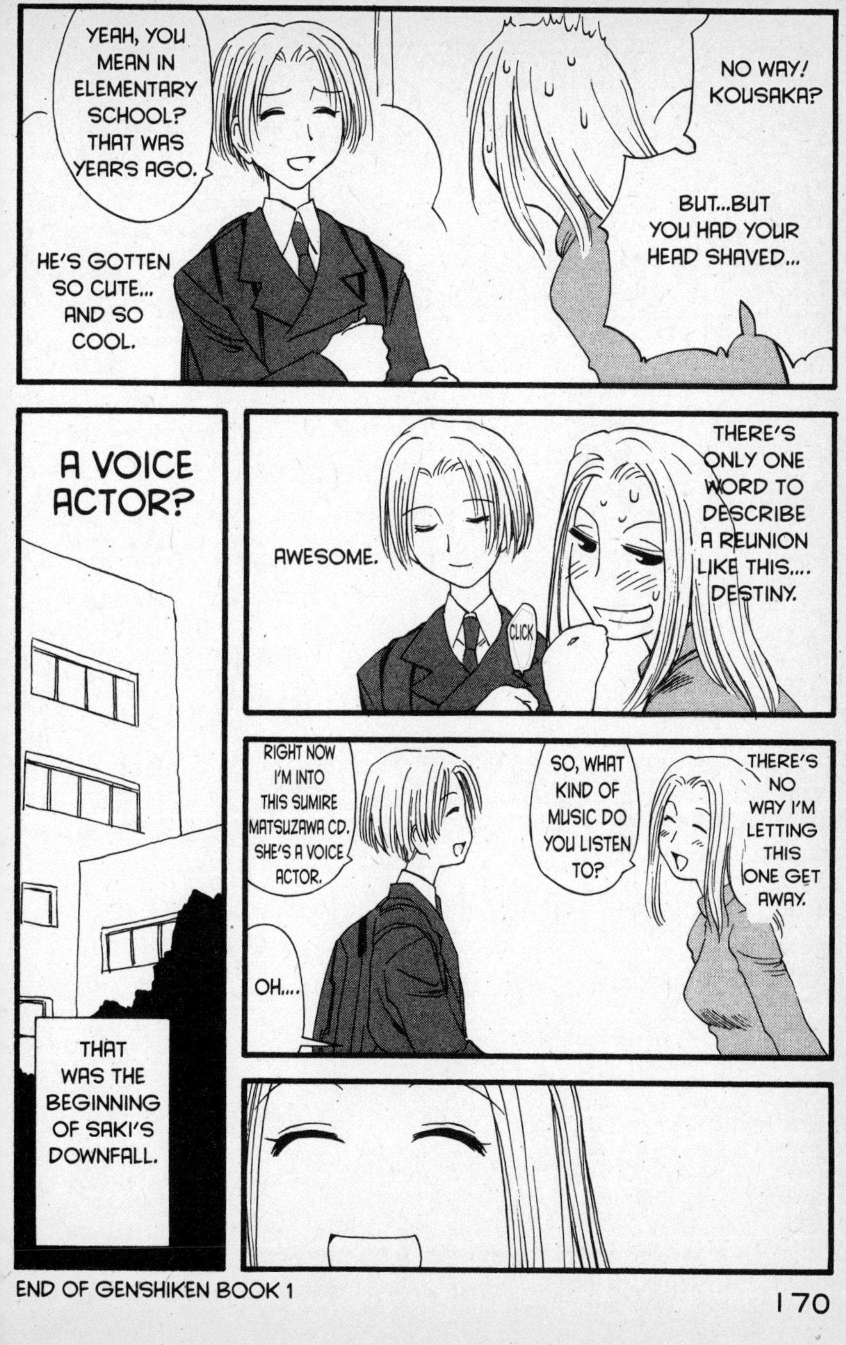
NO WAY! KOUSAKA?
YEAH, YOU MEAN IN ELEMENTARY SCHOOL? THAT WAS YEARS AGO.
BUT...BUT YOU HAD YOUR HEAD SHAVED...
HE'S GOTTEN SO CUTE... AND SO COOL.
THERE'S ONLY ONE WORD TO DESCRIBE A REUNION LIKE THIS.... DESTINY.
AWESOME.
CLICK
THERE'S NO WAY I'M LETTING THIS ONE GET AWAY.
SO, WHAT KIND OF MUSIC DO YOU LISTEN TO?
RIGHT NOW I'M INTO THIS SUMIRE MATSUZAWA CD. SHE'S A VOICE ACTOR.
OH....
A VOICE ACTOR?
THAT WAS THE BEGINNING OF SAKI'S DOWNFALL.

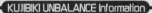

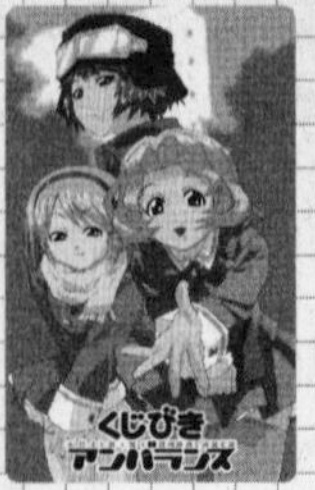
くじびき
アンバランス

くじびき KUJIBIKI UNBALANCE アンバランス

THE INSTITUTION ARTS OF CHARACTERS

A POPULAR MANGA TITLE FROM KOODANSHA'S SHONEN MAGAZOON THAT IS CURRENTLY ON ITS 4TH TANKOBON. AS FANS HAD HOPED AND EXPECTED "KUJIBIKI UNBALANCE" HAS NOW BEEN MADE INTO AN ANIME SERIES. THE PECULIAR HIGH SCHOOL KNOWN AS TATEHASHIIN HIGH SOLVES ALL OF ITS PROBLEMS WITH A KUJIBIKI LOTTERY. EVEN THE ENTRANCE EXAMS ARE DETERMINED BY KUJIBIKI LOTTERY. THE SCHOOL'S STUDENT BODY OFFICERS GENTLY WRESTLE THEIR WAY THROUGH RELATIONSHIPS IN THIS ROMANTIC COMEDY. THIS MONTH WE'LL INTRODUCE THE EIGHT MAIN CHARACTERS. WE'VE EVEN PROVIDED A "RELATIONSHIP MAP" TO HELP YOU GET ACQUAINTED WITH THE CHARACTERS AND HELP YOU LEARN ALL THERE IS TO KNOW ABOUT "KUJIBIKI UNBALANCE."

ANIME DATA

STAFF:
CREATOR..................YUU KUROKI
DIRECTOR..................AKITARO OOZORA
PRODUCER..................YOSHIO URASAWA
CHARACTER DESIGNER......AKEMI MORI
MUSICAL COMPOSER........MIHO KANNO
ART DIRECTOR..............KOUICHI KATO

BROADCAST SCHEDUALE

KUJIBIKI UNBALANCE
SATAIMA TV/ SATURDAYS AT 25:25
CHIBARAGI TV/ TUESDAYS AT 24:30
TEIKYOO TV/ MONDAYS AT 25:55

Tokino Akiyama

THE HEROINE. TOKINO IS A SOPHOMORE AT TATEHASHIIN HIGH SCHOOL. SHE WAS CHOSEN BY KUJIBIKI LOTTERY TO BECOME A CANDIDATE FOR STUDENT BODY PRESIDENT NEXT TERM. SHE'S SMART, SWEET AND VERY CUTE. THE ONLY WEIRD THING ABOUT TOKINO IS THE FACT THAT SHE "LOVES MUSHROOMS." (VOICE ACTOR: YUI HORIE)

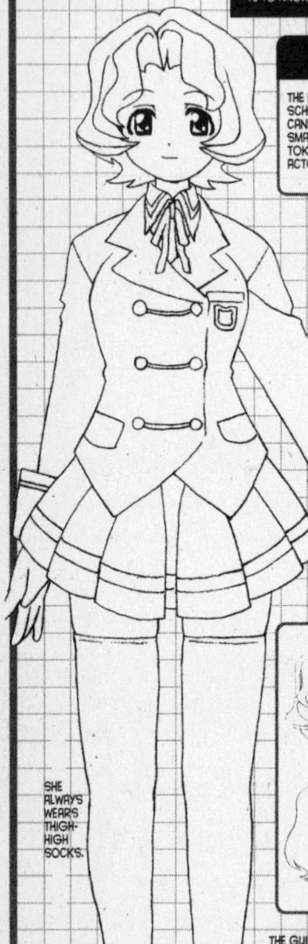

SHE ALWAYS WEARS THIGH-HIGH SOCKS.

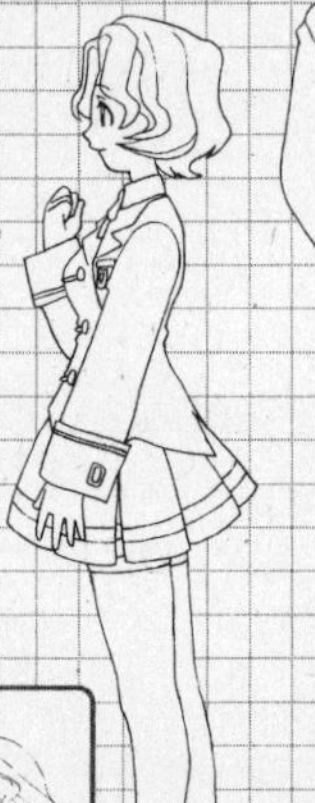

THE TATEHASHIIN HIGH SCHOOL UNIFORM—MOST STUDENTS ALTER THEIR UNIFORMS, BUT TOKINO DOESN'T.

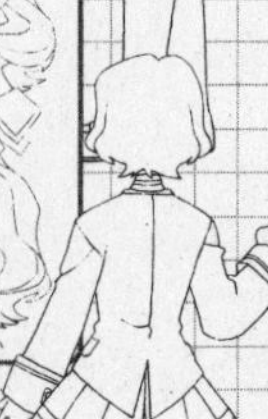

FACIAL EXPRESSIONS

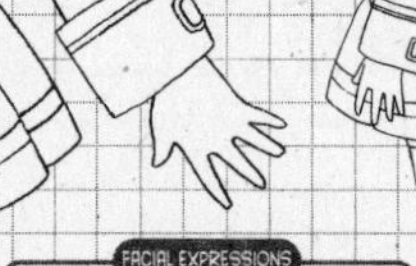

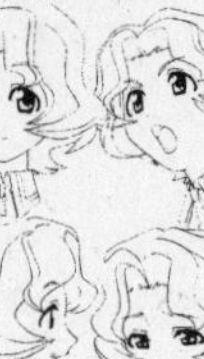
世界のキノコ

THE GUIDE TO MUSHROOMS THAT TOKINO WON'T LET GO OF. A REAL EDITION OF THIS BOOK WILL SOON BE AVAILABLE.

MUSHROOMS OF THE WORLD

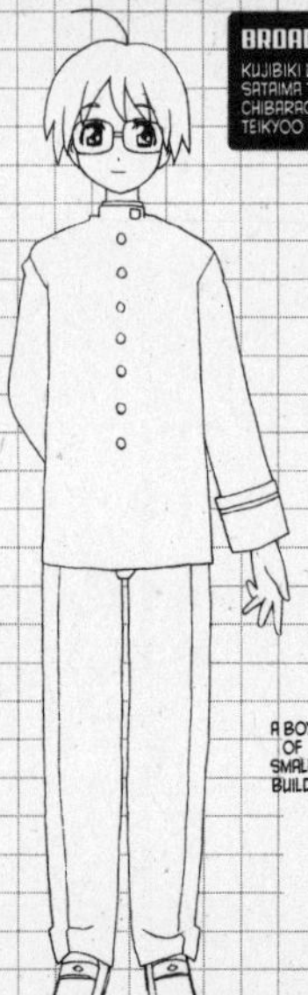

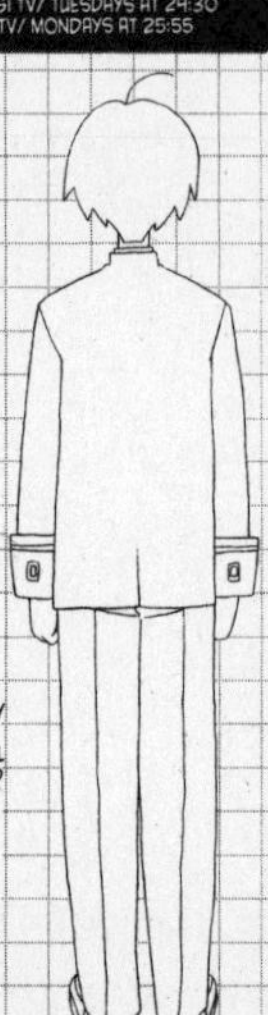

A BOY OF SMALL BUILD

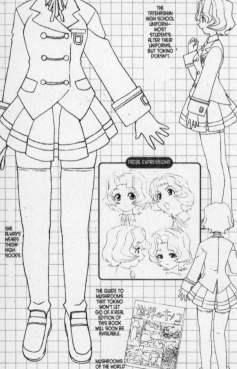

FACIAL EXPRESSIONS

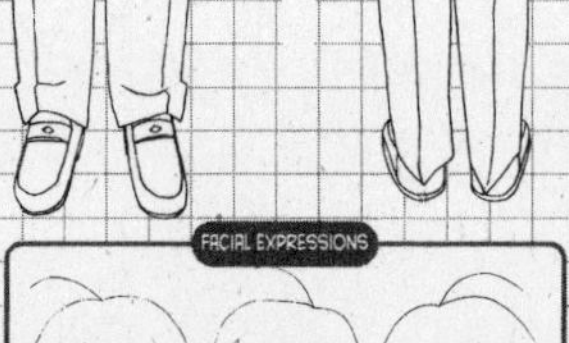

Chihiro Enomoto

HIS NAME SOUNDS LIKE A GIRL'S BUT HE'S DEFINITELY A BOY. IN FACT, HE'S THE MAIN CHARACTER. HE'S A FRESHMAN AT TATEHASHIIN HIGH SCHOOL AND A CANDIDATE FOR STUDENT BODY SECRETARY. HE FELL IN LOVE AT FIRST SIGHT WHEN HE SAW TOKINO AT THE LIBRARY. THEY TEAMED UP TO TRY AND BECOME STUDENT BODY OFFICERS. CHIHIRO IS A GREAT COOK. (VOICE ACTOR: TOKO TAKIMOTO)

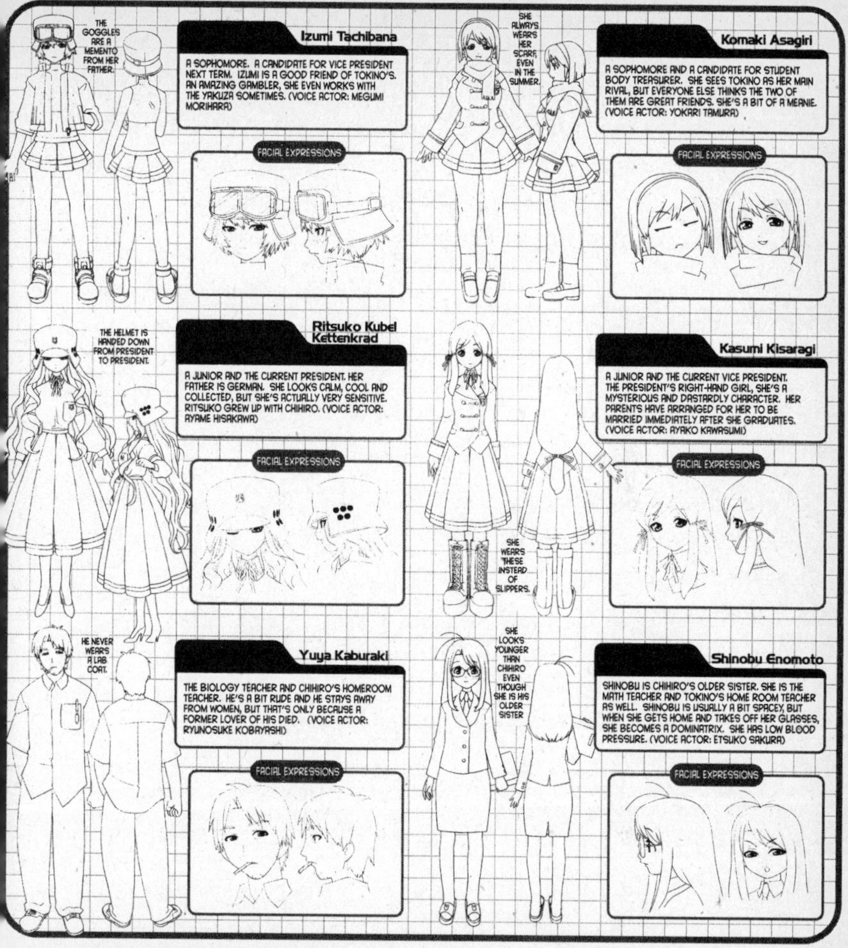
THE GOGGLES ARE A MEMENTO FROM HER FATHER.
Izumi Tachibana
A SOPHOMORE. A CANDIDATE FOR VICE PRESIDENT NEXT TERM. IZUMI IS A GOOD FRIEND OF TOKINO'S. AN AMAZING GAMBLER, SHE EVEN WORKS WITH THE YAKUZA SOMETIMES. (VOICE ACTOR: MEGUMI MORIHARA)
FACIAL EXPRESSIONS
SHE ALWAYS WEARS HER SCARF, EVEN IN THE SUMMER.
Komaki Asagiri
A SOPHOMORE AND A CANDIDATE FOR STUDENT BODY TREASURER. SHE SEES TOKINO AS HER MAIN RIVAL, BUT EVERYONE ELSE THINKS THE TWO OF THEM ARE GREAT FRIENDS. SHE'S A BIT OF A MEANIE. (VOICE ACTOR: YOKARI TAMURA)
FACIAL EXPRESSIONS
THE HELMET IS HANDED DOWN FROM PRESIDENT TO PRESIDENT.
Ritsuko Kubel Kettenkrad
A JUNIOR AND THE CURRENT PRESIDENT. HER FATHER IS GERMAN. SHE LOOKS CALM, COOL AND COLLECTED, BUT SHE'S ACTUALLY VERY SENSITIVE. RITSUKO GREW UP WITH CHIHIRO. (VOICE ACTOR: AYAME HISAKAWA)
FACIAL EXPRESSIONS
Kasumi Kisaragi
A JUNIOR AND THE CURRENT VICE PRESIDENT. THE PRESIDENT'S RIGHT-HAND GIRL, SHE'S A MYSTERIOUS AND DASTARDLY CHARACTER. HER PARENTS HAVE ARRANGED FOR HER TO BE MARRIED IMMEDIATELY AFTER SHE GRADUATES. (VOICE ACTOR: AYAKO KAWASUMI)
FACIAL EXPRESSIONS
SHE WEARS THESE INSTEAD OF SLIPPERS.
HE NEVER WEARS A LAB COAT.
Yuya Kaburaki
THE BIOLOGY TEACHER AND CHIHIRO'S HOMEROOM TEACHER. HE'S A BIT RUDE AND HE STAYS AWAY FROM WOMEN, BUT THAT'S ONLY BECAUSE A FORMER LOVER OF HIS DIED. (VOICE ACTOR: RYUNOSUKE KOBAYASHI)
FACIAL EXPRESSIONS
SHE LOOKS YOUNGER THAN CHIHIRO EVEN THOUGH SHE IS HIS OLDER SISTER
Shinobu Enomoto
SHINOBU IS CHIHIRO'S OLDER SISTER. SHE IS THE MATH TEACHER AND TOKINO'S HOME ROOM TEACHER AS WELL. SHINOBU IS USUALLY A BIT SPACEY, BUT WHEN SHE GETS HOME AND TAKES OFF HER GLASSES, SHE BECOMES A DOMINATRIX. SHE HAS LOW BLOOD PRESSURE. (VOICE ACTOR: ETSUKO SAKURA)
FACIAL EXPRESSIONS

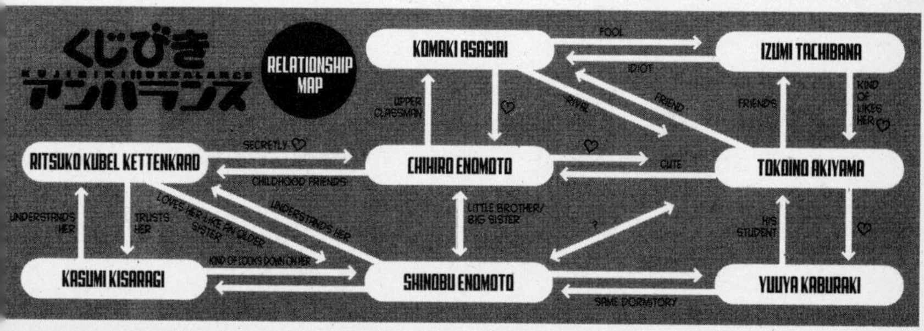
くじびきアンバランス
KUJIBIKI UNBALANCE
RELATIONSHIP MAP
KOMAKI ASAGIRI
IZUMI TACHIBANA
FOOL
IDIOT
UPPER CLASSMAN
RIVAL
FRIEND
FRIENDS
KIND OF LIKES HER
RITSUKO KUBEL KETTENKRAD
SECRETLY
CHIHIRO ENOMOTO
CUTE
TOKINO AKIYAMA
CHILDHOOD FRIENDS
UNDERSTANDS HER
TRUSTS HER
LOVES HER LIKE AN OLDER SISTER
UNDERSTANDS HER
LITTLE BROTHER/ BIG SISTER
?
HIS STUDENT
KIND OF LOOKS DOWN ON HER
KASUMI KISARAGI
SHINOBU ENOMOTO
YUUYA KABURAKI
SAME DORMITORY

Translation Notes

Japanese is a tricky language for most Westerners, and translation is often more art than science. For your edification and reading pleasure, here are notes on some of the places where we could have gone in a different direction in our translation of the work, or where a Japanese cultural reference is used.

College Circles, page 4

Social life in Japanese colleges revolves around participation in interest groups. The activities of these groups, also known as circles, can range from sports to academic studies to anime.

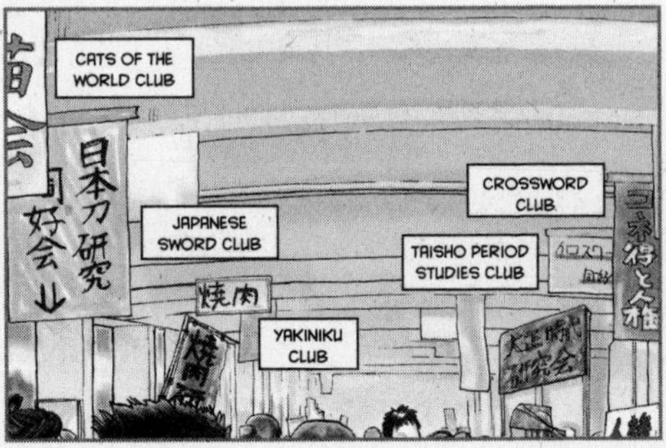
CATS OF THE WORLD CLUB
日本刀研究
好会
JAPANESE SWORD CLUB
焼肉
YAKINIKU CLUB
CROSSWORD CLUB
TAISHO PERIOD STUDIES CLUB
研究会

Yakiniku, page 4

Yakiniku is Korean-style barbecued beef. Yum!

Otaku, page 7

An "otaku" is someone with an obsession of some kind, generally with manga or anime.

FF, page 19

"FF" probably refers to the game "Final Fantasy."

Tenku No Shiro Rapyuta, page 20

Tenku No Shiro Rapyuta, The Castle in the Sky, is a Hayao Miyazaki anime film.

Fan-zines, page 26

Kanji is looking at a doujinshi fan-zine. These fan-zines are written by fans using popular manga characters. The doujinshis are usually a group effort written by college manga club members like the Genshiken guys. They often contain graphic homosexual and adult content.

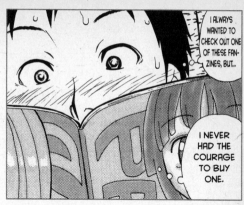

I ALWAYS WANTED TO CHECK OUT ONE OF THESE FAN-ZINES, BUT...

I NEVER HAD THE COURAGE TO BUY ONE.

Gundam, page 32

Kanji is quoting the anime series "Gundam."

Soboro donburi, page 38

Soboro donburi is minced chicken and egg over rice.

Honneamise: Royal Space Force, page 43

Tanaka and Kugayama are referring to the anime film wings of *Honneamise: Royal Space Force*.

Hokaben, page 48

Hokaben is short for Hoka Hoka Tei, a popular bento (boxed lunch) chain.

Akihabara, page 62

Akihabara is the electronics shopping district in Tokyo.

The JR, page 63

JR stands for Japan Railway. It's the largest of all the Japanese railroads.

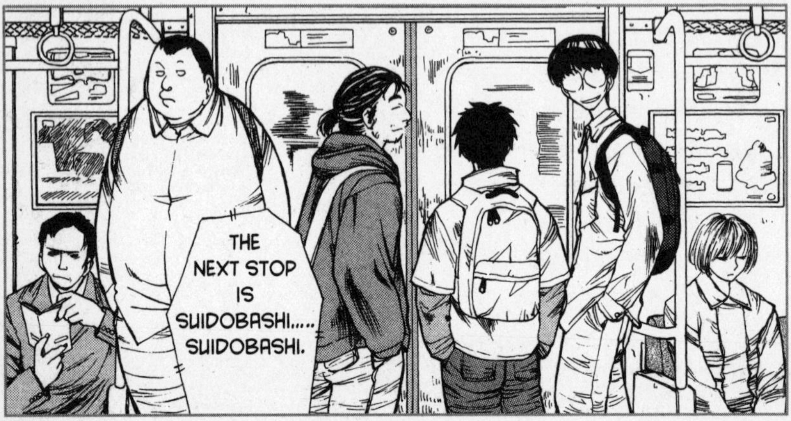
THE NEXT STOP IS SUIDOBASHI..... SUIDOBASHI.

A tight squeeze, page 68

Some stores in Tokyo are so small that they can only allow a certain number of customers to enter at a time.

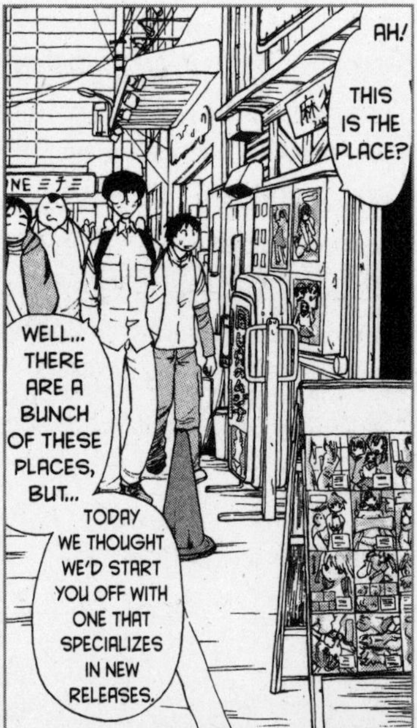
AH!
THIS IS THE PLACE?
WELL... THERE ARE A BUNCH OF THESE PLACES, BUT...
TODAY WE THOUGHT WE'D START YOU OFF WITH ONE THAT SPECIALIZES IN NEW RELEASES.

Pornographic fan-zines, page 71

Usually pornographic fan-zines take characters from regular games or manga and put them in pornographic situations. Kanji is puzzled that someone would make a fan-zine based on something that was already pornographic to start with.

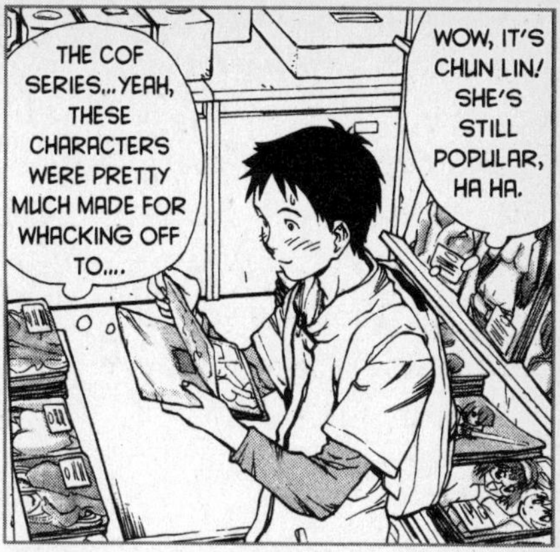

WOW, IT'S CHUN LIN! SHE'S STILL POPULAR, HA HA.
THE COF SERIES...YEAH, THESE CHARACTERS WERE PRETTY MUCH MADE FOR WHACKING OFF TO....

Soramimi Hour, page 78

"Soramimi Hour" is a musical segment on a popular comedy show called *Tamori Club*.

Kugapii, page 94

Kugapii is Saki's nickname for Kugayama.

Why so formal?, page 95

Kanji uses formal Japanese when speaking to Saki.

Mahjong Takes Off, page 98

Mahjong video games, in which a girl removes a piece of clothing after every winning move, are very popular in Japan.

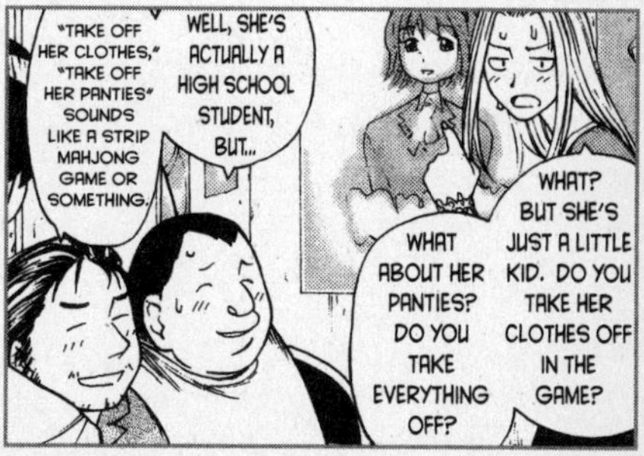

WELL, SHE'S ACTUALLY A HIGH SCHOOL STUDENT, BUT...
"TAKE OFF HER CLOTHES," "TAKE OFF HER PANTIES" SOUNDS LIKE A STRIP MAHJONG GAME OR SOMETHING.
WHAT? BUT SHE'S JUST A LITTLE KID. DO YOU TAKE HER CLOTHES OFF IN THE GAME?
WHAT ABOUT HER PANTIES? DO YOU TAKE EVERYTHING OFF?

Shunga prints, page 100

Shunga were popular, erotic wood block prints from the Edo period of Japanese history.

The Obon holiday, page 125

The Comic-Fest is probably happening during the "Obon" holiday. Obon is a special summer holiday when people visit the graves of their deceased relatives.

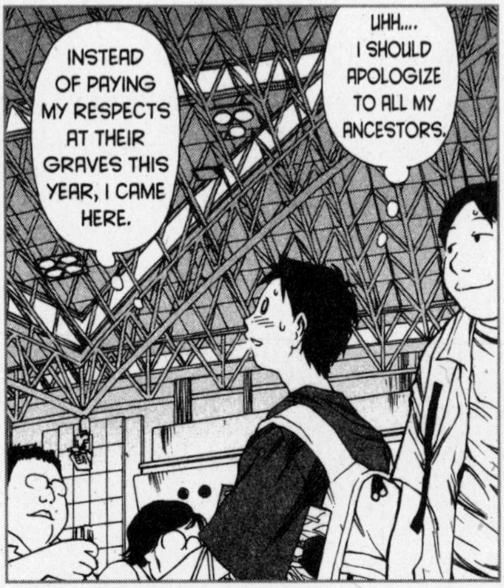
INSTEAD OF PAYING MY RESPECTS AT THEIR GRAVES THIS YEAR, I CAME HERE.
UHH.... I SHOULD APOLOGIZE TO ALL MY ANCESTORS.

Yearly festivals, page 145

Japanese schools hold festivals once a year. During these festivals, school clubs usually engage in an activity to raise money and solicit new members. Popular activities include food stalls, cafes, haunted houses, and dance parties.

Back to school—in Spring, page 150

The Japanese school year begins in April. Since Kanako is transferring from a school in the U.S., she's starting school in September.

Harisen, page 168

A harisen is a paper fan made by rolling up sheets of paper. A famous Osaka comedian used to hit people with a harisen. Apparently it's an Osaka thing.

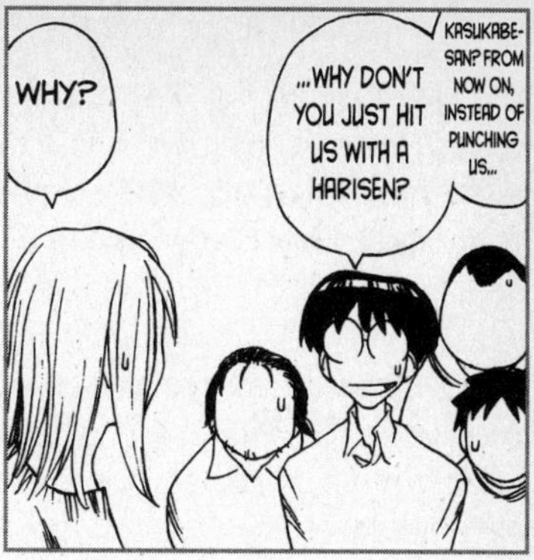
KASUKABE-SAN? FROM NOW ON, INSTEAD OF PUNCHING US...
...WHY DON'T YOU JUST HIT US WITH A HARISEN?
WHY?

Afternoon, page 169

"Genshiken" originally appeared in the magazine *Afternoon*, which is known as a hardcore otaku magazine.

Honorifics

Throughout the Del Rey Manga books, you will find Japanese honorifics left intact in the translations. For those not familiar with how the Japanese use honorifics and, more importantly, how they differ from American honorifics, we present this brief overview.

Politeness has always been a critical facet of Japanese culture. Ever since the feudal era, when Japan was a highly stratified society, use of honorifics—which can be defined as polite speech that indicates relationship or status—has played an essential role in the Japanese language. When addressing someone in Japanese, an honorific usually takes the form of a suffix attached to one's name (example: "Asuna-san"), or as a title at the end of one's name or in place of the name itself (example: "Negi-sensei," or simply "Sensei!").

Honorifics can be expressions of respect or endearment. In the context of manga and anime, honorifics give insight into the nature of the relationship between characters. Many translations into English leave out these important honorifics, and therefore distort the "feel" of the original Japanese. Because Japanese honorifics contain nuances that English honorifics lack, it is our policy at Del Rey not to translate them. Here, instead, is a guide to some of the honorifics you may encounter in Del Rey Manga.

-san: This is the most common honorific and is equivalent to Mr., Miss, Ms., or Mrs. It is the all-purpose honorific and can be used in any situation where politeness is required.

-sama: This is one level higher than "-san" and is used to confer great respect.

-dono: This comes from the word "tono," which means "lord." It is an even higher level than "-sama" and confers utmost respect.

-kun: This suffix is used at the end of boys' names to express familiarity or endearment. It is also sometimes used by men among friends, or when addressing someone younger or of a lower station.

-chan: This is used to express endearment, mostly toward girls. It is also used for little boys, pets, and even among lovers. It gives a sense of childish cuteness.

Bozu: This is an informal way to refer to a boy, similar to the English term "kid" or "squirt."

Sempai: This title suggests that the addressee is one's senior in a group or organization. It is most often used in a school setting, where underclassmen refer to their upperclassmen as "sempai." It can also be used in the workplace, such as when a newer employee addresses an employee who has seniority in the company.

Kohai: This is the opposite of "sempai" and is used toward under-classmen in school or newcomers in the workplace. It connotes that the addressee is of a lower station.

Sensei: Literally meaning "one who has come before," this title is used for teachers, doctors, or masters of any profession or art.

[blank]: Usually forgotten in these lists, but perhaps the most significant difference between Japanese and English. The lack of honorific means that the speaker has permission to address the person in a very intimate way. Usually, only family, spouses, or very close friends have this kind of permission. Known as *yobisute,* it can be gratifying when someone who has earned the intimacy starts to call one by one's name without an honorific. But when that intimacy hasn't been earned, it can also be very insulting.

Preview of Volume 2

We're pleased to present you a preview from Volume 2.
This volume will be available in English in July 26, 2005,
but for now you'll have to make do with Japanese!

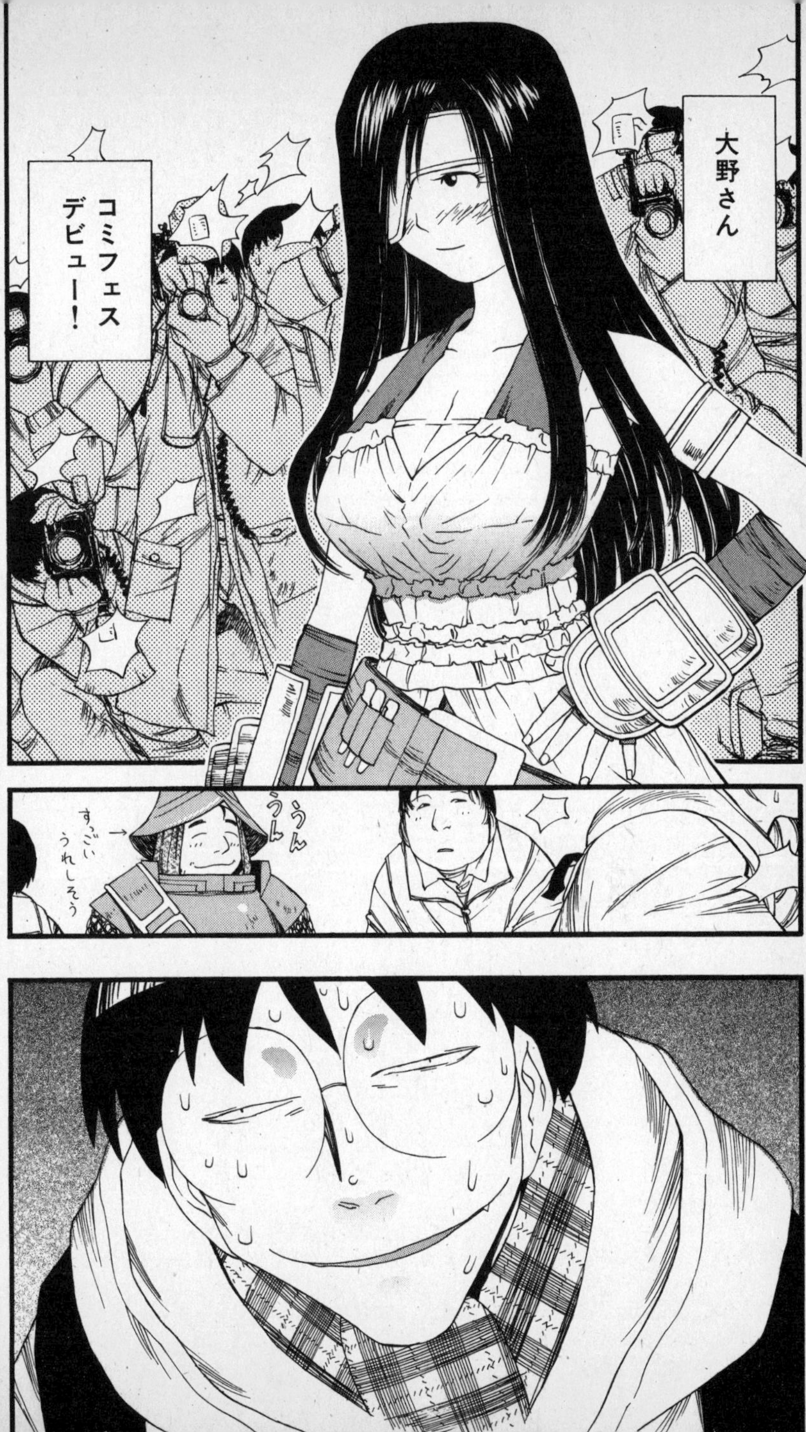
大野さん
コミフェスデビュー!
うんうん
すっごいうれしそう

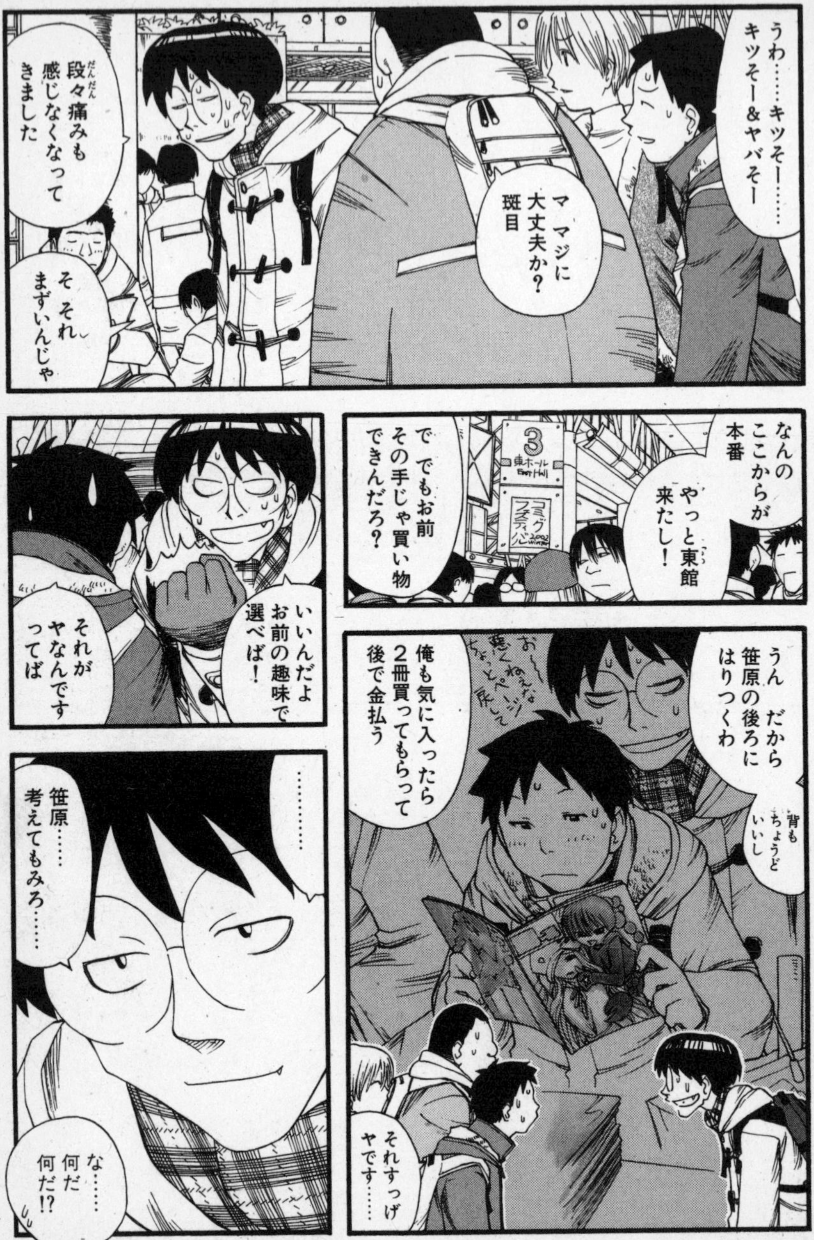
うわ……キツそー……
キツそー&ヤバそー
ママジに大丈夫か？斑目
段々痛みも感じなくなってきました
そ それまずいんじゃ
なんのここからが本番
やっと東館来たし！
3
東ホール East Hall
でもお前その手じゃ買い物できんだろ？
いいんだよお前の趣味で選べば！
それがヤなんですってば
うん だから笹原の後ろにはりつくわ
背もちょうどいいし
俺も気に入ったら2冊買ってもらって後で金払う
おー 悪くねえな ちょっとページ戻して
それすっげヤです……
…………
笹原…… 考えてもみろ……
な…… 何だ 何だ!?

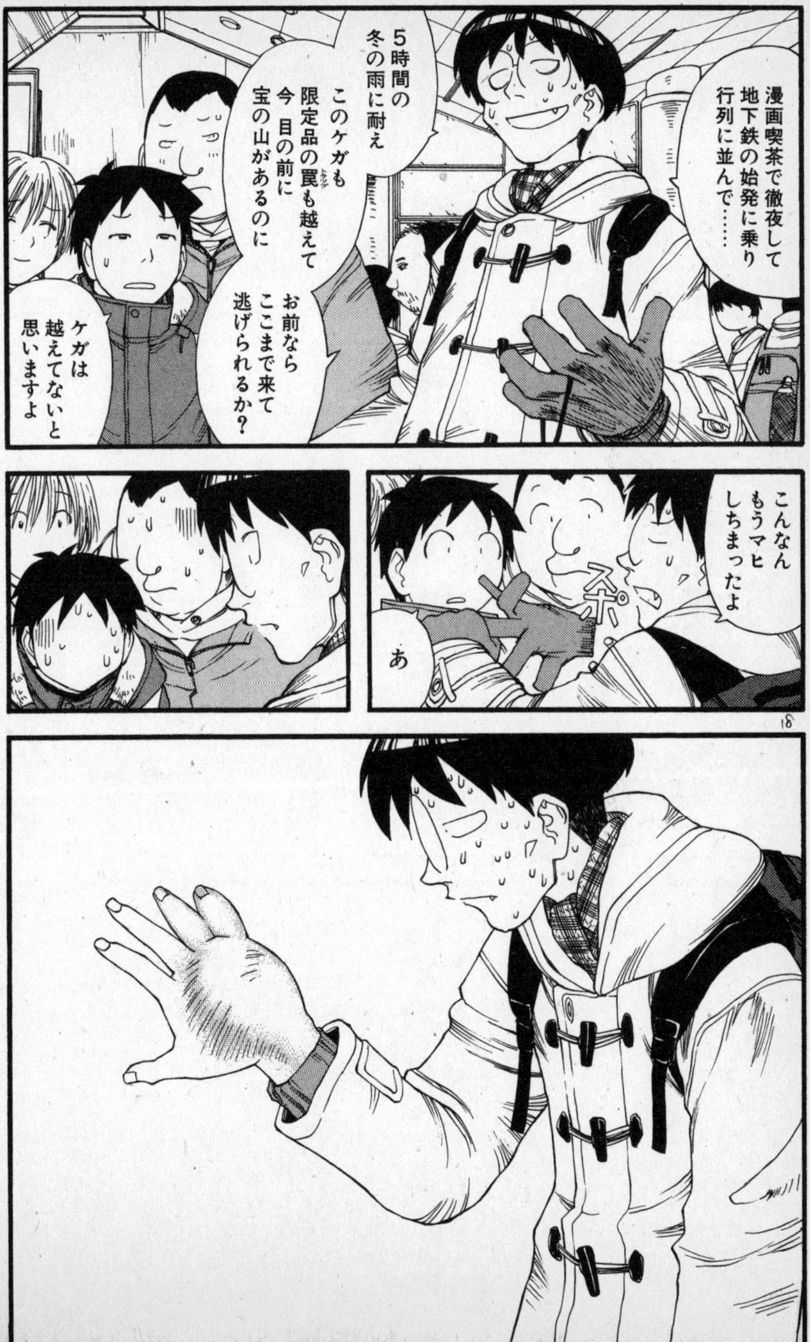
漫画喫茶で徹夜して地下鉄の始発に乗り行列に並んで……
5時間の冬の雨に耐え
このケガも限定品の罠も越えて今目の前に宝の山があるのに
お前ならここまで来て逃げられるか?
ケガは越えてないと思いますよ
こんなんもうマヒしちまったよ
スポッ
あ

Nodame Cantabile

VOLUME 1

BY TOMOKO NINOMIYA

The son of a famous pianist, music student Shinichi Chiaki has always wanted to study abroad and become a conductor like his mentor. However, his fear of planes and water make it impossible for him to follow his dream. As he watches other young students achieve what he has always wanted, Shinichi ponders whether he should quit music altogether.

Then, one day he meets a fellow music student named Megumi Noda, also known as Nodame. This oddball girl cannot cook, clean, or even read her own score, but she can play the piano in incomparable Cantabile style. And she teaches Shinichi something that he has forgotten: to enjoy his music no matter where he is.

1
Nodame Cantabile
TOMOKO NINOMIYA
Winner of the Kodansha Manga of the Year Award

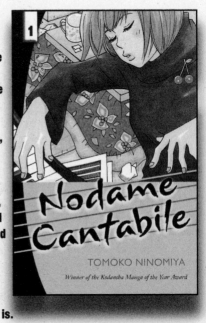

WINNER OF THE 2003 MANGA OF THE YEAR AWARD FROM KODANSHA.

Includes special extras after the story!

VOLUME 1: On sale April 26, 2005

DEL REY

For more information and to sign up for Del Rey's manga e-newsletter, visit www.delreymanga.com

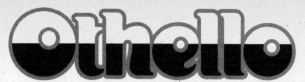

VOLUME 4

BY SATOMI IKEZAWA

Too-shy Yaya is no match for the clever manipulations of the latest transfer student, Megumi Hino—Hino-chan—whose bright, optimistic exterior shields a perfect storm of selfishness, jealousy, and sadism. Hino-chan has her tentacles in all aspects of Yaya's life, including her budding relationship with nice-guy Moriyama and a strange unspoken animosity with rakish, ex-rock star Shôhei. Perhaps Yaya's aggressive alter ego Nana can cut Hino-chan down to size . . . especially when Yaya is pressured into signing a legally binding contract with her arch enemy!

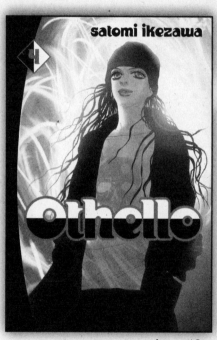

Ages: 16+

Includes special extras after the story!

VOLUME 4: On sale June 28, 2005

For more information and to sign up for Del Rey's manga e-newsletter, visit www.delreymanga.com

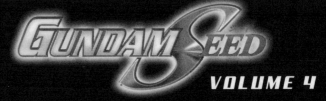

GUNDAM SEED

VOLUME 4

ART BY MASATSUGU IWASE
ORIGINAL STORY BY HAJIME YATATE
AND YOSHIYUKI TOMINO

Devastated by the cruel realities of war, Flay, Athrun, and Miriallia grieve, believing that Kira and Tolle are dead. Even as they mourn and question themselves, the fighting intensifies. Coordinator leader (and Athrun's father) Patrick Zala gains political control over the Plant, and the battle between Zaft and the Earth Army shifts to a military base. When the crew of *Archangel* realize that Earth has used them as bait and betrayed them, they decide to embark on a journey to the neutral state of Aube to start new lives. But on the horizon are new, more powerful mobile suits that may just turn the tide in this war!

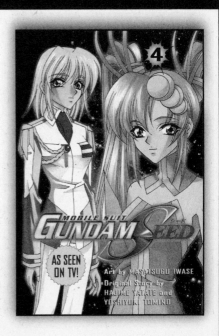

VOLUME 4: On sale March 1, 2005 • VOLUME 5: On sale August 30, 2005

 For more information and to sign up for Del Rey's manga e-newsletter, visit www.delreymanga.com

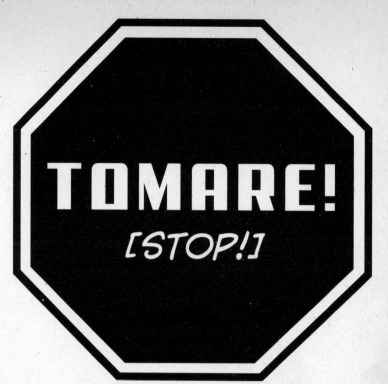

TOMARE! [STOP!]

You are going the wrong way!

Manga is a completely different type of reading experience.

To start at the *beginning,* go to the *end!*

That's right! Authentic manga is read the traditional Japanese way—from right to left. Exactly the *opposite* of how American books are read. It's easy to follow: Just go to the other end of the book, and read each page—and each panel—from right side to left side, starting at the top right. Now you're experiencing manga as it was meant to be.

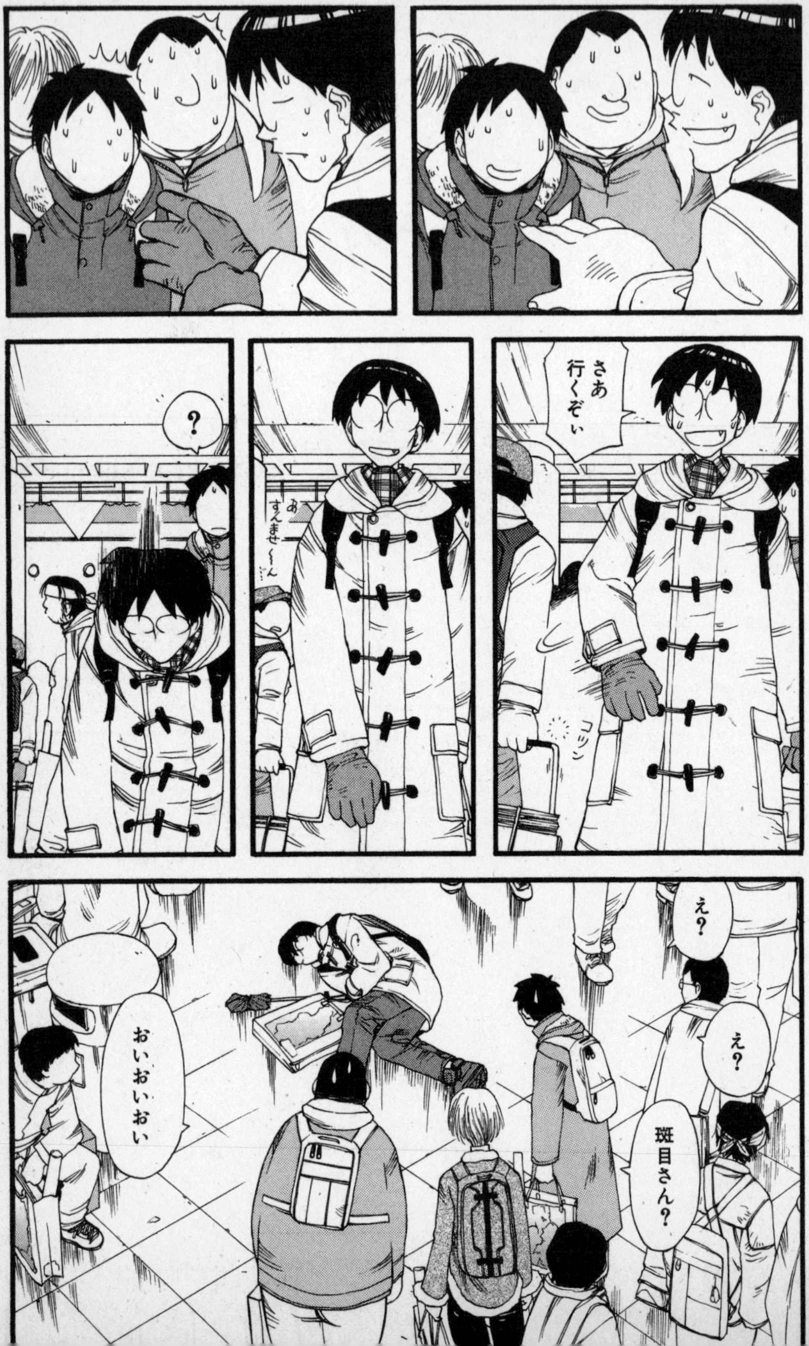
さあ
行くぞぃ
コツン
あ
すんませ〜ん
?
え?
え?
斑目さん?
おいおいおい

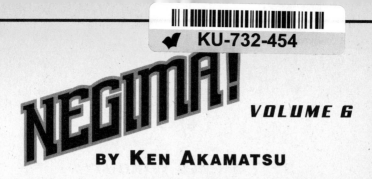

NEGIMA! VOLUME 6

BY KEN AKAMATSU

Ten-year-old Negi Springfield has just graduated from a British school for wizards. After meeting with the school headmaster to discuss his graduate work assignment, he finds that he will be moving to Japan—to teach English at an all-girls high school. Under strict instructions not to show his magic powers, Negi finds that he can't resist using them to help others. Of course, despite his good intentions, sometimes his magic just makes things even worse!

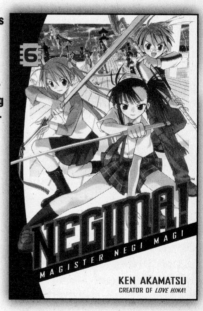

6
NEGIMA!
MAGISTER NEGI MAGI
KEN AKAMATSU
CREATOR OF *LOVE HINA!*

Includes special extras after the story!

VOLUME 6: On sale June 28, 2005

DEL REY

For more information and to sign up for Del Rey's manga e-newsletter, visit www.delreymanga.com